THE SIMMS READER

Selections from the Writings of William Gilmore Simms

THE PUBLICATIONS OF THE
SOUTHERN TEXTS SOCIETY

Michael O'Brien, Editor

THE SIMMS READER

Selections from the Writings of William Gilmore Simms

EDITED BY JOHN CALDWELL GUILDS

University Press of Virginia
Charlottesville and London

The Southern Texts Society gratefully acknowledges generous
funding for this volume by the William Gilmore Simms Society.

THE UNIVERSITY PRESS OF VIRGINIA
© 2001 by the Southern Texts Society
All rights reserved
Printed in the United States of America

First published 2001

⊗ The paper used in this publication meets the minimum requirements
of the American National Standard for Information Sciences—Permanence
of Paper for Printed Library Materials, ANSI Z39.48-1984.

Library of Congress Cataloging-in-Publication Data

Simms, William Gilmore, 1806–1870.
    [Selections. 2001]
    The Simms reader : selections from the writings of William Gilmore
Simms / edited by John Caldwell Guilds.
      p. cm. — (Publications of the Southern Texts Society)
    Includes bibliographical references and index.
    ISBN 0-8139-2019-1 (alk. paper)
    1. Southern States—Fiction. I. Guilds, John Caldwell, 1924–.
II. Title. III. Series.
PS2843 .G84 2001
818'.309—dc21   00-060018

Portions of this book have appeared, in different form, in *Stories and Tales,*
vol. 5 of *The Writings of William Gilmore Simms: Centennial Edition* (Columbia:
University of South Carolina Press, 1974), and in *Simms: A Literary Life*
(Fayetteville: University of Arkansas Press, 1992) and are
reprinted by permission.

Contents

Fiction

Nonfiction

Poetry

Contents / vii

Preface

The very productivity of the writer contributes to the very dearth of his readership—an ironic axiom, indeed, that applies with some truth to William Gilmore Simms. The reader who cares to know Simms faces not the prospect of reading just a volume or two—for Simms has no universally renowned masterpiece to certify him in quick time—but the more daunting challenge of plowing through a whole bevy of books admittedly imperfect that, taken as a whole, reveal an author whose achievement is prodigious. That there has been no single work by Simms that "roll[s] all [his] strength and all / [His] sweetness up into one ball" for the leisurely enjoyment of the twentieth-century reader has prevented his becoming common knowledge to even the literary-minded. Thus I am much indebted to Michael O'Brien and the Southern Texts Society for the opportunity to put together a single, easily available anthology that attempts to catch the essence of Simms the man and writer.

Many scholars and institutions have assisted me in my pleasant, yet formidable task. I am grateful to the University of Arkansas for providing me on a regular basis both financial support and research time; to the University of South Carolina for the special grant that enabled me to devote the summer of 1995 to this project, working full time in the Simms archives in the South Caroliniana Library; and to the University Press of Virginia for the publication of the finished volume. Individuals to whom I am indebted for direct assistance with *The Simms Reader* (not to mention all those who have contributed throughout the years to my understanding of Simms) include the members of the Simms Society's Executive Council, past and present; I am particularly grateful to James E. Kibler, James B. Meriwether, Anne Blythe Meriwether, and David Moltke-Hansen for reading portions of the manuscript and making helpful suggestions. Michael O'Brien, exceptionally generous with his time and ability, was helpful in numerous ways far beyond his role as series editor. Mary Simms Oliphant Furman, who always can be counted upon in matters pertaining to Simms, kindly furnished the previously unpublished photograph that serves as the frontispiece. Special thanks are due to George Terry, director of libraries at the University of

South Carolina, and especially to Allen Stokes and his able staff at the South Caroliniana Library for providing a perfect working environment and sophisticated logistical support. A grant from the Simms Foundation afforded assistance for the preparation of the text for publication; and I am greatly in debt to Eric Roman for his expertise in carrying out the initial stages of this important assignment—with a conscientious fervor that augurs well for his future career as textual scholar and editor. And once the seemingly interminable revising, trimming, and squeezing process was complete, I am especially grateful to my research assistants at the University of Arkansas, Hilary Harris (postdoctoral) and Kevin Collins, for performing with skill and dispatch, and always with good humor and high intelligence, the crucial task of formatting and printing out clear copy. Finally, gratitude to Gertrud Pickar Guilds is encompassed in all I do.

Abbreviations

BJ	*Broadway Journal*
CP	Simms, *The Cub of the Panther,* ed. Miriam J. Shillingsburg (Fayetteville, Ark., 1997).
DLB	*Dictionary of Literary Biography*
EAD	Evert A. Duyckinck
EAP	Edgar Allan Poe
JHH	James Henry Hammond
JL	James Lawson
Letters	*The Letters of William Gilmore Simms,* ed. Mary C. Simms Oliphant, Alfred Taylor Odell, and T. C. Duncan Eaves, 5 vols. (Columbia, S.C., 1952–56)
	The Letters of William Gilmore Simms, vol. 6, ed. Mary C. Simms Oliphant and T.C. Duncan Eaves (Columbia, S.C., 1982)
MCSO	Taped interviews with Mary C. Simms Oliphant, WGS's granddaughter, at her home in Greenville, S.C., June 20, 1978–May 11, 1979
NBT	Nathaniel Beverley Tucker
PDDLC	Simms, *Poems Descriptive, Dramatic, Legendary and Contemplative,* 2 vols. (1853)
PHH	Paul Hamilton Hayne
RWG	Rufus Wilmot Griswold
SLM	*Southern Literary Messenger*
SQR	*Southern Quarterly Review*
SWMMR	*Southern and Western Monthly Magazine and Review*
VRAH	Simms, *Views and Reviews in American Literature, History and Fiction,* first series, ed. C. Hugh Holman (Cambridge, Mass., 1962)
WGS	William Gilmore Simms

THE SIMMS READER

Selections from the Writings of William Gilmore Simms

Introduction

I

The lifetime of William Gilmore Simms (1806–1870), a passionate and articulate man, spans one of the most tumultuous eras of American history. Nullification, unionism, states' rights, abolitionism, secession, Civil War, and reconstruction all were part of Simms's experience; and his responses to these crises are of a significance that, even were he not the pre-eminent man of letters of the Old South, he would nevertheless warrant study by all interested in nineteenth-century America.

This proud, complex, fascinating individual was in many ways a self-made man who came from humble origins. He was born on April 17, 1806, in Charleston, South Carolina, of relatively obscure parents. His father, William Gilmore Simms, Sr., had immigrated from Larne, Ireland, to South Carolina shortly after the American Revolution, residing first in Lancaster District, then moving to Charleston (probably in the 1790s). There he married Harriet Ann Augusta Singleton of a well-established family originally from Virginia, who bore him three sons. Their union, however, was marked by tragedy. The first child, born in 1805, died in infancy shortly after the birth of William Gilmore; and the young mother herself died in childbirth together with the third in January 1808. The strain and shock were too much for Simms Sr., whose business failed almost simultaneously with their loss. Calling Charleston "a place of tombs,"[1] he deserted the city, leaving his young namesake in the care of his maternal grandmother, Jane Miller Singleton Gates,[2] and sought better fortune in the Old Southwest, first in Tennessee and eventually in Mississippi. The son was in effect an orphan at the time of his earliest memories, and the strong sense of alienation that permeated his

---

1. WGS, Personal Memorials, Charles Carroll Simms Collection, South Caroliniana Library, University of South Carolina.

2. The widow of John Singleton, who died in 1799, Jane Miller had later married Jacob Gates, whom she had also survived. The Charleston directories for 1813 and 1816 list "Gates, Mrs. (Widow) King-St. Road" and "Gates, Jane, widow, e side king-st. Road," respectively.

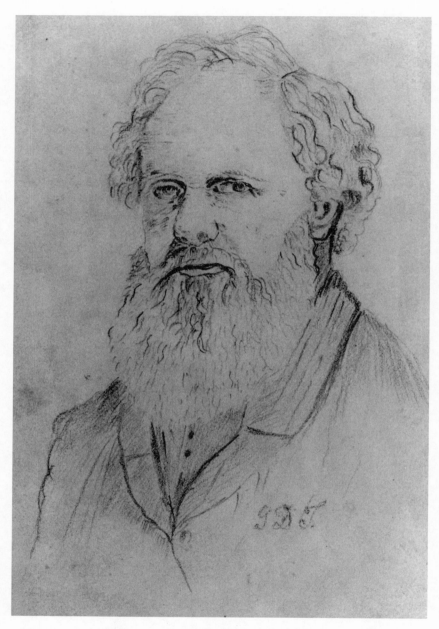

William Gilmore Simms, pencil sketch by Jeanne Davis Tupper, probably about 1870. (Courtesy of Mary Simms Oliphant Furman)

adult life may have originated then. Years later Simms wrote revealingly of "the feeling of isolation in which I found myself at an early age—without father or mother, brother or indeed, kindred of any kind," and as a result, he claimed, he "was always on the look out for opposition and hostility."[3]

Jane Gates, however, did her best for her young grandson. Because she had lived near the Simmses on King Street, she would have had many opportunities to help care for her small grandson even before the family tragedy; and though a strict disciplinarian, she seems to have had a special touch with children. Perhaps the highest tribute Simms paid to his maternal grandmother was his recognition in later life that she was "a stern though affectionate parent" who "taught me the first great lesson without which we learn none—obedience."[4] There can be little doubt that Jane Gates had a profound effect on young Simms in her role as surrogate mother, particularly in her imaginative storytelling ability. As a teenaged girl during the Revolution, Jane Miller had traveled with partisan spies in an open rowboat down the Cooper River into Charleston; the man she married, John Singleton, the colony's tobacco inspector, had fought in the Revolution, and she knew at firsthand the heroic exploits of her wealthy father-in-law, Thomas Singleton, whose activities in the patriot cause led to his arrest in 1780 by the British and his departure on a prison ship to Florida. Jane Singleton Gates was a superstitious yet bookish person steeped in experience, history, literature, and the supernatural;[5] she fascinated her precocious grandson and sparked his interest in the glories of South Carolina, medieval France and Spain, and ghosts of all kinds.[6]

Yet Mrs. Gates failed to give her ward (whether through shortsightedness or financial difficulties) the kind of educational opportunities he needed or the strong emotional support a loving young mother might have given, deficiencies Simms noted in later life. In 1839, answering inquiries about factors shaping his career, Simms acknowledged that "my father left me when an infant to the care of an aged Grandmother" and that the "old lady" (whose "resources were small" and who was "one to economize them to the uttermost") had "wretchedly neglected" his education, which "accordingly was almost wholly nominal."[7] In June 1841 Simms was even more candid concerning Jane Singleton Gates's niggardly ways; he complained that the

3. WGS to JL, Dec. 29, 1839, *Letters* 1 : 164.

4. Ibid., 161.

5. MCSO, June 20, 1978.

6. For insight into the grandmother's influence, see WGS, *Donna Florida: A Tale* (Charleston: Burges & James, 1843), 10, 12, and passim.

7. WGS to JL, Dec. 29, 1839, *Letters* 1 : 161.

"small maternal property" left him was "hoarded so religiously" by his grandmother "as to withhold the appropriations necessary to my education."[8] But
the statement by Simms that most tellingly reveals the impact of his childhood came in a letter of April 14, 1860, to fellow novelist John Esten Cooke,
in which Simms explained that he lost his mother when only an infant: "I grew
up without young associates. I grew *hard* in consequence, hard, perhaps, of
manner; but with a heart craving love beyond all other possessions."[9]

Nevertheless, the bright and energetic boy was not neglected by his dutiful grandmother, who entered her young charge in the public schools of
Charleston in 1812; and despite testimony to the contrary from the adult
Simms, he seems to have obtained the rudiments of an education there. Because most upper-class Charlestonians placed their sons in the hands of private tutors or enrolled them in prestigious private schools, Simms's bitter
thoughts later about his schooling perhaps may be attributed to his sense of
alienation from the proud city's aristocracy as much as to the shortcomings
of the schools themselves. In the 1841 letter in which he first complained of
Mrs. Gates's mismanagement of his inherited property left in her care,
Simms frankly admitted that "the utmost" of his educational attainments
"were those of a grammar school, irregularly attended."[10]

Despite the deficiencies in his schooling, young Gilmore Simms was remarkably well read for his age. An earlier anecdote records the premature
bookishness of Mrs. Gates's ward, who even before he could walk would
crawl up to her bookcase and touch with delight the leather-bound volumes;[11] as a child he was inquisitive enough and precocious enough to become a voracious reader and a facile writer despite inadequacies of his ele-
mentary schooling. Even the boyhood sickness that produced frequent
absences and brought about "almost the conviction with all that I could not
be raised" had "its advantages," Simms recorded. "I got books, devoured
them—books of all kinds without order or discrimination" and as a result,
he asserted, "acquired a thousand times more than I could have done under
the ordinary school advantages."[12] Family tradition has it that as a boy he
worked out an ingenious plan for reading late at night despite his grandmother's decree that the light in his room be out at dusk. By installing in
his room a huge dry-goods box that effectively hid from her watchful eye
the flicker of his burning candle, Gilmore managed to fulfill his thirst for

8. WGS to RWG, June 20, 1841, ibid., 5 : 357.
9. WGS to John Esten Cooke, April 14, 1860, ibid., 4 : 216.
10. WGS to RWG, June 20, 1841, ibid., 5 : 357.
11. MCSO, 3.
12. WGS to RWG, June 20, 1841, *Letters* 5 : 357.

reading and keep peace with his grandmother at the same time. The young scholar's initiative here anticipates the drive and inventiveness he was to demonstrate time and again throughout his long career. In Simms's own memory of his boyhood in Charleston, he was "a student, and an unsleeping one." He declared that his reading was "perhaps not less valuable because it was desultory," noting: "An inquiring, self judging mind . . . can never be hurt by reading mixed books, since it is always resolute to judge for itself, and very soon acquires a habit of discriminating. I soon emptied all the book-cases of my acquaintances."[13] As for Simms's favorites as a boy, he was quoted by Paul Hamilton Hayne as having said, "I used to glow and shiver in turn over 'the Pilgrim's Progress,' and Moses' adventures in 'The Vicar of Wakefield' threw me into paroxysms of laughter."[14]

In the summer of 1816, when Gilmore was ten and had just completed his fourth year in school, an event occurred that was to have great impact upon his life. In leaving his son in Charleston in 1808, the elder William Gilmore Simms had extracted a promise from Mrs. Gates that she would bring his son to him in the Southwest after he had established himself there. Eight years later, the elder Simms called for his son to join him in the Mississippi Territory. When Jane Gates refused either to take or send her ward to his father, William Simms dispatched his brother James to Charleston with legal authorization to get the ten-year-old from his maternal grandmother. According to family archives, James Simms accosted his nephew on the streets of Charleston, and only the frantic resistance of the boy, aided by Mrs. Gates, prevented his being, in effect, kidnapped. The shouts and shrieks of young Gilmore attracted the attention of neighbors, who rushed to his rescue. Foiled in this attempt, the elder William Gilmore Simms— still working through brother James—sought to get custody of his son by court order, and the case was tried before Judge Elihu Hall Bay. James and William Simms retained the services of Benjamin Cudworth Yancey, a distinguished Charleston attorney, to represent them in court; and in return Jane Gates retained John S. Richardson and Robert Y. Hayne, both also well-known members of the Charleston bar. But rather than decide the case himself or have a jury decision, Judge Bay took a surprising action. He left the decision—whether Simms should go to Mississippi to join his father or remain in Charleston with his grandmother—to the ten-year-old boy himself. Under these dramatic circumstances young Simms chose Mrs. Gates and Charleston—and the pattern of his life was set.[15]

13. WGS to JL, Dec. 29, 1839, ibid., 1:161.
14. PHH, "Ante-Bellum Charleston," *Southern Bivouac* 1 (Oct. 1885):261–62.
15. MCSO, 5, 7.

The implications of the boy's decision were far-reaching, having a profound effect upon his life and work. Opting as he did for Charleston, young Simms was turned toward the genteel professions, including the literary. Had he chosen the Southwest, he probably would have been directed away from the arts and toward the practical, the political, and the economic, with success assured him by his championing father. In later years Simms voiced regret, even resentment, about the decision forced upon him as a boy not mature enough to understand its ramifications: "At ten years of age, my answer was relied upon by the Judge, to make his decision. I declared my wish to remain with my Grandmother, and the rights of the father were set aside,—I think now improperly, and as I now believe, to my irretrievable injury in many respects. Had I gone with my father, I should have known less feeling, but more world wisdom . . . I should then have received the additional education the want of which I often feel & shall continue to feel while I live."[16] By choosing Charleston, he rejected his father. A certain ambivalence was the inevitable result of this traumatic boyhood decision: ambivalence toward his father and, perhaps most of all, ambivalence toward Charleston—a love-hate dichotomy that lasted a lifetime. Simms committed himself to Charleston, and with it to the profession of letters, at an early age, but with that commitment he also repudiated his father, whom he scarcely knew but whose image he honored—almost worshiped—so that his filial love became mingled with feelings of guilt. Simms, however, though he wavered and complained, never deserted the city of his birth and never forsook his early commitment to belles lettres. Out of the decision of the boy came the profession of the man.

Simms's penchant for literature began early—at fourteen he composed a drama entitled "The Female Assassin," at fifteen he published verses in the Charleston newspapers, and at sixteen he became a regular contributor. His career as a professional man of letters, it may be said, began in 1825, when at nineteen he became editor of the *Album,* a Charleston literary journal that he wrote extensively for—poetry, fiction, and essays. The *Album* lasted through 1826, and young Simms (who married Anna Malcolm Giles of Charleston on October 19, 1826) waited only a year before assuming the coeditorship of another, more significant Charleston magazine, the *Southern Literary Gazette,* 1828–29. According to Simms primary motivation in editing these early periodicals was to encourage the literary development of his city, region, and nation; but certainly another attraction was the outlet these journals provided for his own creative efforts. Simms published so extensively in the *Southern Literary Gazette*—poetry, fiction, essays, literary criticism; some remarkably good, some obviously mere space fillers—that he

16. WGS to JL, Dec. 29, 1839, *Letters* 1 : 161.

felt constrained to offer the reader an apology, a pithy explanation of the plight of many a magazine editor of the early nineteenth century: "As long as the Editor is compelled, as we have frequently been, to write one half of his book himself, one half of what he writes, must be trash."[17]

In 1829, however, young Simms was still interested in being an editor. When his second effort to establish a literary journal in Charleston failed in November, Simms was not long in deciding to direct his talent as editor into a more profitable channel. Forming a partnership with a printer named E. S. Duryea, he—unwisely, it seems—invested funds from his maternal inheritance in the *City Gazette,* a Charleston daily newspaper then up for sale. Simms served as editor of the *City Gazette* from January 1, 1830, until June 7, 1832, and those thirty months constituted for him one trying experience after another, including the death of Anna Malcolm Giles Simms from tuberculosis in February 1832. His stand against the doctrine of Nullification made for him many personal and political enemies; on at least one occasion in 1831 only Duryea's prudence is said to have saved his partner from attack by an angry mob, to whom the young editor had defiantly shouted, "Cowards!"[18] Simms himself later summed up his ill-fated editorship of the *City Gazette:*

> It [the *Gazette*] had been declining in public estimation long before I purchased it & had got so low that when I—most imprudently—bought it, it must have been discontinued but for the sale and transfer into new hands. It resuscitated somewhat after it fell into my hands, and but for my taking . . . the unpopular side of the question in Carolina, it must have succeeded. But all the sources of income which it derived from the Nullifiers, and which contributed fully one-half of its profits—were suddenly dried up, and at the close of a 2½ years term of mental torture, I was only too happy to give it up.[19]

Young Simms's unflinching support of the Unionist cause in the Nullification crisis reflects his lifelong interest in politics. That his strongest commitment, however, was to letters, not to politics or law (he was admitted to the bar on his twenty-first birthday), became apparent with his next editorial venture—the *Cosmopolitan: An Occasional* (1833), which by design

---

17. *Southern Literary Gazette* n.s. 1 (July 1, 1829): 80.

18. This incident, though important, did not have the lasting significance attributed to it by Trent (*Simms,* 62–64) and by James A. B. Scherer ("William Gilmore Simms," *Library of Southern Literature,* ed. Edwin Anderson Alderman et al., 16 vols [Atlanta, 1907], 11:4795–96), both of whom overdramatize it as evidence of the hostility encountered by WGS in Charleston throughout his life.

19. WGS to JL, Dec. 19, 1839, *Letters* 1:162.

scrupulously avoided politics to concentrate wholly upon the "higher employ" of literature. Coedited with fellow Charlestonians Charles and Edward Carroll, the *Cosmopolitan* contains stories and literary essays by Simms and the Carrolls; beyond its call for a national and regional literature, its importance lies primarily as a stepping-stone in Simms's development as a writer—evidence of which was soon to hit the New York literary market.

The years 1833–34 saw the emergence of young William Gilmore Simms as a promising novelist of national import. Before that time Simms had written more poetry than fiction; but with the publication of *Martin Faber* in 1833 and *Guy Rivers* in 1834 (both by the prestigious New York firm of J. & J. Harper), Simms's "main work" became the novel,[20] the genre for which he was best suited. Both novels were widely reviewed; and with *Guy Rivers,* "the first of my regular novels,"[21] Simms for the first time hit upon the distinctively American theme to which he would turn time and again: society's attempt to encroach upon, civilize, and control a lawless and violent frontier splendid in its brutal resistance to its inevitable exploitation. Before the furor created by *Guy Rivers* had died down, Simms cashed in on his triumphant entry to the national literary scene with two more Harper-published, action-filled dramatic novels, both in 1835: *The Yemassee,* the first of his Indian trilogy, and *The Partisan,* the first of his Revolutionary Romances. Both were fictional representations of American history (a favorite theme for Simms); and each depicted an early era of America's efforts to fulfill its manifest destiny by means of partisan warfare not dissimilar to that practiced on the nineteenth-century frontier. At age twenty-nine Simms had found his niche as a writer.

The following year the young widower achieved social and personal fulfillment to match his literary attainment: he wooed and won Chevillette Eliza Roach, the only daughter of wealthy landowner Nash Roach and the heiress to large twin plantations, Oak Grove and Woodlands, encompassing almost seven thousand acres on the banks of the South Edisto River. With their November 1836 marriage Simms gained admittance to the Southern hegemony, the planter class, and with it the social status from which he had felt excluded. His social ascension suddenly achieved, he focused more than ever on his primary goal: literary immortality. Simms looked upon the noblesse oblige tradition of the Southern planter, heavy in emphasis upon personal and societal responsibility, as additional motivation to excel in his chosen profession. His proprietorship of Woodlands bolstered his commitment

---

20. Ibid., Nov. 1832, 45.
21. WGS, "Dedicatory Epistle to Charles R. Carroll, Esq.," dated Nov. 15, 1854, and published as the preface to the "new and revised" edition of *Guy Rivers* (New York: Redfield, 1855), 10.

to the Southern cause, it is true, and now more than ever he viewed the soil of South Carolina as sacred home turf. While he pointed out and criticized the faults and shortcomings of the South to fellow Southerners like James H. Hammond, he was increasingly defensive about the region's role in national affairs. What was it that motivated Simms to his greatest toil at just the time he seemingly had established himself for life financially and socially? His own words provide the best answer. In writing in July 1834 to James Lawson (the New York critic and businessman who would become one of his best friends), the novelist candidly remarked that "my ambition is such, that having fairly rid myself of one labour, I must necessarily go on to another. I cannot be content, if I would."[22] In another letter to Lawson in June 1835, Simms—after admitting that *The Yemassee* had been "certainly extravagantly" praised—confessed: "Perhaps, if the truth were known, I am still dissatisfied—I am not easily content. My achievements must go on—though upon the Alps, yet would I not slumber while Rome lay beyond them attainable, yet unattained."[23] These passages give extraordinary insight into William Gilmore Simms: as a man marked by a drive that kept him aggressively striving for more and more recognition, appreciation, and power. Incapable of being completely fulfilled, he was incapable of being content. Simms was a workaholic long before the concept came into vogue; relentlessly driven toward success, he was never content to rest upon his laurels or to enjoy a relaxed, leisurely existence. In a letter to Rufus W. Griswold, another New Yorker, in 1841, Simms declared dramatically: "Do not . . . suppose me insensible to the sweet solicitings of fame. It has been the dream of my life, the unnamed inspiration of my boyhood—dearer than life, for which I take cheerfully to toil, and toil on, though I see not the reward."[24] His success in literature, marriage, and public esteem only whetted his insatiable appetite "cheerfully to toil on, and toil on" to the next summit of the Alps or the next Rome. He was fortunate that his greatest joy in life was his work, unfortunate that he never believed his work sufficiently appreciated by his contemporaries. Simms's self-analysis was accurate: I cannot be content, if I would.

The decade following Simms's marriage to Chevillette Roach was marked by untiring literary efforts and high production. From 1837 to 1847 Simms

---

22. WGS to JL, July 19, 1834, *Letters* 1 : 59.

23. Ibid., June 10, 1835, 71. The reference to Hannibal having attained the summit of the Alps, with his ultimate goal of Rome still lying beyond, is expanded upon in the July 19, 1834, letter to JL: "The Alps may have passed but Rome's beyond them, and I shall not be satisfied short of a fine marble and permanent, not to say classically well-built residence in the Eternal City! So much for the love of fame, and human approbation, a terribly large development of which my head possesses" (ibid., 59).

24. WGS to RWG, June 20, 1841, ibid., 5 : 359.

published no fewer than fifteen important titles: two Revolutionary Romances: *Mellichampe* (1837) and *The Scout* (1841); five Border Romances: *Richard Hurdis* (1838), *Border Beagles* (1840), *Confession* (1841), *Beauchampe* (1842), and *Helen Halsey* (1844); two volumes of some of his best short stories in *The Wigwam and the Cabin,* first and second series (1845); two volumes of essays, *Views and Reviews in American Literature, History and Fiction,* first and second series (1845); three books of poetry: *Southern Passages and Pictures* (1839), *Grouped Thoughts and Scattered Fancies* (1845), and *Areytos, or, Songs of the South* (1846); one superb short novel, *Castle Dismal* (1844); a judicious, well-written biography of Chevalier Bayard (1847), the medieval French knight "sans peur et sans reproche"; and a concise history of South Carolina (1840). In addition, twice during this period he edited significant magazines devoted to the development of Southern and American letters, the *Magnolia* (1842–43) and the *Southern and Western* (popularly known as "Simms's Magazine") (1845).

On the personal level, the first six of the fourteen children of the union of Simms and Chevillette Roach were born in the first ten years of their marriage, wreaking havoc on her frail health. During this time Simms developed a staunch friendship with James Henry Hammond (1807–1864), a temperamental, high-toned, articulate intellectual who shared Simms's interest in history, politics, and agriculture and his passion for literature (of which Hammond was a connoisseur, not a practitioner). It was Hammond who, while governor of South Carolina in 1842–44, whetted the political aspirations of his literary friend. As Simms's chief confidant on all matters and his self-appointed adviser on politics, Governor Hammond persuaded Simms to run for the South Carolina legislature, to which Simms was elected in 1844 for a two-year term and served with distinction. Simms, unlike Hammond, held no high hopes for elective office, but the idea of a diplomatic appointment abroad—first hinted at by Simms in 1836—appealed to the author immensely, and with Hammond's strong urging, he vigorously pursued the possibility in the 1840s and 1850s. The failure to secure such an appointment despite repeated efforts was for Simms one of the most frustrating disappointments of his lifetime. That he, as the most distinguished author (and the only nominee) from the South, was repeatedly passed over in favor of "literary men of the North" added to his increasing resentment of what he regarded as condescension toward the South.[25]

As the animosity between North and South grew, Simms, somewhat unexpectedly, found himself recognized as the primary spokesman for the

---

25. WGS to JL, April 7, 1845, ibid., 2:48. Among the Northern writers given the kind of appointment WGS cherished, he identified Edward Everett, Henry Wheaton, Robert Walsh, Theodore S. Fay, and George Bancroft—as well as Washington Irving.

Southern point of view. Though in every magazine he had edited before 1845 — and in numerous essays and lectures — Simms had advocated the development of Southern literature, he had done so as a literary nationalist who recognized the importance of regionalism in the creation of an authentic and distinctive American literature. "To be *national* in literature," he wrote in 1845, "one must needs be *sectional*. No one mind can fully or fairly illustrate the characteristics of any great country; and he who shall depict *one section* faithfully, has made his proper and sufficient contribution to the great work of *national* illustration."[26]

By the mid-1850s Simms, the "ultra American, . . . born Southron"[27] who had seen no inconsistency in the patriotic support of both nation and region, was finding difficulty in reconciling his literary nationalism with the increasingly partisan and separatist cast to his region's politics. Simms's decision in 1849 to accept the editorship of the *Southern Quarterly Review* is telling: his motive was no longer literary but political, for the *SQR* format allowed no fiction or poetry. Though Simms wrote some of his best literary criticism in the *SQR* "Critical Notices" section (for which he was totally responsible), his journal's contents were wholly nonfiction: political, social, and philosophical essays written almost exclusively by Southerners (James Henry Hammond, M. C. M. Hammond, Beverley Tucker, Joel R. Poinsett, Alexander Beaufort Meek, Benjamin F. Perry, J. D. B. DeBow, William Henry Trescot, David Flavel Jamison, Francis Lieber, George Frederick Holmes, Brantz Mayer, Josiah Nott, Robert W. Gibbes, and Mitchell King were among the contributors). Invariably, these writers expressed the Southern points of view. The *Southern Quarterly* was superbly edited by Simms, and his ability to attract prominent contributors to the cause of Southern rights rescued what had been a floundering periodical — rescued it, that is, at least until the end of 1854, when Simms resigned after a long squabble with his niggardly publishers over payment of debts. Without Simms, the *SQR* declined rapidly and finally expired in 1857 — a landmark of the difficulties of editing and publishing in the South as elsewhere in America, be the magazine literary or political.

Though now decidedly pro-Southern in his always strongly held political views, Simms, however, never ceased to be primarily a man of letters. Even while editor of the *SQR,* Simms demonstrated both his productivity and versatility as an author. In 1850 he brought out *The Lily and the Totem,* an imaginative volume of fictional history dealing with the Huguenot settlements in Florida in the sixteenth century, and *Flirtation at the Moultrie House,* a light

---

26. WGS, "Dedication to Nash Roach, Esq., of South Carolina," *The Wigwam and the Cabin,* new and rev. ed. (New York: Redfield, 1856), 4.

27. WGS to George Frederick Holmes, Aug. 15, 1842, *Letters* 1 : 319.

farcical comedy of manners gently satirizing fashionable Charleston society. The third novel in the Revolutionary War series, *Katherine Walton,* which dramatizes the diplomatic and military battle for control of Charleston, followed in 1851. The remarkable year 1852 witnessed the publication of five works that reflect both his diversity and his virtuosity: *The Golden Christmas,* a novelette of social manners set in the South Carolina low country; *The Sword and the Distaff* (later entitled *Woodcraft*), a postwar Revolutionary romance, considered one of Simms's masterpieces; *As Good as a Comedy,* a vernacular comic novel of the Southwestern frontier; and two dramas, *Norman Maurice,* which won critical praise but was never performed, and Simms's last attempt as a dramatist, *Michael Bonham,* published anonymously. Continuing on a sustained creative surge, Simms brought out in 1853 the best collection of his poetry, *Poems Descriptive, Dramatic, Legendary and Contemplative,* and the second novel in his Indian trilogy, *Vasconselos,* set in Florida at the time of De Soto's invasion. *Southward, Ho!*—a collection of short stories—followed in 1854; and in 1855 and 1856 he produced a pair of his best crafted novels, *The Forayers* and *Eutaw,* the Revolutionary Romances dealing with the battle of Eutaw Springs.

Thus 1856 found Simms at the height of his creative powers; yet the year was to be marked by a display of poor judgment and belligerence that threatened Simms's good name with his Northern reading audience. Already vexed by political disappointment and irked by the frustrating conclusion to his editorship of *SQR,* Simms passionately plunged into a tumultuous lecture tour of the North amid one of the most turbulent periods of North-South relations. After Massachusetts senator Charles Sumner in a May 1856 Senate debate impugned the role of South Carolina in the Revolutionary War and was subsequently caned by irate South Carolina representative Preston S. Brooks, political leaders in South Carolina looked to Simms to be their spokesman in the heated controversy. Simms, reluctantly accepting the mantle thrust upon him, invited disaster by allowing impetuosity and righteous indignation to override his usual rationality under fire: his intemperately voiced lecture on "South Carolina in the Revolution," delivered at key cities in the North, evoked a strongly negative audience reaction. The whole imbroglio may have planted a seed that—quickly taking root and spreading throughout the Northeast—would haunt his literary career from that time forward.

Nevertheless, Simms's literary accomplishments and reputation continued to grow—at least for a time. The year 1859 was pivotal for Simms: in it he published perhaps his best novel, *The Cassique of Kiawah,* the last of his Indian trilogy, which won high critical praise, both North and South, and Simms himself was acclaimed the nation's best living novelist; and yet after

1859 he would publish, in book form, no other novel for the rest of his life. This surprising development can be accounted for only by a rapid sequence of events—the Ordinance of Secession in 1860 and the outbreak of Civil War in 1861—that almost automatically cut him off from his main reading audience and from the opportunity to continue publishing in the North, terminated the royalties from his copyrights, and to all intents and purposes ended his career as popular novelist.

Personal tragedy also plagued Simms. After the loss of two sons to yellow fever on the same day in 1858 and the accidental burning of Woodlands in 1862, the year 1863 was marked by the death of his wife of twenty-seven years, the wounding of his namesake son in a Civil War battle, and the death of his most intimate friend in South Carolina, James Henry Hammond. In 1865 Woodlands—after being restored—was burned a second time, and his library destroyed, by stragglers of Sherman's army. By the close of the Civil War, Simms had little to sustain him but pride, determination, and strong will. Though weak and almost constantly wracked with pain (probably the result of colon cancer), Simms persisted in writing, lecturing, and editing for whatever pittances he could get. Forced to forgo writing the kind of stirring historical novels by which he had won national distinction, he demonstrated admirable adaptability by producing for Southern publishers volumes of contemporary history (*Sack and Destruction of the City of Columbia*) and patriotic poetry (*War Poetry of the South*), and by partially recapturing the Northern periodical market with tall tales told in dialect and installment novels that carefully and skillfully avoided evoking images of the plantation South (*Joscelyn, The Cub of the Panther,* and *Voltmeier,* for example).

On June 11, 1870, William Gilmore Simms died in the home of his eldest daughter at 13 Society Street in Charleston, the city of his birth.

II

Simms has importance in American intellectual history in ways other than literary—as an editor of periodicals; as a molder of political strategy; as an articulate spokesman for causes; as an early exponent of environmental protection and agricultural reform; as an antiquarian enamored of history, books, and art. Yet Simms looked upon himself primarily as a creator of belles lettres or a literature understood as encompassing history, for in his eyes no distinct line divided history and literature. Indeed, he believed that only through artistic creativity could the soul of history be captured and given life. In his fiction Simms made use of history in a way and to a degree unmatched by his contemporaries. He attempted to do for American history what Scott had done for Scottish—make it vibrantly alive. "My design is to identify my fiction (D.V.) with every historical scene in South Carolina," Simms wrote in 1856. "It is a vulgar sort of patriotism, no doubt."[28] Simms's multicultural concept of American history began not with British colonization but with French and Spanish exploration. His vision covered the whole span of America's birth and growth as a nation up to his own time; his challenge was to create books that fulfilled that vision.

Simms's advantage in contemplating a series of diverse books variously illustrating "national history," "national consciousness," or "national themes"—an amorphous task to most eyes—was his vision of an organic wholeness in the multiplicity of forces and influences shaping American history from its beginnings to his own times. Fascinated by the symmetry of historical patterns, he sighted threads of unity in the complex cultural woof from which the fabric of a new nation was being woven. To Simms, writing about precolonial America, the English colonies, the Revolutionary War, and the rampaging frontier of his own youth was no disparate effort, but part of a sustained, interconnected narrative covering more than four hundred years. He traced the development of American national consciousness through four centuries in two dozen books that, taken together, constitute a powerful, intense, highly readable epic.

Simms's forte, however, lies in his bold, hard-hitting, and tellingly accurate portrayal of life on American's moving frontier—from the sixteenth to the mid-nineteenth century. Simms's graphic depiction of the frontier, though, is not limited to his Border Romances; nearly all of his fiction, including the precolonial novels, the colonial novels, the Revolutionary Romances, and many of his short novels and stories, portray a frontier environment. In the words of Donald Davidson, "The field of Simms's fictions, if not its essential subject, is the frontier of the lower South. At its farthest stretch of time, it is the frontier from the Spanish explorations of the sixteenth century up to the 'flush times' of the eighteen-thirties when land-speculators and land-pirates were crowding into the newly opened Indian country of Georgia, Alabama, and Mississippi."

"Most important of all," Davidson continues, "the field of action" in Simms's Revolutionary War novels "is frontier South Carolina." Because the Indians were not expulsed until 1838, at the outbreak of the Revolution the frontier "as a social and cultural conditioning element" extended almost to "the gates of Charleston." Even the Southern plantation itself was "in principle and essence a frontier institution," for it not infrequently served as a headquarters to plan military strategy or as a fortress to help repel attack, as

---

28. WGS to James Chesnut, Jr., March 7, 1856, ibid., 3:423.

shown occasionally in Simms's novels.[29] But since the frontier of the lower South, especially South Carolina, is not known to Americans generally, Davidson concludes, "in the same familiar way that the history of frontier Kentucky and Tennessee, the Ohio valley, and the trans-Mississippi West is known," Simms's novels dealing with frontierlike warfare in precolonial Florida and in colonial South Carolina have been "virtually lost to our historical consciousness."[30]

The "interaction between civilization and frontier" is indeed Simms's "real subject,"[31] and the unifying principle of a career devoted largely to historical novels about the development of American identity from 1539 to 1862 — from *Vasconselos: A Romance of the New World* to *Paddy McGann; or, The Demon of the Stump.* Simms traced modes of thought and action in the nation's growing consciousness of itself as a nation and as a civilization. His statement to John R. Thompson in 1856 is particularly illuminating: "My novels aim at something more than the story. I am really, though indirectly, revising history . . . extending somewhat our usual province of His'l. Rom."[32] Later Simms reiterated his desire "to open new clues to the student in [the] province" of historical understanding.[33] He succeeded to a degree that is unmatched by any of his contemporaries in productiveness and surpassed by only a few in the quality of his best work.

Simms's productivity, however, raises a question which in any assessment of him must eventually be answered: how should one measure the accomplishments of a literary man who, in the words of Vernon Parrington, "poured out his material copiously, lavishly, with overrunning measure," producing annually "an incredible amount of work"[34] and a career output of eighty-two books, a total staggering enough for two or three ordinary professional men or women of letters. Though the great authors are best judged by their masterpieces, even a critic as elitist as Poe conceded that in calling Simms "the best novelist which this country has, upon the whole, produced," he had chosen to "take into consideration, of course, as well the amount of what he has written, as the talent he has displayed."[35] Just his output alone is astounding: one poem and one review a week, on average, over forty-plus years.

Simms's reputation is also dependent upon a certain willingness—

---

29. Davidson, "Introduction," ibid., 1 : xxxvii–xxxviii.
30. Ibid., xxxix–xl.
31. Ridgely, *Simms,* 67.
32. WGS to John R. Thompson, Feb. 7, 1856, *Letters* 3 : 421.
33. WGS to Benton John Lossing, May 22, 1856, ibid., 435.
34. Parrington, *Romantic Revolution,* 127.
35. Review of *The Wigwam and the Cabin* in *BJ* 2 (Oct. 4, 1845): 190.

displayed by critics of, say, Dickens, Fielding, Melville, Dreiser, or Wolfe—
to recognize strengths as "major" and blemishes as "minor." Poe's statement
that Simms's "merits lie among the major and his defects among the minor
morals of literature" exemplifies the critical position essential to the status
of Simms as a major writer.[36] No one has seriously questioned his possession
of strong literary virtues, and Simms himself freely acknowledged the presence of defects in even his best writings. In admitting to Beverley Tucker,
the author and law professor at the College of William and Mary, that his
works were "wanting in symmetry and finish" and "grossly disfigured by errors of taste and judgement," Simms explained that he was pointing out his
"crudenesses without endeavoring to excuse them." But, as in an earlier admission to Lawson of deficiency in his writings, Simms also expressed hope
that his friend "discover in them proofs of original force, native character,
and some imagination."[37]

Simms's strengths as a writer are both abundant and distinctive. As recognized by even his detractors, an "extraordinary gusto" permeates his writings, which in vigor, spontaneity, and robustness can compete with any body
of fiction by a single author in pre–Civil War America. Among novelists of
the time, it was Simms alone who (as Parrington astutely observed) captured
much of Whitman's "largeness and coarseness" and delight in the good things
of the earth.[38] In addition, Simms's writings possess power, exuberance, intensity in a measure that anticipate Thomas Wolfe, another Southerner with
boldness, impetuosity, and a sense of alienation and resentment. Donald
Davidson was right in pointing to the oral, folk quality of Simms's best novels and tales. Simms can be appreciated to the fullest only if read aloud. He
himself recognized both that he found it easier to invent a new story than to
repair the defects of an old one, and that when he forgot "himself in the excitement of the story," he wrote with his effortless, free-flowing style.[39] In
describing his habit of composition, Simms more than once remarked that
he wrote "*stans pede in uno,* goon like, literally, as fast as pen could fly over
paper."[40] On another occasion, he used a particularly vivid analogy to elu-
cidate his everyday practice: "I . . . write like steam, recklessly, perhaps
thoughtlessly—can give . . . no idea of the work";[41] yet again, in a passage

36. Ibid.
37. WGS to Beverley Tucker, May 29, April 23, 1849, *Letters* 2 : 528, 504.
38. Parrington, *Romantic Revolution,* 127.
39. WGS to RWG, Dec. 6, 1846, *Letters* 2 : 224–25.
40. WGS to Benjamin F. Perry, July 14, 1842, ibid., 1 : 316.
41. WGS to JL, Sept. 10, 1841, ibid., 278.

revealing remarkable self-awareness, he asserted: "I . . . write usually as I talk; and as the world goes am accounted a somewhat rude, blunt man."[42] Perhaps with the plea of Hammond (and other well-meaning advisers) in mind, Simms acknowledged that his "mode" of composition was "not very favorable to a work of permanent merit," but, he added significantly, it was "particularly suited to a temperament like mine."[43]

Because Simms's natural, seemingly careless writing habits have been widely assailed as being accountable for the lack of polish and refinement in his writings and yet have also been acclaimed as the source for the easy flow and raw power of his lusty, swift-moving prose at its best, the question of the effect of Simms's practices of composition upon the quality of his work needs to be resolved. Though assiduous efforts have been made to demonstrate that Simms revised his writing with more frequency and more effectiveness than commonly believed, the evidence suggests that he wrote his most memorable lines, passages, chapters, and books when he served almost involuntarily as the conduit through which his creativity surged without restraint, almost without direction. This is not to say that Simms never improved a work when he revised it, for there are specific instances when he did; but these revisions were never enough to transform mediocre writing into excellent writing. In Simms's best work he lost himself in the heat of creativity; he wrote "like steam" or "as I talked," "as fast as pen could fly over paper" because he gave himself up to inspiration. When he became conscious of observing literary proprieties, he tended to become awkward, stilted, pretentious, boringly conventional; when he "rolled up his sleeves" and spoke in natural language about the raw frontier he had experienced, he wrote visceral prose marked by a vernacular robustness and vibrancy not found in American letters before Mark Twain. Early in his career Simms detected that his "style was better" when his "feelings were aroused."[44] He later observed, truthfully in his case, that "fame does not so much as follow polish & refinement as Genius—not so much grace and correct delineation as a bold adventurous thought."[45] Whatever Simms did best, he did with passionate intensity, and if he burned himself out with one topic or with one endeavor, he turned to another, a lifelong practice which seemed to refresh his energy and restore his creativity.

Because "bold adventurous thought" was characteristic of Simms the man

---

42. WGS to Sarah Lawrence Drew Griffin, June 8, 1841, ibid., 6:27.
43. WGS to Perry, July 14, 1842, ibid., 1:316.
44. WGS to JL, Dec. 29, 1839, ibid., 162.
45. WGS to Holmes, Jan. 26, 1844, ibid., 400.

and writer, he naturally was attracted to aspects of human behavior other than the timid, the righteous, and the elegant. Though he depicted the civilized virtues of the drawing room and the plantation (at times very effectively in a vein of humorous, ironic satire) as well as the violence and lawlessness of the frontier, Simms, with his penchant for realism and his dramatic awareness, was never reluctant to focus upon the sensational and the horrible with an intensity unusual for his time. Early in his career Simms had written: "I certainly feel that, in bringing the vulgar and the vicious mind into exceeding activity in a story of the borders, I have done mankind no injustice." He was persuaded, he had added, that particularly during periods of war and hostility "vulgarity and crime must always preponderate— dreadfully preponderate."[46] Though Simms's unconventional use of graphic details in his treatment of murder, brutality, and other forms of violence revolted some critics and readers of his day, it is recognition of the existence of violence and disorder as a prominent strain in Southern life that inevitably links him to William Faulkner, Robert Penn Warren, and William Styron— a relationship noted only in passing, if at all, in the exhaustive studies of Southern literature as the preeminent representation of twentieth-century American letters. The roots of Faulkner and Warren are clearly to be found in Simms if the effort is made to read their fiction as emanating from a literary tradition rather than springing full-grown from previously unplowed Southern soil. And Simms's once controversial concept that an artist's role in a national literature is the faithful and meaningful portrayal of his own region is now accepted in the philosophy of composition of most "later Southern writers of fiction [who] write as though their theory was similar to that of Simms."[47] Simms's pivotal role as a kind of ancestral father to modern literature of the South cries for greater recognition. Acknowledging the vagaries of time and place in the establishment and maintenance of literary reputations, Simms without dismay observed late in his career, "My writings are not to be estimated by things of a clique or of a day."[48]

III

It will be helpful to offer a commentary on some of the selections that follow, which fall into various categories: letters, fiction, nonfiction, and poetry.

---

46. *Mellichampe*, 6.
47. Hubbell, *South in American Literature*, 595.
48. WGS to PHH, c. Aug. 1, 1864, *Letters* 4:461.

Letters: No literary man of his time wrote as many, as varied, or as interesting letters as did William Gilmore Simms. Whether one peruses them for the historical perspective of a complicated period in American history or simply for the enjoyment they provide for connoisseurs of epistolary prose, Simms's letters are remarkable. After the death of Simms, John Esten Cooke tried to persuade Paul Hamilton Hayne to use Simms's "delightful" correspondence as the basis for a biography, "letting our noble old Southern Maestro paint himself, his own large generous character, his struggles, trials, successes, and all."[49] More than a century later Louis D. Rubin, Jr., termed Simms's edited letters "the most important single document in the study of ante-bellum Southern cultural life," describing them as "essential not only for matters involving Simms but almost anything having to do with Southern literature, intellectual and political life during those key years when fateful identity of the region was being established."[50] But the significance of Simms the letter writer is not limited to documentation of the South. Because Simms's circle of friends included Northern authors, critics, and publishers; because he visited the North frequently and commented thoughtfully and sometimes pungently on his impressions of the conditions of life there; and because his correspondence covers a wide range of American politics, economics, and philosophy as well as literature and publishing, his letters have national implications and importance.

The selection of a small number of Simms letters from the more than fourteen hundred that have been collected and preserved is a difficult and painstaking task; however, the twenty-four included here represent the versatility, the complexity, the candor, the conviction, and—at times—the humor and the profundity of a letter writer who throughly enjoyed the art.

Fiction: Though Simms's highest accomplishment was in writing novels, his strongest abilities lay perhaps in the short story or novelette, a genre that benefited from his skill at swift-moving narrative even more than did the slower-paced novel. During his career Simms produced enough short fiction for five or six volumes of stories and novelettes of the first magnitude. *The Wigwam and the Cabin* alone contains thirteen stories ranging from Poe's favorite, "Grayling," to the controversial "Caloya, or, The Loves of the Driver," to a half-dozen personal favorites: "The Two Camps," "The Arm-Chair of Tustenuggee," "The Giant's Coffin," "Sergeant Barnacle," "Those

---

49. John Esten Cooke to PHH, April 2, 1873, Hayne Collection, Duke University Library.

50. Louis D. Rubin, Jr., to John C. Guilds, April 10, 1986, in possession of addressee; published in *Long Years of Neglect,* xi.

Old Lunes!" and "Lucas de Ayllon," each with distinctive excellences in the vein of Simms's border writings. In addition, "How Sharp Snaffles Got His Capital and Wife" and "Bald-Head Bill Bauldy" bear witness to Simms's mastery of the tall tale; while "The Humours of the Manager" and *Flirtation at Moultrie House* attest to his capability in humorous and satirical stories of manners. Other titles of interest and significance are "Ephraim Bartlett," "Mesmerides in a Stage-Coach," "Indian Sketch," "The Unknown Masque," and "Geoffrey Rudel." In Simms's "moral imaginative" category fall such tales as "Confessions of a Murderer" (the forerunner to *Martin Faber*), "Carl Werner," and "The Bride of Hate."

Perhaps even more than in the short story, Simms excelled in the writing of the short novel or novelette. In this category of "regularly planned . . . novels in little,"[51] he produced eight examples, beginning in 1833 with *Martin Faber,* a pioneering psychological study, and culminating in 1863 with *Paddy McGann,* whose ironic humor and biting satire make it one of Simms's most telling fictive works. Between *Faber* and *McGann* fall his studies of contemporary Carolina life, *Castle Dismal,* "Maize in Milk," and *The Golden Christmas,* each depicting the Christmas season; his vernacular comic narrative, *As Good as a Comedy,* a lively precursor of Faulkner's *The Reivers;* his Poesque novella set in New Orleans, *Marie de Berniere,* somewhat anticipatory of Kate Chopin; and his artistically pleasing Spanish romance, "The Maroon" (originally subtitled "A Legend of the Caribees"), never published separately as a book as he had hoped. These "novels in little" offer such rich varieties of tone, mood, and substance and display such evidence of literary virtuosity that, combined with his accomplishments in the short story, they testify to Simms's mastery of all forms of fiction, not simply of the novel, in which his greatest achievement lies.[52]

I have chosen five shorter pieces of fiction, one from Simms's earliest days, three from his middle period, one from after the Civil War.

Though "Indian Sketch," first published in 1828 in the *Southern Literary Gazette,* is marred by the clumsy phrasing of an inexperienced young writer hard-pressed with his responsibilities as coeditor of the journal, the unpretentious sketch is nevertheless noteworthy as Simms's earliest fictional portrayal of the Indian. In it the young author-editor mocks the romantically conceived "savage" of "the Poet and the novelist" and insists upon more realism in the treatment of the Indian; he also demonstrates his latent narrative skill and power, particularly in the highly effective final three paragraphs.

---

51. WGS to EAD, Dec. 6, 1854, *Letters* 3: 342.

52. *Selected Fiction of William Gilmore Simms: Arkansas Edition* is bringing out a series of WGS's novels, most of which are out of print.

"Indian Sketch" also marks Simms's earliest successful use of the Southern backwoods as the subject for fiction. Later in his career Simms expanded the germ of the story into a much longer, philosophy-laden version entitled "Oakatibbe, or, The Choctaw Sampson," included in *The Wigwam and the Cabin.*

Edgar Allan Poe, recognizing "Grayling" as one of Simms's "best fictions," singled it out as the "most meritorious" of the tales collected in 1845 in *The Wigwam and the Cabin,* a volume for which he had high praise. Not only did Poe find "Grayling" "full of the richest and most vigorous imagination"; he went on to say, "We have no hesitation in calling it the best ghost story we have ever read."[53] Such high acclaim from the master of the short story in the nineteenth century takes on added significance because of Poe's well-earned reputation as demanding critic as well as consummate artist. Multi-dimensional in characterization and range of tone, "Grayling" is also note-worthy for the artistic blending of the real and the unreal; perhaps more revealing than anything else Simms wrote, "Grayling" displays the lingering effects of the traumatic choice he as a child was forced to make between father and grandmother. Grayling's rejection of his father's rationalism and acceptance of his grandmother's spiritualism seems to reflect the author's own early decision to reject Mississippi, business-politics, and father in fa-vor of Charleston, imaginative literature, and grandmother. But whether or not autobiographical, the framework Simms employs—having the haunting legend emanate "from the lips of an aged relative" who had been "a resident of the seat of most frequent war in Carolina during the Revolution"—is an artful device for obtaining the willing suspension of disbelief requisite to the success of a story of the supernatural.

Perhaps the most artistically satisfying tale in the whole impressive col-lection, *The Wigwam and the Cabin,* first published in 1845, is "The Two Camps: A Legend of the Old North State." In it Simms achieves unity of tone and effect by employing a single vessel of consciousness whose credibility the reader never questions. Once Simms has provided the historical background and introduced the "hale and lusty, but white-headed" frontiersman, Daniel Nelson (who "unfolds from his own budget of experience a rare chronicle"), the entire legend of ubiquitous spiritual mediums on the rugged "southern borders of North Carolina" is put into the quizzical, picturesque dialect of the backwoods. Simms handles skillfully the delicate task of securing willing suspension of disbelief, crucial to the plausibility of Nelson's two visions of a hostile Indian camp.

The final story in *The Wigwam and the Cabin* (1845) and the only one not

---

53. EAP, review of *The Wigwam and the Cabin* in *BJ* 2 (Oct. 4, 1845): 190–91.

to represent "the border history of the south," "Lucas de Ayllon" illustrates Simms's concentration upon the "first period" of American history (c. 1497–c. 1607), during which came "frequent and unsuccessful attempts at colonization in our country by the various people of Europe—the English, French, and Spaniard." Simms's sense of history enabled him to recognize the multiethnic, heterogeneous roots in the establishment of the new nation, one of the few among his contemporaries to make this observation, and to make use of it in his fiction. "Lucas de Ayllon" should be read first and foremost as a love story, but it possesses many other fine qualities: as a ghost story, to be compared favorably with "Grayling"; as a legend of Indian tradition and folklore, to be compared with such stories as "The Arm-Chair of Tustenuggee: A Tradition of the Catawba" and "Jocassee: A Cherokee Legend," with such narrative poems as "The Broken Arrow," "Accabee—A Ballad," "Tzelica: A Tradition of the French Broad," and "The Last Fields of the Biloxi," and with such novels as *The Yemassee, Vasconselos,* and *The Cassique of Kiawah;* and, lastly, as an example of Simms's creation of a new genre, fictional history (as likened to historical fiction), in which fiction is made "simply tributary, and always subordinate to the fact," the words of the author in defining his accomplishment in *The Lily and the Totem, or, The Huguenots in Florida* (1850).[54] The terrifying experience aboard the Spanish slave ship described so vividly by Simms anticipates by some eleven years Herman Melville's celebrated "Benito Cereno," with its own devastating depiction of the horrors existing on another Spaniard slave ship of later vintage. "Lucas de Ayllon" may well be the earliest slave-ship narrative in American literature.

Simms's declaration, in the long footnote at the beginning of "Lucas de Ayllon," that "the essential facts" are "all historical" and his concluding challenge that "it will be difficult for any chronicler to say, of what I have written, more than that he himself knows nothing about it. But his ignorance suggests no good reason why better information should not exist in my possession" pose an interesting problem. While there are conflicting theories about how Lucas de Ayllon died, none coincides with the version Simms gives in this "historical nouvellette." In his own *The History of South Carolina* (1840), Simms cites an unspecified historical account in which De Ayllon and his company "fell victims to the cannibal propensities of the savages"; recognizing the "doubts cast upon" this "not improbable" event, Simms's *History* concludes: "Nothing is positively known of [De Ayllon] after this event, and what we have of, conjecture, describes him as living a life of ignominy,

54. WGS, "Epistle Dedicatory to the Hon. James H. Hammond, of South Carolina," *The Lily and the Totem,* iv.

and dying miserably at last."[55] Simms himself recognized that the "happy obscurity" of De Ayllon's death "leaves the poet at perfect liberty so to shape his catastrophe as to adapt it to the general exigencies of his story."[56] It should be pointed out that the "historian" Simms cites in two instances in the story is Simms himself, and that the "history" he quotes is in his own *History:* the quotation is verbatim except for the "punishment" in the *History* becoming "doom" in the story, a change not without artistic significance.

"How Sharp Snaffles Got His Capital and Wife" is a small masterpiece. Donald Davidson, in his 1952 introduction to Simms's *Letters,* was the first to proclaim that the story "stands almost without a peer, surely, among the 'tall tales' recorded or written in the United States,"[57] but lack of earlier recognition of "Sharp Snaffles" can be attributed largely to one fact: unavailability. Not published until after Simms's death, the story made its first appearance in *Harper's New Monthly Magazine* for October 1870 and was not collected in Simms's works until the publication of *Stories and Tales* a century later—in 1974.

There is evidence that Simms began gathering notes for "Sharp Snaffles" during a 1847 visit to the mountain region of North and South Carolina. "My purpose," he wrote to James Lawson at the time, "is to visit as much fine scenery, and to see & hear as much as I can. I shall make a book of it."[58] Several months later, in another letter to Lawson, Simms reported that his mission had been accomplished: "I have been among the mountaineers, in the very realm of wolf and panther, bear, deer, and other small vermin, with a budget sufficiently stored for a volume."[59] Knowledge of Simms's working habits leads to the conclusion that the 1847 "month . . . spent in a mountain camp, in the midst of hunters" provided him with the basic material for both "How Sharp Snaffles Got His Capital and Wife" and its companion piece, "Bald-Head Bill Bauldy," though he was not to bring his experiences to artistic fruition until some twenty years later.[60] Space limitations preclude the inclusion in *The Simms Reader* of "Bald-Head Bill Bauldy," left in manuscript at Simms's death, but it too is a gem in the tradition of Southwest humor and should be read in conjunction with "Sharp Snaffles." "Sharp Snaffles" and "Bald-Head Bill Bauldy," each told in dialect and each left unpublished at Simms's death, constitute perhaps the finest writing in the special genre of the tall tale in American literature.

---

55. WGS, *History of South Carolina,* 12.
56. *VRAH,* 1st ser., 91.
57. Davidson, "Introduction," *Letters* 1 : lii.
58. WGS to JL, Sept. 23, 1847, ibid., 2 : 350.
59. Ibid., Oct. 20, 1847, 356.
60. Ibid., March 23, 1848, ibid., 404.

Nonfiction: This unsatisfactory term covers many genres at which Simms was adept: social criticism, literary criticism, historical writing, and political observation, mostly embodied in the form of the essay. The untimely death of John R. Welsh in 1975 stopped work on the much-needed volume of Simms's essays scheduled to appear in *The Centennial Edition of the Writings of William Gilmore Simms,* and that scholarly lacuna still exists today; Simms's accomplishments as an essayist remain relatively unknown and neglected. Particularly if pronouncements on literary theory and criticism are included among Simms's essays, his importance as an essayist rises significantly. As a social and philosophical thinker, Simms was an articulate spokesman for fervently held views; he was, however, more an accurate reflector of society than an original thinker—though on occasion he could be a caustic, forward-looking critic of the opinions, customs, and practices of society. But in his prose writings about literature—whether they be critiques of books and authors, or enunciations about nationalism and regionalism in belles lettres, or definitions of genres, or expressions of literary creed—he was among the most imaginative, prescient, and judicious of his time. Simms's basic social theories center upon the importance of home, the need for stability, the value of work, the requirements of leadership, the protection of the environment, and reverence for the past—all consistent with the philosophy of the Southern planter class: noblesse oblige. His views on race and slavery were likewise those of his time and place. As a literary theorist and critic, however (as the essays that follow on Cooper, realism and Americanism in literature, and the function of poetry, among others, clearly show), Simms was an innovator and pioneer, grounded in the practical, but with a vision of the future.

I have arranged the selections chronologically, but it will be helpful here to discuss them by subject matter. First, I have included several of Simms's prefaces (in his day frequently called "advertisements"), which include statements revelatory of his literary technique, creed, and theory. In the "Advertisement" to the first edition of *The Yemassee* (1835), for instance, he anticipated by more than a decade-and-a-half the more famous definition of *romance* given by Hawthorne in *The House of Seven Gables* (1851). Though this early insistence by Simms upon the merits of the romance has caused some misunderstanding of his later espousal of literary realism—demonstrated in the excerpts from the prefaces to Redfield editions of *The Wigwam and the Cabin* (1856) and *Richard Hurdis* (1855)—all three are included here for reader perusal. The longer "Advertisement" to *The Partisan,* published, like *The Yemassee,* in 1835, contains a valuable explanation of Simms's original design for his Revolutionary War series, as well as an illustration of his technique of combining legend with history and encompassing both in fictional narrative, by which process the novel, "made useful[,] . . . ministers to morals, to mankind, and to society." Based upon his belief that "an author, having any real merits, is always the best critic of his own writings," Simms wrote in 1855, "My prefaces afford generally the leading idea of my works."[61]

Further light on his literary views is shed by his "Letter to the Editor" of 1841. Part of the debate over Simms's literary status centers around the long-standing question of whether Simms should be considered a romanticist or a realist—for he undeniably possessed characteristics of both. His early definition of *The Yemassee* as a "romance," not a "novel," and his accompanying contention that the romance was a modern prose epic, approximating "the poem" and "of loftier origin than the novel," are his best-known enunciations of romantic theory. Yet his forthright defense of "The Loves of the Driver" (later entitled "Caloya, or, The Loves of the Driver") and his forward-looking introduction to *The Wigwam and the Cabin* are substantial evocations of tenets of realism. "The Loves of the Driver," an account of the attempted seduction of a young Indian wife by a lustful black driver on a Georgia plantation, created an immediate furor upon its publication in 1841 in the *Magnolia, or, Southern Monthly,* a Savannah literary journal edited by Philip C. Pendleton. When a reader who termed himself "A Puritan" objected to "the low valley" of Simms's story, Pendleton responded with a clear-minded editorial statement defending Simms, and Simms himself came to Pendleton's and his own rescue in "A Letter to the Editor, by the Author of 'The Loves of the Driver.'"

Likewise, I have selected several of his critiques of notable contemporaries: Scott, Cooper, and Poe. Though Simms's indebtedness to Scott has been overemphasized, his admiration for Scott has not. Of all the writers of prose fiction in the English language, Sir Walter Scott in Simms's estimation was simply the best. His recognition of Scott's merit is best revealed in his long essay on "Modern Prose Fiction" (1849),[62] for which Simms made Scott the centerpiece. Likewise, Simms's much admired essay on Cooper, praised by Bryant "as the most illuminating and most judicious treatment of the novelist,"[63] displays the perceptiveness, the hardheadedness, and the open-mindedness that made Simms at his best one of the better critics in nineteenth-century America. Coming as it did when Cooper was distrusted and misunderstood by the reading public, "The Writings of James Fenimore

---

61. WGS to EAD, June 23, 1855, ibid., 3:388.
62. WGS, "Modern Prose Fiction," *SQR* 15 (April 1849): 41–83.
63. William Cullen Bryant, "Simms," *Homes of American Authors* (New York, 1853), 262.

Cooper" is on the whole an admirable piece of writing, demonstrating the critical acumen that was Simms's strength—and at the same time some of the impulsiveness and strong prejudice that were his chief weaknesses as a critic. Simms's thoughtful yet succinct definition of criticism—"justly to discriminate, firmly to establish, wisely to prescribe, and honestly to award—these are the true aims and duties of criticism"[64]—was not to him empty rhetoric; throughout his long career he made a point to single out both merits and defects in books that he reviewed, as illustrated in his treatment of Cooper. Yet the essay is perhaps most notable for its keen analysis of Cooper's character, for its stout defense of the right of an American literary man to be critical both of his own countrymen and the British.[65] Lastly, the brief critique of Poe's *Tales* that Simms wrote for the *Southern and Western* for August 1845 is enlightened, perspicacious, and fair-minded—one of the most discriminating written by a fellow American during Poe's lifetime. Poe and Simms continually crossed literary paths—as editors, writers, and critics—and frequently reviewed each other's works. It was Poe who in 1845, in the *Broadway Journal,* called Simms "the best novelist which this country has, upon the whole, produced."[66]

Simms also ventured biography. During a four-year period in the 1840s, Simms wrote three lives: of Francis Marion (1844), Captain John Smith (1846), and the Chevalier Bayard (1847); though he edited yet another, of Nathanael Greene, in 1849, at first attributed to Simms, he was never to write a book of biography again. Why this midcareer flurry of interest in the lives of other men? One reason was the literary market: in late 1843 Simms observed that because "novel writing at present is not encouraging," he was "engaged on nothing better than biography";[67] another, perhaps more compelling motivation was his conviction that the study of heroic lives helped in making the most of one's own life. In each of Simms's biographies the protagonist confronts the choice of a profession, a subject of continuous interest to Simms; with Bayard, his profession of soldiering had been dictated by his "natural endowments," just as in Simms's eyes his own calling was prescribed by his own inclination toward the literary. Despite the difference between Bayard and himself—soldier and poet—there was an overriding parallel in that neither "chose his vocation; the vocation had chosen him." Why

64. WGS, *Egeria,* 19.

65. First published in 1842 under the title "Cooper: His Genius and Writings," in the *Magnolia, or, Southern Apalachian,* of which WGS was editor, the essay was revised and expanded for inclusion in *VRAH* (1845), the version used as copy-text.

66. EAP, review of *The Wigwam and the Cabin,* in *BJ* 2 (Oct. 4, 1845): 190.

67. WGS to George Frederick Holmes, Oct. 27, 1843, *Letters* 1 : 378–79.

after Bayard, his third and best-written biography, did Simms never seriously undertake another? The best answer: his hard-earned recognition that literary immortality rests upon belles lettres, not biography.

Simms's broader historical and aesthetic philosophy is best understood through his lecture on "Poetry and the Practical" and his essays on "Americanism in Literature" and "The Four Periods of American History." Simms's original assessment of "Poetry and the Practical" was, however, extremely modest; he advised M. C. M. Hammond, at whose home he was to be guest the night before the initial lecture in Augusta, Georgia, on January 6, 1851: "I shall deal generously with you, and will not expect, you, as a friend, to listen to my Lecture. I shall not decieve you with any assurance that it will be worth your hearing, for, in truth, I write nothing nowadays that affords me satisfaction. My mind is jaded, and I merely drivel. I shall try & make it passable, my performance, so as not to fall into discredit; but when I wish my friends to listen, I would achieve something fresh and glorious. This is not my season for such a performance."[68] Whether Simms really had serious misgivings about "Poetry and the Practical," or whether, as was his wont, he merely attempted (with tongue-in-cheek) to keep the expectations of his host low, the lecture when delivered was a success — to such an extent that James Henry Hammond (M. C. M.'s brother) raved, "I have never known any speech to produce such a sensation in Augusta."[69] Despite Simms's disclaimer, he had put much thought into the content of "Poetry and the Practical," and in its actual composition he seems to have experienced one of those creative surges that distinguished his most imaginative works. Perhaps motivated by the spontaneous acclaim of his listening audience, Simms again took up the manuscript and carefully reworked his main ideas, expanding the original lecture into a series of three lectures, which he delivered on special occasions in his honor in 1854.[70]

Simms ranks as one of the nation's staunchest advocates of a distinctive American literature. Rising from an inauspicious beginning as a brash, young author and editor in the South to a position as a recognized spokesman for Young America, he remained throughout his career an ardent and faithful

---

68. WGS to M. C. M. Hammond, Dec. 14, 1850, ibid., 3:80–81.

69. JHH to WGS, Jan. 21, 1851, ibid., 86n.

70. All manuscript versions of "Poetry and the Practical" are located in the Charles Carroll Simms Collection. The longer, three-part manuscript—from which the excerpt in *The Simms Reader* is taken—has been edited by James E. Kibler, Jr., and published for the first time in 1996. Kibler considers "Poetry and the Practical" one of the most important enunciations of poetic theory in nineteenth-century American literature.

champion of "Americanism" in literature, though in time he became convinced that he could best serve national literature by encouraging the development of letters in his own region. In the initial article in "Simms's Magazine" (as the *Southern and Western Monthly Magazine and Review* was popularly called), the editor set the tenor for his new magazine with "Americanism in Literature," ostensibly a review of the oration by that title delivered by Alexander B. Meek at the University of Georgia in August 1844.[71]

Actually the third section of a larger essay entitled "The Epochs and Events of American History, as Suited to the Purposes of Art in Fiction," "The Four Periods of American History" prefigures Simms's lifelong practice of using American history "for the purposes of art in fiction." In this prescient and farsighted essay Simms explained his ideas for "the illustration of national history"—a formula which he had used in writing some of his novels before 1845 and which was to provide him ready-made "national-theme" subjects for future volumes. Simms was the only American author of the nineteenth century to envision, design, initiate, and consummate an epic portrayal of the development of the nation.[72]

A more informal grasp of Simms's view of his society can be gleaned from his travel writing. In 1831 the young Simms, then editor of the Charleston *City Gazette,* made his second visit to the Southwest—a trip occasioned by the death of his father in Mississippi on March 28, 1830. The enterprising twenty-four-year-old editor took full advantage of his journey by publishing in the *City Gazette* a series of ten travel letters entitled "Notes of a Small Tourist," chronicling his impressions of sites in Georgia, Alabama, Louisiana, and Mississippi while en route to his father's plantation in Columbia, Mississippi. "Notes of a Small Tourist—No. 10," appearing in the *City Gazette* of May 17, 1831, documents the last phase of Simms's adventurous travels, earmarked by the young writer's keen observations on subjects as diverse as the early theater in New Orleans and "a journey on horseback . . . into the Yazoo purchase." These first recorded reflections on the newly opened frontier are seminal to Simms's Border Romances and other backwoods writings.

Nonetheless, the key to Simms's social philosophy is the lecture he delivered at the University of Alabama in December 1843, under the title "The Social Principle: The True Source of National Permanence" (later published as a pamphlet by the Erosophic Society of the University). As a youth Simms

---

71. The article was slightly revised for publication as the lead essay in *VRAH,* the copy-text here.

72. "The Four Periods of American History," like "Americanism in Literature," was first published in *SWMMR* before being included in *VRAH.*

had visited Alabama en route to visit his father in Mississippi; thus he knew at first hand the great potential of the Southwest. His resistance to the invitations of his father (and later his uncle) to move west (where he was assured political and economic success), combined with his choice to remain in Charleston and become a writer, was probably the crucial decision in his life. Knowledgeable about both the frontier and the city, as few in his day were, Simms developed in "The Social Principle" an explanation of history based (in the words of John McCardell) upon "the careful balance between permanence, stability, polish, and devotion to home, and innovation, exploration, and the crude, disorderly realities that accompany the progress of a people."[73] The oration created much fanfare in Tuscaloosa (Simms was awarded an honorary doctorate on the occasion) and attracted favorable notice after its publication, one discriminating reviewer terming it "an essay of the very first order of merit."[74] Obsessed as he was with the prospect of literary fame, Simms frequently underestimated (or pretended to underestimate) his productions not clearly in the realm of belles lettres; thus his own modest assessment—"a performance to which I attach no great value myself"—belies its significance as the most important exegesis of a personal and social philosophy visionary for its times.[75]

Simms was a slaveholder, who judged both the system of slavery as well as the individuals in it, the individual and the genus. He recognized that strengths and weaknesses existed in all people, and he learned through experience that some could be trusted, and some could not; that some were compassionate and intelligent, and some were not; that some possessed loyalty and courage, and some did not. Simms made distinctions of these kinds in his relationships with all people—white, black, or red—and in his fiction he portrayed good and bad individuals of all three races. But Simms, like most intellectuals of his time and place, expressed no belief in racial equality; he and they falsely reasoned that patriarchal slavery was a benefit to an inferior black race as a means of self-development. (Interestingly enough, Simms did not defend exploitation of the Native American, whose rights to land and tradition he tacitly acknowledged.) In his creative writing Simms tended away from social propaganda, though having fictive characters take potshots at abolitionists, he considered fair game. His habit, particularly in his fiction, was not to propagandize but simply to reflect the manners, customs, and morals of the region and the people he depicted. But as private

73. McCardell, "Poetry and the Practical," 201.
74. Thomas Caute Reynolds, "Mr. Simms as a Political Writer," *SLM* 9 (Dec. 1843): 755.
75. WGS to John Pendleton Kennedy, June 16, 1844, *Letters* 5:382.

citizen, plantation owner, and spokesman for the South, Simms made clear his support of slavery, his most explicit statement coming in a pamphlet, published in Richmond in 1838, entitled *Slavery in America, Being a Brief Review of Miss Martineau on That Subject,* "By a South Carolinian." Ostensibly a book review of Harriet Martineau's *Society in America* (1837), Simms's essay is actually an answer to Martineau's attack on slavery.[76] Little more than an articulation of the patriarchal philosophy adopted by most intellectuals living in the seaboard South in the 1830s and 1840s, *Slavery in America* won enthusiastic applause from critics in the South and even the *New York Mirror* called it "an admirable critique" of Miss Martineau.[77] While it does not belong to Simms's literary canon, as the author himself recognized, he did consider it "a very successful paper";[78] it is an accurate reflection of the point of view of the Southern planter class to which Simms belonged.

Simms's most significant use of history is not as a professional historian but as a creative artist who draws upon it extensively, especially for use in fiction, but also in poetry, drama, and essays. Simms himself explains this role in his definition of the "true historian": "Hence it is the artist who is the true historian. It is he who gives shape to the unhewn fact, who yields relation to the scattered fragments,—who unites the parts in coherent dependency, and endows, with life and action, the otherwise motionless automata of history. It is by such artists, indeed, that nations live."[79]

Only a few times in his career did Simms write books of history per se — most notably in *The History of South Carolina* (1840) and *Sack and Destruction of the City of Columbia* (1865)—and even in these instances he had agenda other than strictly chronicling and interpreting historical data. But Simms was a historian in another sense: the perceptive and articulate observer of mankind and his environment who recorded for posterity his thoughts and observations. Coming under his scrutiny were subjects as diverse as travel, social principles, politics, military strategy, qualities of leadership, and manners and mores—such as sectional and national prides and prejudices and many smaller individual idiosyncrasies. Probably Simms's most valuable contribution as a historian, however, is his stark, powerful account of the *Sack and Destruction of the City of Columbia, S.C., to Which Is Added a List of Property Destroyed,* an eyewitness record of the pillaging of South Carolina's capi-

---

76. It was entitled "Miss Martineau on Slavery" when first published in *SLM* for Nov. 1837.

77. *New York Mirror,* Mar. 23, 1839.

78. WGS to JL, Dec. 29, 1839, *Letters* 1 : 166.

79. WGS, "The Epochs and Events of American History, as Suited to the Purposes of Art in Fiction," *VRAH,* 1st ser., 36.

tal after its surrender to Sherman's army. It is an important and impressive historical document, recognized by James Kibler as "among Simms's best works" for its graphic description and its "stark and powerful prose style."[80] Ironically, Simms and at least four of his children were in Columbia at the time of Sherman's invasion on February 1 7, 1 86 5, only because Simms had evacuated his family from Woodlands to Columbia, believing it to be safer. But by nightfall of the day on which Sherman's troops entered Columbia, the author had witnessed much uncontrolled destruction of a surrendered city. Simms's explicit account was published in book form in the summer of 1 86 5 after first having appeared in slightly different form in the *Columbia Phoenix* during March and April. Simms's presence in the city and credibility as a historian lend substance to his depiction of the chaos that prevailed in the surrender of the civilian government of Columbia to the military command under Sherman. The fire that demolished the city after one day of Union occupation was attributed by Sherman to causes beyond his control; with unmistakable irony Simms viewed the tragedy differently.

But Simms often wrote history with contemporary purposes. A sample of his political writing is his essay on the Southern Convention held in the summer of 1 8 5 0 in Nashville, Tennessee, with the dual purpose of denouncing Northern interference with the South and designing a strategy for the South in dealing with the North. As editor of the *Southern Quarterly Review,* the most influential "organ of opinion and education" in the South, Simms tried to shape a policy to counteract Northern aggressiveness and, if all else failed, to lead to secession, with South Carolina in the forefront. Thus in his treatise on the convention, Northern injustice to Southern accomplishment in the Revolutionary War and Northern indifference to Southern opinion were central to his argument. Though conciliatory toward Southern delegates not yet committed to a firm stand, Simms's tone from beginning to end, as the excerpts show, was defiant toward the North. "The Southern Convention," appearing in the *Southern Quarterly* for September 1 8 5 0, comes to no hopeful conclusion.

History and politics mingled in 1 8 5 6, when Simms made one of his most devastating political mistakes. Vexed by political defeat and disappointment and irked by the frustrating conclusion to his editorship of the *Southern Quarterly Review,* he passionately and unwisely plunged into a tumultuous lecture tour of the North amid one of the most turbulent periods of North-South relations. Although the inflammatory speech by Massachusetts senator Charles Sumner in a May 1 8 5 6 Senate debate over Kansas was the primary instigator

---

80. James Everett Kibler, Jr., "William Gilmore Simms," *DLB* 7 : 291.

of the worsened state of affairs between North and South, Simms had already written to Northern friends a month earlier that he was contemplating "a course of lectures at the North this coming winter."[81] Well before Sumner's tirade attacking South Carolina senator Andrew Pickens Butler and impugning the role of South Carolina in the Revolutionary War, Simms had expressed the intent to hold at least one lecture in the North "to establish better relations between North & South" and had explained to Boston publisher James T. Fields that he designed "one or two Lectures touching the scenery, the society, habits manners, of the South, especially for your people."[82]

Thus the disastrous Northern lecture tour of 1856 was not originally conceived of as a response to Sumner's condemnation of South Carolina but as a friendly public-spirited mission to create better understanding between two widely divergent parts of the Union. The Sumner-Butler imbroglio, heightened by the caning of Sumner by South Carolina representative Preston S. Brooks, almost certainly altered Simms's attitude toward what he had hoped to accomplish with his lectures: though his purpose was still educational, his outlook changed from one of kindly benevolence intent upon instructing with charm to one of righteous indignation set upon redeeming the honor of South Carolina and South Carolinians in a hostile environment. He changed, in short, from peaceful missionary representing only himself to belligerent aggressor charged with righting a wrong done to his state and his people. Simms's letter of September 7, 1856, to Hammond reveals that political leaders in South Carolina looked to him to be their spokesman in this heated controversy:

> Butler and Evans are flooding me with the attacks of the Northern Press on South Carolina. Butler says "I have no time to answer them. It is the business of the Historian." But his blunderings have provoked them, & he is one of the victims in all the attacks. In brief he wants me to take up the cudgels and fight his battles. It is a pretty thing that one has fed all his life at the treasury bowls, who is still feeding—who is chosen for this very sort of warfare—should call upon me to do the business, whom he & his fraternity have always contrived to keep without feed at all.[83]

The bitter, defiant tone of this letter reveals the state of mind of Gilmore Simms just before he trudged North "to take up the cudgels and fight [the]

---

81. WGS to Mary Lawson, April 17, 1856, *Letters* 3:423–24; see also to EAD, April 18, 1856, ibid., 425.

82. WGS to James T. Fields, April 19, 1856, ibid., 429.

83. WGS to JHH, Sept. 7, 1856, ibid., 446–47. Josiah James Evans (1786–1858) was, like Butler, U.S. senator from South Carolina; he served until his death.

battles" of his fellow citizens, an action that succeeded only in making a bad
situation worse. One would hope that Hammond, at least, had advised his
good friend against throwing himself into a no-win foray with high personal
risk, although Simms's espoused intent, "to disabuse the public of the North
of many mistaken impressions which do us wrong,"[84] reveals his crusading
purpose, and perhaps Hammond, like Simms, felt that Northern cities (especially New York) would give the Southerner a fair hearing out of respect
for his stature. At any rate, Hammond waited until after the calamitous experiences (fully documented in a valuable article by Miriam J. Shillingsburg),
in almost every Northern city in which Simms gave his lecture entitled
"South Carolina in the Revolution," to express his dismay. Writing bluntly
to Simms of his folly, Hammond charged: "You have gone North at a somewhat critical time for *you* & martyred yourself for So Ca, who will not even
buy your books & for Brooks whose course could at best be only *excused*."[85]

The most significant and far-reaching effect of this episode, which caused
Simms to lose credibility with the Northern audience that had provided the
greatest number of readers of his books, may have been, as Shillingsburg suggests, to poison his reputation in the North for the remainder of his life.

Poetry: During his career William Gilmore Simms published two thousand
poems, in magazines, newspapers, and eighteen volumes of poetry, and
wrote many others that never got into print. Thus, beginning early ("I commenced doggrelizing, I think at 8 or 9") and continuing late, the habit of
writing poetry was so ingrained in Simms—came so naturally to him—that
he was scarcely aware of his productivity: "I write daily, on an average from
15 to 22 pages foolscap," he once remarked of his capacity to "write like
steam": "I am afraid to think of what I've done."[86] But writing naturally, or
writing by habit, does not signify writing without purpose or ambition; on
the contrary, Simms held "poetry . . . to be my proper province" and expressed confidence that "I shall someday assert a better rank in verse than . . .
in prose."[87] Upon the publication of his favorite collection, *Poems Descriptive, Dramatic, Legendary and Contemplative,* in 1853, Simms confided to E. A.
Duyckinck: "I flatter myself that my poetical works exhibit the highest phase

84. WGS to George Bancroft, William Cullen Bryant, and others, Nov. 3, 1856,
ibid., 454.

85. JHH to WGS, Nov. 27, 1856, ibid., 465n.

86. WGS to RWG, June 20, 1841, to Sarah Lawrence Drew Griffin, Sept. 27, 1841,
to JL, Sept. 10, 1841, ibid., 5:356, 358, 6:37, 1:278.

87. WGS to George William Bagby, Nov. 9, 1860, to Frederick Saunders, Aug. 10,
1852, ibid., 6:213, 3:190.

of the imaginative faculty which this country has yet exhibited"—a self-judgment which, he admitted disarmingly, "sounds. . . very egotistical, perhaps, but I am now 47 years old, and do not fear to say to a friend what I think of my own labour."[88] Simms's desire to be remembered as a poet is finally being accorded: a new assessment of his poetry is in progress, largely as a result of the publication in 1990 of *Selected Poems of William Gilmore Simms,* a scholarly edition (edited by James E. Kibler, Jr.) that gives substantial evidence of Simms's poetic prowess.

The poems that follow, selected from all phases of Simms's career, reveal the scope, tone, substance, and technique of his poetry. Included are philosophical and religious poems (e.g., "Heedlessness" and "Sonnet—The Age of Gold"); narrative poems of Indian legend or tradition ("The Broken Arrow," "Tzelica," and "Accabee—A Ballad"); highly autobiographical poems ("Sonnet—To My Books," "Invocation," "Life, Struggle and Defeat," and "The Voice of Memory in Exile"); poems of nature, beautiful and serene ("The Grape Vine Swing," "Ashley River," and "Carolina Woods") and poems of nature, wild and violent ("The Wilderness" and "Taming the Wild Horse"); literary poems ("Shakspeare," "Scott," and "The Poet"); patriotic, historical poems ("Hayne—Let the Death-Bell Toll"); poems of the frontier ("The Western Emigrants"); witty, satirical poems ("The Kiss behind the Door," "Politician," and " 'Tis True That Last Night I Adored Thee"); and rollicking drinking songs ("Raisons in Law and Liquor") and folklore ballads ("The Ballad of the Big Belly"). It should be noted that nearly all these poems are Southern in theme and character, and that the most memorable are written in sonorous vernacular language. As a group, the sonnets in particular excel (lending validity to Simms's own observation, "I am vain to think [*Grouped Thoughts and Scattered Fancies*] are the best collection of sonnets ever printed in America");[89] but probably the powerful sweep of his superbly crafted Indian ballads (the most famous of which, "The Cassique of Accabee," is excluded because of length) represents his highest poetic achievement.

To conclude, then, Simms is a poet of more power, originality, and versatility than had been recognized before recent study placing him among the important writers of poetry before the Civil War.[90] As a literary critic and spokesman for belles lettres in general, Simms was among the most influen-

---

88. WGS to EAD, Nov. 24, 1852, ibid. 3 : 261–62.

89. Ibid., Oct. 28, 1845, 2 : 111. With characteristic honesty and ambivalence, however, WGS in a less buoyant mood admitted that his early poems "contained a great deal of very sorry stuff," calling them "overflowing rather than working . . . unseemly . . . too frequently turbid" (to RWG, June 20, 1841, ibid., 1 : 356).

90. Kibler, "Introduction," *Selected Poems,* xi–xxii.

tial of his place and time: a discriminating and powerful, if sometimes biased and volatile force to the good of American and Southern letters. As a writer of drama (for which he held a poorly concealed lifelong passion), he is among the unsuccessful pioneers in a genre late to develop in America as a serious art form, but even here he displayed enough promise to prompt a distinguished literary historian of our time to conclude that if his efforts had been so channeled he could have been a significant playwright.[91] Among our literary letter writers of the nineteenth century, Simms is peculiarly valuable in his importance to both historians and literary scholars. His almost two thousand pieces of correspondence display many of the striking qualities—audacity, frankness, rebelliousness, exuberance, spontaneity, keen insight, and good humor—that characterize the man and his works. While it is remarkable that he accomplished so much in other literary fields—poetry, criticism, drama, letter writing—it is, I believe, as a writer of fiction, and particularly as a novelist, that Simms leaves his most enduring mark. And most of all, Simms's novels and tales breathe with the vitality of the American frontier. The harsh, brutal frontier of Simms's experience and observation contrasts sharply with the idealized frontier of Cooper's imagination and reading. Realistic portrayal of the frontier is uniquely the power and the glory of Simms as an author. The frontier in Simms shifts from the Spanish and the French expeditions in Florida in the sixteenth century, to colonial and Revolutionary times in South Carolina in the seventeenth and eighteenth centuries, to the land-rush settlements of the lower Mississippi Valley in the first half of the nineteenth century. Such comprehensiveness of vision about the frontier experience is found nowhere else in the literature of his day. Within the narrative mode he adapted his talents superbly to the different and difficult tasks of writing the short story, the novelette, and the novel. In short fiction or long, Simms has few peers among his contemporaries, whether gauged by the substantial worth of his work in each genre or by the singular excellence of those efforts adjudged to be his finest.

---

91. Hubbell, *South in American Literature,* 593.

Statement of Editorial Principles

The purpose of *The Simms Reader* is to present selections from the volumi-
nous work of William Gilmore Simms that reflect its variety, depth, and
complexity. Priority has been given to the portrayal of ideas and themes central to Simms and his times, to the demonstration of his artistic technique
and theory, and to the revelation of his personality and character. Writings
from every period of Simms's life, from every phase of his career, and from
every genre in which he worked (except the novel and drama) are included.
Whenever possible, the entire text of a selection is provided: all letters,
short stories, and poems appear in toto; but to obtain a fair sampling of
Simms's essays and historical and biographical writings, I have been forced to
use excerpts of these items. Space limitations also support the policy that
when two viable versions of a text exist, the shorter, more compact version
has precedence; scarcity of space has precluded representation of Simms's
novels.

No attempt has been made to regularize Simms's spelling, capitalization,
or punctuation; for example, in his letters and the manuscript "Poetry and
the Practical" his characteristic spelling of *recieve* has been preserved; in the
case of works published during Simms's lifetime, the nineteenth-century
version has been retained without alteration, except to correct obvious ty-
pographical omissions or errors, indicated by square brackets.

A word about titles: in the bibliography of books by Simms, titles conform precisely to the wording and punctuation on the title page of the original publication (as does information identifying the author and publisher).
Otherwise, throughout *The Simms Reader* titles have been regularized in accordance with modern editorial principles. Individual poems conform, in
indentations and punctuation, to copy-text.

To provide as clear a text as possible, all footnotes in the text other than
the letters are by Simms [*WGS*] (but not every note by Simms has been retained). Headnotes to the letters contain information relevant to a reading
of the text. Unless otherwise noted, the following editions provide copy-
text (with permission from the appropriate press) for the selections in the
The Simms Reader: The Letters of William Gilmore Simms, ed. Mary C. Simms

Oliphant et al., 6 vols. (Columbia: University of South Carolina Press, 1952–82); *Selected Poems of William Gilmore Simms,* ed. James Everett Kibler, Jr. (Athens: University of Georgia Press, 1990); *Stories and Tales,* vol. 5 of *The Writings of William Gilmore Simms: Centennial Edition,* ed. John Caldwell Guilds (Columbia: University of South Carolina Press, 1974); *Views and Reviews in American Literature, History and Fiction* by William Gilmore Simms, 1st ser., ed. C. Hugh Holman (Copyright © 1962 by the President and Fellows of Harvard College, renewed © 1990 by Margaret Holman Stroud. Reprinted by permission of Harvard University Press); *The Cub of the Panther: A Hunter Legend of the "Old North State,"* ed. Miriam Jones Shillingsburg (Fayetteville: University of Arkansas Press, 1997).

Chronology

1806	Born in Charleston, South Carolina, April 17, the son of William Gilmore Simms, an Irish immigrant, and Harriet Ann Augusta Singleton Simms
1808	Mother died; left in the custody of his maternal grandmother by his father, who, frustrated by personal tragedy and business failure, deserted Charleston for the Southwest
1812–16	Attended public schools in Charleston
1816	Made momentous decision to remain in Charleston with grandmother rather than join now-wealthy father in Mississippi
1816–18	Concluded formal education at private school conducted in buildings of the College of Charleston
1818	Apprenticed to apothecary to explore medical career
1824–25	Visited father in Mississippi; witnessed rugged frontier life
1825	Began study of law in Charleston office of Charles Rivers Carroll; edited (and published extensively in) the *Album,* a Charleston literary weekly
1826	Married Anna Malcolm Giles, October 19
1827	Admitted to bar; appointed magistrate of Charleston; published two volumes of poetry; first child, Anna Augusta Singleton Simms, born November 11
1828–29	Founding coeditor, *Southern Literary Gazette*
1830	As editor of Charleston *City Gazette* supported Union in the Nullification crisis
1831	Visited Southwest to settle father's estate
1832	Death of Anna Malcolm Giles Simms February 19; made first visit to New York, where he met James Lawson, who became his literary agent and lifelong friend; published *Atalantis,* his fourth volume of poetry
1833	Published first volume of fiction, *Martin Faber: The Story of a Criminal*
1834	Published first "regular novel," *Guy Rivers: A Tale of Georgia*

1835   Published *The Yemassee: A Romance of Carolina* and *The Partisan: A Tale of the Revolution*

1836   Married Chevillette Eliza Roach, November 15, and moved to Woodlands, a plantation owned by her father; published *Mellichampe: A Legend of the Santee*

1837   Birth of Virginia Singleton Simms, November 15; first of fourteen children born to Chevillette Roach Simms

1838   Published *Richard Hurdis, or, The Avenger of Blood: A Tale of Alabama*

1839   Published *Southern Passages and Pictures,* "some of my best *published* verses"

1840   Published *Border Beagles: A Tale of Mississippi* and *The History of South Carolina*

1841   Published *The Kinsmen, or, The Black Riders of Congaree: A Tale* (later retitled *The Scout*) and *Confession, or, The Blind Heart: A Domestic Story*

1841   Published *Beauchampe, or, The Kentucky Tragedy: A Tale of Passion* (later retitled *Charlemont*)

1842−43   Editor, *Magnolia,* Charleston literary magazine

1844   Elected to South Carolina legislature for 1844−46 term; published *Castle Dismal, or, The Bachelor's Christmas: A Domestic Legend* and *The Life of Francis Marion*

1845   Published *The Wigwam and the Cabin; Helen Halsey, or, The Swamp State of Conelachita: A Tale of the Border;* and *Grouped Thoughts and Scattered Fancies;* editor, *Southern and Western* (popularly known as "Simms's Magazine")

1846   Published *Views and Reviews in American Literature, History and Fiction,* first series (dated 1845); *Areytos, or, Songs of the South;* and *The Life of Captain John Smith*

1847   Published *Views and Reviews,* second series (dated 1845) and *The Life of Chevalier Bayard*

1849−54   Editor, *Southern Quarterly Review*

1850   Published *The Lily and the Totem, or, The Huguenots in Florida*

1851   Published *Katharine Walton, or, The Rebel of Dorchester: An Historical Romance of the Revolution in Carolina* and *Norman Maurice, or, The Man of the People: An American Drama*

1852   Published *The Sword and the Distaff, or, "Fair, Fat and Forty": A Story of the South at the Close of the Revolution* (retitled *Woodcraft*); *The Golden Christmas: A Chronicle of St. John's, Berkeley; As Good as a Comedy, or, the Tennessean's Story;* and *Michael Bonham, or, The Fall of Bexar: A Tale of Texas*

1853   Published *Vasconselos: A Romance of the New World* and a collected edition of *Poems*

1855   Published *The Forayers, or, The Raid of the Dog-Days*

1856   Published *Eutaw: A Sequel to the Forayers . . . ; Charlemont, or, The Pride of the Village. A Tale of Kentucky;* and *Beauchampe, or, The Kentucky Tragedy: A Sequel to Charlemont;* disastrous lecture tour of the North, in which he voiced pro—South Carolina and pro—Southern views

1858   Lost two sons to yellow fever on the same day, September 22: the "crowning calamity" of his life

1859   Published *The Cassique of Kiawah: A Colonial Romance;* the *North American Review, Godey's,* and the *New York Leader* all recognize Simms as the best of America's living novelists

1860   Vigorously supported the secessionist movement; published last collection, *Simms's Poems: Areytos*

1862   Woodlands burned; rebuilt with subscription funds from friends and admirers; birth of last child, Charles Carroll Simms, October 20

1863   Published *Paddy McGann; or, The Demon of the Stump;* Chevillette Roach Simms died September 10: "bolt from a clear sky"

1864   Eldest son William Gilmore Simms, Jr., wounded in Civil War battle in Virginia, June 12; most intimate friend in South Carolina, James Henry Hammond, died November 13

1865   Woodlands burned by stragglers from Sherman's army; witnessed the burning of Columbia, described in *Sack and Destruction of the City of Columbia, S.C.*

1866   Made arduous but largely unsuccessful efforts to reestablish relations with Northern publishers

1867   Published *Joscelyn: A Tale of the Revolution* serially in the magazine *Old Guard*

1869   Published *The Cub of the Panther: A Mountain Legend* serially in *Old Guard;* published *Voltmeier, or The Mountain Men* serially in *Illuminated Western World* magazine

1870   Delivered oration on "The Sense of the Beautiful" May 3; died, after a long bout with cancer, at the Society Street home of his daughter Augusta (Mrs. Edward Roach) in Charleston, June 11, survived by Augusta and five of the fourteen children from his second marriage; June 15 the *Charleston Daily Courier* announced plans for a monument honoring Simms

1879   Commemorative bust of Simms (by John Quincy Adams Ward) unveiled in White Point Gardens, Charleston

Letters

LETTER 1

Addressee: James Lawson / New York City / N.Y.
Postmark: Orangeburg / April 19 [1836]

James Lawson (1798–1880) was Simms's chief correspondent over a span of forty years. Born in Glasgow he emigrated to New York as a young man and established himself there as an astute businessman with literary proclivities; a minor poet, playwright, and editor, he immediately bonded with Simms during the latter's first visit to New York in 1832. He became Simms's literary agent and his chief conduit to New York's circle of writers and publishers. During Simms's annual summer visits in the early 1830s, the two young bachelors courted together, had long talks together, and cemented a relationship that lasted a lifetime. Despite some playful squabbles—Simms complained about Lawson's tardiness and testiness as a letter writer; Lawson, aware of the mutual attraction between his wife and his friend, who cheerfully acknowledged his love for "Lady Lyde" (or "Lady Lide"), experienced spasmodic pangs of jealousy—the two remained loyal and dedicated to each other despite the tensions of the Civil War. The families, too, were close: Lawson named a son for Simms, and Simms named a daughter Mary Lawson. Simms's letters to Lawson are witty and conversational, assertive and frank on literary matters, caring and supportive on personal matters, and—with the exception of politics, which Simms was reluctant to discuss freely with his New York friend—unfailingly candid on all matters.

After Lawson's marriage to Mary Eliza Donaldson in 1835, Simms wrote to his friend in January, 1836: "I fear I shall not soon be so fortunate as yourself."[1] Simms was actively pursuing the "fair, gentle, accomplished" Chevillette Eliza Roach, daughter of Nash Roach, wealthy plantation owner; but he was "determined to marry no woman" until he was "perfectly independent of her resources"[2]—a circumstance referred to again in the following letter joyously announcing his engagement.

My dear Lawson   Orangeburg, So Caro. Apl. 15 [1836]

Ay di me alhama! Sympathise with me, *mon ami,* if you have tears prepare to shed them now!![3] I have been wooing—I have wooed and—have won. The Lady has smiled, and as much, perhaps, to rid herself of my importunacy as any thing else, has said 'Yes'. She sits at a little distance from me now—a dark eyed, dark haired, sad looking little creature, whose fingers

---

1. WGS to JL, Jan. 27, 1836, *Letters* 1:77.
2. Ibid., 78.
3. *Julius Caesar* 3.2.174.

are even now describing a hundred semi-circles in a minute as she whip-stitches one of those most mortal frights in the domestic economy, good on winter nights, which ancient huswifes designate a quilt! Occasionally like Byron's bird, 'she starts into voice a moment and is still'.[4] Sometimes, she looks up at me as I write as if to ask are you talking about me in that letter; and now and then she hums the catch of some pleasant love ditty, as if desiring to call my attention from the scrawl before me to the more pleasant contemplation of myself in her. She is the chosen and she has told me that she loves me, and I have been fond & foolish enough to believe, implicitly and credulously, the sweet assurance. So you may congratulate me as soon as possible on the event—not that I am married, or like to be so, for sometime yet—certainly, not before the next winter, so you will see me, still a Bachelor in N. Y. next summer. But so far I must have your congratulations, and you will do me no small service by letting the fact be known, before I come on, to certain of your feminines who shall be nameless. It will give me, as you well know, a fategiving benefit of future excruciation.

From you l have not heard for a month of Sundays. I got a letter from Mr. Bancroft[5] a few days ago, and only regret that I have not availed myself of your warning a little sooner. It is a performance rather Yankeeish in its character, but of this I shall write you especially. He tells me in his letter that Herbert[6] has written me. You also told me so in one of your first letters. But I have recd. from Herbert no letter, and the probability is that he gave it to the Harpers, and that it lies in one of their sixty drawers awaiting the millenium. From them I have heard nothing for a long season. To you, while in town a few weeks ago I wrote a brief epistle, referring you to a long & tedious one written a little time before, and to both of these you have been silent. I hope that nothing has happened to you or yours.

How does Lady Lide—Mrs. L. rather? Tell her that she had better set about that picture which she promised to execute for me, when a certain event should be realized. She is pledged to it, and I have told the one for whom it was promised, that she may expect the performance from the fingers of a New York Belle. Of course she will forget no such promise, and

---

4. *Childe Harold's Pilgrimage* 3.817–18 reads: "At intervals, some bird from out the brakes / starts into a voice a moment, then is still."

5. Monson Bancroft, in partnership with George W. Holley (who, like Lawson, lived at 15 Le Roy Place in 1836), operated a bookstore at 8 Astor Place and a music store at 395 Broadway.

6. William Henry Herbert (1807–1858) was editor of the *American Monthly Magazine,* to which WGS was a frequent contributor. Under the pseudonym "Frank Forester," Herbert was a prolific writer of articles and books on field sports.

indeed, if she did, I should not. So be sure, and keep her well minded, on this head.

Pray how are all my friends—Wetmore,[7] Leggett,[8] Herbert and the rest. Do not let them forget me. I have seen Herbert's review in the Am. Mon.[9] and in many respects esteem it just, nor am I disposed to regard him with less warmth & good feeling than before. He has erred in several respects, however, since one of his chief objections to the work is its abruptness— a necessary consequence of the plan, which contemplated a series, and re- served the futures of many of the persons for conclusion in a general sequel. He is not less wrong in objecting to humour, simply because his individual taste does not seek it. He should remember the wholesome rule in Shak- speare 'Because thou art virtuous shall there be no more cakes and ale,— aye, and ginger shall be hot in the mouth, too.'[10] But he is right in many other respects. I hear nothing from N. Y. Do enlighten me on the subject of all its lions. I see that Fay[11] has got back and has been praising me up in the Mirror. Have you seen my two Poems in the Knickerbocker—To Flowers in Autumn and the Dirge of the Leaves.[12] How are they relished? On the sub- ject of a memoir of Forrest[13] I wrote to you urgently. Can you not get Leggett to send me not only the material, but such of Forrest's letters as he would like published. I would bring them out with an introduction in our Southern Magazine.[14] But no more. Pray tell all How-dye—give my best respects to all friends—with due good wishes for John & Vesey Street,[15] hold me ever yrs etc.

Simms

My address is Charleston.

---

7. Prosper Montgomery Wetmore (1798–1876) was a New York businessman, poet, and contributor to the *New York Mirror.*

8. William Leggett (1801–1839) was a poet and acting editor (in William Cullen Bryant's absence) of the *New York Evening Post.*

9. Herbert's review of WGS's *The Partisan,* commending the author in general but damning the book, appeared in *American Monthly Magazine,* n.s., 1 (Jan. 1836): 101–4.

10. *Twelfth Night* 2.3.

11. Theodore S. Fay (1807–1898) was one of the editors of the *New York Mirror,* which contained notices of WGS on Jan. 16, Jan. 23, and Feb. 27, 1836 (13:231, 239, 280). Fay was the author of the popular novel *Norman Leslie* (1835) and later another novel, *Hoboken: A Romance of New York* (1843).

12. "Flowers in Autumn," *Knickerbocker* 7 (Feb. 1836): 169; "The Fall of the Leaf," ibid., Jan. 1836, 37.

13. Edwin Forrest (1806–1872), the famous actor, was a close friend of JL.

14. Probably the *Southern Literary Journal* (1836–38), to which WGS contributed heavily.

15. Fashionable district of New York City where WGS and JL had courted.

LETTER 2

Addressee: Armistead Burt / Washington / D.C.
Postmark: Midway SC / Jany 27 [1845]

Armistead Burt (1802–1883), Abbeville criminal lawyer with a reputation for astuteness unrivaled in South Carolina, was elected in 1843 to Congress, where he was noted for timidity rather than boldness. A disciple of Calhoun, he— unlike Simms—had been a strong supporter of Nullification; after the Civil War he was appointed by Governor Benjamin F. Perry to draft labor regulations and a code for the protection of freed slaves. For several years Burt lived on a plantation on the Savannah River, a relatively short distance from Simms at Woodlands.

Among the chief disappointments of Simms's career is that he never received a much cherished diplomatic appointment abroad, a denial that caused him over the years to become increasingly bitter. This letter to Congressman Burt is his first expression of interest in such an appointment; and though Simms initially believed that he had Burt's enthusiastic support, he later came to the conclusion that "our delegation in Congress . . . resolved to make no application in behalf of Carolina." [16]

My dear Sir   Woodlands, Jan 26 [1845]
    I do not desire office for its own sake, but circumstances have never allowed me to travel out of the limits of our own country. Literature has only sufficed to enable me to live like a Gentleman at home, and, after reaching the tolerably mature term of thirty eight years, which I am now, I feel that I may, without overstepping the bounds of modesty, declare my desire to see a little of the outer world. I should like to go to Europe, but it will please me to travel in other regions. I have no particular preferences—after the civilized portions of the old world—for any special region. Of my capacities you all know probably quite as much as I do myself. My studies have been various, my experience not inconsiderable. Though never a commercial man, I am considered a practical one, am a working one, and was born & reared in Charleston, a commercial city. My friends may safely promise that I will faithfully discharge the duties confided to me, as far as my abilities will allow. I can read a little french, and have some slight inkling, which a little time would enable me to improve into an acquisition, of Italian & Spanish. It must be for my friends to determine not only what will suit me best, but what I am most good for. I am, I fancy, rather a prudent man than otherwise,

---

16. WGS to JL, April 7, 1845, *Letters* 2:48.

can understand the wink or nod of a minister,—certainly quite as well as—
Mr Shannon![17]—and in all respects, I am patient to acquire & progress, and
cool enough to see my position fairly. I can keep cool & remain firm, and say
'No!' to the Dons without putting them or myself into a passion.—I have
been friendly to the election of Polk and Dallas,[18] not because I loved them
or cared for them, but because I regarded them as a choice of evils & am totally opposed to South Carolina throwing away her vote. However, I have
taken no part in their election, except to talk a little by the wayside, to
stump it once or twice in favor of Texas, and to aid as a Member of our Legislature in electing the Electors, knowing very well for whom they were to
vote. And this is all! Nay, there is more, I am the author of a very popular
Texan Song[19] which you may have heard our friend Stewart,[20] when fairly
fuddled, singing in the streets & taverns of Columbia. I have also a very
Texan drama,[21] unpublished in my desk, which will make a rumpus, be sure,
if ever it reaches light upon the stage. You may answer for it that I am a genuine Southron, well hated by New England, hostile to the Tariff, Abolition
&c, not to speak of a hundred other Yankee abominations. Whether these are
qualities to recommend me to Mr Polk, I know not. That they secure me
the affections of all genuine Southrons I am very sure.—As a traveller in for-
eigns, I should perhaps be doing the country a service apart from the performance of official duties. I should be a close observer of what is curious in
the traditions, the antiquities & the manners of a people; of these I should
make due record, & future elaborate use in fiction or in history. I have never
sought for office in my life & would not now that my friends should take any
undue pains to force my pretensions. I would not have them do for me,
("crooking the pregnant hinges of the knee,"[22] even though 'thrift should follow fawning,") what I would not do for myself. As for the pecuniary value of
the berth, I care for it only so far as it will enable me with my little family to
maintain the attitude of a Southern Gentleman in a foreign land. And now,

---

17. Wilson Shannon (1807–1877) had been appointed U.S. minister to Mexico on
April 9, 1844, and served until March 1845.

18. George Mifflin Dallas (1792–1864), of Pennsylvania, was vice president under
President James Knox Polk.

19. WGS's "The Texian Hunter's Bride," published on Oct. 11, 1844, in the
Charleston Mercury, later appeared under the title "The Texian Hunter" in *Areytos: or,
Songs of the South* (1846), 21–22.

20. John A. Stuart (1800–1852) was editor of the *Charleston Mercury* from 1831 until early in 1845.

21. *Michael Bonham*, not published until 1852.

22. *Hamlet* 3.2.66–67.

you have the whole, and see the extent of my cravings. I shall write to my old friend, Judge Huger,[23] on the subject, and you will suffer our friend Holmes[24] to read this letter. In your & their hands, I leave the matter wholly to be urged or set aside at your discretion. Thanks for your kind consideration, which I shall remember always while I am,

Yours,
W. Gilmore Simms

LETTER 3

Addressee: Benjamin Franklin Perry / Greenville, C.H. / So Carolina
Postmark: Midway SC / feby 15 [1845]

As young men, Benjamin Franklin Perry (1805–1886) and Simms were both strong Unionists—Simms writing editorials against Nullification in Charleston while Perry was writing them in Greenville. Though Simms over time shifted from Unionist to secessionist, Perry never departed from his early stand—a consistency that won him respect both North and South. As a result, after the Civil War he was named provisional governor of South Carolina. Despite differences in their politics, Perry and Simms shared literary and historical views: both stressed the importance of regional literature in the development of American letters; both were students of the American Revolution and assiduous collectors of Revolutionary War documents and artifacts. They remained steadfast in their friendship and their respect for one another.

This letter is significant in its relevation of important aspects of Simms's ambition, career, personality, and philosophy. The topics discussed—Southern magazines, place in American literature, diplomatic appointment abroad, sectional politics, work "*pro bono publico*"—all offer insight into the make-up of the author.

B. F. Perry, Esq.
My dear Perry.   Woodlands, Feb 13. 1845
It was my hope to have seen you on your late visit to Charleston, of which Yeadon[25] gave me some assurances, but I was compelled to hurry out of town, and when I returned to it you had just taken your departure. It would

---

23. Daniel E. Huger (1779–1854) was U.S. senator, 1842–45.

24. Isaac E. Holmes (1796–1869), of Charleston, was a member of Congress from 1838 to 1850.

25. Richard Yeadon (1802–1870), lifelong friend of WGS and Perry, was editor of the *Charleston Courier* (1832–44) and opponent of both nullification and secession.

have given me great pleasure to have hob-a-nob'd with you over his madeira, and to have discussed the pleasant world and wines of which we were a part. I may have this pleasure next summer if I succeed in doing what I desire— arranging for a trip to the back country. It is probable that you are in reciept of the first number of my Magazine,[26] and I trust that its contents like you. We were somewhat hurried in their preparation, but they are respectable, and with a little time we shall do better. I need not say that I desire you would resume your labors for its pages. You can surely gather up an interesting additional series of revolutionary events, or these failing, the subjects for literary manufacture, in your parts, are sufficiently extensive. My own notion is that we should write as much as possible about home—gather up our own gems & jewels—look about us and within us—what we are, what we have been & what we may be. It is from the use of such materials that author and country alike grow famous. Thus far, for yourself. And now,— it would give me great pleasure if Waddy Thompson[27] could be persuaded to give us a series of sketches about Mexico, its people, its President, its leading men generally. Now that Santa Anna is *hors de combat* his history becomes peculiarly interesting. Thompson who is a sensible man, not wanting in imagination, should be able, I should suppose, to prepare a series equally thoughtful and picturesque which would be creditable to his name in a new department. Can he not be persuaded to it. If you thought it better, I should, though personally unknown to him, write to him myself; but I think it likely that you can do more for our object than any body beside. Broach it to him, *mon ami,* if you second my notions, & let me have the result as soon as possible.——There is a matter which concerns myself, upon which I communicate *sub rosa.*——I have some friends, in Washington & Tennessee, who are disposed to present my name to the new President as one for whom they would like to procure a foreign appointment. The movement is with my approbation. The difficulty is in finding out what is available which would suit me. Will it be in your way to sound Thompson as to the nature of [the] situation while in Mexico—how he relished that city & country and in how far it was agreeable & desirable to himself. To these questions, cautiously urged, he might yield sufficient answer, without suspecting their object. Perhaps, too, his old experiences in Congress might enable him to give some

---

26. The *Southern and Western Monthly Magazine and Review* (familiarly known as "Simms's Magazine"), of which WGS was editor and chief contributor, was established in Charleston in Jan. 1845 and died in December of that year.

27. Waddy Thompson (1798–1868) was congressman from South Carolina, 1835–41, and U.S. minister to Mexico, 1842–44.

information as to the eligibility of appointments to Italy—the Sicilies for example,—Rome &c. I am in very ample ignorance of the advantages or disadvantages of almost every berth which might be found available.—I am very far from sanguine in my expectations. I have been no clamorer for Mr. Polk, have thrown up no hat, and simply took him for my man, as an alternative. I have no doubt that he is a worthy man, but very far from a great one. Still his choice of ministers & friends may be judicious, & I may be one of them!—And now to close,—do nothing & say nothing in these matters which shall not be perfectly agreeable to yourself. You are, as I would have all whom I esteem, perfectly at liberty.—Yet no,—you must work for the Magazine, *pro bono publico*. It is a cheap work, and will be purely native. Be sure of that. Let your Editor do his duty, & set some of your young men to work to beat up subscribers. Present me very respectfully—my wife joins me—to Mrs. P. & the family of Mrs. McCall.[28]

Yours faithfully
W. Gilmore Simms

LETTER 4

Addressee: Evert Augustus Duyckinck / New York
Postmark: Midway SC / March 17 [1845]

A Simms correspondent for more than twenty-five years, Columbia University–graduate Evert A. Duyckinck (1816–1878) was a lawyer-editor in the circle of New York literati who befriended Simms and sponsored his literary career. In 1845 Duyckinck was coeditor of *Arcturus* and a contributor to many journals, including Simms's *Southern and Western;* in June of that year, when he became editor of Wiley and Putnam's Library of American Books, Simms wrote him: "You are now in a situation to do a real service to American literature."[29] Sharing Simms's view that American authors should write on American themes, Duyckinck published in the series both *The Wigwam and the Cabin* (the "collection of 'Tales of the South'" mentioned in the letter below) and *Views and Reviews.* Like fellow New Yorker James Lawson, Duyckinck remained a close friend and steady correspondent with Simms throughout the strain of war, though their letters were primarily literary, mostly avoiding controversial political topics.

This letter contains a remarkably perceptive and judicious commentary on

---

28. Mrs. Hext McCall was Perry's mother-in-law.
29. WGS to EAD, June 25, 1845, *Letters* 2:77.

Poe, one to be compared with Simms's public assessment (see "On Poe's *Tales*" below) and his personal letter to Poe himself (see letter 6).

My dear D.   Woodlands, 15th. March 1845

I left Charleston this morning early but have heard nothing of your friend Mr. Fraser.[30] Your letter, dated the 10th. I find awaiting me at the plantation. I trust you gave Mr. F. instructions to find his way up to us. If his object be to waste time, a week or two with us in the country would not be amiss. We are not in Charleston (the family) during winter & spring, only in summer & autumn. My daughter has been down for a month attending balls & parties, and I run down every two weeks or so, to show myself & pick up matters and see to business. But our town house is always closed during this period. I shall be pleased to see Mr. F. and will give him welcome whenever we encounter. I quite regret that No. 3 of the Wallet[31] did not come to hand, as I should like to have carried on the Nos. regularly. Our March no. is through my hands. Our papers are quite too long for our pages, and it so happens that the subjects taken up seem to require it. We shall amend as we advance—perhaps—in this as other respects. In our April no. there is an attack on the North American[32]—based on its circular. It is rather too long. I see your Mr. Briggs[33] does not like us. I mortally offended his *amour propre*,—as I fear—not only in my paper touching Mathews,[34]—but in a conversation had in his presence at Mathews' office, in which, having no cue, I spoke rather freely—not once suspecting him of being a professed humourist—one of your crack men in that department. You know my notion upon humour generally, and American humour, so called, in particular. These naturally annoyed him, and I suspect, he is not of a forgiving nature. But *Sessa* — let it pass. Your paper on Jones[35] is a good & *kind* one. He has his kinks, but he has his merits also. I am glad that you think and speak well of Poe, which Mathews was not disposed to do though I tried to open his eyes

---

30. Probably Robert F. Fraser, New York art critic and friend of EAD.

31. "Time's Wallet," nos. 1 and 2, literary commentary by EAD, had appeared in the first two issues of *SWMMR* (1 [Jan. 1845]: 61–66 and [Feb. 1845]: 100–106).

32. "A Passage with 'The Veteran Quarterly,'" ibid., 1 (May 1845): 297–311. WGS was the author of the article, signed "M"; in the copy of the magazine owned by Mary C. Simms Oliphant, WGS had inscribed his initials at the end of this article.

33. Charles Frederick Briggs (1804–1877), frequently called "Harry Franco" from his novel of the same name, was editor of the *Broadway Journal,* which ridiculed *SWMMR* in its Feb. 1, 1845 (1:77), issue.

34. Cornelius Matthews (1817–1889) was a New York poet, critic, and humorous writer.

35. "Sketches of American Prose Writers: William A. Jones," *BJ* 1 (Jan. 11, 1845): 26–28.

to the singular merits of that person. Poe is no friend of mine, as I believe. He began by a very savage attack on one of my novels—the Partisan.[36] I cannot say that he was much out in his estimate. In some respects, as a story for example,—& in certain matters of taste & style, that was one of the very worst of the books I have ever written. Poe's critique, however, paid little heed to what was really good in the thing, and he did injustice to other portions which were not quite so good. Besides, he was rude & offensive & personal, in the manner of the thing, which he should not have been, in the case of anybody,—still less in mine. My deportment had not justified it. He knew, or might have known, that I was none of that miserable gang about town, who beg in the literary highways. I had no clique, mingled with none, begged no praise from anybody, and made no conditions with the herd. He must have known what I was personally—might have known—& being just should not have been rude. What should we think of an executioner who mocks the carcass after he has taken off the head. I tell you all this to satisfy you of my sense of verities. I do not puff the man when I say I consider him a remarkable one. He has more real imaginative power than 99 in the 100 of our poets & tale writers. His style is clear & correct, his conceptions bold & fanciful, his fancies vivid, and his taste generally good. His bolder effects are impaired by his fondness for *detail* & this hurts his criticism which is too frequently given to the analysis of the inferior points of style, making him somewhat regardless of the more noble features of the work. But, I repeat, he is a man of remarkable power, to whom I shall strive one day to do that justice which a great portion of our public seems desirous to withhold. This may be owing to the fact that he is something of an Ishmaelite. He seems too much the subject of his moods—not sufficiently so of principle. I suspect he frequently says bitter things through a wanton consciousness of power. This is an unhappy immorality which all good men resent, and the blow, however, well dealt, is thus apt to recoil upon him who gives it. His private life, I am told, has been irregular, but this, I take it, is owing to his poverty, which, I also learn, has been extreme. Is it any better now?—I should like to hear something more of the plan of W & P. Will they want any thing from me? Why not a collection of "Tales of the South"—selected carefully & closely revised, making a handsome volume—Pray get them to send me Miss Fuller's

---

36. EAP reviewed *The Partisan* in *SLM* 2 (Jan. 1836): 117–21. In the critique he finds the character Porgy "a most insufferable bore," states that the author's English is "shockingly bad," and claims that "instances of bad taste—villainously bad taste—occur frequently in the book." He concedes, however, that "in spite . . . of its manifest and manifold blunders and impertinences, 'The Partisan' is no ordinary work."

book,[37]—and tell Jay[38] or Wetmore[39] to send me the Report or Essay of Broadhead. Send me also Poe's Lecture.[40] As for Lawson, don't leave any thing for him to do for—aside from his business, to which he is punctually devoted—he is the most remiss rascal in the world. When you write *me,* address to Midway—when to the publishers, write to Charleston.

In haste. God bless you &c
W. G. S.

LETTER 5

Addressee: James Henry Hammond / Silverton, / So. Carolina
Postmark: Midway SC / May 21 [1845]

James Henry Hammond (1807–1864), whom Simms had known since the Nullification crisis (in which they had taken opposite sides), but with whom he became intimate in the 1840s, ultimately became the author's chief confidant. A flamboyant elitist who rivaled Simms in wit and impetuosity and likewise burned with a passion for the intellectual, Hammond as a young man served briefly in Congress (1835–36), and six years later he ran successfully for the governorship of South Carolina, during which tenure Simms acted as his chief adviser and speechwriter. A midcareer scandal (see letter 7) almost ruined Hammond's political aspirations; but he persevered, bolstered in no small part by Simms's loyalty and support, and was elected to the U.S. Senate in 1857. Both Hammond and Simms were strong, outspoken men with common political and literary views, and—more important perhaps to their bonding—they shared a sense of alienation from the Southern society they both loved. Highly ambitious and strongly motivated, they goaded each other to higher achievement, one primarily in politics and the other in literature, but each with significant interests in both directions. Simms expanded Hammond's literary horizons just as Hammond sharpened the writer's political awareness. Their correspondence reveals that they addressed each other with remarkable candor on almost any subject, keeping little hidden. Their friendship was strong enough that neither hesitated to chide the other for poor taste or poor judgment when warranted. Hammond recognized Simms's talent as few close associates did and encouraged him to concentrate his efforts on a magnum opus rather than fritter

---

37. Margaret Fuller's *Summer on the Lakes, in 1843.*
38. John Jay (1817–1894) was a New York lawyer, author, and diplomat.
39. For Prosper Wetmore, see note 7 above.
40. EAP lectured on "Poets and Poetry of America" in New York on Feb. 28, 1845.

away time, energy, and genius on ephemeral projects. But somewhat contra-
dictorily, it was the well-meaning Hammond who also persuaded his literary
friend that he could have success in politics as well.

This letter well illustrates the humor and candor with which Simms addresses Hammond: as the editor of the *Southern and Western,* Simms lightly
praises (but significantly does not publish) "verses to Carolina" while advising his
friend to "stick to the prose"; he reveals his sensitivity to his own lack of formal
education and perhaps as a result, his uneasiness with pretentious titles; and he
lays bare some of the alienation, resentment, and ambition that motivate his life.

My dear Hammond   Woodlands May 20 [1845]

Your verses to Caroline will have an early place. They are as smoothly
turned as if you had frequently practiced at the lathe. But stick to the prose
and do more of it. You were right in giving your letters to Pemberton.[41] I
have no doubt they will do you credit, and maintain the reputation which
you have everywhere got by the first. As for the reluctance to publish that
which you have deliberately written, and which is wholly without its use unless put in circulation, that, permit me to say, is one of your little affectations
which do not become you. You are too much of a genuine man to indulge in
such pettinesses. You see I deal with you frankly as a friend should do. While
in this frank mood let me beg that you will forbear giving me any title other
than those which are in ordinary use. The courtesy of well meaning but mis-
judging friends have conferred upon me distinctions which, as I have but
little pretension to any legitimate claim in these respects, I feel great reluctance to appropriate. To a stranger, I should be loth to say this, for I would
not give pain to those by whom I have been thus most unwisely distinguished; but to you, to whom I may speak in safety, I repeat the wish that
I may neither be called Dr. nor Col.[42] I am no military man, and have long
since learned to smile, at your parade soldiers, of whom when the season of
action comes, we seldom hear anything. I confess too it always seems to me
to degrade the man to dress him up like a monkey or a peacock. If men must
fight, let them go into battle as Cromwell's fire-eaters did in plain buff coats,
resolute apart from the guns & trumpets, the glitter & the gewgaws.——I have
as little claim to be a Dr. of Laws as any literary man in the country. Never
was education so worthless as mine,——i. e. in a classical point of view. I
am very little of the linguist, am versed in no sciences, cannot play with

41. A. H. Pemberton, of Columbia, editor and publisher of the *South-Carolinian,*
published as a pamphlet JHH's *Letter . . . to the Free Church of Glasgow, on the Subject of Slavery,* dated June 21, 1844.

42. In 1842 WGS received the Doctor of Laws degree from the University of Alabama, and during Hammond's governorship he served as colonel on his staff.

chemistry as you do, and exult in agriculture. In brief, my dear fellow, if I were called upon to say in what respect my knowledge was thorough, I should be at great loss to happen upon one element. I have a smattering of this & that, picked up, heaven knows how. Of my reputation & how it has grown, you know as much as myself. All that I can claim is this, that what I am I am *in spite of friends,* of fortune, and all the usual aids of the ambitious. I have worked in the face of fortune and many foes. I have never known what was cordial sympathy, in any of my pursuits among men. I have been an exile from my birth, and have learned nothing but to drudge with little hope, and to think and feel and act for myself. Through painful necessities I have come to the acquisition of an Independent Mind.——You will say that I have egotism enough at least. That is one of the evil consequences of my isolation. It is per-haps inseperable from independence. But, here ends. You mistook a hint (probably) which I gave in a previous letter, & hence what I have said about these titles. I must submit to be called Dr. & Col. by that silly class of per-sons who attach much importance to these things. To you I may safely de-clare myself & I do so.——There.——I owe you no letter.——But I write in pain, suffering from a swollen testicle!——I think it likely I shall leave for the city on the 29th. inst.——I am on that cursed com'tee for the examination of the Bank concerns. Can you give me any hints.

Yours &c
Simms

LETTER 6

Addressee: Edgar Allan Poe
Postmark: none [July 1846]

Despite striking differences in background, philosophy, and personality, Poe (1809–1849) and Simms had much in common: as the dominant Southern lit-erary figures of their time, they were among America's first professional men of letters, attempting to sustain themselves through editing, lecturing, reviewing books, giving readings, and doing literary hackwork of all sorts while laboring prodigiously at belles lettres. As literary critics, they both derided the "puffery" of American authors, both choosing to set high standards as the best means of developing a national literary consciousness. And though Poe was an advocate of a cosmopolitan literature committed only to aesthetics, and Simms an artic-ulate supporter of Americanism in literature, in practice they each recognized the genius (as well as limitations) of the other's work. It was Poe who said of Simms: "In invention, in vigor, in movement, in the power of exciting interest, and in the artistical management of his themes, he has surpassed, we think, any of his countrymen:—that is to say, he has surpassed any of them in the aggregate of these high qualities."[43]

Poe had been engaging in "The War of the *Literati*," writing satirical sketches of literary personages for *Godey's Lady's Book,* when he wrote to Simms outlining his financial and physical (as well as literary) problems and apparently seeking his advice and assistance in all these matters. (Poe's letter to which Simms is responding is unlocated.) In a literary letter to the *Southern Patriot* dated July 15, 1846, Simms wrote that Poe's articles were causing "no little rattling among the dry bones of our Grub street"; of Poe's health and mental status, Simms added: "He . . . is in obscurity, somewhere in the country [at Fordham], and sick, according to a report which reached me yesterday [from Poe?], of brain fever."[44]

Edgar A Poe, Esq.
Dear Sir   New York July 30. 1846
I recieved your note a week ago, and proceeded at once to answer it, but being in daily expectation of a newspaper from the South, to which, in a Letter, I had communicated a paragraph concerning the matter which you had suggested in a previous letter, I determined to wait until I could enclose it to you. It has been delayed somewhat longer than I had anticipated, and has in part caused my delay to answer you. I now send it you, and trust that it will answer the desired purpose; though I must frankly say that I scarcely see the necessity of noticing the sort of scandal to which you refer.—I note with regret the very desponding character of your last letter. I surely need not tell you how deeply & sincerely I deplore the misfortunes which attend you— the more so as I see no process for your relief and, extrication but such as must result from your own decision and resolve. No friend can well help you in the struggle which is before you. Money, no doubt, can be procured; but this is not altogether what you require. Sympathy may soothe the hurts of Self-Esteem, and make a man temporarily forgetful of his assailants;—but in what degree will this avail, and for how long, in the protracted warfare of twenty or thirty years. You are still a very young man, and one too largely & too variously endowed, not to entertain the conviction—as your friends entertain it—of a long & manful struggle with, and a final victory over, fortune. But this warfare, the world requires you to carry on with your own unassisted powers. It is only in your manly resolution to use these powers, after a legitimate fashion, that it will countenance your claims to its regards

43. EAP, review of *The Wigwam and the Cabin* in *BJ* 2 (Oct. 4, 1845): 190—91.
44. WGS, "From Our Correspondent," *Southern Patriot*, July 20, 1846, in *Letters* 2: 174n.

& sympathy; and I need not tell you how rigid & exacting it has ever been in the case of the poetical genius, or, indeed, the genius of any order. Suffer me to tell you frankly, taking the privilege of a true friend, that you are now perhaps in the most perilous period of your career——just in that position——just at that time of life——when a false step becomes a capital error——when a single leading mistake is fatal in its consequences. You are no longer a boy. "At thirty wise or never!" You must subdue your impulses; &, in particular, let me exhort you to discard all associations with men, whatever their talents, whom you cannot esteem as men. Pardon me for presuming thus to counsel one whose great natural & acquired resources should make him rather the teacher of others. But I obey a law of my own nature, and it is because of my sympathies that I speak. Do not suppose yourself abandoned by the worthy and honorable among your friends. They will be glad to give you welcome *if you will suffer them.* They will rejoice——I know their feelings and hear their language——to countenance your return to that community——that moral province in society—— of which let me say to you, respectfully and regretfully,——you have been, according to all reports but too heedlessly and, perhaps, too scornfully indifferent. Remain in obscurity for awhile. You have a young wife——I am told a suffering & interesting one,——let me entreat you to cherish her, and to cast away those pleasures which are not worthy of your mind, and to trample those temptations underfoot, which degrade your person, and make it familiar to the mouth of vulgar jest. You may [do] all this, by a little circumspection. It is still within your power. Your resources from literature are probably much greater than mine. I am sure they are quite as great. You can increase them, so that they shall be ample for all your legitimate desires; but you must learn the worldling's lesson of prudence;——a lesson, let me add, which the literary world has but too frequently & unwisely disparaged. It may seem to you very impertinent,——in most cases it is impertinent——that he who gives nothing else, should presume to give counsel. But one gives that which he can most spare, and you must not esteem me indifferent to a condition which I can in no other way assist. I have never been regardless of your genius, even when I knew nothing of your person. It is some years, since I counseled Mr. Godey to obtain the contributions of your pen. He will tell you this. I hear that you reproach him. But how can you expect a Magazine proprietor to encourage contributions which embroil him with all his neighbours. These broils do you no good——vex your temper, destroy your peace of mind, and hurt your reputation. You have abundant resources upon which to draw even were there no Grub Street in Gotham. Change your tactics & begin a new series of papers with your publisher.—— The printed matter which I send you, might be quoted by Godey, and might be ascribed to me.[45] But, surely, I need not say to you that, to a Southern man, the annoyance of being mixed up in a squabble with persons whom he does not know, and does not care to know,—and from whom no Alexandrine process of cutting loose, would be permitted by society—would he an intolerable grievance. I submit to frequent injuries & misrepresentations, content, though annoyed by the slaver, that the viper should amuse himself upon the file, at the expense of his own teeth. As a man, as a writer, I shall always be solicitous of your reputation & success. You have but to resolve on taking & asserting your position, equally in the social & the literary world, and your way is clear, your path is easy, and you will find true friends enough to sympathize in your triumphs. Very Sincerely though Sorrowfully, Yr frd & Servt.

W Gilmore Simms

P. S. If I could I should have been to see you. But I have been & am still drudging in the hands of the printers, kept busily employed night and day. Besides, my arrangements are to hurry back to the South where I have a sick family. A very few days will turn my feet in that direction.

LETTER 7

Addressee: James Henry Hammond
Postmark: none [December 1846]

See Letter 5 for Hammond.

The scandal associated with Hammond, now well documented, broke while Hammond was governor in 1843; unfortunately for Hammond's reputation and political aspirations, it involved accusations from his brother-in-law, Wade Hampton, that Hammond had sexually exploited (among others) Hampton's teen-aged daughter, a niece of Hammond. Hampton did everything in his power to ruin Hammond politically; the whisper campaign against Hammond became even more vehement in 1846 when Hammond unsuccessfully made his first bid for a U.S. Senate seat. This letter reveals Simms's loyalty to his tarnished friend, despite recognition that Hammond "had some atonement" to make. It is significant that Simms was tolerant of the fallibility and indiscretions of a trusted friend; as a realist not expecting always exemplary conduct from anyone, Simms accepted imperfection in others better than most people did. As Simms himself put it to Paul Hamilton Hayne years later, "I always find some excuse in

---

45. The "printed matter" WGS refers to apparently was a clipping from the Charleston *Southern Patriot,* but *Godey's* contains no quotation from WGS. See *Letters* 2:176n.

my own heart, for what seems the shortcoming of my friend."[46] For his part Hammond felt that he "owed a life" to Simms for his "generous and abiding confidence"; it "compensates me a thousand fold for all I have suffered. . . . God bless you."[47]

My dear Hammond.   Woodlands. Decr. 11. 1846

I had hopes to meet you a few days ago at the Court House, having been assured that you were to be present. It was there that I was first advised of the result of the Senatorial election which, when you look at the anxious among the solicitors, and the anxious lawyers seeking to be solicitors, is perhaps easy to be accounted for. But, when I left Columbia, it was not supposed that Butler[48] would run—that he would be so foolish as to risk a permanency, for an office from which it is not improbable that in two years he will be ousted. He is not the man to keep in Calhoun's harness, and if seriously or strongly opposed at the regular election will be beaten. Elmore[49] could not have beaten you by a larger vote, and Butler was the only man in the State (in my opinion) after Elmore, by whom you could have been beaten. Nor could he have done it relying on his intrinsic strength. The Judgeship gave him 25 votes, at least.—I cannot say that I regret that you were run, since my impression is that the contest results in placing you *rectus in curia*. That I should have urged your running, had I been in Columbia, is doubtful. I might have been scared from it by the threats of your enemies, and by my own conviction that you had some atonement to make. But now that it is over, I feel that you have gained a point in the game which is of immense importance to you hereafter. It will not be possible for Hampton and his friends to commit a second time the monstrous blunder of which they have been guilty—a blunder which, while it might have forced upon you the admission of error, subjected themselves to an exposure than which nothing could be more unhappy. In your case, what the outer world conjectured was no doubt much more ugly than the truth. You had suffered the worst. Actual revelation could not have done you greater harm; and such a development must have only injured those to whom it was of importance that the thing should remain equivocal. My notion is that you could have lost

---

46. WGS to PHH, Mar. 26, 1870, *Letters* 5 : 303.

47. JHH to WGS, Dec. 8, 1846, ibid., 2 : 235n.

48. Judge Andrew Pickens Butler (1796–1857) was the successful candidate for the U.S. Senate seat vacated by George McDuffie (1790–1851) in 1846. Butler was re-elected in 1848 and again in 1854.

49. Franklin Harper Elmore (1799–1850), at the time president of the Bank of the State, chose not to run for the Senate in 1846. After having earlier served in Congress (1836–39), he succeeded John C. Calhoun in the Senate in 1850.

few votes by it. Your friends have been encouraged & strengthened. They will stick to you. They will increase, as they will naturally absorb all those in the State whom the vast shadows of some two or three persons have kept from the sunshine of public favor. 'Young Carolina' will probably make you a rallying point for a new party. At least, many of those to whom this cry is becoming grateful, as it promises release from bondage, are, I know, looking to you as to a centre. I need not exhort you to patience. Perhaps, an excess of coolness—a something too much of *recoil* and stoicism—is your foible. I wish you had a little more of the boy in you—a little more of enthusiasm & faith. It was your misfortune to have been caught too young—to have been but too little of the boy. Boyhood is the term for the training—not the crushing or stifling of the faith. You, I fear, believe too little in your neighbours.—But you will wait, & you will triumph. I look around, and see the unavoidable necessity of the young men of the country turning to you. Where else? What are the public men? The good are too weak. The strong are too selfish and not wise. Barnwell,[50] Colcock & a few others of this class, are worthy fellows but can do nothing. And of another class, Rhett, Pickens, Davie,—not absolutely weak—nay smart, all of them, each in his way—yet not one of them with the slightest claim to wisdom. Elmore has something of this. This is his secret. He is wise rather than smart. He has that species of social prudence, which is a minor sort of wisdom, by which he passes for more than he is worth himself, and persuades others to a conviction of his necessity to them: I think him equal to all that I have named, put together, in the capacity of being useful—which I hold to be the first essential of a good politician. He has one faculty which you perhaps do not sufficiently use—that of persuading others that they are in reality turning the wheel on whose spokes they only revolve. You have too much will for this,—yet the art is a useful one.—But none of these men will answer for the approaching emergency.—I had almost said crisis. And I see no young ones starting up in the shade. Do you?—As for myself, I am pretty well tired of a game in which it is so easy to be beaten.[51] Besides, I am ill at ease at home. My affairs are in a doubtful way, my prospects gloomy, my wife in very bad health, and I myself very much dissatisfied with what I have done & what I am. I have almost come to persuade myself that my career has deluded nobody but myself, and that I should regard my recent defeats as a sufficient

50. Robert W. Barnwell (1801–1882), president of South Carolina College (1835–41), was appointed to fill the unexpired Senate term left vacant in 1850 by Elmore's death.

51. WGS had lost the election for lieutenant governor of South Carolina by a small margin to W. A. Cain of Pineville. See JHH's letter of condolence, Dec. 18, 1846, *Letters* 2 : 237n.

proof that I am not the person that I suppose myself & possess but few of the endowments upon which I had but too easily been satisfied to count. In my present frame of mind, I should consent to run for nothing, to hope for nothing, to think of nothing, the gift of which might depend upon the people from whom alone one might confidently look for anything. God bless you.

W. Gilmore Simms

J. H. Hammond Esq.

LETTER 8

Addressee: Nathaniel Beverley Tucker / Williamsburg, / Va.
Postmark: Midway SC / April 8 [1849]

Nathaniel Beverley Tucker (1784–1851), novelist, essayist, and professor of law at the College of William and Mary, was a member of the group of iconoclastic, intellectual Southerners—Simms, Hammond, Holmes, and agriculturist Edmund Ruffin were the others—so vividly portrayed in Drew Faust, *A Sacred Circle: The Dilemma of the Intellectual in the Old South, 1840–1860.* Tucker and Simms shared passionate views on literature and politics and—indeed—entered into relationship noted by its candor, warmth, and trust. Though they corresponded regularly and faithfully beginning in 1849, they met face-to-face only once, when Simms visited him in Williamsburg and traveled with him to Capon Springs just before Tucker's death in 1851. In 1854 Simms named a son Beverley Hammond Simms in honor of his two closest friends—one deceased, one living.

In his first letter to Tucker—dated March 15, 1849—Simms, newly appointed editor of the *Southern Quarterly Review,* specifically requested that Tucker "represent the Old Dominion in our pages,"[52] an invitation that prompted the "warm tone" of Tucker's response. Years later Simms still remembered a similar incidence involving Tucker: "I once wrote a letter to old B. Tucker of your precinct," Simms wrote to John Esten Cooke in 1859, "and closed it with '*Yours Lovingly.*' I forget what were the terms of the old man's response, but it showed that his heart was touched by the use of a word which men employ femininely only,—and in their dealings with women."[53]

My dear Sir.   Woodlands, April 5. 1849.

My first impulse, on the reciept of your letter, was to sit down immediately and answer it. Its tone was so warm, its sentiment so frank and Southern, that it made its way at once to my heart. But I restrained the impulse in

---

52. WGS to NBT, March 15, 1849, ibid., 497.
53. WGS to John Esten Cooke, July 26, 1859, ibid., 4:164.

regard to a consideration of more selfish character. I was anxious to answer
you about the Review of Macaulay. As you conjectured, the subject had been
assigned to one of the old contributors of the Review—the Honorable
Mr. Grayson[54]—formerly in Congress from this State and now Collector
of the Port of Charleston,—a very amiable and intelligent Gentleman. He
consented to prepare the article, but proved dilatory; and, suspecting (what
proved to be the truth) that he had done little or nothing towards it, instead
of writing to you I wrote to him, frankly telling him that I was particularly
anxious if his own progress had not been so far as to interest him in the subject, that it should be yielded up to you. His answer has just been recieved
and is such as I could wish. He, himself, is anxious that you should take
Macaulay in hand for two reasons. He wishes to have your pen enlisted in
behalf of the Review and he is curious to see what are your objections to
a writer, in whose work he has found everything to delight him. Opinions,
even less indulgent to Macaulay than your own, have met his ears in
Charleston. He writes—"I find that my enthusiasm in his favour is not
shared by every body here. Some are so irreverent as to call him a Humbug."
This Macaulay certainly is not. He may pretend to some things beyond his
measure, but he is unquestionably a man of considerable research and sometimes forcible though perhaps not very profound reflection. His misfortune
is, perhaps, to prefer a point to a truth, and his ambition at uniform brilliance is fatal to that *repose* which we desire mostly in the perusal of works
which require patient and calm consideration. But I need not prate of him
to you. I have read nothing of his present work but his introduction, which
seems to me stiff and frigid, though comprehensive and perhaps complete,
as regards the generalization which he intended. I shall be quite happy to recieve your article[55] by the fifteenth of May. It will then be in season. Could
I get it earlier, it should have, what I desire to give it, an earlier place in the
number. Hammond will probably furnish the initial article,[56] which is devoted to Elwood Fisher['s] pamphlet comparing North & South. Your opinion with regard to Hammond, is one to which I fully respond. He is one of
the most remarkable men that the South has produced. We singularly agree

---

54. William John Grayson (1788–1863), poet, is remembered for his individual
poem "The Hireling and the Slave," published in 1854 in a volume of the same title. A
strong defender of slavery, he also wanted to preserve the Union. Like Simms, Grayson
had strong sympathy with Native Americans, demonstrated in *Chicora, an Indian Legend*
(1856).

55. NBT, "Macaulay's History of England," *SQR* 15 (July 1849): 374–410.

56. JHH, "The North and the South," *SQR* 15 (July 1849): 273–311.

on the subject of the Yankees. Their great deficiency is in the imaginative faculty. In argument, because of this deficiency, they are incapable of generalization & deal only in details. And this is the remarkable respect in which their Congressional speeches differ from those of Southern men. Did you ever see such a race of rhymers, men and women, without a thought or fancy of their own to go all fours upon?——The Southern Review up to a late period, *was* edited, as you conjecture, by a Yankee;[57] a consummate ass, who had not the slightest notion of the length of his own ears, and who was as obtrusive & impudent as the most indurated pedlar of his race. He was *bought* out by a certain number of our Gentlemen, not so much, I believe, with the view of making the Review successful, as to relieve the South of the discredit of such a representative. In taking charge of the work, I feel my own deficiencies sufficiently, and my policy is to arm myself with good contributors. In a little time we shall be able to shake off some of those who have been deluging us with stupidity & commonplace; but we shall, for a while, be burdened with some few of the Balaamites. Our forthcoming number is cumbered by heavy and I fear unattractive articles. But when I consented to take charge of the work, not an article was written, and the number already due. We had no alternative, but to take just such stuff as we could lay hands upon. To reform this altogether will depend upon the favour of a select body of Contributors which I trust we shall be able in season to secure.——Gradually, we may attempt some of the improvements which you counsel. At present it is perhaps better to forbear experiments. There is a vulgar notion that reviews are merely grave & learned things. To be witty or playful, or to employ other forms of Art than such as distinguish the grave essay upon a printed book, such as constitutes the common character of our reviews at present, would seem to such people exceedingly undignified. I am sure I could wish to be allowed to go aside from the beaten track at times; since I should sometimes find it easier to put forth a story than a critique and by far more pleasant.——I knew you to be a State rights man before I wrote you. I was very far from wanting in the knowledge of your various resources. I had read George Balcome[58] when it was first published with the greatest pleasure; and I felt sure that I could rely upon you in any department, or in the

---

57. Massachusetts-born Daniel K. Whitaker (1801–1881), founder of the *Southern Literary Journal* in Charleston in 1835 and founding editor of *SQR* in New Orleans in 1842. In 1843 he moved *SQR* to Charleston and remained as its editor until 1847.

58. NBT, *George Balcombe,* 2 vols. (New York, 1836). WGS had referred to *George Balcombe* as Tucker's "excellent and thoughtful novel" (WGS to JHH, c. April 4, 1847, *Letters* 2 : 300).

treatment of any subject which it would please you to adopt. Perhaps, the better course, in choosing your subjects, would be to do so and simply write me what you design. It shall then be my care to reserve the topic & a place for you exclusively. With very great respect & regard, I presume, as you permit me, to subscribe myself very faithfully

Your friend &c
W. Gilmore Simms

P. S. Compelled to write hurriedly, and after a day of exhausting labor at the desk, reading and revising *proof* & MS., I am heartily ashamed of the rude & crude epistle I have scribbled you. But you will make the necessary allowance. I trust we shall have more leisure for correspondence hereafter. I was at Hammond's a few weeks ago, where we both very much wished for you. Have you ever visited Carolina? Don't let it be too late. We should both rejoice to welcome you,—and it is so little satisfactory to make a letter answer the purpose of conversation—at least to Southern men. We occupy places in the same district though fifty miles apart. Had your town been less off the route, I should have found my way to you years ago. I have usually visited the North every summer, for the last 16 or 17 years, sometimes through Virginia, and I have greatly longed to linger, when I did so. I do not yet despair that we shall find our way to the same neighbourhood. Your 'life in Virginia' would afford a good subject for the incidental & enlivening portions of a review article. There is something in Carolina life which has struck me as deserving description. The rural attractions of both have a value but little understood & seldom dwelt upon. But I am again at the bottom of my sheet.

Very sincerely Yours &:
W. Gilmore Simms

Please address me at this place, "Midway, P. O. S. C." I am 72 miles from Charleston at our country seat.

LETTER 9

Addressee: John Pendleton Kennedy
Postmark: none [May 1851]

John Pendleton Kennedy (1795–1870), of Baltimore, was second only to Simms among the novelists of the Old South. His two chief works, *Swallow Barn* and *Horse-Shoe Robinson* (a Revolutionary War novel set in South Carolina), were especially admired by Simms, who wrote appreciative reviews. Simms's affection for Kennedy is demonstrated by the dedication of *Count Julian* "to the Hon.

John P. Kennedy," a tribute graciously acknowledged by Kennedy in a letter to Simms stating, "I am no better than a laggard in the glorious path where you have become a leader."[59] Like Simms, Kennedy was a lawyer and a politician as well as a writer; he served as speaker of the Maryland House of Delegates, as a member of Congress, and as secretary of the U.S. Navy.

This letter to a contemporary writer he likes and admires candidly reflects the highs and lows of Simms's thinking in 1851: the frustrations of the editorship of *SQR*, the "Grist Mill" that keeps him "costive" and "churlish"; his appreciation of *Swallow Barn* as a literary work that answers the abolitionists ("if they *would* be answered"); and his passionate contempt for abolitionism, which he sees leading inevitably to secession. All these troubled thoughts, however, do not mitigate the affectionate tone of an otherwise genial personal note to a trusted colleague.

My dear Kennedy.   Woodlands S. C. May 12. [1851]
I have suffered your letter to lie in my sight for two months, while obeying calls which, if infinitely less agreeable, were infinitely more exacting than those of friendship. The business of the Review, as incessant as that of a Grist Mill, keeps me costive, and almost churlish in my correspondence; and in the increasing feebleness of my social virtues, I have only to console myself with a growing faith in the charities of my friends. That I should have so long foreborne to express my sympathies for your ailments, has however left you ample time to recover from them, and the hope that you have done so, it is much more grateful to me now to declare, than would have been the expression of my regrets a month ago. I have also had my ailments, which, when my *lachesse* is the subject of reflection, you will please take into the account; thus finding for me those apologies which I will not tediously thrust into your ears. As I propose to go north this summer, taking Balto. *en route,* let me hope that I shall be in condition to congratulate you on being no better physically (certainly no worse) than I trust then to find myself. To spend an hour, or day, with you, and hear from your own lips a better story of your own industry than your letter affords, is among the prospects & promises which I have been fashioning in Fancy for all the months of July & August.—— I am glad to hear that we are to have a new edition of Swallow Barn. Its genial & natural pictures of Virginia Life, are equally true of Southern life generally among the old & wealthy families, and are in fact the most conclusive answers to the abolitionists, (if they *would* be answered) that could be made. But they are not a people to need or to tolerate an answer. They will not listen any more than Pilate, to the very truths which they profess to solicit.

---

59. John Pendleton Kennedy to WGS, March 18, 1846, *Letters* 2 : 160n.

They have done the mischief which wiser and better men will fail to repair and have utterly subverted the only bond (that of sympathy) by which the people of our separate sections were ever truly held together. Common cause, common necessities, and the belief in a common feeling—these were the true articles of confederation. Abolitionism has pretty well obliterated them all from the compact. You will see for yourself what position S. C. occupies. I take no part in affairs publicly, & would wish not to do so privately, and am quite opposed to individual state action;—but I hold it now to be inevitable. The action of our Legislature, by decreeing a convention of the people, reduced us to a dilemma—either to *recede* from our position, with discredit, *a la mode Virginia,*[60] or to *secede,* at our peril. There is a third course which may be taken, but the State is not in the mood, does not possess the wisdom or the true courage, perhaps, to fall back upon it. The recent convention in Charleston,[61] meant to *coerce* to action the State Convention,[62] will have its effect. Its action has been nearly unanimous.—I am glad to hear that you meditate work hereafter. Braddock's career[63] is properly left to you. The material besides, in the same region, is both abundant & rich. Boone, Rogers Clarke, & others, afford ample room & verge enough to the writer of prose fiction; & by making yourself familiar with the scene, (which is an important matter) you have all that is necessary to your hands.—I thank you for the Green Mount Cemetery address which I read with great pleasure. I shall look for Swallow Barn with expectations. Where is the memoir of Cooke?[64] Do not forget to send it. I should like to have it by the 1st. July. With best regards, Believe me

Very faithfully Yours &c
W. Gilmore Simms

---

60. The General Assembly of Virginia in March 1851 resolved to do nothing to imperil the Union.

61. The Southern Rights Association of South Carolina resolved that South Carolina could not submit to the aggressive federal government and "that it is necessary to relieve herself therefrom, whether with or without the co-operation of other Southern States."

62. Held in Columbia, April 26–30, 1852.

63. In 1755 Gen. Edward Braddock (?1695–1755) was defeated at Fort Duquesne, "one in the chain of events which brought about the National Independence" (WGS to John Pendleton Kennedy, Feb. 16, 1851, *Letters* 3:92). Kennedy did not take WGS's suggestions to write about Braddock, or Daniel Boone (1734–1820) or George Rogers Clark (1752–1818).

64. Kennedy had promised a memoir of Philip Pendleton Cooke (1816–1850), his kinsman, for *SQR* (Kennedy to WGS, March 8, 1851, *Letters* 3:92). The memoir did not appear in *SQR*.

LETTER 10

Addressee: George Frederick Holmes
Postmark: none [July 1853]

A close neighbor of Simms when he taught school at Orangeburg, a short distance from Woodlands, George Frederick Holmes (1820–1897) early became
a protégé of Simms, with whom he shared literary, social, and political views.
Holmes was an ambitious, articulate, well-educated Englishman who emigrated
to South Carolina and who, with Simms's help, quickly rose to prominence in
Southern literary and educational circles. He wrote frequently for the magazines Simms edited and once was editorially associated with the *Southern Quarterly Review*. Moving to Virginia, he held professorships at Richmond College,
the College of William and Mary, and the University of Virginia and at one time
served as president of the University of Mississippi. With an affinity for South
Carolina social and political life, he was disappointed that even with Simms's
support, he was unable to secure a position at South Carolina College, where
William C. Preston, his uncle-in-law, was president from 1845 to 1851.

   This letter offers insight into the problems confronting the editor of a magazine published in the South; it also gives important details about publishers and
printers in general and the plight of a literary man in a sparsely settled region.
It aptly portrays Simms, who once admitted, "I cannot not be content if I
would,"[65] in one of his characteristic despondent moods.

OFFICE "SOUTHERN QUARTERLY REVIEW."

My dear Professor   Charleston, S. C., July 15. 1853.
   I can afford you only a short and sluggish note in reply to your long and
kindly toned letter. I am still a most unhappy drudge, fettered to the desk,
as the galley slave to his oar. It is this great & unrelenting doom of drudgery
in most part, which is breaking me down in strength & spirit, and which
must account to you for the dreary tone of my previous epistle. That I am
compelled to work incessantly, & mostly in vain, is a necessity which will
finally overcome any will, and subdue the elastic in any spirit. I am in debt,
my family increases, my resources diminish, and every hope upon which I
persuade myself to build, seems doom'd to disappointment, until I sometimes feel like throwing down the burden, and resolving desperately, I will
struggle no [more.] You understand what it is to be doomed to strive for the
palm, yet not be in the field. A literary man, residing in the South, may be
likened to the blooded horse locked up in the stable, and miles away from
the course, at the moment when his rivals are at the starting post. Do what

---

65. WGS to JL, July 19, 1834, *Letters* 1 : 59.

we may, it is impossible in such cases, that we can stand any chance of success. My true policy is to live in one of our great Northern cities. Yet my
wife is an only child; her father is in declining health & years; she cannot
leave him, and I cannot separate from her & my children, except for a brief
period. I am thus compelled to remain here, in my stable, when I ought to
be speeding over the track. My labours here are profitless. The Review does
not pay me. I have just given the publishers to know that with this year my
Editorship terminates[66] unless I am regularly paid, though it be the pittance
of a $1000 only which they have hitherto professed their willingness to al-
low. Our difficulty is that we really have no publishers. Our people of this
order, are in fact only printers & know nothing & do nothing for the work,
which would be a fortune to one who was capable, & who prosecuted his
labors earnestly. *Voila tout.* My family is all well, I am glad to say, and spite
of drudgery, I still maintain a full front. But though the top of the tree is still
green, there is much rot at the core. My friends do not see; but my brain is
troubled, overwrought, and I look to drop down some sunny day, in the harness. Well!—Your article makes 48 pages, the initial article of our October
issue. Draw for $48 on the publishers, as soon as the number is out, i. e.
Oct. 1. Have you seen & read our July issue. Write me what you think of it.
In haste but

Very truly Yours, &c
W. Gilmore Simms

LETTER 11

Addressee: Mary Lawson
Postmark: none [July 1854]

Mary Lawson (1839–1893), the second child and second daughter of James
Lawson (see letter 1) and Mary Elyse Donaldson Lawson (Simms's "Lady
Lyde"), was in 1854 a bright, inquisitive fifteen-year-old who idolized Simms,
the literary friend of her parents and a frequent guest in her home. In 1865 she
married Thomas Sarjeant Sandford, a New York lawyer.

The recorded correspondence between Simms and Mary Lawson begins in
1854 with this letter (a reply to Mary's "kind little epistle") and ends in November 1859 with a note from Simms inviting her to visit Woodlands: "Come,
at all events, early in December, when we generally have fine weather."[67] (That

66. WGS eventually resigned as editor in Dec. 1854.
67. WGS to Mary Lawson, Nov. 15, 1859, ibid., 4:179.

their friendly relationship continued, however, even after her marriage, is ascertained by a Simms letter in 1868 introducing and recommending "with perfect trust and confidence" Sandford and "his young wife," a "very sweet, well bred & intelligent woman, the daughter of one of my oldest Northern friends.") [68] The letter that follows displays a side of Simms not frequently seen: his warm, gentle yet firm, inspirational yet practical, encouraging yet cautionary touch with young people. It also shows Simms's recognition of the intellectual and spiritual endowment of women and of their capability and need to accomplish things in life other than the domestic. Simms's exhortation, "Let me entreat you . . . not to trouble yourself so much to be a fine young lady, as a noble thoughtful performing woman," reveals that in his letter writing, as in his fiction, Simms demonstrates an awareness of the worth of woman long before the advent of a feminist movement.

Miss Mary Lawson.
dear Mary.   Charleston, July 13. 1854.
    I am grateful for your attention and the kind little epistle which I owe to your hands. I am particularly delighted to see what a nice letter you can write. It is so well concieved, in such excellent taste, so gracefully expressed, and withal so well thought and so appropriate, that I have been exceedingly gratified by its perusal, by the promise it gives of your mind in future, and by the proofs which it affords that you have not been neglectful of your acquisitions. I trust you will exercise as much as possible, with the view to your own continued improvement that rarely beautiful instrument, a young, generous, ardent and susceptible nature. Now is the time for you to read; and read variously, and read ambitiously. If I might counsel you, it is now proper that you should direct your attention in especial to a class of works which young ladies rarely attempt—history, biography, travels. I would have you make yourself familiar with Plutarch, Anacharsis, Froissart &c, and while I counsel such volumes for general reading, I would urge you to some special study,—Botany for example, Natural history—Art—exercising your mind & taste *practically,* on one or other of these studies. With such opportunities as you possess, Botany might become one of your positive possessions; and if your taste inclined you to the Fine Arts, you have even greater opportunities for making yourself a mistress of one or other of their many branches. Belles Lettres, at all events, might be easily attainable, and would be a perpetual spring of satisfaction to one whose tastes and sensibilities have already prepared her for rapid acquisition. Let me entreat you, therefore, not to trouble yourself so much to be a fine young lady, as a noble

---

68. WGS to Joseph Henry, Dec. 5, 1868, ibid., 5: 179.

thoughtful performing woman, using her mind, as a Godlike instrument from which she may, at all periods, extract the most soul solacing harmonies.

Let me repeat my thanks for your letter which supplies to me, for the first time, much of the information which I desired in respect to your father, and the condition of your family, for which I sought vainly of all other sources. I need not tell you how greatly I have been relieved and rejoiced by the account of your father's recovery.[69] That he is still an invalid is a discouragement, it is true; but that he is rescued from the great peril which he suffered, is a subject of fervent gratitude among the whole of us. Were I with him, I think it might be easy to put his right arm again in piscatorial condition; and the description which you give of the beautiful scenery where you harbour makes me really desirous to pop in upon you suddenly some day and see for myself. When I shall come north, I cannot now say from the condition of my family, over the destinies of which there hangs just now a certain anxiety;[70] but all things turning out well, I do not despair of getting North early in August. My daughter Augusta has suddenly resolved not to go north this season, as it has so far advanced already. But next year she builds on for the adventure. When I visit N. Y. I shall surely run up to see your father the first thing, and your mother the next thing, and their sons & daughters the third thing. In the meantime I send you a kiss for each which you will please to advance on my account; make a memorandum of the number thus bestowed, and when I come on I will repay you for all with proper interest. My wife & Augusta send their loves with mine for all of you, & your little namesake Mary Lawson expresses very earnest wishes to convey hers in proper person. Very lovingly Mary,

Your sincere friend
W. Gilmore Simms

LETTER 12

Addressee: Justus Starr Redfield
Postmark: none [May 1856]

Justus Starr Redfield (1810–1888), Simms's favorite publisher, first opened a bookstore in New York, in 1841, and became a part of the city literary network,

---

69. In an April 30, 1854, letter to JL, Simms expressed relief that JL was "sufficiently restored" after "a severe struggle with the first and last natural enemy of man" (*Letters* 3:294).

70. Chevillette Simms was pregnant with Beverley Hammond Simms, born July 17, 1854.

leading him eventually to establish his own printing and publishing firm. In 1853, after Simms became exasperated with futile attempts to have his collected poems published in Charleston, Redfield offered to publish not only his poetical works but a series of his prose works as well. The resulting "Redfield edition" constitutes by far the best nineteenth-century collection of Simms's writings. Even after the Redfield publishing house failed in 1860 and was succeeded by W. J. Widdleton, Simms continued to trust and rely upon Redfield's judgment, frequently calling upon him for help with Northern publishers after the Civil War. As late as 1870, when Redfield was contemplating returning to his "first love," the author—slowly dying of cancer—wrote the publisher a long letter of encouragement ending, "Concentrate yourself upon your business, & leave Banks, Custom Houses & Politics to go to the Devil, with whom most of them originate."[71]

In addition to testifying to the good working relationship between author and publisher, this letter contains what is perhaps Simms's most explicit statement of his religious beliefs. Simms was not reluctant to discuss religion with Redfield because he knew of Redfield's interest in spiritualism: Redfield was the publisher of a number of books on the topic.

My dear Publisher.   Woodlands, May 4. 1856

I have just got home after a two week's absence and find your letter of the 23d. I have not recieved my copy of Eutaw[72] from Russell, though it will probably come up this week in a bundle which I expect. I had a glimpse of a copy in a Passenger's hands on the Rail Road a few days ago. I trust that the latter portion of the book contains no flagrant error. That it possibly may is still my anxiety. If so, our only remedy is the correction in a new edition, for which, I hope, as you do, that our pleasant public will have proper cravings in due season. In respect to the future series we may pause until we can confer this summer in a pleasant *tête a tête*. But, meanwhile, it appears to me a proper policy to have "*Vasconselos*"[73] illustrated and formally avowed in a new preface or letter to our excellent friend, Dr. Francis. This, as the work is stereotyped, will add but little to your outlay, and the vol. will be kept selling in setts. No copies of that need be given to editors, except in some few special instances, where they were not bestowed before. Again, "The Wigwam & the Cabin" is stereotyped & the plates belong to me. The page, in size & type closely corresponds with your edition. The difference is too slight to occasion remark, or even excite attention. Now, you shall have the plates for $100. The work is near 500 pages. You will then need only the

71. WGS to J. S. Redfield, Feb. 16, 1870, ibid., 5 : 297.
72. Redfield issued the first edition of *Eutaw* in May 1856.
73. Redfield had published the first edition of *Vasconselos* in 1853. The second edition (1857) contains a new dedication to John Wakefield Francis.

illustrations from Darley,[74] to be able to include it in the collection which with the Yemassee, Southward Ho and the Poems, Vasconselos would then constitute a library of 19 volumes[75]—7 Rev; 6 Border; 2 Poems; & Wig & Cab. These 2 additional volumes, Vasconselos & The Wigwam, might be put forth at proper intervals between this and November. I am sure that, in the South, the collection will sell spiritedly, *as a whole.*—Thanks for your suggestion touching the Lectures.—Do you know one Geo. Peckham,[76] of the House of Eno. Roberts & Co? I met him in the cars a few days ago, & he was introduced to me through the means of a Member of Congress, and a bottle of *wheat* whiskey. He broached the subject of Lectures[77] to me, and gave me to understand that he was the Ruling Spirit for all such matters for the good city of Gotham. He said to me,—"You will hear from our Merc. Association. I will have you invited, &c." There is another matter to which I crave your attention. I have been considerably impressed of late with the subject of Spiritualism. My mind has always, in fact, been governed by an earnestness of tendency, approaching to Religion, and but two considerations have ever kept me from actually taking to the Pulpit. One of these considerations was the painful conviction that I was not sufficiently virtuous myself—not sufficiently superior to my own passions—with no adequate restraint of will over desire,—and found sin too pleasant, perhaps, to shake off its company;—the next was that my own mind stubbornly opposed every creed of every Christian Church extant. I rejected the Old Testament as a religious authority altogether, & satisfied myself that the New was, however true and good, & wise & pure in many things, a wonderfully corrupt narrative. Spiritualism as a philosophy is in more complete accordance with my own speculations, felt & pursued for 30 years, than any other system. I naturally desire to *know* — substituting my own certain, for the alleged experiences of other people. Now, if God spares me to visit the North this summer, you must endeavour to secure me the *entree* of some of these magic circles, the character of whose members is beyond suspicion. I am resolved to see & study the matter for myself whenever I can get a chance. I am not the man to dread ridicule; and still less am I so little earnest, as to shrink from an investigation involving so vital and absorbing an interest. If you have any of the

74. F. O. C. Darley (1822—1888) was the noted illustrator of WGS's novels issued by Redfield.

75. With the later addition of *The Cassique of Kiawah* (1859) and *The History of South Carolina* (1860), Redfield published twenty-one volumes of WGS.

76. There was James Peckham on the Committee of Arrangements that invited WGS to lecture in New York on Nov. 18, 21, and 25, 1856.

77. WGS's proposed lecture tour in the North (see Letter 16).

Spiritual Documents & Records, and can spare me some of them, send them. I have forborne to draw from the Bal. reported in your Jan. account. But I shall shortly have to do so.

God forgive you.

Yours &c

W. Gilmore Simms

LETTER 13

Addressee: James Henry Hammond
Postmark: none [December 1856]

See letter 5 for Hammond.

This letter should be read in conjunction with Simms's essay entitled "South Carolina in the Revolution: A Lecture" (see below). After Simms's lecture debacle in 1856, Hammond's outrage that Simms had foolishly "martyred" himself and his subsequent query, "What Demon possessed you, mon ami, to do this?"[78] prompted Simms to write as he does here, more in defense than in explanation. Hammond confided to Simms his own error in judgment and expressed some contrition for failing to give good advice: "I put on a good face, and rather believed that curiosity would make the Yankees flock to you for a 'sensation.' . . . In this I was mistaken. The feeling is more intensely hostile than I suspected. You ought to have known better than a recluse like me. And you ought to have known there is no gratitude in the South and that a man is a fool who would sacrifice a red cent for her."[79] Two months later Hammond redeemed himself somewhat by the wise counsel he gave his author friend: "As to your own affairs you must not suppose that I can ever be otherwise but deeply and sincerely interested in them. For what I can see your rebuff at the North is likely to be fine Southern Capital and yield you a good per cent. I am sure it will be if you demean yourself prudently . . . . You have lost nothing South."[80] Hammond's prediction probably induced Simms, almost immediately thereafter, to schedule a lecture tour in the South to replace his aborted Northern itinerary, thereby recouping some of his financial loss, as well as restoring ego.

My dear Hammond.   Woodlands, Decr. 8. 1856.

My time has been so entirely employed, for some time past, and my mind so troubled, that I have not had a chance to write to you as I several times desired. You perhaps do me some injustice. Properly, there was nothing in

---

78. JHH to WGS, Nov. 27, 1856, *Letters* 3:465n.
79. Ibid., 465–66n.
80. Ibid., Jan. 23 and 31, 1857, 466n.

my Lecture which should have given offence. I forbore wherever I could to say what was offensive. I gave the true history, of S. C. and referred to other regions only where it was necessary to establish a just standard by which to judge of what ought to be expected of S. C. in the Revolution. I made no allusion to Brooks, directly or indirectly. I did to Sumner, as the wanton assailant of S. C. in the Chamber of Commerce Council, & when she (S. C.) was not a subject of discussion. I had to do this, in order to show why, & on what points, I had undertaken to correct the vulgar mistakes or misrepresentations of her history. But such is the rancorous temper of Black republicanism; so completely does New England rule N. Y.; and so malignantly do they all regard S. C., that the very subject re-aroused all the hostility. Besides, the Black republicans were grateful for any new occasion for keeping up the excitements by which they live. I was a new brand of pitch pine to fling into the furnace. I grant you that I could have used other Lectures in themselves innocuous. But I had set out on this my mission, had prepared these Lectures, by way of disabusing them of those errors which were leading them on to ruin; and my own blood was in a ferment. But for the freshness of their disappointment under the recent defeat of their hopes & party, I fancy I should have had no difficulty. The mistake which I made, was, in not taking into account the probable effect of the election.[81] I am the loser,— self-sacrificing you say—but in money matters only. I have preserved my self respect & the honour of our section. They saw no faltering in me. I spoke to crowded houses at Rochester & Buffalo, more than 1200 people in each, and they howled under the arguments which they could not answer. At N. Y. the first night, I had but 150. They had seen the furious demonstrations of the Buffalo press. But, in truth, my Lectures were badly advertised. As for the Herald,[82] it is a budget of the most foul & reckless lies. For example, the second night was not advertised at all in a single paper of the day. The night was one of storm & rain. Numbers came, but the church was unopened. It had been arranged, in the interval between the first & second night, that we were to abandon the field. The Committee came to me the day after the first lecture. They said—"Such is the feeling in the community on account of the allusion to Sumner—such, in regard to certain passages of

---

81. In the 1856 presidential election, James Buchanan (Democrat of Pennsylvania) defeated Millard Fillmore (National American of New York) and John Charles Frémont (Republican of California). The election results hardened increasing sectional animosity.

82. The *New York Herald,* Nov. 19, 1856, condemned both WGS and his lecture on "South Carolina in the Revolution." The Buffalo *Evening Post,* Nov. 12, 1856, called the WGS lecture of Nov. 11 "an ill-digested, bitter and to at least nine-tenths of the audience, offensive defence of South Carolina politicians of the Brooks school."

your discourse,—that we cannot only not sell tickets, but we cannot give them away—the language being "D———n S. C. & all that belongs to her—we want to hear no *blowing* about S. Car." This report was confirmed by others, who agreed that the rancorous feeling in the city was such that they were willing to listen to nothing from the South. What remained to me, but to release the Committee from a contract in which they were to suffer loss. I did so promptly. They paid over the money to my publisher,[83] and I ordered him to bestow it on public charities. I could have gone farther—could have carried out my contracts elsewhere,—got the money; but could I have taken it under such circumstances? Could I hope that if I could not secure a hearing in N. Y. I should be more successful farther East. I could, it is true, have used subjects which should not give offence. But would not that have made me appear as shrinking from the very mission which I came upon;—as recoiling under the storm that I had raised. If I had gone farther, I should certainly have given no other than my Southern subjects, and these they were prepared everywhere to ignore. I grant you that, if, at the outset, I had dreamed that I should have been denounced because of my local subjects, I would have taken others; but the step once taken, it was matter of pride & honor, that I should insist upon these or none. And who could have fancied that the rancour had become so universal & so universally blinding. You are right in saying that S. C. had no claim of self-sacrifice upon me. But, mon ami, neither you nor I,—are quite capable, whatever the wrongs or neglect we suffer—to contemn, discard, or escape from our own impulses. My *heart* (suffer me to have one) was *slavishly* in these topics of S. C. I could no more fling them off from it, than I could fly. And my mind followed my heart. In this field, I was the champion; and my heroism did not stop to ask whether I should ever win thanks or a smile from the disdainful sovereign whom I was prepared to serve with my life. Do not *you* reproach me with this *weakness,* in which I could not suffer a selfishness to share. I expect nothing from S. C., but I have been too long accustomed to toils & sacrifice for her, to feel her injustice now. My losses are all pecuniary. She will never make them up to me. She will probably never acknowledge my performances. But I have the precious consciousness of both the toil & the sacrifice, and the proud feeling that if I have never recieved her favours, I am free from obligations; and though she may allow of none to me, I, at least, have a conviction on that score which is singularly compensative.—I have not forgotten your commission among the Spiritualists, though I have not been able to achieve much, or much, on your account, that will prove satisfactory. Of these I shall write hereafter, when I am able to collect & arrange my papers. Enough that I have been very much

---

83. For J. S. Redfield, see Letter 12, above.

impressed on my own account, even when I asked nothing about myself—when, in fact, with your queries in my hand, I was speaking only for you and never dreaming of my own affairs. Then I was suddenly awakened with tidings of those (of my own blood) in waiting and desiring to be heard. I have the name of a medium[84] for you, who proposes to visit the South in the spring, and whom you should invite to your house, even if you reward him highly. My affectionate regards to your wife, & such of your children as may be with you. God bless you. Write me soon.

Yours &c
W G S.

LETTER 14

Addressee: Orville James Victor
Postmark: none [September? 1859]

Orville James Victor (1827–1910), New York author-publisher, was editor of the *Cosmopolitan Art Journal* from 1856 to 1861. He was married to Metta Victoria Fuller (1831–1885), a minor poet whose *The Arctic Queen* Simms called "a remarkable blank verse poem . . . much better than that of all our lady poets"[85]—a position he later tempered. After the Civil War, Victor became editor of the *Illuminated Western World* and arranged with Simms for the serial publication of *Voltmeier* in 1869, at a time when the author was having difficulty finding publishers for his works.

In July 1859 Simms invited John Esten Cooke to write a biographical sketch of him to be used "by Mr. Victor, of the Art Journal of New York—a quarto of large circulation and much merit. Of this Victor I know but little, having seen him only twice or thrice last summer."[86] Cooke's sketch of Simms was published with a portrait of Simms in the December 1859 number of the *Cosmopolitan Art Journal*. Simms's letter to Victor, though brief, contains biographical details found nowhere else. Particularly interesting, in the light of Simms's lifelong passion for acting, caricature, and mimicry, is his statement that he "could imi-

---

84. George A. Redman (b. 1835), of Boston. Some weeks later, in a long letter devoted almost entirely to spiritualism, WGS said to JHH: "I learned from Redfield that he had made an engagement for me, with a Mr. Redman, one of the most remarkable mediums of the country. This Mr. R. is a *writing* medium" (Dec. 30, 1856, *Letters* 3:480). Redman was the author of *Mystic Hours; or, Spiritual Experiences* (New York, 1859).

85. WGS to John Esten Cooke, July 26, 1859, *Letters* 4:166.

86. Ibid.

tate [Indians] in speech; imitate the backwoodsmen, mountaineers, swamp suckers, &c." Late in 1859 Simms offended society-minded gentry at an elegant dinner party at Middleton Place near Charleston by acting out (in his own words) "my character as a backwoodsman."[87]

My dear Mr. Victor.   [September? 1859]

I hasten to send you the sketch of myself which I have just recieved from Mr. Cooke. I might add a good many details, but his summary seems to cover them. You may state, if necessary that I am a Cotton Planter, and reside on the plantation of 'Woodlands,' Barnwell District, some eight months in the year; that I have a wife and seven children living. I have lost seven. I have now four girls and three boys,— the eldest of the former married. Four months in the year, from June to Sept. inclusive my family & self reside in Charleston where we own a residence. We sometimes travel; and I usually make a flying visit north every summer. You may also throw into Mr. Cooke's sketch somewhere, that from my earliest years, I have been a hard student & perpetual reader, rarely even now retiring at night untill the short hours; that I have travelled, in early years, greatly in the South & South West on horseback, seeing the whole region from Carolina to Mississippi personally, and as far back as 1825 when $\frac{2}{3}$ was an Indian Country; that I saw the red men in their own homes; could imitate them in speech; imitate the backwoodsmen, mountaineers, swamp suckers, &c. Mr. John Russell, who left Charleston in the Steamer on Thursday, takes on a couple of pictures (photographs) one full face, the other profile, from which you are to choose. Your engraver will need to open the eyes a little. Being once a sufferer from coup de soleil, the least condensation of light upon my eyes, even for a moment, causes the delicate muscles of that region to wince & contract, so that the eye nearly closes, & there is a swelling & corrugation all around it, & the very nose is slightly lifted. To correct this, get the engraved portrait published by Redfield and let the engraver work out from the two. My friends here are of the opinion that this engraving would be the best after all for you. You will see that one of the pictures is a profile, which I think will make really the best picture. But suit yourself. You will find Mr. Cooke's article well written & with great spirit. He uses here, a portion of a paper which he published in the South. Messenger.[88] Yours in haste, but

Ever truly
W. Gilmore Simms

---

87. WGS to Williams Middleton, Nov. 2, 1859, ibid., 6:208.
88. John Esten Cooke, "William Gilmore Simms," *SLM* 28 (May 1859): 355–70.

LETTER 15

Addressee: James Lawson
Postmark: none [December 1860]

See Letter 1 for Lawson.

Lawson's son Jimmy, a good friend of Simms's son Gilmore Jr., was a guest at Woodlands when on December 20, 1860, the Ordinance of Secession was unanimously adopted in Charleston. Earlier, in a letter of November 20, Simms had tried to persuade his Northern colleague that "there will be no war. A war would destroy the whole confederacy of the North, & make the South supreme."[89] In addition to the invitation to Jimmy—with the promise "I will take care of him"—Simms also had coaxed Lawson: "Come yourself. Settle here alongside of me, as a Cotton Planter. . . . I will get or give you a farm."[90]

My dear Lawson.   Woodlands, 31 Decr. 1860.

Jimmy is preparing to go to Charleston, and thence to Savannah. I have just had a long talk with him. The Charleston Steamers are stopt. Possibly, within the next 3 days, the Savannah Steamers will be stopt also. Possibly, this very night, an attempt will be made upon Fort Sumter. I have said to Jimmy—"You can go to Charleston & to Dr. Fuller, and the cost will be trifling, & the risk nothing. But, if the Savannah Steamers, as well as the Charleston have stopt running, you must go home by land. In that event, come home, *here,* to *me;* & go hence by the Wilmington R Road. *Your father's son shall have the means,* though I steal 'em; but your father's son must not have a hair of his head endangered." Accordingly, I have *ordered* him, if there be any fighting on the Seaboard, "do you come back to *me.*" I will give him letters of credit to Charleston & Savannah, for such small amounts as he will need, enough to keep & carry him home; even though his father's credit should fail; which is not likely. It is to you much more important that the boy should be safe, than that he should be in a hurry to get home. He is safe with me, and under my counsel. We are on the eve of war, and our boys are not to be kept bridled much longer. A dirty trick has been played upon us; Mr. Buchanann pledged that the forts should be kept in their present *status.* And while we have kept faith with him, the *status* has been changed.

In brief, the Federal Government, is one of dirty rascals, with whom no faith should be kept. The *Venue* changed, we shall have harder work; and with the loss of more lives. We could have captured all the forts weeks ago,—but we wished the work to end peaceably. This is denied. War is inevitable! And—God defend the right! I know not what is to be done. I am not in a

---

89. WGS to JL, Nov. 20, 1860, *Letters* 4: 268.
90. Ibid., 269.

position to know or to do any thing, and I am a small volcano in a canebrake: ready to boil over & burst; but without doing more than making the canes explode. Gilmore has been suddenly summoned back to Columbia, to drill the other boys. Head of the first class,[91] he is thus thrown back. He chafes; is anxious to go to Charleston—anxious to volunteer; will fight like the devil, if I will let him; but *I* cannot afford it. He is the last hope of the family. Fortunately, he is an invalid. He has been afflicted, ever since Jimmy came on, with blood boils, or tumours, on his neck, which have kept him in the house, with head awry, with constant poultices, from which he is not yet freed. Sooner than he shall enter into the fray, I will go myself!—In respect to Jimmy, it is with pleasure that I tell you that all parties speak of him with favour. He is an intelligent boy, and a modest boy, and wins his way with grace and propriety. We are all fond of him, & would keep him longer. If I find that there is any difficulty in Charleston, by the papers tomorrow, I shall probably not suffer him to go thither. I shall keep him out of danger. He shall stay *here,* till I hear from you. Here, there is no danger.—He, & Carroll,[92] Gilmore & myself have been playing whist till this moment. All are gone to bed but myself, & as I have several letters to write tonight, I bid you God E'en, & God be with you.

Yours ever
W. G. S.

LETTER 16

Addressee: William Porcher Miles / Charleston, / South Carolina
Postmark: Midway SC / January 1/61

William Porcher Miles (1822–1899), one of Simms's closest Charleston friends, had a distinguished career. A graduate of the College of Charleston with highest honors, he served on the faculty of his alma mater, practiced law, was mayor of Charleston, and was elected to both the U.S. Congress and the Confederate Congress. Noted as an orator, he was much in demand as a public speaker. A close friend to Simms's family, he was named godfather at the birth of Harriet Myddleton Simms; tradition has it that his brother, Episcopal minister James Warley Miles, was at Simms's bedside when the author died. Simms dedicated *The Cassique of Kiawah* to William Porcher Miles and memorialized him with "Sonnet.—To W. Porcher Miles," including the express lines, "No brother more devoted!—More than friend, / Beloved evermore,—behold me thine!"

---

91. At the Citadel Academy, Charleston.

92. Francis Fishburne Carroll (b. 1833), physician and planter, a neighbor of WGS, was the son of Charles Rivers Carroll, under whom WGS studied law, to whom he dedicated *Early Lays* and *Guy Rivers,* and for whom he named his youngest son.

In November 1860 Simms urged then Congressman Miles to consider running for the governorship of South Carolina because after secession "it will be, for a time at least, the Presidency of a new Republic"[93]—evidence of Simms's trust in Miles's political acumen if not a demonstration of his own. All during the events leading up to war, and after its outbreak, Simms wrote Miles (and David Flavel Jamison, president of the Secession Convention) lengthy letters outlining military strategy in general and the defense of Charleston Harbor in particular. These letters in copious detail demonstrate that among other accomplishments Simms was a knowledgeable military tactician. But the succinct letter below is a revelation of Simms's mood—his quiet desperation, yet firm resolution—at a time of crisis.

dear Miles. Woodlands, 31 Decr. [1860]

Keep yourself warm with the scarf. My wife will never forget you, nor will I. God bless you & yours.—We are all here on the *qui vive* of expectation, & today the rascally mails failed us, & we have neither Mercury nor Courier. I have written to Jamison. It was an oversight to let Anderson[94] transfer himself from Moultrie to Sumter. I told Jamison, long ago, that Ft. Sumter held control over all the forts in the harbour, & must be had first, to secure the rest. Your *Guarda Costas* should have been flying between, day & night. Now, so far as I can see, you have but two processes left you. You must either starve out or smoke out the garrison. You should certainly not suffer them to mount a cannon; but by incessant cannonade, from the landside, wear them out. In the smallness of the garrison is your hope. Do not attempt *escalade,* until all other means have failed. I am here, like a bear with a sore head, & chained to the stake. I chafe, and roar & rage, but can do nothing. Do not be rash, but, do not let this old city forget her *prestige.* Charleston is worth all New England.

God be with you!
W. Gilmore Simms.

LETTER 17

Addressee: William Gilmore Simms, Jr.
Postmark: none [November 1861]

William Gilmore Simms, Jr. (1843–1912), Simms's fifth child and first son, called "Gilly," was especially close to his father, whose love and paternal concern included instilling in his offspring the discipline, as well as the sense of

93. WGS to W. P. Miles, Nov. 12, 1860, *Letters* 4:263.

94. Maj. Robert Anderson (1805–1871), without orders from Washington, removed his command from Fort Moultrie to Fort Sumter.

responsibility, needed to meet the challenge of life. A vigorous boy who loved hunting, fishing, swimming, pistol shooting, and horseback riding, he grew up holding his literary, philosophical father in reverence—as did all members of Simms's family, beginning with Chevillette, whose unselfish love for her husband was manifest in all she did and served as an exemplary role model for her children. Though Gilly never attended college—somewhat surprising in the light of the high premium his father placed on education—after the war he studied law and helped his father in the management of Woodlands. Though Simms at times—inadvertently, perhaps—gave evidence of disappointment in his elder son's lack of intellectual prowess, he loved him no less passionately and tried to give him the paternal guidance he himself had so sorely missed in his own youth. William Gilmore Simms, Jr., closed out his career by serving for many years as clerk of court in Barnwell County.

(Letter 17 should be read in conjunction with Letter 15.) In the words of Simms, who had lost three sons within three years, he had scarcely "buried another son," Sydney Hammond Simms, who died on or about July 2, 1861, before his eldest son received the call to report for active duty, on or about November 7, 1861, when Union forces attacked and captured Port Royal on the South Carolina coast. Written that same day, the letter of William Gilmore Simms to his namesake son and heir is memorable; combining practical and philosophical advice, this calm, almost matter-of-fact letter must have been calculated by the father to have a steadying influence upon the son. Certainly, by intention, it reveals none of the terrible anxiety the father must have felt at the time.

Woodlands, Thursday Afternoon. [November 7, 1861]

You had better, my dear Son, get a belt and pocket of leather, for your revolver, and not burden yourself with carrying the box. It will not be necessary to you. If you have enough of bullets, even the bullet mould & all the appurtenances of powder flask &c. may be left with the box. The same flask from which you load your musket, will afford you powder for your pistol. But as in the musket you may probably use cartridges, then carry the powder flask of the pistol. But be sure & strip yourself of all unnecessary incumbrances, which the Romans called *Impedimenta*. Be as lightly armed as you can. It would be better that I should provide you with moulded bullets than that you should carry mould & lead with you. Leave box, mould & all that sort of thing with your sister. Advise me, as soon as you can, of your whereabouts & the mode of reaching you, in the event of our desiring to send you any thing. See that your provision for clothing is warm & sufficient. Leave every thing that you do not need, with your sister; and remember that nobody is more lighthearted than he who has fewest cares, whether of brain or body. Your bowie knife may be very useful. You are to remember that you are to defend your mother country, & your natural mother, from a hoard of mercenaries & plunderers, and you will make your teeth meet in the flesh.

The less you fear for yourself, the more your security. 'He who would save his life, the same shall lose it!' This is a biblical warning against that lack of firmness, that overcaution, always trembling consequences, & calculating chances, which was the infirmity of Hamlet, and which is fatal to all heroism. And this audacity & courage are not inconsistent with the utmost prudence and circumspection. All generalship, in fact, is so much military prudence, as reconciles valour with judgment & wisdom. Mere inconsiderate rage is not so much valour as blindness, ignorance, presumption & insanity. Obey orders, do your duty faithfully & cheerfully & patiently, and wait your time, & watch your time, and keep your head so, that where your leader may falter, you shall be able to keep him up, counsel him on, & where he falls, take the lead yourself. A strong will, a brave heart & clear head, in the moment of danger, these constitute the essentials of heroism. Let nothing, at any time, divert your mind, from the immediate duty which is before you. This is *first* & therefore *over* all. It will be time enough tomorrow for other matters. But I will not bore you with laws and maxims. Be a man, my son, faithful & firm, and put yourself in God's keeping. All that the love & confidence of parents can do for you will be done. Yourself, with God's aid, must do the rest. We are in his hands, all of us! Pray to him. It will not lessen your strength & courage to do so, even on the abyss of battle! We are all well except your father. I am suffering from neuralgia in the head, from ear ache, and tooth ache, all at once. The latter will probably compel me to visit the city on Monday next, & I may go to the Mills House or Charleston Hotel. I trust you have the dressing case by this time. Better take out of it a single razor, get it *set* by the Barber, take a small box of the ointment & the Brush & leave the case with your sister. It would only encumber you. A mere pinch of the ointment is put upon the face, and the brush, wet with water is then applied briskly. In laying the razor to cheek or chin, let it be as flat as possible. It will then cut the beard better, and will be less likely to cut the skin. Besides, it will keep the razor longer from being dulled.—The news which reaches us is exciting without being satisfactory. I have for six months predicted the attempt of the enemy on Beaufort, with a formidable force, with which they would expect to make Beaufort a base of operations, against Charleston & Savannah equally. I expected them in September. What our troops will need is numerous small steamers & boats so as to have ready access from one island to another. What I fear is the cutting off of small bodies on isolated spots. We require, now, that we have made the issue on the sea islands where the naval force of the enemy can be employed, to sustain our batteries against launches landing infantry & light troops. Any small bodies landing, we can cut off. To concentrate our troops in sufficient bodies against a formidable force will be more difficult, and, in the end, in all probability, we may be reduced to a guerilla warfare along the main fronting the sea islands. Write when you get a chance. God be with you, my son,

> Your father
> W. G. S.

LETTER 18

Addressee: Paul Hamilton Hayne
Postmark: none [September 1863]

Paul Hamilton Hayne (1830–86) came from one of South Carolina's most distinguished families: Robert Y. Hayne, the opponent of Webster, was his uncle; Colonel Isaac Hayne, a martyred hero of the Revolutionary War (see Simms's poem "Haynes—Let the Death-Bell Toll" below), was his ancestor. Hayne himself was a child prodigy. Before he was thirty, he already had established a reputation as poet, the author of three books of high promise, if not high accomplishment. Next to Simms, and perhaps Timrod, he ranks as the most gifted writer to come from Charleston's horde of talented literati. Though Hayne as a young man had always looked up to Simms as his mentor, the two did not become truly intimate until the 1860s, when—particularly after the death of James Henry Hammond—Hayne became Simms's confidant, the only South Carolinian with whom he candidly discussed both literary and personal matters. Simms and Hayne may well have had the most positive, most mutually supportive relationship to exist between an old literary lion and a young protégé in all of nineteenth-century America—the kind of ideal relationship Henry James touched upon (not without irony) in "The Lesson of the Master."

Just two weeks before Simms wrote this letter, his wife of twenty-seven years, Chevillette Eliza Roach Simms, died after a short illness. If during her life he had taken her too much for granted, upon her demise he suddenly realized both the intricacy of his love for her and the depth of his dependency upon her. Recognition that he had undervalued Chevillette, it appears, led him to question whether he had valued other things too highly: in this intense confessional letter to Hayne, the author who had always burned with ambition seemed to renounce it as an ill-advised addiction. Even, however, in this reflective and chastened mood, in which he admitted to feeling "much older—much feebler," Simms spoke hopefully of Hayne as "the younger brother of his guild" who would seek honors in the future.

My dear Paul.   Woodlands, Sep. 23. [1863]
    I am under the impression that I answered all your letters. I have a vague notion that our two last letters crossed on the route, & I left it to you, as the

youngest, to reopen the correspondence. I perfectly recollect the remarkable event you refer to, in respect to poor Ramsay[95]—on these subjects, as you are probably aware I am not an incredulous man. The spiritual world is in close contact with us. I believe that my beloved dead are ever with me and I would not willingly give up the belief.—I have been ill my friend, I may say dangerously ill, from the moment when I was struck down by the heaviest bolt of all that ever shattered my roof-tree. I was, I think, insane. I neither slept nor ate for four days and nights. Fever seized me, and I should have gone mad but for the administration of timely opiates. I am once more on my legs, but very weak. Today, is the first that I have given to the desk, and this I could do only in snatches of brief period. I move about the house & try to see to things. But every thing seems blank, & waste, & very cheerless. I am alone! Alone! For near 30 years, I had one companion in whose perfect fidelity, I felt sure. To her I could go, and say, 'I suffer!'—or 'I am glad,' always satisfied that she would partake the feeling with me, whatever its character. Your eulogy is not mere varnish & gilding. She was all that you describe,—a dutiful wife, a devoted mother, and the most guileless of women. Ah! God! And I am lone!

We live too much for the world, my dear Paul. It is a poor affair. This ambitious struggle after greatness, is a vanity. Our sole justification must lie in the will & wish to *do,* irrespective of the profit and the loss. What does Milton say in Lycidas—I half forget the passage

> 'But not *the praise,*
> Phoebus replied, & toucht my trembling ears—
> Fame is no plant that grows on mortal soil—
> &c.[']

Write me, my young friend. The old man has grown much older—much feebler—& it is becoming, the ministration of you, the younger brother of his guild, to assist his palsying eylids, and point his sight, and say—'here place your staff—set your foot here, & now—sit. There is a prospect before you of a glorious valley, purple in a generous sunset.' God be with [you] & yours in mercy.

Your old friend
W. Gilmore Simms

---

95. Maj. David Ramsay (1830–1863) died on Aug. 4 of wounds he suffered on Morris Island as commander of the Charleston Battalion.

LETTER 19

Addressee: Edward Spann Hammond
Postmark: none [November 1864]

Edward Spann Hammond (1834–1921), the son of James Henry Hammond (see Letter 5), was a graduate of the University of Pennsylvania who returned to South Carolina to enter politics, practice law, and become a planter. Serving in the South Carolina House of Representatives during 1858–59, he was a major on the staff of Gen. Milledge Luke Bonham in 1861 and editor of the Richmond *Whig* during 1863–64.

The death of James Henry Hammond on November 13, 1864, prompted this remarkable letter, in which Simms poured out his feelings for his most intimate friend and gave his most memorable characterization of him. In closing, Simms presaged the downfall of South Carolina, and eventually of the South as a whole, with the eerily prophetic lines about the "requisite audacity" of Sherman and the eventuality of his "overrunning . . . Carolina!"

My dear Spann.   Woodlands, Nov. 20. 1864

Language fails me in any effort to embody my feelings in words. I will not speak of my loss, in comparison with that of your mother—you—all of you. Yet your father was my most confidential friend for near twenty five years. Never were thoughts more intimate than his & mine. We had few or no secrets from each other—we took few steps in life without mutual consultation. We had,—I am sure I had—perfect confidence in him. I believe he had in me. I felt that there was something kindred in our intellectual nature. Certainly, there was much, very much, in common between us. Never did man more thoroughly appreciate his genius—its grasp—its subtlety—its superiority of aim. And most deeply did I sympathize with him, under that denial of his aim, and the exercise of his powers,—which, permitted, I verily believe he would have lived to a mature old age—lived for far higher triumphs even than those which he achieved. But the will of God be done. His faith & mine, recognized the future as compensative—regarded immortal life, as enabling us to develope fully those immortal endowments to which this mean under world denied opportunity & occasion. So let us all hope, for our own sakes, not less than his.—I would have liked much to have been with him in his last days—not his last hours—for I could not well have borne to witness his loss of consciousness—to behold that intellect wandering, which so often spelled my own—to hear meanin[g]less words from lips that were ever so governed by the magnetic mind. I should have been with him, and purposed to do so—made an engagement with

Gregg,[96] and even wrote of my coming to your father; but a letter from Gregg advised me that he could no longer see his friends. From the first intimation of his case, I feared the worst. This day, I feel doubly alone. I have seen committed to the grave, year after year, children, wife & friends. The fiery circle of Fate is drawing rapidly around me. We shall meet before many days, and, I trust in God, that we shall meet not only for the renewal of old ties, but for the exercise of those faculties, in which I felt proudly that we were kindred. Preserve all his papers. I hope some day to render a proper tribute to his memory. We have no chance for this now. There is no organ. There are no means. Do not suffer his *revised* publications to be mislaid. Have them carefully preserved, compactly put up & sealed against mischance. With God's blessing, I hope to put on record my appreciation of his claims and to illustrate them by his works. And I propose, if possible, some time this winter to visit you, when your minds & my own heart, are more reconciled to this dispensation. I trust that your fears in respect to your mother are ill founded. She is too strong a woman, too pure & pious a Christian, to forget that she has now double duties to perform—Children & Grandchildren to watch & to rear, to admonish, counsel & console. Besides, she has no reproach upon her conscience. Never have I known a woman more tenderly & thoroughly devoted to her husband. She has consecrated her whole life to his—to his need, his want, his very existence, with all a woman's tenderness & a wife's love. Let her turn to the All Consoler, & she will be strengthened. Her own soul at peace, from the conviction of cares nobly borne, and duties piously done, it only needs that she should cast herself upon God, to be rendered strong for the duties which lie before her. I fear nothing for her. If ever woman was nobly strengthened during life for her mission, and duly sensible of it, & rigidly observant of all its requisitions, your mother is that woman. And shall she falter now. I hope not, and believe not.—But I write with painful effort. I have been too much staggered by recent events fully to command the resources of my mind. I cannot *will* myself to thought. I can only fold hands, & wonder, and perhaps pray. What awaits us in the future, is perhaps foreshown to us by our Past, of trial and loss and suffering. Or it may be that God designs that we should surrender in sacrifice our choicest possessions, that we may become worthy of the great boon of future Independence. Yet while I write, and hope, and pray, the day grows more

---

96. William Gregg (1800–1867), close friend of Hammond, was at one time president of the South Carolina Institute for the Promotion of Art, Mechanical Ingenuity, and Industry. Gregg was the leading Southern cotton manufacturer of his day, the founding president of the Graniteville Manufacturing Company in Edgefield District, which began operation in 1848.

clouded. I trembled & had sore misgivings when Johnson[97] was removed from the army, & Hood[98] put in his place. I predicted evil then to your father & to others. He concurred with me. And when Hood removed from Sherman's front, I then declared my opinion that if Sherman had the requisite audacity—it did not need Genius,—he would achieve the greatest of his successes, by turning his back on the enemy in his rear, & march boldly forward towards the Atlantic coast. I fear that such is his purpose. If so,— what have we to oppose him? I dare not look upon the prospect before us. It may become necessary for you, for me, & all to prepare as we can, for the overrunning of Carolina! All's very dark;—doubtful, perhaps; but the probabilities are as I relate. Commend me with affectionate sympathy to your mother, and God be with your household in mercy.

Your father's friend & your own.

W. Gilmore Simms.

LETTER 20

Addressee: Benjamin Franklin Perry
Postmark: none [March 1865]

See Letter 3 for Perry.

As Simms had fearfully prophesized, Sherman did penetrate into the interior of South Carolina, entering Columbia (where Simms had sought refuge with seven of his children) on February 17, 1865, on which night the city burst into flames and was almost completely destroyed (see Simms's eyewitness account in the *Sack and Destruction of . . . Columbia,* below). In Columbia the Simmses were housed in the "obscure dwelling" of the George E. Isaacses, "humble but excellent people," in the words of the novelist, "who are connected by marriage with my eldest daughter."[99]

Hon. Judge Perry
My dear Perry.   Columbia 6th. March '65.

Mr. Isaacs, who will hand you this, will tell you fully of the fate of Columbia, & of its present condition. I am here, perforce, in a sort of durance,

---

97. Gen. Joseph Eggleston Johnston (1807–1891), commander of the Confederate Army of the Tennessee, was relieved of his command on July 17, 1864, after falling back before Sherman's assault.

98. Gen. John Bell Hood (1831–79), who replaced Johnston, attacked Sherman in two pitched battles on July 20 and 22, 1864, but suffered heavy losses and retreated into Atlanta's entrenchments. On Sept. 1 he was forced to evacuate Atlanta, and on the following day Sherman occupied the city.

99. WGS to Harry Hammond, Jan. 24, 1865, ibid., 4:483–84.

with my little family, & cannot, for the present, get away; & know not the fate or state of my plantation.[100] Several reports lead me to apprehend that my house & every thing has been destroyed. Can any small cottage, however humble, be bought in your precinct, with our present currency? Of this, & in bonds, I can command some $15,000. How much land can this procure? I am at a place of refuge, and care not much for the rudeness of the dwelling, if there be a moderate, but sufficient, quantity of land along with it—say a few acres. Will you interest yourself for me in these questions, & report through Mr. Isaacs, who will advise you, no doubt, of the period of his return to Columbia. I will also thank you to procure for me a small supply of *candles,* for which I will pay you at a future day. We are here, and my money is mostly in the Union Bank, which has gone Heaven knows where—probably to Charlotte. We have only an occasional voice from the outer world, and there is not a shop left in Columbia. Fortunately, I had made provision in *meat & bread* for my family, and though some of it was burned, I have still enough to last us awhile longer. But of small comforts, such as candles—almost indispensable to me, with my habits—matches, medicines, weapons, firewood &c.—we are almost utterly stript. The incendiary & Robber have done their work most effectually with the wretched people of this town. No less than 8000 persons are depending for their daily food, upon a short ration of meal & lean beef, distributed by the Authorities. Half of the population, male & female, have been robbed of all the clothes they had, save those they wore, and of these many have had overcoat, hat & shoes taken from them. Watches & purses were appropriated at every corner; and the amount of treasure & wealth, in cloth, gold, silver & other booty borne away by the Huns & Vandals of the Century, is incomputable. Seven-eights of the best portions of Columbia have been destroyed. In fact, what remains unburnt are, almost exclusively, the suburban precincts. All is wreck, confusion & despair. With best regards to your family, & the renewal of old pledges, believe me

Ever truly Your friend
W. Gilmore Simms

P. S. A little good smoking tobacco would be very acceptable. Here we can only get a villainous substitute of stem & weed, for that glorious plant which Spenser calls "divine." Mr. Isaacs will probably be soon coming down in person, and will be pleased to bring any thing you may send me. I am lodging in his House, where my *little* flock of *seven* enjoys two rooms. The humbleness & obscurity of our abode, constituted its security. It held forth too little

---

100. Unknown to WGS at the time, Woodlands had been burned by stragglers from Sherman's army, on or about Feb. 20, 1865.

promise to the plunderers, and so escaped the fire. Few of the finer dwellings of the city have escaped, & but one small house remains on the whole length of Main St. from Cotton town, inclusive, to a point considerably beyond the capital!

W. G. S.

LETTER 21

Addressee: Evert Augustus Duyckinck
Postmark: none [November 1869]

See Letter 4 for Duyckinck.

This letter demonstrates the plight of Simms in late 1869, when he has been reduced by poverty to the selling of treasured items from his Revolutionary War archives, such as the manuscript letter from General Francis Marion being bartered for him in New York by his good friend Duyckinck; and when he has been reduced by disease to such physical agony that he can "sit to write" for only "a brief period at a time." But the strength of Simms's will—"the strength to endure" he admired so much in Voltmeier, title-character in his just published novel—comes through vividly even in his painful incapacity. There can be no doubt that Simms knew he was dying, but he retained his wry sense of humor until the end.

Nov. 25. 1869.
My dear Duyckinck. 				Charleston S. C.

I have no reason to doubt the genuineness of the Marion letter, save the single one of its great superiority over all others that I have seen. The general type is that of Marion, but there was more uniformity in this, and the letters seemed more pronounced & sharply cut. There is no evidence, one way or the other, beyond the face of the letter itself, & during the 30 years, more or less, that it has been in my possession, I never once doubted that it was genuine throughout, untill the moment when I was about to send it off for sale as *genuine*. I then, for the first time felt a scruple in saying so; and being no less scrupulous on the subject, now as then, I commit the sale wholly to your discretion. Get for it what you can, as much as you can of course, (without taking too much trouble upon yourself in seeking a market for it[)]. I shall be quite satisfied with any result which, in your discretion, you may arrive at. Were it *certain* that the whole letter was from his pen, it would be extremely valuable among collectors; and could I be sure, I would not be at a loss to decide what it should bring; but as I am not sure, I prefer to leave it with you & the few *gentlemanly experts* who deal in these rarities. It is probable that these parties will be much more able than myself to speak for its genuineness. I do not know that Marion ever had a secretary, though one of his aids may have written it. As a Colonel, only, & acting only in a detached command, he would have no aid (special as such) and the letter is evidently from the hand of one, who, like Marion, had enjoyed very few advantages of the schools. What you do in the business please do as quickly as you can. I am living in the city for the present, simply that my Physician may note the successive phases of my malady, under the action of his medicine, and shall leave for Woodlands just as soon as he can pronounce definitely on my condition. My expenses here are necessarily far greater than they would be on the plantation, & as I have been earning no money for some time past, recieving little & able to do no profitable work, my resources are pretty well dried up. I earned a moderate quid, a few days ago, writing an address for the opening of a new theatre in this city, and I command a few creature comforts from the newspapers for an occasional editorial, &—that is all. I am glad to tell you that I am physically better; that some of my most suspicious & painful symptoms have undergone mitigation, and that I am in hopes of restoration to strength & comparative health, in a very few weeks, unless surprised by some unexpected & unfavorable change, which I have no reason & no desire to anticipate. My brain is in excellent order, & as free to respond to any drafts made upon it as ever. But I cannot sit to write for more than a brief period at a time. My whole abdominal region suffers, & there is a continued soreness at all times in the lower part of the bowels, such as is natural in dysenteric affections, and mine are partly of this nature, complicated possibly with a diseased condition of the kidneys.—The Pirate's Book [101] was duly recieved & in good order, thanks to you & Kernot. [102] And many thanks for your kindly sympathies & generous expressions. Were you here with me, and I talking with you, while stretched at length upon my sofa, you certainly would be slow to conjecture that I was suffering pain the while. There is a wild Arabian tale of a living head that delivered oracles while joined to a dead or petrified body. I sometimes think of that story, while I am talking here to some one or other of my circles,—talking oracularly too, as some of them think,—with no failure of voice or memory; but reminded of my mortality when I forget my pain & seek to rise & illustrate my thought

---

101. Capt. Charles Johnson (pseud.?), *A General History of the Pyrates,* 2 vols. (London, 1724—25), was purchased for WGS by EAD in New York.

102. Henry Kernot (1806—1874) was a New York bookseller friend of EAD. In the Charleston *Mercury* of Feb. 1, 1854, WGS describes Kernot as "my old bookseller friend . . . who looks upon an author with a degree of sympathy with might almost suffice to convert him also into a creator of the books which he catalogues and vends."

by action. It is then that the body pulls me down from my perch. Terrible, that a man's brains should be at the mercy of his bowels.

Ever faithfully Yours
W. Gilmore Simms

LETTER 22

Addressee: Paul Hamilton Hayne
Postmark: none [December 1869]

See Letter 18 for Hayne.

Another letter revealing Simms's determination to work assiduously despite pain and poverty, this one is also highly personal and highly literary, demonstrating that Simms has retained the quality to live the "full life"—the pleasures of the senses and the stimulation of the imagination. The two books that Simms has just completed under arduous circumstances are *Voltmeier* and *The Cub of the Panther,* both published serially in 1869. Earlier Simms had written Hayne: "I am writing from morning to night. If I get my daily bread from my daily work, I am content."[103] Simms has in no sense relinquished his role as man of letters.

My dear Paul.   Woodlands, Midway P. O.   S. C. Decr. 22. [1869]

Your letter of the 19th. reached me last night, & it gave me great pleasure to find that you could write with such buoyant spirits. It is so long since I have heard from you that I feared you had forgotten me in the variety of your cares or pleasures. I have been duly advised that your mind was always busy, & have seen from time to time some of your sweet & fanciful poems in the papers. For my part, and for the last six months, I have been literally *hors de combat,* from overwork of the brain—brain sweat—as Ben Jonson called it,—and no body sweat—no physical exercise. In the extremity of my need, I took contracts in N. Y. in the autumn of 1868 for no less than three romances, all to be worked, at the same time. I got advances of money on each of these books, and the sense of obligation pressing upon me, I went rigidly to work, concentrating myself at the desk from 20th. Oct. 1868 to the 1st. July 1869.—nearly 9 months, without walking a mile in a week, riding but twice and absent from work but half a day on each of these occasions. The consequence was that I finished two of the books & broke down on the third, having written during that period some 3000 pages of the measure of these which I now write to you. Dyspepsia, in its most aggravated

---

103. WGS to PHH, March 15, 1867, *Letters* 5:26.

forms,—Indigestion, Constipation, Nausea, frequent vomitings, occasional vertigo, and, as the safety valve to this, hemorrhoids. From July, when I went North, to the present moment, I have been suffering more or less acutely, and at no time without constant abdominal uneasiness. And so it continues even now, though the symptoms are mitigated. I have been forbidden the studio, & do little beyond my correspondence which, at all times has been very exacting. I am here, for the Holidays, & shall return to the city for a space, where I reside with my daughter, Mrs. Roach at 13 Society Street.—I have sent two articles to the Cosmopolitan,[104] & am glad that you are to be associated with that work. Take moderate pay, but be sure that you get some pay. Do not work without a quid of some nature. It is sometimes that *a Publisher can send you supplies when he can not send you money.* Get these, whether money or supplies weekly, or as promptly as possible. Beyond these, and an occasional paper to the Eclectic, the 19th. Century,[105] &c. I have done & am doing nothing. I am revising for the Eclectic my Sketches in Greece, which you will remember as being very vilely printed, in the Richmond Weekly, and shall furnish them with certain others, not yet published. But, as yet, they pay me *nothing.* I am willing to help them in order that *the South shall have an organ.* Of the six magazines in the South, all will perish, in all probability, after a struggle of one or two years. They will need to unite on some central situation, Baltimore or Charleston, & one

---

104. *Cosmopolitan Monthly* (Atlanta) succeeded *Scott's Monthly Magazine* (Dec. 1866–Dec. 1869) but apparently died after a single Jan. 1870 issue (unlocated). *Scott's Monthly Magazine* 8 (Dec. 1869): 970 had announced that the first issue of the *Cosmopolitan Monthly* (of which PHH was literary editor) would contain "the opening chapters of a new serial" by WGS entitled "Major Martinet; or, The Lost Half Hour. The Record of a City Bachelor."

105. *New Eclectic Magazine* (Baltimore) published the following contributions by WGS: "The Passage of the Red Sea," 5 (Oct. 1869): 399–403; and three of his "Sketches in Hellas": "The Peace in Elis," "Scene at Actium," and "The Lions of Mycenae," 6 (Jan., Feb., and May 1870): 8–12, 173–76, 532–34. The *XIX Century* (Charleston), a monthly edited by Felix Gregory de Fontaine and William Watkins Hicks, published the following contributions by WGS: "Bells," 1 (June 1869): 42–45; "Intellectual Growth in the Southern States," 1 (July 1869): 133–39; "Our Early Authors," 1 (Aug. 1869): 169–77 and 1 (Sept. 1869): 27–83; "Among the Ruins," 1 (Sept. 1869): 263–64; "Intellectual Progress in the South," 1 (Oct. 1869): 335–42; "My Tricksy Spirit," 2 (Dec. 1869): 541–43; "Early Literary Progress in South Carolina," 2 (Jan. 1870): 631–67; "Early Writers of South Carolina," 2 (Feb. 1870): 695–700; "Fancy in Siesta," 2 (April 1870): 832–36; and "Reminiscences of South Carolina: Literary Progress," 2 (May 1870): 920–24. The "Richmond Weekly" referred to was *Seminary Magazine.*

good one, is worth a dozen poor ones. John Bruns [106] has lately written me. As you say, his letters are apt to be lugubrious. But who in the South can write cheerfully in these ill aspects of society. He is all you say of him, a brilliant fellow, with one difficulty—that he is too impatient to wait for his time of battle. My son Gilmore, & my son in law, Major Rowe, [107] work the plantation, or so much of the land as we can find capital & labour for. You are aware that I was burned out by Sherman, and had to rebuild, restore, replenish & provide. You may ascribe all my physical sufferings to this necessity, for this could not be done without money, and my only capital was in my poor brain. And my brain has played the devil with my bowels, and that these have not yet played the devil with my brains, is due to a resolute will & to a good physique. How long these will endure, under the continued troubles of the bowels, is the question. I have been ill & very ill, and the problem is yet unsolved whether I shall recover, or go through a protracted condition of suffering down to very imbecility. I am doing nothing, and for 6 months have been earning little. My boys are likely to do better the coming year, which God grant, but I, too, have need to be doing something. I have built up a *wing* of my house, have helped them to stock &c. furniture, food &c. and have devolved every thing upon them. If they shall develope the proper manhood, every thing will go well, in spite of the boars, vultures & monkeys.—I enjoy your picture of your fine fires at Copse Hill, [108] and your violets & mosses,—but the violets were omitted from the letter—and [I] feel an unctuous & pervading consciousness of a peculiar & grateful odor from the [*one word illegible*] cordial of which you speak—coming from a mysterious source. May the draughts from this mysterious source never fail you. I am compelled to rely upon whiskey & lager, occasional supplies of which come from certain friends for whom I do little labours, *en passant*. I write an occasional article for the Courier, for which I recieve occasional whiskey, segars & tobacco. An occasional Sermon, Lecture or Oration, for some friend, caught by an appointment which terrifies him, and he sends me some trifling creature comforts, fruits, liquor & segars. Recently, I wrote the address for the opening of the Charleston Theatre, for which I recieved $30. To this may be added $25 more from an unknown source, as a supplementary & complimentary compensation for the address. All my labours, if

---

106. John Dickson Bruns (1836–1883), Charleston poet, in 1869 was practicing medicine in New Orleans.

107. Donald Jacob Rowe, the son of a relative of WGS, Captain Henry Rowe of Orangeburg, had married Chevillette Simms on Christmas Day in 1865.

108. PHH's home near Augusta, Georgia.

charged for by a Lawyer, would give me a splendid income. But I have good
& devoted friends, who show me much solicitude & I drive no bargains.——
You say that your son is at school in Charleston. My son, Govan, who is at
Gadsden & Porter's School, came home for the Holidays two days ago, &
tells me of a smart boy, named Hayne, at the same school, who promises to
be a Poet. I assume, now, that he is your son. You will tell me. My boy promises nothing as yet. He rides like a trooper, swims like a duck, can shoot,
drive wagon, oxen, mules & stallions, without fear or scruples, and will
fight, if need be, like a Gaul. It is my hope that the school will develope his
moral manhood. I have six children left me, of 15, and I have 3 grandchildren of 6. I wish to live long enough to see them fairly embarked on the voyage of life, with a proper knowledge of the helm. After that, what matters.
Beyond these, life has few objects for me,——but these suffice to make me desire that I may be permitted to die in harness, spurs at my heels, lance in rest,
and in the heat of a desperate charge. This sinking into the lean & slippered
pantaloon, dealing in old saws and drowsy proverbs does not suit my taste.
I am for action to the last for all life is so much warfare against Sin, the Devil,
and Tom Walker. With best regards to your wife & mother, hold me ever
faithfully Yours

W. Gilmore Simms.

LETTER 23

Addressee: William Cullen Bryant
Postmark: none [April 1870]

Among the first Americans to perceive the poetic merits of William Cullen
Bryant (1794–1878), Simms named Bryant the "First American Poet" in one of
his juvenile journals. By 1832, well established as a major literary figure, Bryant
was eagerly sought out by Simms on his first trip to the Northeast. Their meeting at that time marked the beginning of a personal as well as literary relationship. Thereafter Simms and his family frequently visited the Bryants in Great
Barrington, Massachusetts; and the Bryants reciprocated with visits to Woodlands in 1843 and 1849. Bryant immortalized his first stay at Woodlands with a
highly favorable portraiture of Simms and Southern plantation life in *Homes of
American Authors.* Indicative of the relationship between the two families, Augusta Simms and Fanny Bryant became such close friends that Augusta lived for
a while with the Bryants so that she and Fanny might attend school together in
Great Barrington. Though Simms and Bryant became somewhat estranged during Civil War hostilities, their friendship was renewed and strengthened before
Simms's death.

This letter, the last Simms was to write to Bryant, and one of the few he was known to write before he died two months later, shows the author still proud, still suffering but unbowed, still appreciative of good friends and good literature, and still with a sense of humor.

Wm. Cullen Bryant, Esq.
My dear Bryant.   Charleston, Aprl. 9. [1870]

I cannot well tell you how delighted I was at the reciept of your kind and genial letter, so happily reviving ancient memories, now of nearly forty years ago. I should have said *youthful* memories; for neither of us then anticipated the picture in our mirrors of those gray bearded men, as you & I now are, and as we present ourselves before that pleasant public, which, in your case, has not forgotten Jacob. Nothing has afforded me greater satisfaction than the vigour you are displaying in your old age; the wonderful industry, the surprising will, and the more than surprising command which you have of memory, & the intellectual powers, which were the pride of your middle manhood. You, in your province, & I in mine, have nearly survived all the contemporaries of youth. I see that Verplanck, who was one of the few men left on your plane, has suddenly passed from it; and since the departure of Halleck, Irving, Cooper, &c.[109] I really—looking about for *you*—know not where to turn to find you a contemporary. Here, in the last few years, I have lost a score of my best friends, & the ablest men in all the South. I feel myself very much alone. My people honour me, and the young men gather around me with proofs of love and reverence, and in my advancing years, suffering as I have done with a malady, which I fear is chronic, which keeps me perpetually uneasy, & frequently in pain, it is one of my great consolations that our young men come & minister to me, with the reverence, which they can no longer yield to better abler men. My children, besides, are all dutiful & devoted. I have six left me of 15; and I have several grandchildren. My eldest son carries on the plantation at Woodlands, on a small scale, in accordance with his very limited resources. I alternate between the plantation & the city, staying, when in town, with my daughter, Mrs. Roach, whom you will remember as Augusta. I suppose Julia will hardly remember me; but you may tell her that an old man's blessing can do her no harm. I presume that she is your constant companion.—Thanks for the 1st. Homer. I have been reading in it without pause, ever since recieved, & last night regretfully closed the 12th. Book.[110] I am delighted with it. Its manly simplicity, its

---

109. Gulian C. Verplanck died on March 18, 1870, Fritz Greene Halleck in 1867, Washington Irving in 1859, and James Fenimore Cooper in 1851.
110. WGS had published an editorial about Bryant's translation of the first twelve books of *The Iliad* in the *Charleston Courier* of Feb. 26, 1870.

directness of aim, the absence of all that might be involved & circuitous, and the avoidance of all effort, in any place, to *graft* yourself upon your original. This seems to me to have been among the difficulties in the way of most translators. Above all, I rejoice, though I did not doubt, that you would choose the good, stout, manly English heroic blank as your medium of translation. *That* is the great verse of our language, and for several reasons. But of all this hereafter. I write now under the pleasant impulse which makes me say how grateful I am for your letter.

Yours faithfully as Ever
W. Gilmore Simms.

P. S. My health has been somewhat improving in the last two weeks. My liver seems disposed to do its duty for the first time in 8 months. I sleep well, & my appetite improves. But I have not tasted meat for two months, and my chief diet has been eggs & fruit, in minimum quantities. Had I pursued a physical training such as yours, I should be a giant even now.

LETTER 24

Addressee: William Hawkins Ferris
Postmark: none [May 1870]

William Hawkins Ferris was unique among Simms's circle of New York friends in that he was neither a writer nor a publisher. A highly successful businessman who for years was associated with the New York branch of the U.S. Treasury, Ferris was an admirer of literary personages and a collector of their autographs and letters. Simms frequently visited Ferris during his annual trips to New York, and Simms tried to persuade him to buy the plantation of David Flavel Jamison, Burwood, when it became available after the Civil War, so that they might be neighbors. Ferris was probably the most active of Simms's Northern friends in raising money to help Simms when he was left destitute after the war. In 1867 Simms characterized Ferris as "an excellent gentleman & worthy friend of mine. He is not a litterateur exactly, but a great admirer of men of letters."[111]

On May 3 Simms literally rose from the sickbed to deliver his last oration, "The Sense of the Beautiful"; on May 27 he wrote to Ferris his last letter; on June 11 he died.

dear Ferris. Charleston 27 May. [1870]
    I spent a couple of weeks very gratefully at Woodlands, and felt quite a physical improvement there; came to the city last Saturday, was quite well

---

111. WGS to Charles E. A. Gayarre, April 12, 1867, *Letters* 5 : 43.

that day & Sunday, but Sunday night had one of my atrocious paroxysms & have been suffering ever since. For two successive nights I never slept a wink. I am better today—i.e. easier;—but I am still under the action of medicine & quite feeble. All are well save myself. I write simply to tell you that I still live. God bless you & yours.

W. Gilmore Simms

Fiction

Indian Sketch

(1 8 2 8)

During a short excursion, some few years since in the Western country, I
found, after a long and fatiguing ride over bad roads, on a hot and sultry day
in June, that I was at length approaching something like a human settlement.
The indication of the traces of human perseverance are to be met with in the
wilderness some miles in advance of the habitations of the wanderers themselves. The long cross rail fence, the opening in the trees upon the sky, the
clear whistle of the wind among the few remaining giants of the forest, and
the distant hum of happy voices—together with the more clearly marked
and intelligible lowing of cattle, neighing of horses, cackling of geese, and
now and then the dark apparition of some bristly hog half wild and half tame,
brushing suddenly by you, to your infinite alarm, particularly if night fall be
at hand. Travelling, (as in all new countries, one must, if he wishes to travel
without inconvenience from creeks running over their banks by frequent
freshets, felled trees and often compelled to take a new road) on horseback,
is calculated to render, after a long day's ride, the sight of a farm house one
of those somethings in life, which, while we should blush to give it the character or appellation of a pleasure, is nevertheless an object of no little moment and concern. I found the one to which I was fast approaching a perfect
cure to my fatigue and ill-humour of the day. Whether it was that I had already begun to calculate on the smoking and enticing supper of fried bacon,
eggs, fresh water trout, fresh butter, and round and glowing biscuits made
of new Ohio flour—or that the natural tendency of the frame to repose and
quietude, induced the feeling of gratitude and pleasure that I enjoyed, I leave

to bookmen, apt at enquiries of this nature, to determine. Certain it was that I was more than pleased. I had ridden the whole day through a seemingly interminable forest, that, when I had emerged from the density of one seemed to show forth a denser and darker in which I had to embowel myself—that I had at length arrived safe at my resting place for the night, and all that was left for me to do, was to see my horse fed, rubbed down, and watered (a duty which no traveller ought to neglect) and to provide for the content and appetite of his equally hungering and jaded master. It required no great effort to make the inmates of this well stocked but humble cottage understand the nature of my wants, and provide for them accordingly, practised as they were, by an almost daily recurrence of similar duties. The supper table of neat pine was quickly furnished forth—a white cotton cloth with fringe from its sides a foot deep, was soon spread over it, and the rude but well relished dainties of country life were before me, and I nothing loth, ready for the repast.

I ate my supper in silence. My host was a half breed, who had married an Indian woman of the Nation (Choctaw) and under the sanction of the tribe, had commenced the business of Innkeeper upon their principal road. It is never the character of the Indian to be communicative; and nature has in this simple particular provided him with an education, which makes him more polite than the civilized man. His native independence and secluded and wandering habits, by removing him from the necessity of society, throws him upon himself, and his mind becomes actively employed, while his tongue may be said to slumber. The half-breed has so much of the aborigine still about him, that he partakes of nearly the same ascetic and taciturn disposition. His words are always significant and full of meaning—his looks are taught to have a language of their own for the better filling out and illustrating the brief and pithy accents of his speech. The Indian women are of a degraded *caste* in the opinion of the men. They are considered and used as mere beasts of burthen. Seldom, if ever admitted to the confidence of equality or affection, they are kept at a humble distance from their superiors, who assume to themselves in practice, the full supremacy as Lords of the creation. Nothing can be more amusing to one who is at all intimate with the Indian character, than the various pictures which are given of them by the Poet and the novelist. Nothing more idle and extravagant. The glory of the Indians (as they were) is the hunt and the battle field; and in robbing them of the extent of country sufficient for the one pursuit, and exercising such a powerful restraint upon them, as a ready and well-armed frontier, in the other, we seem to have robbed them of all of that pride, love of adventure and warlike enthusiasm, which is the only romance, the North American Indian ever had in his character.

As I have said, my supper was discussed in silent solemnity. My host sat before me at the head of the table, eating only occasionally. His consort, a large, strapping Indian woman *stood up behind* his chair and waited upon us throughout the meal. The looks of both of them as well as of two young and tolerably well looking savages who sat in the corner of the room, seemed full of gravity and sadness. Although naturally gloomy and sullen, I could easily perceive that something unusual had taken place, and accordingly as soon as our repast was ended, after a preliminary compliment on my part of a twist of Tobacco, which seemed to have stirred up the spirit to an effort, I began my enquiries of the youngest of the group whom I soon ascertained to be the most communicative and intelligent. From him, I gathered the following interesting communication. There had been, it seems, (I use my own language, as his was broken and scarcely intelligible) a number of Indians, young men and women, employed by a neighbouring planter (a white man) to pick a quantity of cotton which he had on hand. For some days they pursued their labor, with a diligence and assiduity, which, accustomed as we are to hear of the indisposition of the Indians to all manner of employment, except that of hunting, was, at least to me, new and interesting.

At length on the last day of the time for which they had been employed, the Planter, after rewarding them for their labor, produced the all inviting jug of whiskey—and placed it before them. This there was no withstanding. Those who had tasted the "Fire water" before, now set the example for those as yet ignorant of its perniciously seductive influence, and they all, with the exception of Mewanto became immediately intoxicated. This young man, who amidst the general example thus placed before him and from a society, than which, he could have no other restraint, could thus stoically resist, it must be supposed was a man of no ordinary strength of mind. He was in fact the pride of his people, and amidst their general depravity they felt the moral superiority of the man, and were "ashamed of their nakedness." Mewanto, had among the many who had thus bartered the higher energies of their original character, for a sensual and momentary indulgence, one intimate, closely allied and dear friend, called Oolatibbe. He strove for a long while to prevent this young man from falling into the dangerous habits of his associates—but in vain. The prevalence of custom proved more effective than the advice and entreaties of friendship, and the youth, unaccustomed to the liquor, became in a short time deeply intoxicated. His friend, with some difficulty led him away from the small grove or thicket where the rest of the party were still carousing, and represented to him in the simple language of truth, the danger and the error of his present licentious and unhappy indulgence. He spoke with much warmth and a good deal of that native eloquence with which this people are said to be so admirably gifted—and I remember, my informant having used (for he adopted the figurative mode of speech so common, not only with them but every savage people) as the language of the young savage on this occasion, the following sentence. Alluding to the prostration of his people on the appearance of the whites, "that they had been as many as the leaves on the trees about them, but the white man had been the whirlwind that shook them down, and the remaining few were falling one by one, blighted and blasted by the cunning of their enemy, otherwise, wholly unable to remove them." The drunken man listened to him with a sort of stupid attention for some time, but at length suddenly starting back as if he had encountered some fearful object, he tore the knife from his belt, and before his friend could avoid the danger plunged it quickly into the bosom of Mewanto, who fell dead upon the spot.

He remained in a sort of stupor for a moment—but suddenly became sobered on the instant to behold with horror the dead body before him. A shriek or howl, which is indicative of some matter of death, and peculiar to the Indians, was the result of his first awakening to sensibility and reason. This, the rest of the Indians perfectly well understood, and it had the effect of bringing them all to their proper senses. A loud, wild and melancholy cry was sent up in general by the party—the murderer preceding them to the great council of the nation. They placed no restraint whatever upon him— and without any compunction he voluntarily delivered himself up to the council and demanded to be led to death. "To-morrow," said my informant in conclusion, "he will be shot." [1] And where is he now, said I, anxious to gather from the youth as much more as possible, for his fit of talkativeness seemed to be nearly exhausted. "By your side," he returned. I started and beheld the same young man, whose countenance had first struck me while at the supper table. The question involuntarily rose and I asked with some astonishment—"and is he not confined—and will he not escape." "He cannot fly, for did he not help to make the law himself." Thus was the powerfully moral rule of all christian denominations, "Do not unto others what you would not others should do unto you," faithfully and honestly obeyed on the most trying occasion in the annals of humanity, as if it had been one of the simplest duties of the domestic hearth.

I was curious to witness the final termination of this, to me, wonderful characteristic of a people, whom we have learned to despise, before we have been taught to understand. I turned round and fixed my gave upon the condemned. What could a spectator, unacquainted with the circumstances, have met with there. Nothing of the precise and awful matter of fact, that connected itself with the fortunes and life of the object of observation. I addressed him—I brought him to the subject so deeply interesting to himself.

He spoke of it, as of those common occurrences which we often speak of unconsciously. He took up the handle of a tomahawk and employed himself in
carving upon it, a space for a bit of flattened silver which he labored to introduce into it. He spoke in detached sentences, during this little effort. In
reply to a question which I put, touching the commission of the crime, and
whether he was conscious that he was doing it or not, he replied—"Yes—
he knew it all—he knew it was the one of himself, the best part—but he
had put on a horrible shape and the evil one darkened his eye sight—that
while he struck the blow, he knew perfectly well that it was his friend he
struck, but that he was made to do it."

We conversed at intervals till a late hour—he seemed to sing at times
or rather muttered a few broken catches of song, monotonous and highly
solemn—at length, the rest having withdrawn, he threw himself upon a
bear skin before the door, and I attended the little boy, who was with
difficulty aroused from a deep sleep, to my chamber, which he pointed out.

It may be supposed, I slept little that night. I was filled with thoughts of
the strange obedience which this ignorant savage manifested to his rude and
barbarous, but really equitable laws. The highest moral obligation however
instructing him, "that he must not expect others to do, what he would not
do himself."

The next morning, a large crowd had assembled within and around the
house in which I slept. I rose and went to the window. The open space in
front of the house was covered with the Indians. A great deal of excitement
seemed to run through them all. I dressed myself as quickly as possible and
went down among them. They were crowded in the house as well as in the
area before it. I looked about for the principal in this extraordinary spectacle—his were the only features unmoved in the assembly. He seemed
busily employed in gathering up sundry little articles as well of ornament as
necessity in the Indian's life. His dress seemed more studied—it consisted of
a pair of pantaloons, seemingly much worn, and probably the cast off dona-
tion of some passing traveller. There was a buckskin hunting shirt on him,
with several falling capes, all thickly covered with fringe, a belt of wampum,
studded with beads of various colours, tolerably well arranged, encircled his
waist—while his legs, which were well formed, were admirably fitted by a
pair of leggings loaded with beads. Several other little ornaments were
thrown about him, particularly over his neck and shoulders.

A difference of sentiment seemed to operate upon, and form a division
among the assembled multitude, an air of anger, impatience and exultation,
fully indicated the friends of the deceased thirsting for the blood of his murderer—while an appearance of sadness and concern, pointed out those who

were more tenderly disposed toward him. At length, the victim himself made the first signal of preparation. He arose, and giving to a little boy who followed him, a bundle which he had been making up of beads, hatchets, arrow heads, knives, tobacco-pouch and some other little things, he led the way. I joined in the mournful procession. Our way lay through a long grove of stunted pines—at the end of which we were met, and accompanied by the three men appointed as his executioners, who were armed with rifles, which they wore under the left arm.

Never did I behold a man with a step so firm on any occasion, or head so unbent—a countenance so unmoved, and yet without any of the effort common to most men who endeavor to assume an aspect of heroism upon an event so trying. He walked as to a victory. The triumphal arch seemed above him, and instead of an ignominious death, a triumph over a thousand hearts seemed depicted before him.

The grave was in sight. I watched his brow attentively. I felt myself shudder and grow pale, but saw no change in him. He began a low song, apparently consisting of monosyllables only. He grew more impassioned— more deeply warm. I could not understand a single word he uttered—but, even though he stood as firm, proud and unbending as a Roman might be supposed to have stood, as if he disdained the addition of action to his words, the cadence, the fall, the melody and wild intonation of this high-souled savage's voice was to me an active eloquence, which I could not misunderstand. He paused at length. Then moving with an even pace, he took his place at the head of the grave prepared for him—beckoned the boy near, who had followed him, with the simple utensils of savage life, and when he had retired, motioned the executioners. I saw them prepare their rifles, and take their aim—I looked upon the features of the victim—they were steady and calm—I turned my head away with a strange sickness. I heard the single report of the three rifles, and when I turned my eye upon the spot so lately occupied by the unfortunate victim of an infatuation, which has slain more than the sword, they were slowly shovelling the earth into the grave of the murderer.

---

1. *WGS* We annex a poem by a native writer upon this subject, which (as we believe it has never been quoted before) may serve as an apt illustration of this article.

> At midnight did the Chiefs convene,
> With many a shriek of wild alarm,
> 'Till solemn silence hushed the scene,
> As in prophetic charm;
> When, wild the cry of horror broke,
> As thus a dark brow'd warrior spoke

"I come to die—no vain delay,
Nor trembling pulse unnerves my soul;
Ye fellow Chiefs, prepare the way—
Let death's dark clouds about me roll;
My bosom feels alone life's dread—
There is no feeling with the dead!

Our tribe has lost its bravest steel—
'Tis well the scabbard follow too,
Since life no longer can reveal
Aught that can glad my view:
From its own home, I madly tore
The jewel, that my bosom wore.

He cross'd me in my hour of wrath,
And still with cruel love pursued—
An evil spirit dimn'd my path,
A film o'er spread my gaze—I view'd
No more, the friend I lov'd so well,
But some insatiate foe from hell!

My hand had grasp'd its kindred knife,
A struggle, and I heard a cry—
It was the shriek of parting life,
For it is hard to die,
A friend or kindred soul to leave—
Now, there are none, for me will grieve!

Too late, too late I knew my friend,
Too late, had wish'd the deed undone!
'Twere vain, my bosom's grief to blend
With tears, that can restore me none,
(Tho' in unending streams they fell)
Of all the friend, I loved so well.

Far, wand'ring on the distant hills,
Yet, watching for the morning's dawn,
His spirit lingers near the rills,
Now anxious to be gone:
And only waits my kindred shade,
To bear it to the grave I made.

His hatchet seen in gleaming light,
When first the war hoop's cry is heard,
I've placed to meet his walking sight,
When carols first the morning bird!
Nor did my bosom's care forget,
His rifle, knife and calumet!

Prepare the grave, I long to fly,
To that far distant realm of bliss,
Where nought can dim the spirit's eye,

Or, lead the heart like this;
Where, morning owns no clouded shade,
And life is light, and undecay'd.

Oh, brother, whom I madly slew,
Then shall our kindred spirits join;
At morn the red-deer's path pursue—
At eve the tented camp entwine;
Close at one time the mutual eye,
And on one blanket's bosom, lie."

No longer spoke the Warrior Chief,
But sullen sternness clothed his brow,
Whilst fate and anguish, fix'd and brief,
Proclaim'd him—ready now!
No counsel spoke—no pray'r was made—
No pomp—no mock'ry—no parade.

He walk'd erect, unaw'd, unbound;
He stood upon the grave's dread brink,
And look'd with careless eye around;
Nor did his spirit shrink,
The deadly riflers aim to greet,
His bosom long'd its death to meet.

A moment's pause—no sound was heard;
He gazed—then with unchanging look,
He spoke in pride, the signal word,
With which the valley shook—
And when the smoke had cleared away,
The dark-eyed Chief before me lay.

Grayling, or, "Murder Will Out"

(1845)

CHAPTER 1.

The world has become monstrous matter-of-fact in latter days. We can no longer get a ghost story, either for love or money. The materialists have it all their own way; and even the little urchin, eight years old, instead of deferring with decent reverence to the opinions of his grandmamma, now stands up stoutly for his own. He believes in every "ology" but pneumatology. "Faust" and the "Old Woman of Berkeley" move his derision only, and he would laugh incredulously, if he dared, at the Witch of Endor. The whole armoury of modern reasoning is on his side; and, however he may admit at seasons that belief can scarcely be counted matter of will he puts his veto on all sorts of credulity. That cold-blooded demon called Science has taken the place of all the other demons. He has certainly cast out innumerable devils, however he may still spare the principal. Whether we are the better for his intervention is another question. There is reason to apprehend that in disturbing our human faith in shadows, we have lost some of those wholesome moral restraints which might have kept many of us virtuous, where the laws could not.

The effect, however, is much the more seriously evil in all that concerns the romantic. Our story-tellers are so resolute to deal in the real, the actual only, that they venture on no subjects the details of which are not equally vulgar and susceptible of proof. With this end in view, indeed, they too commonly choose their subjects among convicted felons, in order that they may avail themselves of the evidence which led to their conviction; and, to prove more conclusively their devoted adherence to nature and the truth, they depict the former not only in her condition of nakedness, but long before she has found out the springs of running water. It is to be feared that some of the coarseness of modern taste arises from the too great lack of that veneration which belonged to, and elevated to dignity, even the errors of preceding ages. A love of the marvellous belongs, it appears to me, to all those who love and cultivate either of the fine arts. I very much doubt whether the poet, the painter, the sculptor, or the romancer, ever yet lived, who had not some strong bias—a leaning, at least,—to a belief in the wonders of the invisible world. Certainly, the higher orders of poets and painters, those who create and invent, must have a strong taint of the superstitious in their composition. But this is digressive, and leads us from our purpose.

It is so long since we have been suffered to see or hear of a ghost, that a visitation at this time may have the effect of novelty, and I propose to narrate a story which I heard more than once in my boyhood, from the lips of an aged relative, who succeeded, at the time, in making me believe every word of it; perhaps, for the simple reason that she convinced me she believed every word of it herself. My grandmother was an old lady who had been a resident of the seat of most frequent war in Carolina during the Revolution. She had fortunately survived the numberless atrocities which she was yet compelled to witness; and, a keen observer, with a strong memory, she had in store a thousand legends of that stirring period, which served to beguile me from sleep many and many a long winter night. The story which I propose to tell was one of these; and when I say that she not only devoutly believed it herself, but that it was believed by sundry of her contemporaries, who were themselves privy to such of the circumstances as could be known to third parties, the gravity with which I repeat the legend will not be considered very astonishing.

The revolutionary war had but a little while been concluded. The British had left the country; but peace did not imply repose. The community was still in that state of ferment which was natural enough to passions, not yet at rest, which had been brought into exercise and action during the protracted seven years' struggle through which the nation had just passed. The state was overrun by idlers, adventurers, profligates, and criminals. Disbanded soldiers, half-starved and reckless, occupied the highways,—outlaws, emerging from their hiding-places, skulked about the settlements with an equal sentiment of hate and fear in their hearts;—patriots were clamouring for justice upon the tories, and sometimes anticipating its course by judgments of their own; while the tories, those against whom the proofs were too strong for denial or evasion, buckled on their armour for a renewal of the struggle. Such being the condition of the country, it may easily be supposed that life and property lacked many of their necessary securities. Men generally travelled with weapons which were displayed on the smallest provocation: and few who could provide themselves with an escort ventured to travel any distance without one.

There was, about this time, said my grandmother, and while such was the condition of the country, a family of the name of Grayling, that lived somewhere upon the skirts of "Ninety-six" district. Old Grayling, the head of the family, was dead. He was killed in Buford's massacre. His wife was a fine woman, not so very old, who had an only son named James, and a little girl, only five years of age, named Lucy. James was but fourteen when his father was killed, and that event made a man of him. He went out with his rifle in company with Joel Sparkman, who was his mother's brother, and joined himself to Pickens's Brigade. Here he made as good a soldier as the best. He had no sort of fear. He was always the first to go forward; and his rifle was always good for his enemy's button at a long hundred yards. He was in several fights both with the British and tories; and just before the war was ended he had a famous brush with the Cherokees, when Pickens took their country from them. But though he had no fear, and never knew when to stop killing while the fight was going on, he was the most bashful of boys that I ever knew; and so kind-hearted that it was almost impossible to believe all we heard of his fierce doings when he was in battle. But they were nevertheless quite true for all his bashfulness.

Well, when the war was over, Joel Sparkman, who lived with his sister, Grayling, persuaded her that it would be better to move down into the low country. I don't know what reason he had for it, or what they proposed to do there. They had very little property, but Sparkman was a knowing man, who could turn his hand to a hundred things; and as he was a bachelor, and loved his sister and her children just as if they had been his own, it was natural that she should go with him wherever he wished. James, too, who was restless by nature—and the taste he had enjoyed of the wars had made him more so—he was full of it; and so, one sunny morning in April, their wagon started for the city. The wagon was only a small one, with two horses, scarcely larger than those that are employed to carry chickens and fruit to the market from the Wassamaws and thereabouts. It was driven by a negro fellow named Clytus, and carried Mrs. Grayling and Lucy. James and his uncle loved the saddle too well to shut themselves up in such a vehicle; and both of them were mounted on fine horses which they had won from the enemy. The saddle that James rode on,—and he was very proud of it,—was one that he had taken at the battle of Cowpens from one of Tarleton's own dragoons, after he had tumbled the owner. The roads at that season were excessively bad, for the rains of March had been frequent and heavy, the track was very much cut up, and the red clay gullies of the hills of "Ninety-six" were so washed that it required all shoulders, twenty times a day, to get the wagon-wheels out of the bog. This made them travel very slowly;—perhaps, not more than fifteen miles a day. Another cause for slow travelling was the necessity of great caution, and a constant look-out for enemies both up and down the road. James and his uncle took it by turns to ride a-head, precisely as they did when scouting in war, but one of them always kept along with the wagon. They had gone on this way for two days, and saw nothing to trouble and alarm them. There were few persons on the high-road, and these seemed to the full as shy of them as they probably were of strangers. But just as they were about to camp, the evening of the second day, while they were splitting light-wood, and getting out the kettles and the frying-pan, a person rode up and joined them without much ceremony. He was a short thick-set man, somewhere between forty and fifty: had on very coarse and common garments, though he rode a fine black horse of remarkable strength and vigour. He was very civil of speech, though he had but little to say, and that little showed him to be a person without much education and with no refinement. He begged permission to make one of the encampment, and his manner was very respectful and even humble; but there was something dark and sullen in his face—his eyes, which were of a light gray colour, were very restless, and his nose turned up sharply, and was very red. His forehead was excessively broad, and his eyebrows thick and shaggy—white hairs being freely mingled with the dark, both in them and upon his head. Mrs. Grayling did not like this man's looks, and whispered her dislike to her son; but James, who felt himself equal to any man, said, promptly—

"What of that, mother! we can't turn the stranger off and say 'no;' and if he means any mischief, there's two of us, you know."

The man had no weapons—none, at least, which were then visible; and deported himself in so humble a manner, that the prejudice which the party had formed against him when he first appeared, if it was not dissipated while he remained, at least failed to gain any increase. He was very quiet, did not mention an unnecessary word, and seldom permitted his eyes to rest upon those of any of the party, the females not excepted. This, perhaps, was the only circumstance, that, in the mind of Mrs. Grayling, tended to confirm the hostile impression which his coming had originally occasioned. In a little while the temporary encampment was put in a state equally social and war-like. The wagon was wheeled a little way into the woods, and off the road; the horses fastened behind it in such a manner that any attempt to steal them would be difficult of success, even were the watch neglectful which was yet to be maintained upon them. Extra guns, concealed in the straw at the bottom of the wagon, were kept well loaded. In the foreground, and between the wagon and the highway, a fire was soon blazing with a wild but cheerful gleam; and the worthy dame, Mrs. Grayling, assisted by the little girl, Lucy, lost no time in setting on the frying pan, and cutting into slices the haunch of bacon, which they had provided at leaving home. James Grayling patrolled the woods, meanwhile for a mile or two round the encampment, while his uncle, Joel Sparkman, foot to foot with the stranger, seemed—if the absence of all care constitutes the supreme of human felicity—to realize the most perfect conception of mortal happiness. But Joel was very far from being the careless person that he seemed. Like an old soldier, he simply hung out false colours, and concealed his real timidity by an extra show of confidence and courage. He did not relish the stranger from the first, any more than his sister; and having subjected him to a searching examination, such as was considered, in those days of peril and suspicion, by no means inconsistent with becoming courtesy, he came rapidly to the conclusion that he was no better than he should be.

"You are a Scotchman, stranger," said Joel, suddenly drawing up his feet, and bending forward to the other with an eye like that of a hawk stooping over a covey of partridges. It was a wonder that he had not made the discovery before. The broad dialect of the stranger was not to be subdued; but Joel made slow stages and short progress in his mental journeyings. The answer was given with evident hesitation, but it was affirmative.

"Well, now, it's mighty strange that you should ha' fou't with us and not agin us," responded Joel Sparkman. "There was a precious few of the Scotch, and none that I knows on, saving yourself, perhaps,—that didn't go dead a gin us, and for the tories, through thick and thin. That 'Cross Creek settlement' was a mighty ugly thorn in the sides of us whigs. It turned out a raal bad stock of varmints. I hope,—I reckon, stranger,—you aint from that part."

"No," said the other; "oh no! I'm from over the other quarter. I'm from the Duncan settlement above."

"I've hearn tell of that other settlement, but I never know'd as any of the men fou't with us. What gineral did you fight under? What Carolina gineral?"

"I was at Gum Swamp when General Gates was defeated;" was the still hesitating reply of the other.

"Well, I thank God, *I* warn't there, though I reckon things wouldn't ha' turned out quite so bad, if there had been a leetle sprinkling of Sumter's, or Pickens's, or Marion's men, among them two-legged critters that run that day. They did tell that some of the regiments went off without ever once emptying their rifles. Now, stranger, I hope you warn't among them fellows."

"I was not," said the other with something more of promptness.

"I don't blame a chap for dodging a bullet if he can, or being too quick for a bag net, because, I'm thinking, a live man is always a better man than a dead one, or he can become so; but to run without taking a single crack at the inimy, is downright cowardice. There's no two ways about it, stranger."

This opinion, delivered with considerable emphasis, met with the ready assent of the Scotchman, but Joel Sparkman was not to be diverted, even by his own eloquence, from the object of his inquiry.

"But you ain't said," he continued, "who was your Carolina gineral. Gates was from Virginny, and he stayed a mighty short time when he come. You didn't run far at Camden, I reckon, and you joined the army ag'in, and come in with Greene? Was that the how?"

To this the stranger assented, though with evident disinclination.

"Then, mou'tbe, we sometimes went into the same scratch together? I was at Cowpens and Ninety Six, and seen sarvice at other odds and eends, where there was more fighting than fun. I reckon you must have been at 'Ninety-Six,'—perhaps at Cowpens, too, if you went with Morgan?"

The unwillingness of the stranger to respond to these questions appeared to increase. He admitted, however, that he had been at "Ninety-six," though, as Sparkman afterwards remembered, in this case, as in that of the defeat of Gates at Gum Swamp, he had not said on which side he had fought. Joel, as he discovered the reluctance of his guest to answer his questions, and perceived his growing doggedness, forbore to annoy him, but mentally resolved to keep a sharper look-out than ever upon his motions. His examination concluded with an inquiry, which, in the plain-dealing regions of the south and south-west, is not unfrequently put first.

"And what mou't be your name, stranger?"

"Macnab," was the ready response, "Sandy Macnab."

"Well, Mr. Macnab I see that my sister's got supper ready for us; so we mou't as well fall to upon the hoecake and bacon."

Sparkman rose while speaking, and led the way to the spot, near the wagon, where Mrs. Grayling had spread the feast. "We're pretty nigh on to the main road, here, but I reckon there's no great danger now. Besides, Jim Grayling keeps watch for us, and he's got two as good eyes in his head as any scout in the country, and a rifle that, after you once know how it shoots, 'twould do your heart good to hear its crack, if so be that twa'n't your heart that he drawed sight on. He's a perdigious fine shot, and as ready to shoot and fight as if he had a nateral calling that way."

"Shall we wait for him before we eat?" demanded Macnab, anxiously.

"By no sort o' reason, stranger," answered Sparkman. "He'll watch for us while we're eating, and after that I'll change shoes with him. So fall to, and don't mind what's a coming."

Sparkman had just broken the hoecake, when a distant whistle was heard.

"Ha! That's the lad now!" he exclaimed, rising to his feet. "He's on trail. He's got a sight of an inimy's fire, I reckon. 'Twon't be on reasonable, friend Macnab, to get our we'pons in readiness;" and, so speaking, Sparkman bid his sister get into the wagon, where the little Lucy had already placed herself, while he threw open the pan of his rifle, and turned the priming over with his finger. Macnab, meanwhile, had taken from his holsters, which he had before been sitting upon, a pair of horseman's pistols, richly mounted with figures in silver. These were large and long, and had evidently seen service. Unlike his companion, his proceedings occasioned no comment. What he did seemed a matter of habit, of which he himself was scarcely conscious. Having looked at his priming, he laid the instruments beside him without a word, and resumed the bit of hoecake which he had just before received from Sparkman. Meanwhile, the signal whistle, supposed to come from James Grayling, was repeated. Silence ensued then for a brief space, which Sparkman employed in perambulating the grounds immediately contiguous. At length, just as he had returned to the fire, the sound of a horse's feet was heard, and a sharp quick halloo from Grayling informed his uncle that all was right. The youth made his appearance a moment after accompanied by a stranger on horseback; a tall, fine-looking young man, with a keen flashing eye, and a voice whose lively clear tones, as he was heard approaching, sounded cheerily like those of a trumpet after victory. James Grayling kept along on foot beside the new-comer; and his hearty laugh, and free, glib, garrulous tones, betrayed to his uncle, long ere he drew nigh enough to declare the fact, that he had met unexpectedly with a friend, or, at least, an old acquaintance.

"Why, who have you got there, James?" was the demand of Sparkman, as he dropped the butt of his rifle upon the ground.

"Why, who do you think, uncle? Who but Major Spencer—our own major?"

"You don't say so!—what!—well! Li'nel Spencer, for sartin! Lord bless you, major, who'd ha' thought to see you in these parts; and jest mounted too, for all natur, as if the war was to be fou't over ag'in. Well, I'm raal glad to see you. I am, that's sartin!"

"And I'm very glad to see you, Sparkman," said the other, as he alighted from his steed, and yielded his hand to the cordial grasp of the other.

"Well, I knows that, major, without you saying it. But you've jest come in the right time. The bacon's frying, and here's the bread;—let's down upon our haunches, in right good air nest, camp fashion, and make the most of what God gives us in the way of blessings. I reckon you don't mean to ride any further tonight, major?"

"No," said the person addressed, "not if you'll let me lay my heels at your fire. But who's in your wagon? My old friend, Mrs. Grayling, I suppose?"

"That's a true word, major," said the lady herself, making her way out of the vehicle with good-humoured agility, and coming forward with extended hand.

"Really, Mrs. Grayling, I'm very glad to see you." And the stranger, with the blandness of a gentleman and the hearty warmth of an old neighbor, expressed his satisfaction at once more finding himself in the company of an old acquaintance. Their greetings once over, Major Spencer readily joined the group about the fire, while James Grayling—though with some reluctance—disappeared to resume his toils of the scout while the supper proceeded.

"And who have you here?" demanded Spencer, as his eye rested on the dark, hard features of the Scotchman. Sparkman told him all that he himself had learned of the name and character of the stranger, in a brief whisper, and in a moment after formally introduced the parties in this fashion—

"Mr. Macnab, Major Spencer. Mr. Macnab says he's true blue, major, and fou't at Camden, when General Gates run so hard to 'bring the d——d militia back.' He also fou't at Ninety-Six, and Cowpens—so I reckon we had as good as count him one of us."

Major Spencer scrutinized the Scotchman keenly—a scrutiny which the latter seemed very ill to relish. He put a few questions to him on the subject of the war, and some of the actions in which he allowed himself to have been concerned; but his evident reluctance to unfold himself—a reluctance so unnatural to the brave soldier who has gone through his toils honourably—had the natural effect of discouraging the young officer, whose sense of delicacy had not been materially impaired amid the rude jostlings of military life. But, though he forbore to propose any other questions to Macnab, his eyes continued to survey the features of his sullen countenance with curiosity and a strangely increasing interest. This he subsequently explained to Sparkman, when, at the close of supper, James Grayling came in, and the former assumed the duties of the scout.

"I have seen that Scotchman's face somewhere, Sparkman, and I'm convinced at some interesting moment; but where, when, or how, I cannot call to mind. The sight of it is even associated in my mind with something painful and unpleasant; where could I have seen him?"

"I don't somehow like his looks myself," said Sparkman, "and I mislists he's been rether more of a tory than a whig; but that's nothing to the purpose now; and he's at our fire, and we've broken hoecake together; so we cannot rake up the old ashes to make a dust with."

"No, surely not," was the reply of Spencer. "Even though we knew him to be a tory, that cause of former quarrel should occasion none now. But it should produce watchfulness and caution. I'm glad to see that you have not forgot your old business of scouting in the swamp."

"Kin I forget it, major?" demanded Sparkman, in tones which, though whispered, were full of emphasis, as he laid his ear to the earth to listen.

"James has finished supper, major—that's his whistle to tell me so; and I'll jest step back to make it cl'ar to him how we're to keep up the watch to-night."

"Count me in your arrangements, Sparkman, as I am one of you for the night," said the major.

"By no sort of means," was the reply. "The night must be shared between James and myself. Ef so be you wants to keep company with one or t'other of us, why, that's another thing, and, of course, you can do as you please."

"We'll have no quarrel on the subject, Joel," said the officer, good-naturedly, as they returned to the camp together.

CHAPTER 2.

The arrangements of the party were soon made. Spencer renewed his offer at the fire to take his part in the watch; and the Scotchman, Macnab, volunteered his services also; but the offer of the latter was another reason why that of the former should be declined. Sparkman was resolute to have everything his own way; and while James Grayling went out upon his lonely rounds, he busied himself in cutting bushes and making a sort of tent for the use of his late commander. Mrs. Grayling and Lucy slept in a wagon. The Scotchman stretched himself with little effort before the fire; while Joel Sparkman, wrapping himself up in his cloak, crouched under the wagon body, with his back resting partly against one of the wheels. From time to time he rose and thrust additional brands into the fire looked up at the night, and round upon the little encampment, then sunk back to his perch and stole a few moments, at intervals, of uneasy sleep. The first two hours of the watch were over, and James Grayling was relieved. The youth, however, felt in no mood for sleep, and taking his seat by the fire, he drew from his pocket a little volume of Easy Reading Lessons, and by the fitful flame of the resinous light-wood, he prepared, in this rude manner, to make up for the precious time which his youth had lost of its legitimate employments, in the stirring events of the preceding seven years consumed in war. He was surprised at this employment by his late commander, who, himself sleepless, now emerged from the bushes and joined Grayling at the fire. The youth had been rather a favorite with Spencer. They had both been reared in the same neighbourhood, and the first military achievements of James had taken place under the eye, and had met the approbation of his officer. The difference of their ages was just such as to permit of the warm attachment of the lad without diminishing any of the reverence which should be felt by the inferior. Grayling was not more than seventeen, and Spencer was perhaps thirty four—the very prime of manhood. They sat by the fire and talked of old times and told old stories with the hearty glee and good-nature of the young. Their mutual inquiries led to the revelation of their several objects in pursuing the present journey. Those of James Grayling were scarcely, indeed, to be considered his own. They were plans and purposes of his uncle, and it does not concern this narrative that we should know more of their nature than has already been revealed. But, whatever they were, they were as freely unfolded to his hearer as if the parties had been brothers, and Spencer was quite as frank in his revelations as his companion. He, too, was on his way to Charleston, from whence he was to take passage for England.

"I am rather in a hurry to reach town," he said, "as I learn that the Falmouth packet is preparing to sail for England in a few days, and I must go in her."

"For England, major!" exclaimed the youth with unaffected astonishment.

"Yes, James, for England. But why—what astonishes you?"

"Why, lord!" exclaimed the simple youth, "if they only knew there, as I do, what a cutting and slashing you did use to make among their red coats, I reckon they'd hang you to the first hickory."

"Oh, no! scarcely," said the other, with a smile.

"But I reckon you'll change your name, major?" continued the youth.

"No," responded Spencer, "if I did that, I should lose the object of my voyage. You must know, James, that an old relative has left me a good deal of money in England, and I can only get it by proving that I am Lionel Spencer; so you see I must carry my own name, whatever may be the risk."

"Well, major, you know best; but I do think if they could only have a guess of what you did among their sodgers at Hobkirk's and Cowpens, and Eutaw, and a dozen other places, they'd find some means of hanging you up, peace or no peace. But I don't see what occasion you have to be going cl'ar away to England for money, when you've got a sight of your own already."

"Not so much as you think for," replied the major, giving an involuntary and uneasy glance at the Scotchman, who was seemingly sound asleep on the opposite side of the fire. "There is, you know, but little money in the country at any time, and I must get what I want for my expenses when I reach Charleston. I have just enough to carry me there."

"Well, now, major, that's mighty strange. I always thought that you was about the best off of any man in our parts; but if you're strained so close, I'm thinking, major,—if so be you wouldn't think me too presumptuous,—you'd better let me lend you a guinea or so that I've got to spare, and you can pay me back when you get the English money."

And the youth fumbled in his bosom for a little cotton wallet, which, with its limited contents, was displayed in another instant to the eyes of the officer.

"No, no, James," said the other, putting back the generous tribute; "I have quite enough to carry me to Charleston, and when there I can easily get a supply from the merchants. But I thank you, my good fellow, for your offer. You *are* a good fellow, James, and I will remember you."

It is needless to pursue the conversation farther. The night passed away without any alarms, and at dawn of the next day the whole party was engaged in making preparation for a start. Mrs. Grayling was soon busy in getting breakfast in readiness. Major Spencer consented to remain with them until it was over; but the Scotchman, after returning thanks very civilly for his accommodation of the night, at once resumed his journey. His course seemed, like their own, to lie below; but he neither declared his route nor betrayed the least desire to know that of Spencer. The latter had no disposition to renew those inquiries from which the stranger seemed to shrink the night before, and he accordingly suffered him to depart with a quiet farewell, and the utterance of a good-natured wish, in which all the parties joined, that he might have a pleasant journey. When he was fairly out of sight, Spencer said to Sparkman,

"Had I liked that fellow's looks, nay, had I not positively disliked them, I should have gone with him. As it is, I will remain and share your breakfast."

The repast being over, all parties set forward; but Spencer, after keeping along with them for a mile, took his leave also. The slow wagon-pace at which the family travel led, did not suit the high-spirited cavalier; and it was necessary, as he assured them, that he should reach the city in two nights more. They parted with many regrets, as truly felt as they were warmly expressed; and James Grayling never felt the tedium of wagon travelling to be so severe as throughout the whole of that day when he separated from his favorite captain. But he was too stout-hearted a lad to make any complaint; and his dissatisfaction only showed itself in his unwonted silence, and an over-anxiety, which his steed seemed to feel in common with himself, to go rapidly ahead. Thus the day passed, and the wayfarers at its close had made a progress of some twenty miles from sun to sun. The same precautions marked their encampment this night as the last, and they rose in better spirits with the next morning, the dawn of which was very bright and pleasant, and encouraging. A similar journey of twenty miles brought them to the place of bivouac as the sun went down; and they prepared as usual for their securities and supper. They found themselves on the edge of a very dense forest of pines and scrubby oaks, a portion of which was swallowed up in a deep bay—so called in the dialect of the country—a swamp-bottom, the growth of which consisted of mingled cypresses and bay trees, with tupola, gum, and dense thickets of low stunted shrubbery, cane grass, and dwarf willows, which filled up every interval between the trees, and to the eye most effectually barred out every human intruder. This bay was chosen as the background for the camping party. Their wagon was wheeled into an area on a gently rising ground in front, under a pleasant shade of oaks and hickories, with a lonely pine rising loftily in occasional spots among them. Here the horses were taken out, and James Grayling prepared to kindle up a fire; but, looking for his axe, it was unaccountably missing, and after a fruitless search of half an hour, the party came to the conclusion that it had been left on the spot where they had slept last night. This was a disaster, and, while they meditated in what manner to repair it, a negro boy appeared in sight, passing along the road at their feet, and driving before him a small herd of cattle. From him they learned that they were only a mile or two from a farm stead where an axe might be borrowed; and James, leaping on his horse, rode forward in the hope to obtain one. He found no difficulty in his quest; and, having obtained it from the farmer, who was also a tavern-keeper, he casually asked if Major Spencer had not stayed with him the night before. He was somewhat surprised when told that he had not.

"There was one man stayed with me last night," said the farmer, "but he didn't call himself a major, and didn't much look like one."

"He rode a fine sorrel horse,—tall, bright colour, with white fore foot, didn't he?" asked James.

"No, that he didn't! He rode a powerful black, coal black, and not a bit of white about him."

"That was the Scotchman! But I wonder the major didn't stop with you. He must have rode on. Isn't there another house near you, below?"

"Not one. There's ne'er a house either above or below for a matter of fifteen miles. I'm the only man in all that distance that's living on this road and I don't think your friend could have gone below, as I should have seen him pass. I've been all day out there in that field before your eyes, clearing up the brush."

CHAPTER 3.

Somewhat wondering that the major should have turned aside from the track, though without attaching to it any importance at that particular moment, James Grayling took up the borrowed axe and hurried back to the encampment, where the toil of cutting an extra supply of light-wood to meet the exigencies of the ensuing night, sufficiently exercised his mind as well as his body, to prevent him from meditating upon the seeming strangeness of the circumstance. But when he sat down to his supper over the fire that he had kindled, his fancies crowded thickly upon him, and he felt a confused doubt and suspicion that something was to happen, he knew not what. His conjectures and apprehensions were without form, though not altogether void; and he felt a strange sickness and a sinking at the heart which was very unusual with him. He had, in short, that lowness of spirits, that cloudy apprehensiveness of soul which takes the form of presentiment, and makes us look out for danger even when the skies are without a cloud, and the breeze is laden, equally and only, with calm and music. His moodiness found no sympathy among his companions. Joel Sparkman was in the best of humours, and his mother was so cheery and happy, that when the thoughtful boy went off into the woods to watch, he could hear her at every moment breaking out into little catches of a country ditty, which the gloomy events of the late war had not yet obliterated from her memory.

"It's very strange!" soliloquized the youth, as he wandered along the edges of the dense bay or swamp-bottom, which we have passingly referred to,— "it's very strange what troubles me so! I feel almost frightened, and yet I know I'm not to be frightened easily, and I don't see anything in the woods to frighten me. It's strange the major didn't come along this road! Maybe he took another higher up that leads by a different settlement. I wish I had asked the man at the house if there's such another road. I reckon there must be, however, for where could the major have gone?"

The unphilosophical mind of James Grayling did not, in his farther meditations, carry him much beyond this starting point; and with its continual recurrence in soliloquy, he proceeded to traverse the margin of the bay, until he came to its junction with, and termination at, the high road. The youth turned into this, and, involuntarily departing from it a moment after, soon found himself on the opposite side of the bay thicket. He wandered on and on, as he himself described it, without any power to restrain himself. He knew not how far he went; but, instead of maintaining his watch for two hours only, he was gone more than four; and, at length, a sense of weariness which overpowered him all of a sudden, caused him to seat himself at the foot of a tree, and snatch a few moments of rest. He denied that he slept in this time. He insisted to the last moment of his life that sleep never visited his eyelids that night,—that he was conscious of fatigue and exhaustion, but not drowsiness—and that this fatigue was so numbing as to be painful, and effectually kept him from any sleep. While he sat thus beneath the tree, with a body weak and nerveless, but a mind excited, he knew not how or why, to the most acute degree of expectation and attention, he heard his name called by the well-known voice of his friend, Major Spencer. The voice called him three times,—"James Grayling!—James!—James Grayling!" before he could muster strength enough to answer. It was not courage he wanted,—of that he was positive, for he felt sure as he said, that something had gone wrong, and he was never more ready to fight in his life than at that moment, could he have commanded the physical capacity; but his throat seemed dry to suffocation,—his lips effectually sealed up as if with wax, and when he did answer, the sounds seemed as fine and soft as the whisper of some child just born.

"Oh! major, is it you?"

Such, he thinks, were the very words he made use of in reply; and the answer that he received was instantaneous, though the voice came from some little distance in the bay, and his own voice he did not hear. He only knows what he meant to say. The answer was to this effect.

"It is, James!—It is your own friend, Lionel Spencer, that speaks to you; do not be alarmed when you see me! I have been shockingly murdered!"

James asserts that he tried to tell him that he would not be frightened, but his own voice was still a whisper, which he himself could scarcely hear. A moment after he had spoken, he heard something like a sudden breeze that rustled through the bay bushes at his feet, and his eyes were closed without his effort, and indeed in spite of himself. When he opened them, he saw Major Spencer standing at the edge of the bay, about twenty steps from him. Though he stood in the shade of a thicket, and there was no light in the heavens save that of the stars, he was yet enabled to distinguish perfectly, and with great ease, every lineament of his friend's face.

He looked very pale, and his garments were covered with blood; and James said that he strove very much to rise from the place where he sat and approach him;—"for, in truth," said the lad, "so far from feeling any fear, I felt nothing but fury in my heart; but I could not move a limb. My feet were fastened to the ground; my hands to my sides; and I could only bend forward and gasp. I felt as if I should have died with vexation that I could not rise; but a power which I could not resist, made me motionless, and almost speechless. I could only say 'Murdered!'—and that one word I believe I must have repeated a dozen times."

"'Yes, murdered!—murdered by the Scotchman who slept with us at your fire the night before last. James, I look to you to have the murderer brought to justice! James!—do you hear me, James?'

"These," said James, "I think were the very words, or near about the very words, that I heard; and I tried to ask the major to tell me how it was, and how I could do what he required; but I didn't hear myself speak, though it would appear that he did, for almost immediately after I had tried to speak what I wished to say, he answered me just as if I had said it. He told me that the Scotchman had waylaid, killed, and hidden him in that very bay; that his murderer had gone to Charleston; and that if I made haste to town, I would find him in the Falmouth packet which was then lying in the harbour and ready to sail for England. He farther said that everything depended on my making haste,—that I must reach town by tomorrow night if I wanted to be in season, and go right on board the vessel and charge the criminal with the deed. 'Do not be afraid,' said he, when he had finished; 'be afraid of nothing, James, for God will help and strengthen you to the end.' When I heard all I burst into a flood of tears, and then I felt strong. I felt that I could talk, or fight, or do almost anything; and I jumped up to my feet, and was just about to run down to where the major stood, but, with the first step which I made forward, he was gone. I stopped and looked all around me, but I could see nothing; and the bay was just as black as midnight. But I went down to it, and tried to press in where I thought the major had been standing; but I couldn't get far, the brush and bay bushes were so close and thick. I was now bold and strong enough, and I called out, loud enough to be heard half a mile. I didn't exactly know what I called for, or what I wanted to learn, or I have forgotten. But I heard nothing more. Then I remembered the camp, and began to fear that something might have happened to mother and uncle, for I now felt, what I had not thought of before, that I had gone too far round the bay to be of much assistance, or, indeed, to be in time for any, had they been suddenly attacked. Besides, I could not think how long I had been gone; but it now seemed very late. The stars were shining their brightest, and the thin white clouds of morning were beginning to rise and run towards the west. Well, I bethought me of my course,—for I was a little bewildered and doubtful where I was; but, after a little thinking, I took the back track, and soon got a glimpse of the camp-fire, which was nearly burnt down; and by this I reckoned I was gone considerably longer than my two hours. When I got back into the camp, I looked under the wagon, and found uncle in a sweet sleep, and though my heart was full almost to bursting with what I had heard, and the cruel sight I had seen, yet I wouldn't waken him; and I beat about and mended the fire, and watched, and waited, until near daylight, when mother called to me out of the wagon, and asked who it was. This wakened my uncle, and then I up and told all that had happened, for if it had been to save my life, I couldn't have kept it in much longer. But though mother said it was very strange, Uncle Sparkman considered that I had been only dreaming, but he couldn't persuade me of it; and when I told him I intended to be off at daylight, just as the major had told me to do, and ride my best all the way to Charleston, he laughed, and said I was a fool. But I felt that I was no fool, and I was solemn certain that I hadn't been dreaming; and though both mother and he tried their hardest to make me put off going, yet I made up my mind to it, and they had to give up. For, wouldn't I have been a pretty sort of a friend to the major, if, after what he told me, I could have stayed behind, and gone on only at a wagon-pace to look after the murderer! I don't think if I had done so that I should ever have been able to look a white man in the face again. Soon as the peep of day, I was on horseback. Mother was mighty sad, and begged me not to go, but Uncle Sparkman was mighty sulky, and kept calling me fool upon fool, until I was almost angry enough to forget that we were of blood kin. But all his talking did not stop me, and I reckon I was five miles on my way before he had his team in traces for a start. I rode as briskly as I could get on without hurting my nag. I had a smart ride of more than forty miles before me, and the road was very heavy. But it was a good two hours from sunset when I got into town, and the first question I asked of the people I met was, to show me where the ships were kept. When I got to the wharf they showed me the Falmouth packet, where she lay in the stream, ready to sail as soon as the wind should favour."

CHAPTER 4.

James Grayling, with the same eager impatience which he has been suffered to describe in his own language, had already hired a boat to go on board the British packet, when he remembered that he had neglected all those means, legal and otherwise, by which alone his purpose might be properly effected. He did not know much about legal process, but he had common sense enough, the moment that he began to reflect on the subject, to know that some such process was necessary. This conviction produced another difficulty; he knew not in which quarter to turn for counsel and assistance; but here the boatman who saw his bewilderment, and knew by his dialect and dress that he was a back-countryman, came to his relief, and from him he got directions where to find the merchants with whom his uncle, Sparkman, had done business in former years. To them he went, and without circumlocution, told the whole story of his ghostly visitation. Even as a dream, which these gentlemen at once conjectured it to be, the story of James Grayling was equally clear and curious; and his intense warmth and the entire absorption, which the subject had effected, of his mind and soul, was such that they judged it not improper, at least to carry out the search of the vessel which he contemplated. It would certainly, they thought, be a curious coincidence—believing James to be a veracious youth—if the Scotchman should be found on board. But another test of his narrative was proposed by one of the firm. It so happened that the business agents of Major Spencer, who was well known in Charleston, kept their office but a few rods distant from their own; and to them all parties at once proceeded. But here the story of James was encountered by a circumstance that made somewhat against it. These gentlemen produced a letter from Major Spencer, intimating the utter impossibility of his coming to town for the space of a month, and expressing his regret that he should be unable to avail himself of the opportunity of the foreign vessel, of whose arrival in Charleston, and proposed time of departure, they had themselves advised him. They read the letter aloud to James and their brother merchants, and with difficulty suppressed their smiles at the gravity with which the former related and insisted upon the particulars of his vision.

"He has changed his mind," returned the impetuous youth; "he was on his way down, I tell you,—a hundred miles on his way,—when he camped with us. I know him well, I tell you, and talked with him myself half the night."

"At least," remarked the gentlemen who had gone with James, "it can do no harm to look into the business. We can procure a warrant for searching the vessel after this man, Macnab; and should he be found on board the packet, it will be a sufficient circumstance to justify the magistrates in detaining him, until we can ascertain where Major Spencer really is."

The measure was accordingly adopted, and it was nearly sunset before the warrant was procured, and the proper officer in readiness. The impatience of a spirit so eager and so devoted as James Grayling, under these delays, may be imagined; and when in the boat, and on his way to the packet where the criminal was to be sought, his blood became so excited that it was with much ado he could be kept in his seat. His quick, eager action continually disturbed the trim of the boat, and one of his mercantile friends, who had accompanied him, with that interest in the affair which curiosity alone inspired, was under constant apprehension lest he would plunge overboard in his impatient desire to shorten the space which lay between. The same impatience enabled the youth, though never on shipboard before, to grasp the rope which had been flung at their approach, and to mount her sides with catlike agility. Without waiting to declare himself or his purpose, he ran from one side of the deck to the other, greedily staring, to the surprise of officers, passengers, and seamen, in the faces of all of them, and surveying them with an almost offensive scrutiny. He turned away from the search with disappointment. There was no face like that of the suspected man among them. By this time, his friend, the merchant, with the sheriff's officer, had entered the vessel, and were in conference with the captain. Grayling drew nigh in time to hear the latter affirm that there was no man of the name of Macnab, as stated in the warrant among his passengers or crew.

"He is—he must be!" exclaimed the impetuous youth. "The major never lied in his life, and couldn't lie after he was dead. Macnab is here—he is a Scotchman—"

The captain interrupted him—

"We have, young gentleman, several Scotchmen on board, and one of them is named Macleod—"

"Let me see him—which is he?" demanded the youth.

By this time, the passengers and a goodly portion of the crew were collected about the little party. The captain turned his eyes upon the group, and asked,

"Where is Mr. Macleod?"

"He is gone below—he's sick!" replied one of the passengers.

"That's he! That must be the man!" exclaimed the youth. "I'll lay my life that's no other than Macnab. He's only taken a false name."

It was now remembered by one of the passengers, and remarked, that Macleod had expressed himself as unwell, but a few moments before, and had gone below even while the boat was rapidly approaching the vessel. At this statement, the captain led the way into the cabin, closely followed by James Grayling and the rest.

"Mr. Macleod," he said with a voice somewhat elevated, as he approached the berth of that person, "you are wanted on deck for a few moments."

"I am really too unwell, captain," replied a feeble voice from behind the curtain of the berth.

"It will be necessary," was the reply of the captain. "There is a warrant from the authorities of the town, to look after a fugitive from justice."

Macleod had already begun a second speech declaring his feebleness, when the fearless youth, Grayling, bounded before the captain and tore away, with a single grasp of his hand, the curtain which concealed the suspected man from their sight.

"It is he!" was the instant exclamation of the youth, as he beheld him. "It is he—Macnab, the Scotchman—the man that murdered Major Spencer!"

Macnab,—for it was he,—was deadly pale. He trembled like an aspen. His eyes were dilated with more than mortal apprehension, and his lips were perfectly livid. Still, he found strength to speak, and to deny the accusation. He knew nothing of the youth before him—nothing of Major Spencer—his name was Macleod, and he had never called himself by any other. He denied, but with great incoherence, everything which was urged against him.

"You must get up, Mr. Macleod," said the captain; "the circumstances are very much against you. You must go with the officer!"

"Will you give me up to my enemies?" demanded the culprit. "You are countryman—a Briton. I have fought for the king, our master, against these rebels, and for this they seek my life. Do not deliver me into their bloody hands!"

"Liar!" exclaimed James Grayling—"Didn't you tell us at our own camp-fire that you were with us? that you were at Gates's defeat, and Ninety Six?"

"But I didn't tell you," said the Scotchman, with a grin, "which side I was on!"

"Ha! remember that!" said the sheriff's officer. "He denied, just a moment ago, that he knew this young man at all; now, he confesses that he did see and camp with him."

The Scotchman was aghast at the strong point which, in his inadvertence, he had made against himself; and his efforts to excuse himself, stammering and contradictory, served only to involve him more deeply in the meshes of his difficulty. Still he continued his urgent appeals to the captain of the vessel, and his fellow-passengers, as citizens of the same country, subjects to the same monarch to protect him from those who equally hated and would destroy them all. In order to move their national prejudices in his behalf, he boasted of the immense injury which he had done, as a tory, to the rebel cause; and still insisted that the murder was only a pretext of the youth before him, by which to gain possession of his person, and wreak upon him the revenge which his own fierce performances during the war had naturally enough provoked. One or two of the passengers, indeed, joined with him in entreating the captain to set the accusers adrift and make sail at once; but the stout Englishman who was in command, rejected instantly the unworthy counsel. Besides, he was better aware of the dangers which would follow any such rash proceeding. Fort Moultrie, on Sullivan's Island, had been already refitted and prepared for an enemy; and he was lying, at that moment, under the formidable range of grinning teeth, which would have opened upon him, at the first movement, from the jaws of Castle Pinckney.

"No, gentlemen," said he, "you mistake your man. God forbid that I should give shelter to a murderer, though he were from my own parish."

"But I am no murderer," said the Scotchman.

"You look cursedly like one, however," was the reply of the captain. "Sheriff, take your prisoner."

The base creature threw himself at the feet of the Englishman, and clung, with piteous entreaties, to his knees. The latter shook him off, and turned away in disgust.

"Steward," he cried, "bring up this man's luggage."

He was obeyed. The luggage was brought up from the cabin and delivered to the sheriff's officer, by whom it was examined in the presence of all, and an inventory made of its contents. It consisted of a small new trunk, which, it afterwards appeared, he had bought in Charleston, soon after his arrival. This contained a few changes of raiment, twenty-six guineas in money, a gold watch, not in repair, and the two pistols which he had shown while at Joel Sparkman's camp fire; but with this difference, that the stock of one was broken off short just above the grasp, and the butt was entirely gone. It was not found among his chattels. A careful examination of the articles in his trunk did not result in anything calculated to strengthen the charge of his criminality; but there was not a single person present who did not feel as morally certain of his guilt as if the jury had already declared the fact. That night he slept—if he slept at all—in the common jail of the city.

CHAPTER 5.

His accuser, the warm-hearted and resolute James Grayling, did not sleep. The excitement, arising from mingling and contradictory emotions,—sorrow for his brave young commander's fate, and the natural exultation of a generous spirit at the consciousness of having performed, with signal success, an arduous and painful task combined to drive all pleasant slumbers from his eyes; and with the dawn he was again up and stirring, with his mind still full of the awful business in which he had been engaged. We do not care to pursue his course in the ordinary walks of the city, nor account for his employments during the few days which ensued, until, in consequence of a legal examination into the circumstances which anticipated the regular work of the sessions, the extreme excitement of the young accuser had been renewed. Macnab or Macleod,—and it is possible that both names were fictitious,—as soon as he recovered from his first terrors, sought the aid of an attorney—one of those acute, small, chopping lawyers, to be found in almost every community, who are willing to serve with equal zeal the sinner and the saint, provided that they can pay with equal liberality. The prisoner was brought before the court under *habeas corpus,* and several grounds submitted by his counsel with the view to obtaining his discharge. It became necessary to ascertain, among the first duties of the state, whether Major Spencer, the alleged victim, was really dead. Until it could be established that a man should be imprisoned, tried, and punished for a crime, it was first necessary to show that a crime had been committed, and the attorney made himself exceedingly merry with the ghost story of young Grayling. In those days, however, the ancient Superstition was not so feeble as she has subsequently become. The venerable judge was one of those good men who had a decent respect for the faith and opinions of his ancestors; and though he certainly would not have consented to the hanging of Macleod under the sort of testimony which had been adduced, he yet saw enough, in all the circumstances, to justify his present detention. In the meantime, efforts were to be made, to ascertain the whereabouts of Major Spencer; though, were he even missing,—so the counsel for Macleod contended,—his death could be by no means assumed in consequence. To this the judge shook his head doubtfully. "'Fore God!" said he, "I would not have you to be too sure of that." He was an Irishman, and proceeded after the fashion of his country. The reader will therefore *bear* with his *bull*. "A man may properly be hung for murdering another, though the murdered man be not dead; ay, before God, even though he be actually unhurt and uninjured, while the murderer is swinging by the neck for the bloody deed!"

The judge,—who it must be understood was a real existence, and who had no small reputation in his day in the south,—proceeded to establish the correctness of his opinions by authorities and argument, with all of which, doubtlessly, the bar were exceedingly delighted; but, to provide them in this place would only be to interfere with our own progress. James Grayling, however, was not satisfied to wait the slow processes which were suggested for coming at the truth. Even the wisdom of the judge was lost upon him, possibly, for the simple reason that he did not comprehend it. But the ridicule of the culprit's lawyer stung him to the quick, and he muttered to himself, more than once, a determination "to lick the life out of that impudent chap's leather." But this was not his only resolve. There was one which he proceeded to put into instant execution, and that was to seek the body of his murdered friend in the spot where he fancied it might be found— namely, the dark and dismal bay where the spectre had made its appearance to his eyes.

The suggestion was approved—though he did not need this to prompt his resolution—by his mother and uncle, Sparkman. The latter determined to be his companion, and he was farther accompanied by the sheriff's officer who had arrested the suspected felon. Before daylight, on the morning after the examination before the judge had taken place, and when Macleod had been remanded to prison, James Grayling started on his journey. His fiery zeal received additional force at every added moment of delay, and his eager spurring brought him at an early hour after noon, to the neighborhood of the spot through which his search was to be made. When his companions and himself drew nigh, they were all at a loss in which direction first to proceed. The bay was one of those massed forests, whose wall of thorns, vines, and close tenacious shrubs, seemed to defy invasion. To the eye of the townsman it was so forbidding that he pronounced it absolutely impenetrable. But James was not to be baffled. He led them round it, taking the very course which he had pursued the night when the revelation was made him; he showed them the very tree at whose foot he had sunk when the supernatural torpor—as he himself esteemed it—began to fall upon him; he then pointed out the spot, some twenty steps distant, at which the spectre made his appearance. To this spot they then proceeded in a body, and essayed an entrance, but were so discouraged by the difficulties at the outset that all, James not excepted, concluded that neither the murderer nor his victim could possibly have found entrance there.

But, lo! a marvel! Such it seemed, at the first blush, to all the party. While they stood confounded and indecisive, undetermined in which way to move, a sudden flight of wings was heard, even from the centre of the bay, at a little distance above the spot where they had striven for entrance. They looked up, and beheld about fifty buzzards—those notorious domestic vultures of the south—ascending from the interior of the bay, and perching along upon the branches of the loftier trees by which it was overhung. Even were the character of these birds less known, the particular business in which they had just then been engaged, was betrayed by huge gob bets of flesh which some of them had borne aloft in their flight, and still continued to rend with beak and bill, as they tottered upon the branches where they stood. A piercing scream issued from the lips of James Grayling as he beheld this sight, and strove to scare the offensive birds from their repast.

"The poor major! the poor major!" was the involuntary and agonized exclamation of the youth. "Did I ever think he would come to this!"

The search, thus guided and encouraged, was pressed with renewed diligence and spirit; and, at length, an opening was found through which it was evident that a body of considerable size had but recently gone. The branches were broken from the small shrub trees, and the undergrowth trodden into the earth. They followed this path, and, as is the case commonly with waste tracts of this description, the density of the growth diminished sensibly at every step they took, till they reached a little pond, which, though circumscribed in area, and full of cypresses, yet proved to be singularly deep. Indeed, it was an alligator-hole, where, in all probability, a numerous tribe of these reptiles had their dwelling. Here, on the edge of the pond, they discovered the object which had drawn the keen-sighted vultures to their feast, in the body of a horse, which James Grayling at once identified as that of Major Spencer. The carcass of the animal was already very much torn and

lacerated. The eyes were plucked out, and the animal completely disem-
bowelled. Yet, on examination, it was not difficult to discover the manner of
his death. This had been effected by fire-arms. Two bullets had passed
through his skull, just above the eyes, either of which must have been fatal.
The murderer had led the horse to the spot, and committed the cruel deed
where his body was found. The search was now continued for that of the
owner, but for some time it proved ineffectual. At length, the keen eyes of
James Grayling detected, amidst a heap of moss and green sedge that rested
beside an overthrown tree, whose branches jutted into the pond, a whitish,
but discoloured object, that did not seem native to the place. Bestriding the
fallen tree, he was enabled to reach this object, which, with a burst of grief,
he announced to the distant party was the hand and arm of his unfortunate
friend, the wristband of the shirt being the conspicuous object which had
first caught his eye. Grasping this, he drew the corse, which had been thrust
beneath the branches of the tree, to the surface; and, with the assistance of
his uncle, it was finally brought to the dry land. Here it underwent a careful
examination. The head was very much disfigured; the skull was fractured in
several places by repeated blows of some hard instrument, inflicted chiefly
from behind. A closer inspection revealed a bullet-hole in the abdomen, the
first wound, in all probability, which the unfortunate gentleman received,
and by which he was, perhaps, tumbled from his horse. The blows on the
head would seem to have been unnecessary, unless the murderer—whose
proceedings appeared to have been singularly deliberate,—was resolved
upon making "assurance doubly sure." But, as if the watchful Providence had
meant that nothing should be left doubtful which might tend to the complete
conviction of the criminal, the constable stumbled upon the butt of the
broken pistol which had been found in Macleod's trunk. This he picked up
on the edge of the pond in which the corse had been discovered, and while
James Grayling and his uncle, Sparkman, were engaged in drawing it from
the water. The place where the fragment was discovered at once denoted
the pistol as the instrument by which the final blows were inflicted. "'Fore
God," said the judge to the criminal, as these proofs were submitted on the
trial, "you may be a very innocent man after all, as, by my faith, I do think
there have been many murderers before you; but you ought, nevertheless,
to be hung as an example to all other persons who suffer such strong proofs
of guilt to follow their innocent misdoings. Gentlemen of the jury, if this
person, Macleod or Macnab, didn't murder Major Spencer, either you or I
did; and you must now decide which of us it is! I say, gentlemen of the jury,
either you, or I, or the prisoner at the bar, murdered this man; and if you
have any doubts which of us it was, it is but justice and mercy that you should
give the prisoner the benefit of your doubts; and so find your verdict. But,

before God, should you find him not guilty, Mr. Attorney there can scarely do anything wiser than to put us all upon trial for the deed."

The jury, it may be scarcely necessary to add, perhaps under certain becoming fear of an alternative such as his honour had suggested, brought in a verdict of "Guilty," without leaving the panel; and Macnab, *alias* Macleod, was hung at White Point, Charleston, somewhere about the year 178——.

"And here," said my grandmother devoutly, "you behold a proof of God's watchfulness to see that murder should not be hidden, and that the murderer should not escape. You see that he sent the spirit of the murdered man— since, by no other mode could the truth have been revealed—to declare the crime, and to discover the criminal. But for that ghost, Macnab would have got off to Scotland, and probably have been living to this very day on the money that he took from the person of the poor major."

As the old lady finished the ghost story, which, by the way, she had been tempted to relate for the fiftieth time in order to combat my father's ridicule of such superstitions, the latter took up the thread of the narrative.

"Now, my son," said he, "as you have heard all that your grandmother has to say on this subject, I will proceed to show you what you have to believe, and what not. It is true that Macnab murdered Spencer in the manner related; that James Grayling made the discovery and prosecuted the pursuit, found the body and brought the felon to justice; that Macnab suffered death, and confessed the crime alleging that he was moved to do so, as well because of the money that he suspected Spencer to have in his possession, as because of the hate which he felt for a man who had been particularly bold and active in cutting up a party of Scotch loyalists to which he belonged, on the borders of North Carolina. But the appearance of the spectre was nothing more than the work of a quick imagination, added to a shrewd and correct judgment. James Grayling saw no ghost, in fact, but such as was in his own mind; and, though the instance was one of a most remarkable character, one of singular combination, and well depending circumstances, still, I think it is to be accounted for by natural and very simple laws."

The old lady was indignant.

"And how could he see the ghost just on the edge of the same bay where the murder had been committed, and where the body of the murdered man even then was lying?"

My father did not directly answer the demand, but proceeded thus:——

"James Grayling, as we know, mother, was a very ardent, impetuous, sagacious man. He had the sanguine, the race-horse temperament. He was generous, always prompt and ready, and one who never went backward. What he did, he did quickly, boldly, and thoroughly! He never shrank from trouble of any kind; nay, he rejoiced in the constant encounter with difficulty and trial; and his was the temper which commands and enthrals mankind. He felt deeply and intensely whatever occupied his mind, and when he parted from his friend he brooded over little else than their past communion and the great distance by which they were to be separated. The dull travelling wagon-gait at which he himself was compelled to go, was a source of annoyance to him; and he became sullen, all the day, after the departure of his friend. When, on the evening of the next day, he came to the house where it was natural to expect that Major Spencer would have slept the night before, and he learned the fact that no one stopped there but the Scotchman, Macnab, we see that he was struck with the circumstance. He mutters it over to himself, "Strange, where the major could have gone!" His mind then naturally reverts to the character of the Scotchman; to the opinions and suspicions which had been already expressed of him by his uncle, and felt by himself. They had all, previously, come to the full conviction that Macnab was, and had always been, a tory, in spite of his protestations. His mind next, and very naturally, reverted to the insecurity of the highways; the general dangers of travelling at that period; the frequency of crime, and the number of desperate men who were everywhere to be met with. The very employment in which he was then engaged, in scouting the woods for the protection of the camp, was calculated to bring such reflections to his mind. If these precautions were considered necessary for the safety of persons so poor, so wanting in those possessions which might prompt cupidity to crime, how much more necessary were precautions in the case of a wealthy gentleman like Major Spencer? He then remembered the conversation with the major at the camp-fire, when they fancied that the Scotchman was sleeping. How natural to think then that he was all the while awake; and, if awake, he must have heard him speak of the wealth of his companion. True, the major, with more prudence than himself, denied that he had any money about him, more than would bear his expenses to the city; but such an assurance was natural enough to the lips of a traveller who knew the dangers of the country. That the man, Macnab, was not a person to be trusted, was the equal impression of Joel Sparkman and his nephew from the first. The probabilities were strong that he would rob and perhaps murder, if he might hope to do so with impunity; and as the youth made the circuit of the bay in the darkness and solemn stillness of the night, its gloomy depths and mournful shadows, naturally gave rise to such reflections as would be equally active in the mind of a youth, and of one somewhat familiar with the arts and usages of strife. He would see that the spot was just the one in which a practised partisan would delight to set an ambush for an unwary foe. There ran the public road, with a little sweep, around two-thirds of the extent of its dense and impenetrable thickets. The ambush could lie concealed, and at ten steps command the bosom of its victim. Here, then, you perceive that the mind of James Grayling, stimulated by an active and sagacious judgment, had by gradual and reasonable stages come to these conclusions: that Major Spencer was an object to tempt a robber; that the country was full of robbers; that Macnab was one of them; that this was the very spot in which a deed of blood could be most easily committed, and most easily concealed; and, one important fact, that gave strength and coherence to the whole, that Major Spencer had not reached a well-known point of destination, while Macnab had.

"With these thoughts, thus closely linked together, the youth forgets the limits of his watch and his circuit. This fact, alone, proves how active his imagination had become. It leads him forward, brooding more and more on the subject, until, in the very exhaustion of his body, he sinks down beneath a tree. He sinks down and falls asleep; and in his sleep, what before was plausible conjecture, becomes fact, and the creative properties of his imagination give form and vitality to all his fancies. These forms are bold, broad, and deeply coloured; in due proportion with the degree of force which they receive from probability. Here, he sees the image of his friend; but, you will remark—and this should almost conclusively satisfy any mind that all that he sees is the work of his imagination,—that, though Spencer tells him that he is murdered, and by Macnab, he does not tell him how, in what manner, or with what weapons. Though he sees him pale and ghostlike, he does not see, nor can he say, where his wounds are! He sees his pale features distinctly, and his garments are bloody. Now, had he seen the spectre in the true appearances of death, as he was subsequently found, he would not have been able to discern his features, which were battered, according to his own account, almost out of all shape of humanity, and covered with mud; while his clothes would have streamed with mud and water, rather than with blood."

"Ah!" exclaimed the old lady, my grandmother, "it's hard to make you believe anything that you don't see; you are like Saint Thomas in the Scriptures; but how do you propose to account for his knowing that the Scotchman was on board the Falmouth packet? Answer to that!"

"That is not a more difficult matter than any of the rest. You forget that in the dialogue which took place between James and Major Spencer at the camp, the latter told him that he was about to take passage for Europe in the Falmouth packet, which then lay in Charleston harbour, and was about to sail. Macnab heard all that."

"True enough, and likely enough," returned the old lady; "but, though you show that it was Major Spencer's intention to go to Europe in the Falmouth packet, that will not show that it was also the intention of the murderer."

"Yet what more probable, and how natural for James Grayling to imagine such a thing! In the first place he knew that Macnab was a Briton; he felt convinced that he was a tory; and the inference was immediate, that such a person would scarcely have remained long in a country where such characters laboured under so much odium, disfranchisement, and constant danger from popular tumults. The fact that Macnab was compelled to disguise his true sentiments and affect those of the people against whom he fought so vindictively, shows what was his sense of the danger which he incurred. Now, it is not unlikely that Macnab was quite as well aware that the Falmouth packet was in Charleston, and about to sail, as Major Spencer. No doubt he was pursuing the same journey, with the same object, and had he not murdered Spencer, they would, very likely, have been fellow-passengers together to Europe. But, whether he knew the fact before or not, he probably heard it stated by Spencer while he seemed to be sleeping; and, even supposing that he did not then know, it was enough that he found this to be the fact on reaching the city. It was an after-thought to fly to Europe with his ill-gotten spoils; and whatever may have appeared a politic course to the criminal, would be a probable conjecture in the mind of him by whom he was suspected. The whole story is one of strong probabilities which happened to be verified; and if proving anything, proves only that which we know—that James Grayling was a man of remarkably sagacious judgment, and quick, daring imagination. This quality of imagination, by the way, when possessed very strongly in connexion with shrewd common sense and well-balanced general faculties, makes that particular kind of intellect which, because of its promptness and powers of creation and combination, we call genius. It is genius only which can make ghosts, and James Grayling was a genius. He never, my son, saw any other ghosts than those of his own making!"

I heard my father with great patience to the end, though he seemed very tedious. He had taken a great deal of pains to destroy one of my greatest sources of pleasure. I need not add that I continued to believe in the ghost, and, with my grandmother, to reject the philosophy. It was more easy to believe the one than to comprehend the other.

The Two Camps:
A Legend of the Old North State

(1 8 4 5)

"These, the forest born
And forest nurtured—a bold, hardy race,
Fearless and frank, unfettered, with big souls
In hour of danger."

CHAPTER I.

It is frequently the case, in the experience of the professional novelist or tale-writer, that his neighbour comes in to his assistance when he least seeks, and, perhaps, least desires any succour. The worthy person, man or woman, however,—probably some excellent octogenarian whose claims to be heard are based chiefly upon the fact that he himself no longer possesses the faculty of hearing,—has some famous incident, some wonderful fact, of which he has been the eyewitness, or of which he has heard from his great-grandmother, which he fancies is the very thing to be woven into song or story. Such is the strong possession which the matter takes of his brain, that, if the novelist whom he seeks to benefit does not live within trumpet-distance, he gives him the narrative by means of post, some three sheets of stiff foolscap, for which the hapless tale-writer, whose works are selling in cheap editions at twelve or twenty cents, pays a sum of one dollar sixty-two postage. Now, it so happens, to increase the evil, that, in ninety-nine cases in the hundred, the fact thus laboriously stated is not worth a straw—consisting of some simple deed of violence, some mere murder, a downright blow with gun butt or cudgel over the skull, or a hidden thrust, three inches deep, with dirk or bowie knife, into the abdomen, or at random among the lower ribs. The man dies and the murderer gets off to Texas, or is prematurely caught and stops by the way—and still stops by the way! The thing is fact, no doubt. The narrator saw it himself? or his brother saw it, or—more solemn, if not more certain testimony still—his grandmother saw it, long before he had eves to see at all. The circumstance is attested by a cloud of witnesses—a truth solemnly sworn to—and yet, for the purposes of the tale-writer, of no manner of value. This assertion may somewhat conflict with the received opinions of many, who, accustomed to find deeds of violence recorded in almost every work of fiction, from the time of Homer to the present day, have rushed to the conclusion that this is all, and overlook that labour of the artist, by which an ordinary event is made to assume the character of novelty; in other words, to become an extraordinary event. The least difficult thing in the world, on the part of the writer of fiction, is to find the assassin and the bludgeon; the art is to make them appear in the right place, strike at the right time, and so adapt one fact to another, as to create mystery, awaken curiosity, inspire doubt as to the result, and bring about the catastrophe, by processes which shall be equally natural and unexpected. All that class of sagacious persons, therefore, who fancy they have found a mare's nest, when, in fact, they are only gazing at a goose's, are respectfully counselled that no fact—no tradition—is of any importance to the artist, unless it embodies certain peculiar characteristics of its own, or unless it illustrates some history about which curiosity has already been awakened. A mere brutality, in which John beats and bruises Ben, and Ben in turn shoots John, putting eleven slugs, or thereabouts, between his collar-bone and vertebrae—or, maybe, stabs him under his left pap, or any where you please, is just as easily conceived by the novelist, without the help of history. Nay, for that matter, he would perhaps rather not have any precise facts in his way, in such cases, as then he will be able to regard the picturesque in the choice of his weapon, and to put the wounds in such parts of the body, as will better bear the examination of all persons. I deem it right to throw out this hint, just at this moment, as well for the benefit of my order as for my own protection. The times are hard, and the post-office requires all its dues in hard money. Literary men are not proverbially prepared at all seasons for any unnecessary outlay—and to be required to make advances for commodities of which they have on hand, at all times, the greatest abundance, is an injustice which, it is to be hoped, that this little intimation will somewhat lessen. We take for granted, therefore, that our professional brethren will concur with us in saying to the public, that we are all sufficiently provided with "disastrous chances" for some time to come—that our "moving accidents by flood and field" are particularly numerous, and of "hair-breadth 'scapes" we have enough to last a century. Murders, and such matters, as they are among the most ordinary events of the day, are decidedly vulgar; and, for mere cudgelling and bruises, the taste of the belles-lettres reader, rendered delicate by the monthly magazines, has voted them equally gross and unnatural.

But, if the character of the materials usually tendered to the novelist by the incident-mongers, is thus ordinarily worthless as we describe it, we sometimes are fortunate in finding an individual, here and there, in the deep forests,—a sort of recluse, hale and lusty, but white-headed,—who unfolds from his own budget of experience a rare chronicle, on which we delight to linger. Such an one breathes life into his deeds. We see them as we listen to his words. In lieu of the dead body of the fact, we have its living spirit—subtle, active, breathing and burning, and fresh in all the provocations and associations of life. Of this sort was the admirable characteristic narrative of Horse-Shoe Robinson, which we owe to Kennedy, and for which he was indebted to the venerable hero of the story. When we say that the subject of the sketch which follows was drawn from not dissimilar sources, we must beg our readers not to understand us as inviting any reference to that able and national story—with which it is by no means our policy or wish to invite or provoke comparison.

CHAPTER II.

There are probably some old persons still living upon the upper dividing line between North and South Carolina, who still remember the form and features of the venerable Daniel Nelson. The old man was still living so late as 1817. At that period he removed to Mississippi, where, we believe, he died in less than three months after his change of residence. An old tree does not bear transplanting easily? and does not long survive it. Daniel Nelson came from Virginia when a youth. He was one of the first who settled on the southern borders of North Carolina, or, at least in that neighbourhood where he afterwards passed the greatest portion of his days.

At that time the country was not only a forest, but one thickly settled with Indians. It constituted the favourite hunting-grounds for several of their tribes. But this circumstance did not discourage young Nelson. He was then a stalwart youth, broad-chested, tall, with a fiery eye, and an almost equally fiery soul—certainly with a very fearless one. His companions, who were few in number, were like himself. The spirit of old Daniel Boone was a more common one than is supposed. Adventure gladdened and excited their hearts,—danger only seemed to provoke their determination,—and mere hardship was something which their frames appeared to covet. It was as refreshing to them as drink. Having seen the country, and struck down

some of its game,—tasted of its bear-meat and buffalo, its deer and turkey,—all, at that time, in the greatest abundance,—they returned for the
one thing most needful to a brave forester in a new country,—a good, brisk,
fearless wife, who, like the damsel in Scripture, would go whithersoever
went the husband to whom her affections were surrendered. They had no
fear, these bold young hunters, to make a home and rear an infant family in
regions so remote from the secure walks of civilization. They had met and
made an acquaintance and a sort of friendship with the Indians, and, in the
superior vigour of their own frames, their greater courage, and better weapons, they perhaps had come to form a too contemptuous estimate of the savage. But they were not beguiled by him into too much confidence. Their log
houses were so constructed as to be fortresses upon occasion, and they lived
not so far removed from one another, but that the leaguer of one would be
sure, in twenty-four hours, to bring the others to his assistance. Besides,
with a stock of bear-meat and venison always on hand, sufficient for a winter, either of these fortresses might, upon common calculations, be maintained for several weeks against any single band of the Indians, in the small
numbers in which they were wont to range together in those neighbour-
hoods. In this way these bold pioneers took possession of the soil, and paved
the way for still mightier generations. Though wandering, and somewhat
averse to the tedious labours of the farm, they were still not wholly unmind-
ful of its duties; and their open lands grew larger every season, and increasing comforts annually spoke for the increasing civilization of the settlers.
Corn was in plenty in proportion to the bear-meat, and the squatters almost
grew indifferent to those first apprehensions, which had made them watch
the approaches of the most friendly Indian as if he had been an enemy. At the
end of five years, in which they had suffered no hurt and but little annoyance
of any sort from their wild neighbours, it would seem as if this confidence in
the security of their situation was not without sufficient justification.

But, just then, circumstances seemed to threaten an interruption of this
goodly state of things. The Indians were becoming discontented. Other
tribes, more frequently in contact with the larger settlements of the
whites,—wronged by them in trade, or demoralized by drink,—complained of their sufferings and injuries, or, as is more probable, were greedy
to obtain their treasures, in bulk, which they were permitted to see, but
denied to enjoy, or only in limited quantity. Their appetites and complaints
were transmitted, by inevitable sympathies, to their brethren of the interior,
and our worthy settlers upon the Haw, were rendered anxious at signs which
warned them of a change in the peaceful relations which had hitherto existed
in all the intercourse between the differing races. We need not dwell upon

or describe these signs, with which, from frequent narratives of like character, our people are already sufficiently familiar. They were easily understood by our little colony, and by none more quickly than Daniel Nelson. They rendered him anxious, it is true, but not apprehensive; and, like a good husband, while he strove not to frighten his wife by what he said, he deemed it necessary to prepare her mind for the worst that might occur. This task over, he felt somewhat relieved, though, when he took his little girl, now five years old, upon his knee that evening, and looked upon his infant boy in the lap of his mother, he felt his anxieties very much increase; and that very night he resumed a practice which he had latterly abandoned, but which had been adopted as a measure of strict precaution, from the very first establishment of their little settlement. As soon as supper was over, he resumed his rifle, thrust his *couteau de chasse* into his belt, and, taking his horn about his neck, and calling up his trusty dog, Clinch, he proceeded to scour the woods immediately around his habitation. This task, performed with the stealthy caution of the hunter, occupied some time, and, as the night was clear, a bright starlight, the weather moderate, and his own mood restless, he determined to strike through the forest to the settlement of Jacob Ransom, about four miles off, in order to prompt him, and, through him, others of the neighbourhood, to the continued exercise of a caution which he now thought necessary. The rest of this night's adventure we propose to let him tell in his own words, as he has been heard to relate it a thousand times in his old age, at a period of life when, with one foot in his grave, to suppose him guilty of falsehood, or of telling that which he did not himself fervently believe, would be, among all those who knew him, to suppose the most impossible and extravagant thing in the world.

CHAPTER III.

"Well, my friends," said the veteran, then seventy, drawing his figure up to its fullest height, and extending his right arm while his left still grasped the muzzle of his ancient rifle, which he swayed from side to side, the butt resting on the floor—"Well, my friends, seeing that the night was cl'ar, and there was no wind, and feeling as how I didn't want for sleep, I called to Clinch and took the path for Jake Ransom's. I knew that Jake was a sleepy sort of chap, and it the redskins caught any body napping, he'd, most likely, be the man. But I confess, 'twarn't so much for his sake, as for the sake of all,— of my own as well as the rest;—for, when I thought how soon; if we warn't all together in the business, I might see, without being able to put in, the long yellow hair of Betsy and the babies twirling on the thumbs of some painted devil of the tribe,——I can't tell you how I felt, but it warn't like a human, though I shivered mightily like one,——'twas wolfish, as if the hair was turned in and rubbing a gin the very heart within me. I said my prayers, where I stood, looking up at the stars, and thinking that, after all, all was in the hands and the marcy of God. This sort o' thinking quieted me, and I went ahead pretty free, for I knew the track jest as well by night as by day, though I didn't go so quick, for I was all the time on the look-out for the enemy. Now, after we reached a place in the woods where there was a gully and a mighty bad crossing, there were two roads to get to Jake's—one by the hollows, and one jest across the hills. I don't know why, but I didn't give myself time to think, and struck right across the hill, though that was rather the longest way.

"Howsomedever, on I went, and Clinch pretty close behind me. The dog was a good dog, with a mighty keen nose to hunt, but jest then he didn't seem to have the notion for it. The hill was a sizeable one, a good stretch to foot, and I began to remember, after awhile, that I had been in the woods from blessed dawn; and that made me see how it was with poor Clinch, and why he didn't go for'ad; but I was more than half way, and wasn't guine to turn back till I had said my say to Jake. Well, when I got to the top of the hill, I stopped, and rubbed my eyes. I had cause to rub 'em, for what should I see at a distance but a great fire. At first I was afeard lest it was Jake's house, but I considered, the next moment, that he lived to the left, and this fire was cl'ar to the right, and it did seem to me as if 'twas more near to my own. Here was something to scare a body. But I couldn't stay there looking, and it warn't now a time to go to Jake's; so I turned off, and, though Clinch was mighty onwilling, I bolted on the road to the fire. I say road, but there was no road; but the trees warn't over-thick, and the land was too poor for undergrowth; so we got on pretty well, considering. But, what with the tire I had had, and the scare I felt, it seemed as if I didn't get for'ad a bit. There was the fire still burning as bright and almost as far off as ever. When I saw this I stopt and looked at Clinch, and he stopped and looked at me, but neither of us had any thing to say. Well, after a moment's thinking, it seemed as if I shouldn't be much of a man to give up when I had got so far, so I pushed on. We crossed more than one little hill, then down and through the hollow, and then up the hill again. At last we got upon a small mountain the Indians called Nolleehatchie, and then it seemed as if the fire had come to a stop, for it was now burning bright, on a little hill below me, and not two hundred yards in front. It was a regular camp fire, pretty big, and there was more than a dozen Indians sitting round it. 'Well,' says I to myself, 'it's come upon us mighty sudden, and what's to be done? Not a soul in the settlement knows it but myself, and nobody's on the watch. They'll be sculped, every human of them, in their very beds, or, moutbe, waken up in the blaze, to be shot with arrows as they run.' I was in a cold sweat to think of it. I didn't know what to think and what to do. I looked round to Clinch, and the strangest thing of all was to see him sitting quiet on his haunches, looking at me, and at the stars, and not at the fire jest before him. Now, Clinch was a famous fine hunting dog, and jest as good on an Indian trail as any other. He know'd my ways, and what I wanted, and would give tongue, or keep it still, jest as I axed him. It was sensible enough, jest then, that he shouldn't bark, but, dang it!—he didn't even seem to see. Now, there warn't a dog in all the settlement so quick and keen to show sense as Clinch, even when he didn't say a word;— and to see him looking as if he didn't know and didn't care what was a-going on, with his eyes sot in his head and glazed over with sleep, was, as I may say, very onnatural, jest at that time, in a dog of any onderstanding. So I looked at him, half angry, and when he saw me looking at him, he jest stretched himself off, put his nose on his legs, and went to sleep in 'arnest. I had half a mind to lay my knife-handle over his head, but I considered better of it, and though it did seem the strangest thing in the world that he shouldn't even try to get to the fire, for warm sake, yet I recollected that dog natur', like human natur', can't stand every thing, and he hadn't such good reason as I had, to know that the Indians were no longer friendly to us. Well, there I stood, a pretty considerable chance, looking, and wondering, and onbeknowing what to do. I was mighty beflustered. But at last I felt ashamed to be so oncertain, and then again it was a needcessity that we should know the worst one time or another, so I determined to push for'ad. I was no slouch of a hunter, as you may suppose; so, as I was nearing the camp, I begun sneaking; and, taking it sometimes on hands and knees, and sometimes flat to the ground, where there was neither tree nor bush to cover me, I went ahead, Clinch keeping close behind me, and not showing any notion of what I was after. It was a slow business, because it was a ticklish business; but I was a leetle too anxious to be altogether so careful as a good sneak ought to be, and I went on rather faster than I would advise any young man to go in a time of war, when the inimy is in the neighbourhood. Well, as I went, there was the fire, getting larger and larger every minute, and there were the Indians round it, getting plainer and plainer. There was so much smoke that there was no making out, at any distance, any but their figures, and these, every now and then, would be so wrapt in the smoke that not more than half of them could be seen at the same moment. At last I stopped, jest at a place where I thought I could make out all that I wanted. There was a sizeable rock before me, and I leaned my elbows on it to look. I reckon I warn't more than thirty yards from the fire. There were some bushes betwixt us, and what with the bushes and the smoke, it was several minutes before I could separate man from man, and see what they were all adoing, and when I did, it was only for a moment at a time, when a puff of smoke would wrap them all, and make it as difficult as ever. But when I did contrive to see clearly, the sight was one to worry me to the core, for, in the midst of the redskins, I could see a white one, and that white one a woman. There was no mistake. There were the Indians, some with their backs, and some with their faces to me; and there, a little a-one side, but still among them, was a woman. When the smoke blowed off, I could see her white face, bright like any star, shining out of the clouds, and looking so pale and ghastly that my blood cruddled in my veins to think lest she might be dead from fright. But it couldn't be so, for she was sitting up and looking about her. But the Indians were motionless. They jest sat or lay as when I first saw them—doing nothing—saying nothing, but jest as motionless as the stone under my elbow. I couldn't stand looking where I was, so I began creeping again, getting nigher and nigher, until it seemed to me as if I ought to be able to read every face. But what with the paint and smoke, I couldn't make out a single Indian. Their figures seemed plain enough in their buffalo-skins and blankets, but their faces seemed always in the dark. But it wasn't so with the woman. I could make her out clearly. She was very young; I reckon not more than fifteen, and it seemed to me as if I knew her looks very well. She was very handsome, and her hair was loosed upon her back. My heart felt strange to see her. I was weak as any child. It seemed as if I could die for the gal, and yet I hadn't strength enough to raise my rifle to my shoulder. The weakness kept on me the more I looked; for every moment seemed to make the poor child more and more dear to me. But the strangest thing of all was to see how motionless was every Indian in the camp. Not a word was spoken—not a limb or finger stirred. There they sat, or lay, round about the fire, like so many effigies, looking at the gal, and she looking at them. I never was in such a fix of fear and weakness in my life. What was I to do? I had got so nigh that I could have stuck my knife, with a jerk, into the heart of any one of the party, yet I hadn't the soul to lift it; and before I knew where I was, I cried like a child. But my crying didn't make 'em look about 'em. It only brought my poor dog Clinch leaping upon me, and whining, as if he wanted to give me consolation. Hardly knowing what I did, I tried to set him upon the camp, but the poor fellow didn't seem to understand me; and in my desperation, for it was a sort of madness growing out of my scare, I jumped headlong for'ad, jest where I saw the party sitting, willing to lose my life rather than suffer from such a strange sort of misery.

CHAPTER IV.

"Will you believe me! there were no Indians, no young woman, no fire! I stood up in the very place where I had seen the blaze and the smoke, and there was nothing! I looked for'ad and about me—there was no sign of fire any where. Where I stood was covered with dry leaves, the same as the rest of the forest. I was stupefied. I was like a man roused out of sleep by a strange dream, and seeing nothing. All was dark and silent. The stars were overhead, but that was all the light I had. I was more scared than ever, and, as it's a good rule when a man feels that he can do nothing himself, to look to the great God who can do every thing, I kneeled down and said my prayers—the second time that night that I had done the same thing, and the second time, I reckon, that I had ever done so in the woods. After that I felt stronger. I felt sure that this sign hadn't been shown to me for nothing; and while I was turning about, looking and thinking to turn on the back track for home, Clinch began to prick up his ears and waken up. I clapped him on his back, and got my knife ready. It might be a *painter* that stirred him, for he could scent that beast a great distance. But, as he showed no fright, only a sort of quickening, I knew there was nothing to fear. In a moment he started off, and went boldly ahead. I followed him, but hadn't gone twenty steps down the hill and into the hollow, when I heard something like a groan. This quickened me, and keeping up with the dog, he led me to the foot of the hollow, where was a sort of pond. Clinch ran right for it, and another groan set me in the same direction. When I got up to the dog, he was on the butt-end of an old tree that had fallen, I reckon, before my time, and was half buried in the water. I jumped on it, and walked a few steps for'ad, when, what should I see but a human, half across the log, with his legs hanging in the water, and his head down. I called Clinch back out of my way, and went to the spot. The groans were pretty constant. I stooped town and laid my hands upon the person, and, as I felt the hair, I knew it was an Indian. The head was clammy with blood, so that my fingers stuck, and when I attempted to turn it, to look at the face, the groan was deeper than ever; but 'twarn't a time to suck one's fingers. I took him up, clapped my shoulders to it, and, fixing my feet firmly on the old tree, which was rather slippery, I brought the poor fellow out without much trouble. Though tall, he was not heavy, and was only a boy of fourteen or fifteen. The wonder was how a lad like that should get into such a fix. Well, I brought him out and laid him on the dry leaves. His groans stopped, and I thought he was dead, but I felt his heart, and it was still warm, and I thought, though I couldn't be sure, there was a beat under my fingers. What to do was the next question. It was now pretty late in the night. I had been all day a-foot, and, though still willing to go, yet the thought of such a weight on my shoulders made me stagger. But 'twouldn't do to leave him where he was to perish. I thought, if so be I had a son in such a fix, what would I think of the stranger who should go home and wait till daylight to give him help! No, darn my splinters, said I,—though I had just done my prayers,—if I leave the lad—and, tightening my girth, I give my whole soul to it, and hoisted him on my shoulders. My cabin, I reckoned, was good three miles off. You can guess what trouble I had, and what a tire under my load, before I got home and laid the poor fellow down by the fire. I then called up Betsy, and we both set to work to see if we could stir up the life that was in him. She cut away his hair, and I washed the blood from his head, which was chopped to the bone, either with a knife or hatchet. It was a God's blessing it hadn't gone into his brain, for it was fairly enough aimed for it, jest above the ear. When we come to open his clothes, we found another wound in his side. This was done with a knife, and, I suppose, was pretty deep. He had lost blood enough, for all his clothes were stiff with it. We knew nothing much of doctoring, but we had some rum in the cabin, and after washing his wounds clean with it, and pouring some down his throat, he began to groan more freely, and by that we knew he was coming to a nateral feeling. We rubbed his body down with warm cloths, and after a little while, seeing that he made some signs, I give him water as much as he could drink. This seemed to do him good, and having done every thing that we thought could help him, we wrapped him up warmly before the fire, and I stretched myself off beside him. 'Twould be a long story to tell, step by step, how he got on. It's enough to say that he didn't die that bout. We got him on his legs in a short time, doing little or nothing for him more than we did at first. The lad was a good lad, though, at first, when he first came to his senses, he was mighty shy, wouldn't look steadily in our faces, and, I do believe, if he could have got out of the cabin, would have done so as soon as he could stagger. But he was too weak to try that, and, meanwhile, when he saw our kindness, he was softened. By little and little, he got to play with my little Lucy, who was not quite six years old; and, after a while, he seemed to be never better pleased than when they played together. The child, too, after her first fright, leaned to the lad, and was jest as willing to play with him as if he had been a cl'ar white like herself. He could say a few words of English from the beginning, and learnt quickly; but, though he talked tolerable free for an Indian, yet I could never get him to tell me how he was wounded, or by whom. His brow blackened when I spoke of it, and his lips would be shut together, as if he was ready to fight sooner than to speak. Well, I didn't push him to know, for I was pretty sure the head of the truth will be sure to come some time or other, if you once have it by the tail, provided you don't jerk it off by straining too hard upon it.

CHAPTER V.

"I suppose the lad had been with us a matter of six weeks, getting better every day, but so slowly that he had not, at the end of that time, been able to leave the picket. Meanwhile, our troubles with the Indians were increasing. As yet, there had been no bloodshed in our quarter, but we heard of murders and sculpings on every side, and we took for granted that we must have our turn. We made our preparations, repaired the pickets, laid in ammunition, and took turns for scouting nightly. At length, the signs of Indians got to be thick in our parts, though we could see none. Jake Ransom had come upon one of their camps after they had left it; and we had reason to apprehend every thing, inasmuch as the outlyers didn't show themselves, as they used to do, but prowled about the cabins and went from place to place, only by night, or by close skulking in the thickets. One evening after this, I went out as usual to go the rounds, taking Clinch with me, but I hadn't got far from the gate, when the dog stopped and gave a low bark;—then I knew there was mischief, so I turned round quietly, without making any show of scare, and got back safely, though not a minute too soon. They trailed me to the gate the moment after I had got it fastened, and were pretty mad, I reckon, when they found their plan had failed for surprising me. But for the keen nose of poor Clinch, with all my skill in scouting,—and it was not small even in that early day,—they'd 'a had me, and all that was mine, before the sun could open his eyes to see what they were after. Finding they had failed in their ambush, they made the woods ring with the war-whoop, which was a sign that they were guine to give us a regular siege. At the sound of the whoop, we could see the eyes of the Indian boy brighten, and his ears prick up, jest like a hound's when he first gets scent of the deer, or hears the horn of the hunter. I looked closely at the lad, and was dub'ous what to do. He moutbe only an enemy in the camp, and while I was fighting in front, he might be cutting the throats of my wife and children within. I did not tell you that I had picked up his bow and arrows near the little lake where I had found him, and his hunting-knife was sticking in his belt when I brought him home. Whether to take these away from him, was the question. Suppose I did, a billet of wood would answer pretty near as well. I thought the matter over while I watched him. Thought runs mighty quick in time of danger! Well, after turning it over on every side, I concluded 'twas better to trust him jest as if he had been a sure friend. I couldn't think, after all we had done for him, that he'd be false, so I said to him—'Lenatewá!'—'twas so he called himself—'those are your people!' 'Yes!' he answered slowly, and lifting himself up as if he had been a lord—he was a stately-looking lad, and carried himself like the son of a Micco,[2] as he was—'Yes, they are the people of Lenatewá—must he go to them?' and he made the motion of going out. But I

---

2. *WGS:* A prince or chief.

stopped him. I was not willing to lose the security which I had from his being a sort of prisoner. 'No,' said I; 'no, Lenatewá, not to-night. To-morrow
will do. To-morrow you can tell them I am a friend, not an enemy, and
they should not come to burn my wigwam.' 'Brother—friend!' said the lad,
advancing with a sort of freedom and taking my hand. He then went to
my wife, and did the same thing,—not regarding she was a woman,—
'Brother—friend!' I watched him closely, watched his eye and his motions,
and I said to Betsy, 'The lad is true; don't be afeard!' But we passed a weary
night. Every now and then we could hear the whoop of the Indians. From
the loop-holes we could see the light of three fires on different sides, by
which we knew that they were prepared to cut off any help that might come
to us from the rest of the settlement. But I didn't give in or despair. I worked
at one thing or another all night, and though Lenatewá gave me no help, yet
he sat quietly, or laid himself down before the fire, as if he had nothing in the
world to do in the business. Next morning by daylight, I found him already
dressed in the same bloody clothes which he had on when I found him. He
had thrown aside all that I gave him, and though the hunting-shirt and leggins which he now wore, were very much stained with blood and dirt, he
had fixed them about him with a good deal of care and neatness, as if preparing to see company. I must tell you that an Indian of good family always has
a nateral sort of grace and dignity which I never saw in a white man. He was
busily engaged looking through one of the loop-holes, and though I could
distinguish nothing, yet it was cl'ar that he saw something to interest him
mightily. I soon found out that, in spite all my watchfulness, he had contrived to have some sort of correspondence and communication with those
outside. This was a wonder to me then, for I did not recollect his bow and
arrows. It seems that he had shot an arrow through one of the loop-holes, to
the end of which he had fastened a tuft of his own hair. The effect of this was
considerable, and to this it was owing that, for a few hours afterwards, we
saw not an Indian. The arrow was shot at the very peep of day. What they
were about, in the meantime, I can only guess, and the guess was only easy,
after I had known all that was to happen. That they were in council what to
do was cl'ar enough. I was not to know that the council was like to end in
cutting some of their own throats instead of ours. But when we did see the
enemy fairly, they came out of the woods in two parties, not actually separated, but not moving together. It seemed as if there was some strife among
them. Their whole number could not be less than forty, and some eight or
ten of these walked apart under the lead of a chief, a stout, dark-looking fellow, one-half of whose face was painted black as midnight, with a red circle
round both his eyes. The other party was headed by an old white-headed
chief, who couldn't ha' been less than sixty years—a pretty fellow, you may

be sure, at his time of life, to be looking after sculps of women and children. While I was kneeling at my loop-hole looking at them, Lenatewá came to me, and touching me on the arm, pointed to the old chief, saying—'Micco Lenatewá Glucco,' by which I guessed he was the father or grandfather of the lad. 'Well,' I said, seeing that the best plan was to get their confidence and friendship if possible,—'Well, lad, go to your father and tell him what Daniel Nelson has done for you, and let's have peace. We can fight, boy, as you see; we have plenty of arms and provisions; and with this rifle, though you may not believe it, I could pick off your father, the king, and that other chief, who has so devilled himself up with paint.' 'Shoot!' said the lad quickly, pointing to the chief of whom I had last spoken. 'Ah! he is your enemy then?' The lad nodded his head, and pointed to the wound on his temple, and that in his side. I now began to see the true state of the case. 'No,' said I; 'no, Lenatewá, I will shoot none. I am for peace. I would do good to the Indians, and be their friend. Go to your father and tell him so. Go, and make him be my friend.' The youth caught my hand, placed it on the top of his head, and exclaimed, 'Good!' I then attended him down to the gate, but, before he left the cabin, he stopped and put his hand on the head of little Lucy,—and I felt glad, for it seemed to say, 'you shan't be hurt—not a hair of your head!' I let him out, fastened up, and then hastened to the loop-hole.

CHAPTER VI.

"And now came a sight to tarrify. As soon as the Indians saw the young prince, they set up a general cry. I couldn't tell whether it was of joy, or what. He went for'ad boldly, though he was still quite weak, and the king at the head of his party advanced to meet him. The other and smaller party, headed by the black chief, whom young Lenatewá had told me to shoot, came forward also, but very slowly, and it seemed as if they were doubtful whether to come or go. Their leader looked pretty much beflustered. But they hadn't time for much study, for, after the young prince had met his father, and a few words had passed between them, I saw the finger of Lenatewá point to the black chief. At this, he lifted up his clenched fists, and worked his body as if he was talking angrily. Then, sudden, the war-whoop sounded from the king's party, and the other troop of Indians began to run, the black chief at their head; but he had not got twenty steps when a dozen arrows went into him, and he tumbled for'a'ds, and grappled with the earth. It was all over with him. His party was scattered on all sides, but were not pursued. It seemed that all the arrows had been aimed at the one person, and when he sprawled, there was an end to it: the whole affair was over in five minutes.

CHAPTER VII.

"It was a fortunate affair for us. Lenatewá soon brought the old Micco to terms of peace. For that matter, he had only consented to take up the red stick because it was reported by the black chief—who was the uncle of the young Micco, and had good reasons for getting him out of the way—that he had been murdered by the whites. This driv' the old man to desperation, and brought him down upon us. When he knew the whole truth, and saw what friends we had been to his son, there was no end to his thanks and promises. He swore to be my friend while the sun shone, while the waters run, and while the mountains stood, and I believe, if the good old man had been spared so long, he would have been true to his oath. But, while he lived, he kept it, and so did his son when he succeeded him as Micco Glucco. Year after year went by, and though there was frequent war between the Indians and the whites, yet Lenatewá kept it from our doors. He himself was at war several times with our people, but never with our settlement. He put his *totem* on our trees, and the Indians knew that they were sacred. But, after a space of eleven years, there was a change. The young prince seemed to have forgotten our friendship. We now never saw him among us, and, unfortunately, some of your young men—the young men of our own settlement—murdered three young warriors of the Ripparee tribe, who were found on horses stolen from us. I was very sorry when I heard it, and began to fear the consequences; and they came upon us when we least looked for it. I had every reason to think that Lenatewá would still keep the warfare from my little family, but I did not remember that he was the prince of a tribe only, and not of the nation. This was a national warfare, in which the whole Cherokee people were in arms. Many persons, living still, remember that terrible war, and how the Carolinians humbled them at last; but there's no telling how much blood was shed in that war, how many sculps taken, how much misery suffered by young and old, men, women, and children. Our settlement had become so large and scattered that we had to build a sizeable blockhouse, which we stored, and to which we could retreat whenever it was necessary. We took possession of it on hearing from our scouts that Indian trails had been seen, and there we put the women and children, under a strong guard. By day we tended our farms, and only went to our families at night. We had kept them in this fix for five weeks or thereabouts, and there was no attack. The Indian signs disappeared, and we all thought the storm had blown over, and began to hope and to believe that the old friendship of Lenatewá had saved us. With this thinking, we began to be less watchful. The men would stay all night at the farms, and sometimes, in the day, would carry with them the women, and sometimes some even the children. I cautioned them agin this, but they mocked me, and said I was gitting old and scary. I told them, 'Wait and see who'll scare first.' But, I confess, not seeing any Indians in all my scouting, I began to feel and think like the rest, and to grow careless. I let Betsy go now and then with me to the farm, though she kept it from me that she had gone there more than once with Lucy, without any man protector. Still, as it was only a short mile and a half from the block, and we could hear of no Indians, it did not seem so venturesome a thing. One day we heard of some very large b'ars among the thickets—a famous range for them, about four miles from the settlement; and a party of us, Simon Lorris, Hugh Darling, Jake Ransom, William Harkless, and myself, taking our dogs, set off on the hunt. We started the b'ar with a rush, and I got the first shot at a mighty big she b'ar, the largest I had ever seen—lamed the critter slightly, and dashed into the thickets after her! The others pushed, in another direction, after the rest, leaving me to finish my work as I could.

"I had two dogs with me, Clap and Claw, but they were young things, and couldn't be trusted much in a close brush with a b'ar. Old Clinch was dead, or he'd ha' made other guess-work with the varmint. But, hot after the b'ar, I didn't think of the quality of the dogs till I found myself in a fair wrestle with the brute. I don't brag, my friends, but that *was* a fight. I tell you my breath was clean gone, for the b'ar had me about the thin of my body, and I thought I was doubled up enough to be laid down without more handling. But my heart was strong when I thought of Betsy and the children, and I got my knife, with hard *jugging*—though I couldn't use my arm above my elbow—through the old critter's hide, and in among her ribs. That only seemed to make her hug closer, and I reckon I was clean gone, if it hadn't been that she blowed out before me. I had worked a pretty deep window in her waist, and then life run out plentiful. Her nose dropped agin my breast, and then her paws; and when the strain was gone, I fell down like a sick child, and she fell on top of me. But she warn't in a humour to do more mischief. She roughed me once or twice more with her paws, but that was only because she was at her last kick. There I lay a matter of half an hour, with the dead b'ar alongside o' me. I was almost as little able to move as she, and I vomited as if I had taken physic. When I come to myself and got up, there was no sound of the hunters. There I was with the two dogs and the b'ar, all alone, and the sun already long past the turn. My horse, which I had fastened outside of the thicket, had slipped his bridle, and, I reckoned, had either strayed off grazing, or had pushed back directly for the block. These things didn't make me feel much better. But, though my stomach didn't feel altogether right, and my ribs were as sore as if I had been sweating uncler a coating of hickory, I felt that there was no use and no time to stand there grunting. But I made out to skin and to cut up the b'ar, and a noble mountain of fat she made. I took the skin with me, and, covering the flesh with bark, I whistled off the dogs, after they had eat to fill, and pushed after my horse. I followed his track for some time, till I grew fairly tired. He had gone off in a scare and at a full gallop, and, instead of going home, had dashed down the lower side of the thicket, then gone aside, to round some of the hills, and thrown himself out of the track, it moutbe seven miles or more. When I found this, I saw there was no use to hunt him that day and afoot, and I had no more to do but turn about, and push as fast as I could for the block. But this was work enough. By this time the sun was pretty low, and there was now a good seven miles, work it how I could, before me. But I was getting over my b'ar-sickness, and though my legs felt weary enough, my stomach was better, and my heart braver; and, as I was in no hurry, having the whole night before me, and knowing the way by night as well as by light, I began to feel cheerful enough, all things considering. I pushed on slowly, stopping every now and then for rest, and recovering my strength this way. I had some parched meal and sugar in my pouch which I ate, and it helped me mightily. It was my only dinner that day. The evening got to be very still. I wondered I had seen and heard nothing of Jake Ransom and the rest, but I didn't feel at all oneasy about them, thinking that, like all other hunters, they would naterally follow the game to any distance. But, jest when I was thinking about them, I heard a gun, then another, and after that all got to be as quiet as ever. I looked to my own rifle and felt for my knife, and put forward a little more briskly. I suppose I had walked an hour after this, when it came on close dark, and I was still four good miles from the block. The night was cloudy, there were no stars, and the feeling in the air was damp and oncomfortable. I began to wish I was safe home, and felt queerish, almost as bad as I did when the b'ar was 'bracing me; but it warn't so much the body-sickness as the heart-sickness. I felt as if something was going wrong. Jest as this feeling was most worrisome, I stumbled over a human. My blood cruddled, when, feeling about, I put my hand on his head, and found the sculp was gone. Then I knew there was mischief. I couldn't make out who 'twas that was under me, but I reckoned 'twas one of the hunters. There was nothing to be done but to push for'ad. I didn't feel any more tire. I felt ready for fight, and when I thought of our wives and children in the block, and what might become of them, I got wolfish, though the Lord only knows what I was minded to do. I can't say I had any raal sensible thoughts of what was to be done in the business. I didn't trust myself to think whether the Indians had been to the block yet or no; though ugly notions came across me when I remembered how we let the women and children go about to the farms. I was in a complete fever and agy. I scorched one time and shivered another, but I pushed on, for there was now no more feeling of tire in my limbs than if they were made of steel. By this time I had reached that long range of hills where I first saw that strange campfire, now eleven years gone, that turned out to be a deception, and it was nateral enough that the thing should come fresh into my mind, jest at that moment. While I was thinking over the wonder, and asking myself, as I had done over and often before, what it possibly could mean, I reached the top of one of the hills, from which I could see, in daylight, the whole country for a matter of ten miles or more on every side. What was my surprise, do you reckon, when there, jest on the very same hill opposite where I had seen that apparition of a camp, I saw another, and this time it was a raal one. There was a rousing blaze, and though the woods and undergrowth were thicker on this than on the other side, from which I had seen it before, yet I could make out that there were several figures, and them Indians. It sort o' made me easier to see the enemy before, and then I could better tell what I had to do. I was to spy out the camp, see what the red-devils were thinking to do, and what they had already done. I was a little better scout and hunter this time than when I made the same sort o' search before, and I reckoned that I could get nigh enough to see all that was going on, without stirring up any dust among 'em. But I had to keep the dogs back. I couldn't tie 'em up, for they'd howl; so I stripped my hunting-shirt and put it down for one to guard, and I gave my cap and horn to another. I knew they'd never leave 'em, for I had l'arned 'em all that sort of business—to watch as well as to fetch and carry. I then said a sort of short running prayer, and took the trail. I had to work for'ad slowly. If I had gone on this time as I did in that first camp transaction, I'd ha' lost my sculp to a sartainty. Well, to shorten a long business, I tell you that I got nigh enough, without scare or surprise, to see all that I cared to see, and a great deal more than I wished to see; and now, for the first time, I saw the meaning of that sight which I had, eleven years before, of the camp that come to nothing. I saw that first sight over again, the Indians round the fire, a young woman in the middle, and that young woman my own daughter, my child, my poor, dear Lucy!

CHAPTER VIII.

"That was a sight for a father. I can't tell you—and I won't try—how I felt. But I lay there, resting upon my hands and knees, jest as if I had been turned into stone with looking. I lay so for a good half hour, I reckon, without stirring a limb; and you could only tell that life was in me, by seeing the big drops that squeezed out of my eyes now and then, and by a sort of shivering that shook me as you sometimes see the canebrake shaking with the gust of the pond inside. I tried to pray to God for help, but I couldn't pray, and as for thinking, that was jest as impossible. But I could do nothing by looking, and, for that matter, it was pretty cla'r to me, as I stood, with no help—by myself—one rifle only and knife—I couldn't do much by moving. I could have lifted the gun, and in a twinkle, tumbled the best fellow in the gang, but what good was that guine to do me? I was never fond of blood-spilling, and if I could have been made sure of my daughter, I'd ha' been willing that the red devils should have had leave to live for ever. What was I to do? Go to the block? Who know'd if it warn't taken, with every soul in it? And where else was I to look for help? Nowhere, nowhere but to God! I groaned—I groaned so loud that I was dreadful 'feared that they'd hear me; but they were too busy among themselves, eating supper, and poor Lucy in the midst, not eating, but so pale, and looking so miserable—jest as I had seen her, when she was only a child—in the same fix, though 'twas only an appearance—eleven years ago! Well, at last, I turned off. As I couldn't say what to do, I was too miserable to look, and I went down to the bottom of the hill and rolled about on the ground, pulling the hair out of my head and groaning, as if that was to do me any good. Before I knew where I was, there was a hand on my shoulder. I jumped up to my feet, and flung my rifle over my head, meaning to bring the butt down upon the stranger—but his voice stopped me.

"'Brother,' said he, 'me Lenatewá!'

"The way he talked, his soft tones, made me know that the young prince meant to be friendly, and I gave him my hand; but the tears gushed out as I did so, and I cried out like a man struck in the very heart, while I pointed to the hill—'My child, my child!'

"'Be man!' said he, 'come!' pulling me away.

"'But, will you save her, Lenatewá?'

"He did not answer instantly, but led me to the little lake, and pointed to the old tree over which I had borne his lifeless body so many years ago. By that I knew he meant to tell me, he had not forgotten what I had done for him; and would do for me all he could. But this did not satisfy me. I must know how and when it was to be done, and what was his hope; for I could see from his caution, and leading me away from the camp, that he did not command the party, and had no power over them. He then asked me, if I had not seen the paint of the warriors in the camp. But I had seen nothing but the fix of my child. He then described the paint to me, which was his way of showing me that the party on the hill were his deadly enemies. The paint about their eyes was that of the great chief, his uncle, who had tried to murder him years ago, and who had been shot, in my sight, by the party of his father. The young chief, now in command of the band on the hill was the son of his uncle, and sworn to revenge the death of his father upon him, Lenatewá. This he made me onderstand in a few minutes. And he gave me farther to onderstand, that there was no way of getting my child from them on less by cunning. He had but two followers with him, and they were even then busy in making preparations. But of these preparations he either would not or could not give me any account; and I had to wait on him with all the patience I could muster; and no easy trial it was, for an Indian is the most cool and slow-moving creature in the world, unless he's actually fighting, and then he's about the quickest. After awhile, Lenatewá led me round the hill. We fetched a pretty smart reach, and before I knew where I was, he led me into a hollow that I had never seen before. Here, to my surprise, there were no less than twelve or fourteen horses fastened, that these red devils had stolen from the settlement that very day, and mine was among them. I did not know it till the young prince told me.

"'Him soon move,' said he, pointing to one on the outside, which a close examination showed me to be my own—'Him soon move,'—and these words gave me a notion of his plan. But he did not allow me to have any hand in it—not jest then, at least. Bidding me keep a watch on the fire above, for the hollow in which we stood was at the foot of the very hill the Indians had made their camp on—though the stretch was a long one between—he pushed for'ad like a shadow, and so slily, so silently, that, though I thought myself a good deal of a scout before, I saw then that I warn't fit to hold a splinter to him. In a little time he had unhitched my horse, and quietly led him farther down the hollow, half round the hill, and then up the opposite hill. There was very little noise, the wind was from the camp, and, though they didn't show any alarm, I was never more scary in my life. I followed Lenatewá, and found where he had fastened my nag. He had placed him several hundred yards from the Indians, on his way to the block; and, where we now stood, owing to the bend of the hollow, the camp of the Indians was between us and where they had hitched the stolen horses. When I saw this, I began to guess something of his plan. Meantime, one after the other, his two followers came up, and made a long report to him in their own language. This done, he told me that three of my hunting companions had been sculped, the other, who was Hugh Darling, had got off cl'ar, though fired upon twice, and had alarmed the block, and that my daughter had been made prisoner at the farm to which she had gone without any company. This made me a little easier, and Lenatewá then told me what he meant to do. In course, I had to do something myself towards it. Off he went, with his two men, leaving me to myself. When I thought they had got pretty fairly round the hill, I started back for the camp, trying my best, you may be sure, to move as slily as Lenatewá. I got within twenty-five yards, I reckon, when I thought it better to lie by quietly and wait. I could see every head in the huddle, and my poor child among them, looking whiter than a sheet, beside their ugly painted skins. Well, I hadn't long to wait, when there was such an uproar among the stolen horses in the hollow on the opposite side of the hill—such a trampling, such a whinnying and whickering, you never heard the like. Now, you must know, that a stolen horse, to an Indian, is jest as precious as a sweetheart to a white man; and when the rumpus reached the camp, there was a rush of every man among them, for his critter. Every redskin, but one, went over the hill after the horses, and he jumped up with the rest, but didn't move off. He stood over poor Lucy with his tomahawk, shaking it above her head, as if guine to strike every minute. She, poor child—I could see her as plain as the fire-light, for she sat jest on one side of it—her hands were clasped together. She was praying, for she must have looked every minute to be knocked on the head. You may depend, I found it very hard to keep in. I was a'most biling over, the more when I saw the red devil making his flourishes, every now and then, close to the child's ears, with his bloody we'pon. But it was a needcessity to keep in till the sounds died off pretty much, so as not to give them any scare this side, till they had dashed ahead pretty far 'pon the other. I don't know that I waited quite as long as I ought to, but I waited as long as my feelings would let me, and then I dropped the sight of my rifle as close as I could fix it on the breast of the Indian that had the keeping of my child. I took aim, but I felt I was a little tremorsome, and I stopped. I know'd I had but one shoot, and if I didn't onbutton him in that one, it would be a bad shoot for poor Lucy. I didn't fear to hit *her*, and I was pretty sure I'd hit him. But it must be a dead shot to do good, for I know'd if I only hurt him, that he'd sink the tomahawk in her head with what strength he had left him. I brought myself to it again, and this time I felt strong. I could jest hear a little of the hubbub of men and horses afar off. I knew it was the time, and, resting the side of the muzzle against a tree, I give him the whole blessing of the bullet. I didn't stop to ask what luck, but run in, with a sort o' cry, to do the finishing with the knife. But the thing was done a'ready. The beast was on his back, and I only had to use the knife in cutting the vines that fastened the child to the sapling behind her. The brave gal didn't scream or faint. She could only say, 'Oh, my father!' and I could only say, 'Oh! my child!' And what a precious hug followed; but it was only for a minute. We had no time to waste in hugging. We pushed at once for the place where I had left the critter, and if the good old nag ever used his four shanks to any purpose, he did that night. I reckon it was a joyful surprise to poor Betsy when we broke into the block. She had given it out for sartin that she'd never see me or the child again, with a nateral sculp on our heads.

CHAPTER IX.

"There's no need to tell you the whole story of this war between our people and the redskins. It's enough that I tell you of what happened to us, and our share in it. Of the great affair, and all the fights and burnings, you'll find enough in the printed books and newspapers. What I tell you, though you can't find it in any books, is jest as true, for all that. Of our share in it, the worst has already been told you. The young chief, Oloschottee—for that was his name—the cousin and the enemy of Lenatewá, had command of the Indians that were to surprise our settlements; and though he didn't altogether do what he expected and intended, he worked us quite enough of mischief as it was. He soon put fire to all our farms to draw us out of the block, but finding that wouldn't do, he left us; for an Indian gets pretty soon tired of a long siege where there is neither rum nor blood to git drunk on. His force was too small to trouble us in the block, and so he drawed off his warriors, and we saw no more of him until the peace. That followed pretty soon after General Middleton gave the nation that licking at Echotee,— a licking, I reckon, that they'll remember long after my day. At that affair Lenatewá got an ugly bullet in his throat, and if it hadn't been for one of his men, he'd ha' got a bag'net in his breast. They made a narrow run with him, head foremost down the hill, with a whole swad of the mounted men from the low country at their heels. It was some time after the peace before he got better of his hurt, though the Indians are naterally more skilful in cures than white men. By this time we had all gone home to our farms, and had planted and rebuilt, and begun to forget our troubles, when who should pop into our cabin one day, but Lenatewá. He had got quite well of his hurts. He was a monstrous fine-looking fellow, tall and handsome, and he was dressed in his very best. He wore pantaloons, like one of us, and his hunting shirt was a raally fine blue, with a white fringe. He wore no paint, and was quite nice and neat with his person. We all received him as an old friend, and he stayed with us three days. Then he went, and was gone for a matter of two weeks, when he came back and stayed with us another three days. And so, off and on, he came to visit us, until Betsy said to me one day, 'Daniel, that Indian, Lenatewá, comes here after Lucy. Leave a woman to guess these things.' After she told me, I recollected that the young prince was quite watchful of Lucy, and would follow her out into the garden, and leave us, to walk with her. But then, again, I thought—'What if he is favourable to my daughter? The fellow's a good fellow; and a raal, noble-hearted Indian, that's sober, is jest as good, to my thinking, as any white man in the land.' But Betsy wouldn't hear to it. 'Her daughter never should marry a savage, and a heathen, and a redskin, while her head was hot':—and while her head was so hot, what was I to do? All I could say was this only, 'Don't kick, Betsy, till you're spurred. 'Twill be time enough to give the young Chief his answer when he asks the question; and it won't do for us to treat him rudely, when we consider how much we owe him.' But she was of the mind that the boot was on the other leg,—that it was he and not us that owed the debt; and all that I could do couldn't keep her from showing the lad a sour face of it whenever he came. But he didn't seem much to mind this, since I was civil and kind to him. Lucy too, though her mother warned her against him, always treated him civilly as I told her; though she naterally would do so, for she couldn't so easily forget that dreadful night when she was a prisoner in the camp of the enemy, not knowing what to expect, with an Indian tomahawk over her head, and saved, in great part, by the cunning and courage of this same Lenatewá. The girl treated him kindly, and I was not sorry she did so. She walked and talked with him jest as if they had been brother and sister, and he was jest as polite to her as if he had been a born Frenchman.

"You may be sure, it was no pleasant sight to my wife to them two go out to walk. 'Daniel Nelson,' said she, 'do you see and keep an eye on those people. There's no knowing what may happen. I do believe that Lucy has a liking for that redskin, and should they run!'—'Psho!' said I,—but that wouldn't do for her, and so she made me watch the young people sure enough. 'Twarn't a business that I was overfond of, you may reckon, but I was a rough man and didn't know much of woman natur'. I left the judgment of such things to my wife, and did pretty much what she told me. Whenever they went out to walk, I followed them, rifle in hand, but it was only to please Betsy, for if I had seen the lad running old with the girl, I'm pretty sure, I'd never ha' been the man to draw trigger upon him. As I said before, Lenatewá was jest as good a husband as she could have had. But, poor fellow, the affair was never to come to that. One day, after he had been with us almost a week, he spoke softly to Lucy, and she got up, got her bonnet and went out with him. I didn't see them when they started, for I happened to be in the upper story,—a place where we didn't so much live, but where we used to go for shelter and defence whenever any Indians came about us. 'Daniel,' said my wife, and I knew by the quickness and sharpness of her voice what 'twas she had to tell me. But jest then I was busy, and, moreover, I didn't altogether like the sort of business upon which she wanted me to go. The sneaking after an enemy, in raal warfare, is an onpleasant sort of thing enough; but this sneaking after one that you think your friend is worse than running in a fair fight, and always gave me a sheepish feeling after it. Besides, I didn't fear Lenatewá, and I didn't fear my daughter. It's true, the girl treated him kindly and sweetly, but that was owing to the nateral sweetness of her temper, and because she felt how much sarvice he had been to her and all of us. So, instead of going out after them, I thought I'd give them a look through one of the loop-holes. Well, there they went, walking among the trees, not far from the picket, and no time out of sight. As I looked at them, I thought to myself 'Would n't they make a handsome couple!' Both of them were tall and well made. As for Lucy, there wasn't, for figure, a finer set girl in all the settlement, and her face was a match for her figure. And then she was so easy in her motion, so graceful, and walked, or sate, or danced,— jest, for all the world, as if she was born only to do the particular thing she was doing. As for Lenatewá, he was a lad among a thousand. Now, a young Indian warrior, when he don't drink, is about the noblest-looking creature, as he carries himself in the woods, that God ever did make. So straight, so proud, so stately, always as if he was doing a great action—as if he knew the whole world was looking at him. Lenatewá was pretty much the handsomest and noblest Indian I had ever seen; and then, I know'd him to be raally so noble. As they walked together, their heads a little bent downwards, and Lucy's pretty low, the thought flashed across me that, jest then, he was telling her all about his feelings; and perhaps, said I to myself, the girl thinks about it pretty much as I do. Moutbe now, she likes him better than any body she has ever seen, and what more nateral? Then I thought, if there is any picture in this life more sweet and beautiful than two young people jest beginning to feel love for one another, and walking together in the innocence of their hearts, under the shady trees,—I've never seen it! I laid the rifle on my lap, and sat down on the floor and watched 'em through the loop until I felt the water in my eyes. They walked backwards and for'ads, not a hundred yards off, and I could see all their motions, though I couldn't hear their words. An Indian don't use his hands much generally, but I could see that Lenatewá was using his,—not a great deal, but as if he felt every word he was saying. Then I began to think, what was I to do, if so be he was raally offering to marry Lucy, and she willing! How was I to do? what was I to say?— how could I refuse him when I was willing? how could I say 'yes,' when Betsy said 'no!'

"Well, in the midst of this thinking, what should I hear but a loud cry from the child, then a loud yell,—a regular war-whoop,—sounded right in front, as if it came from Lenatewá himself. I looked up quickly, for, in thinking, I had lost sight of them, and was only looking at my rifle; I looked out, and there, in the twinkle of an eye, there was another sight. I saw my daughter flat upon the ground, lying like one dead, and Lenatewá staggering back as if he was mortally hurt; while, pressing fast upon him, was an Indian warrior, with his tomahawk uplifted, and striking—once, twice, three times— hard and heavy, right upon the face and forehead of the young prince. From the black paint on his face, and the red ring about his eyes, and from his figure and the eagle feathers in his head, I soon guessed it was Oloschottee and I then knew it was the old revenge for the killing of his father; for an Indian never forgets that sort of obligation. Of course, I didn't stand quiet to see an old friend, like Lenatewá, tumbled in that way, without warning, like a bullock; and there was my own daughter lying flat, and I wasn't to know that he hadn't struck her too. It was only one motion for me to draw sight upon the savage, and another to pull trigger; and I reckon he dropped jest as soon as the young Chief. I gave one whoop for all the world as if I was an Indian myself, and run out to the spot; but Lenatewá had got his discharge from further service. He warn't exactly dead, but his sense was swimming. He couldn't say much, and that warn't at all to the purpose. I could hear him, now and then, making a sort of singing noise, but that was soon swallowed up in a gurgle and a gasp, and it was all over. My bullet was quicker in its working than Oloschottee's hatchet; he was stone dead before I got to him. As for poor Lucy, she was not hurt, either by bullet or hatchet; but she had a hurt in the heart, whether from the scare she had, or because she had more feeling for the young prince than we reckoned, there's no telling. She warn't much given to smiling after that. But, whether she loved Lenatewá, we couldn't know, and I never was the man to ask her. It's sartain she never married, and she had about as many chances, and good ones, too, as any girl in our settlement. You've seen her—some among you—and warn't she a beauty—though I say it myself—the very flower of the forest!"

Lucas de Ayllon: A Historical Nouvellette

(1 8 4 5)

CHAPTER I.

The Snare of the Pirate

Sebastian Cabot is supposed to have been the first European voyager who ever laid eyes upon the low shores of Carolina.[3] He sailed along the coast and looked at it, but did not attempt to land,—nor was such a proceeding necessary to his objects. His single look, according to the laws and morals of that day, in civilized Europe, conferred a sufficient right upon the nation by which he was employed, to all countries which he might discover, and to all people, worshipping at other than Christian altars, by whom they might

---

3. *WGS:* The three chapters which constitute this narrative, originally formed part of a plan which I meditated of dealing with the early histories of the South, somewhat in the manner of Henry Neele, in his Romance of English history. Of course I did not mean to follow slavishly in the track pointed out by him, nor, indeed, would the peculiar and large difference between our respective materials, admit of much similarity of treatment. The reader must understand that the essential facts, as given in these sketches, are all historical, and that he is in *fact* engaged in the perusal of the real adventures of the Spanish voyager, enlivened only by the introduction of persons of whom history says nothing in detail—speaking vaguely, as if but too much her wont, of those whose deficient stature fails to inform or to influence her sympathies. It is the true purpose of fiction to supply her deficiencies, and to correct her judgments. It will be difficult for any chronicler to say of what I have written, more than that he himself knows nothing about it. But his ignorance suggests no good reason why better information should not exist in my possession.

be occupied. The supposed right, however, thus acquired by Cabot, was not then asserted by the English whom he served. It was reserved for another voyager, who, with greater condescension, surveyed the coast and actually set foot upon it. This was Lucas Velasquez de Ayllon, whose adventures in Carolina we propose briefly to relate. Better for him that he had never seen it!—or, seeing it, if he had posted away from its shores for ever. They were the shores of destiny for him. But he was a bad man, and we may reasonably assume that the Just Providence had ordained that his crimes should there meet with that retribution which they were not likely to encounter any where else. Here, if he found paganism, he, at the same time, found hospitality; and here, if he brought cunning, he encountered courage! Fierce valour and generous hospitality were the natural virtues of the Southern Indians.

But we must retrace our steps for a brief period. Some preliminaries, drawn from the history of the times, are first necessary to be understood.— The feebleness of the natives of Hayti, as is well known, so far from making them objects of pity and indulgence in the sight of other Spanish conquerors, had the contrary effect of converting an otherwise brave soldiery into a reckless band of despots, as brutal in their performances as they were unwise in their tyrannies. The miserable Indians sunk under their domination. The blandness of their climate, its delicious fruits, the spontaneous gifts of nature, had rendered them too effeminate for labour and too spiritless for war. Their extermination was threatened; and, as a remedial measure, the benevolent father, Las Casas,—whose humanity stands out conspicuously in contrast with the proverbial cruelty and ferocity of his countrymen,—suggested the policy of making captures of slaves, to take the places of the perishing Haytians, from the Caribbean Islands and from the coasts of Florida. The Hardy savages of these regions, inured to war, and loving it for its very dangers and exercises, were better able to endure the severe tasks which were prescribed by the conquerors. This opened a new branch of business for these bold and reckless adventurers. Predatory incursions were made along the shores of the Gulf, and seldom without profit. In this way one race was made to supersede another, in the delicious country which seems destined never to rear a population suited to its characteristics. The stubborn and sullen Caribbean was made to bend his shoulders to the burden, but did not the less save the feeble Haytian from his doom. The fierce tribes of Apalachia took the place of the delicate limbed native of the Ozama; and, in process of years, the whole southern coasts of North America became tributary, in some degree, to the novel and tyrannical policy which was yet suggested by a spirit of the most genuine benevolence.

The business of slave capture became somewhat more profitable than the fatiguing and protracted search after gold—a search much more full of delusions than of any thing substantial. It agreed better with the hardy valour of those wild adventurers. Many bold knights adopted this new vocation. Among these was one Lucas Velasquez de Ayllon, already mentioned as succeeding Cabot in his discovery of Carolina. He was a stern, cold man, brave enough for the uses to which valour was put in those days; but having the narrow contracted soul of a miser, he was incapable of noble thoughts or generous feelings. The love of gold was the settled passion of his heart, as it was too much the passion of his countrymen. He soon distinguished himself by his forays, and was among the first to introduce his people to a knowledge of Carolina, where they subsequently made themselves notorious by their atrocities. Some time in the year 1520, he set forth, in two ships, on an expedition of this nature. He seems to have been already acquainted with the region. Wending north, he soon found himself in smooth water, and gliding along by numberless pleasant islands, that broke the billows of the sea, and formed frequent and safe harborages along the coasts of the country. Attracted by a spacious opening in the shores, he stood in for a prominent headland, to which he gave the name of Cape St. Helena; a name which is now borne by the contiguous sound. The smoothness of the waters; the placid and serene security of this lovely basin; the rich green of the verdure which encountered the eyes of the adventurers on all sides, beguiled them onward; and they were at length rejoiced at the sight,—more grateful to their desire than any other, as it promised them the spoils which they sought—of numerous groups of natives that thronged the lands-ends at their approach. They cast anchor near the mouth of a river, which, deriving its name from the Queen of the country, is called, to this day, the Combahee.

The natives were a race as unconscious of guile as they were fearless of danger. They are represented to have been of very noble stature; graceful and strong of limb; of bright, dark flashing eyes, and of singularly advanced civilization, since they wore cotton clothes of their own manufacture, and had even made considerable progress in the arts of knitting, spinning and weaving. They had draperies to their places of repose; and some of the more distinguished among their women and warriors, wore thin and flowing fringes, by way of ornament, upon which a free and tasteful disposition of pearls might occasionally be seen. Like many other of the native tribes, they were governed by a queen whose name has already been given. The name of the country they called Chicora, or, more properly, Chiquola.

Unsuspecting as they were brave, the savages surrounded the vessels in their boats, and many of them even swam off from shore to meet them, being quite as expert in the water as upon the land. The wily Spaniard spared no arts to encourage and increase this confidence. Toys and implements of a kind likely to attract the eyes, and catch the affections, of an ignorant people, were studiously held up in sight; and, by little and little, they grew bold enough, at length, to clamber up the sides of the ships, and make their appearance upon the decks. Still, with all their arts, the number of those who came on board was small, compared with those who remained aloof. It was observed by the Spaniards that the persons who forbore to visit them were evidently the persons of highest consequence. Those who came, as constantly withdrew to make their report to others, who either stayed on the land, or hovered in sight, but at a safe distance, in their light canoes. De Ayllon shrewdly conjectured that if he could tempt these more important persons to visit his vessels, the great body of the savages would follow. His object was numbers; and his grasping and calculating soul scanned the crowds which were in sight, and thought of the immense space in his hold, which it was his policy and wish to fill. To bring about his object, he spared none of the customary modes of temptation. Beads and bells were sparingly distributed to those who came and they were instructed by signs and sounds to depart, and return with their companions. To a certain extent, this policy had its effect, but the appetite of the Spaniard was not easily glutted.

He noted, among the hundred canoes that darted about the bay, one that was not only of larger size and better construction than the rest, but which was fitted up with cotton stuffs and fringes like some barge of state. He rightly conjectured that this canoe contained the Cassique or sovereign of the country. The canoe was dug from a single tree, and was more than forty feet in length. It had a sort of canopy of cotton stuff near the stern, beneath which sat several females, one of whom was of majestic demeanour, and seemed to be an object of deference with all the rest. It did not escape the eyes of the Spaniards that her neck was hung with pearls, others were twined about her brows, and gleamed out from the folds of her long glossy black hair, which, streaming down her neck, was seen almost to mingle with the chafing billows of the sound. The men in this vessel were also most evidently of the better order. All of them were clad in fringed cotton stuffs of a superior description to those worn by the gathering multitude. Some of these stuffs were dyed of a bright red and yellow, and plumes, similarly stained, were fastened in many instances to their brows, by narrow strips of coloured fringe, not unfrequently sprinkles artfully with seed pearl.

The eyes of De Ayllon gloated as he beheld this barge, from which he did not once withdraw his glance. But, if he saw the importance of securing this particular prize, he, at the same time, felt the difficulty of such a performance. The Indians seemed not unaware of the special value of this canoe. It was kept aloof, while all the rest ventured boldly alongside the Spanish vessels. A proper jealousy of strangers,—though it does not seem that they had any suspicion of their particular object—restrained the savages. To this natural jealousy, that curiosity which is equally natural to ignorance, was opposed. De Ayllon was too sagacious to despair of the final success of this superior passion. He redoubled his arts. His hawk's bells were made to jingle from the ship's side; tinsel, but bright crosses—the holiest sign in the exercise of his religious faith—were hung in view, abused as lures for the purposes of fraud and violence. No toy, which had ever yet been found potent in Indian traffic, was withheld from sight; and, by little and little, the unconscious arms of the Indian rowers impelled the destined bark nearer and nearer to the artful Spaniards. Still, the approach was slow. The strokes of the rowers were frequently suspended, as if in obedience to orders from their chiefs. A consultation was evidently going on among the inmates of the Indian vessels. Other canoes approached it from the shore. The barge of state was surrounded. It was obvious that the counsellors were averse to the unnecessary exposure of their sovereigns.

It was a moment of anxiety with De Ayllon. There were not twenty Indians remaining on his decks; at one time there had been an hundred. He beheld the hesitation, amounting to seeming apprehension among the people in the canoes; and he now began to reproach himself with that cupidity, which, grasping at too much, had probably lost all. But so long as curiosity hesitates there is hope for cupidity. De Ayllon brought forth other lures: he preferred fraud to fighting.

"Look!" said a princely damsel in the canoe of state, as a cluster of bright mirrors shone burningly in the sunlight. "Look!"—and every eye followed her finger, and every feminine tongue in the vessel grew clamorous for an instant, in its own language, expressing the wonder which was felt at this surpassing display. Still, the canoe hung, suspended on its centre, motionless. The contest was undecided: a long, low discussion was carried on between a small and select number in the little vessel. De Ayllon saw that but from four to five persons engaged in this discussion. One of these, only, was a woman—the majestic but youthful woman, of whom we have already given a brief description. Three others were grave middle-aged men; but the fourth was a tall, bright-eyed savage, who had scarcely reached the term of manhood, with a proud eager aspect, and a form equally combining strength and symmetry. He wore a coronet of eagle feathers, and from his place in the canoe, immediately next that of the queen, it was inferred correctly by the Spanish captain that he was her husband. He spoke earnestly, almost angrily; pointed several times to the ships, whenever the objects of attraction were displayed; and, from his impatient manner, it was very clear that the counsel to which he listened did not correspond with the desires which he felt. But the discussion was soon ended. De Ayllon waved a bright scimitar above his head, and the young chief in the canoe of state started to his feet, with an unrestrainable impulse, and extended his hand for the gift. The brave soul of the young warrior spoke out without control when he beheld the true object of attraction. De Ayllon waved the weapon encouragingly, and bowed his head, as if in compliance with his demand. The young savage uttered a few words to his people, and the paddles were again dipped in water; the bark went forward, and, from the Spanish vessel, a rope was let down to assist the visitors as soon as they were alongside.

The hand of the young chief had already grasped the rope, when the fingers of Combahee, the queen, with an equal mixture of majesty and grace, were laid upon his arm.

"Go not, Chiquola," she said, with a persuasive, entreating glance of her deep, dark eyes. He shook off her hand impatiently, and, running up the sides of the vessel, was already safely on the deck, before he perceived that she was preparing to follow him. He turned upon her, and a brief expostulation seemed to follow from his lips. It appeared as if the young savage was only made conscious of his imprudence, by beholding hers. She answered him with a firmness of manner, a dignity and sweetness so happily blended, that the Spanish officers, who had, by this time, gathered round them, looked on and listened with surprise. The young chief, whom they learned to call by the name of Chiquola—which they soon understood was that of the country, also—appeared dissatisfied, and renewed his expostulations, but with the same effect. At length he waved his hand to the canoe, and, speaking a few words, moved once more to the side of the ship at which she had entered. The woman's eye brightened; she answered with a single word, and hurried in the same direction. De Ayllon, fearing the loss of his victims, now thought it time to interfere. The sword, which had won the eyes of the young warrior at first, was again waved in his sight, while a mirror of the largest size was held before the noble features of the Indian princess. The youth grasped the weapon, and laughed with a delighted but brief chuckle as he looked on the glittering steel, and shook it hurriedly in the air. He seemed to know the use of such an instrument by instinct. In its contemplation, he forgot his own suspicions and that of his people; and no more renewing his suggestions to depart, he spoke to Combahee only of the beauties and the use of the new weapon which had been given to his hands.

The woman seemed altogether a superior person. There was a stern mournfulness about her, which, while it commanded respect, did not impair the symmetry and sweetness of her very intelligent and pleasing features. She had the high forehead of our race, without that accompanying protuberance of the cheek bones, which distinguished hers. Her mouth was very small and sweet, like that which is common to her people. Her eyes were large, deeply set, and dark in the extreme, wearing that pensive earnestness of expression which seems to denote presentiment of many pangs and sorrows. Her form, we have already said, was large and majestical; yet the thick masses of her glossy black hair streamed even to her heels. Superior to her companions, male as well as female, the mirror which had been put into her hands—a glance at which had awakened the most boisterous clamours of delight among her female attendants, all of whom had followed her into the Spanish vessel—was laid down, after a brief examination, with perfect indifference. Her countenance, though not uninformed with curiosity, was full of a most expressive anxiety. She certainly felt the wonder which the others showed, at the manifold strange objects which met their eyes; but this feeling was entertained in a more subdued degree, and did not display itself in the usual language of surprise. She simply seemed to follow the footsteps of Chiquola, without participating in his pleasures, or in that curiosity which made him traverse the ship in every accessible quarter, from stem to stern, seeking all objects of novelty, and passing from one to the other with an appetite which nothing seemed likely soon to satiate.

Meanwhile, the example set by their Queen, the Cassiques, the Iawas, or Priests, and other headmen of the Nation, was soon followed by the common people; and De Ayllon had the satisfaction, on exchanging signals with his consort, to find that both ships were crowded with quite as many persons as they could possibly carry. The vessel under his immediate command was scarcely manageable from the multitudes which thronged her decks, and impeded, in a great measure, all the operations of the crew. He devised a remedy for this evil, and, at the same time, a measure very well calculated to give complete effect to his plans. Refreshments were provided in the hold; wines in abundance; and the trooping savages were invited into that gloomy region, which a timely precaution had rendered more cheerful in appearance by the introduction of numerous lights. A similar arrangement conducted the more honourable guests into the cabin, and a free use of the intoxicating beverages, on the part of the great body of the Indians, soon rendered easy all the remaining labours of the wily Spaniard. The hatches were suddenly closed when the hold was most crowded, and two hundred of the unconscious and half stupid savages were thus entrapped for the slave market of the City of Columbus.

In the cabin the same transaction was marked by some distinguishing differences. The wily De Ayllon paid every attention to his guests. A natural homage was felt to be the due of royalty and rank, even among a race of savages; and this sentiment was enforced by the obvious necessity of pursuing that course of conduct which would induce the confidence of persons who had already shown themselves so suspicious. De Ayllon, with his officers, himself attended Chiquola and the Queen. The former needed no persuasion. He freely seated himself on the cushions of the cabin, and drank of the proffered wines, till his eyes danced with delight, his blood tingled, and his speech, always fee, became garrulity, to the great annoyance of Combahee. She had followed him with evident reluctance into the interior of the vessel; and now, seated with the rest, within the cabin, she watched the proceedings with a painful degree of interest and dissatisfaction, increasing momently as she beheld the increasing effect upon him of the wine which he had taken. She herself utterly declined the proffered liquor; holding herself aloof with as much natural dignity as could have been displayed by the most polished princess of Europe. Her disquiet had made itself understood by her impatience of manner, and by frequent observations in her own language, to Chiquola. These, of course, could be understood only by themselves and their attendants. But the Spaniards were at no loss to divine the purport of her speech from her tones, the expression of her face, and the quick significant movements of her hands.

At length she succeeded in impressing her desires upon Chiquola, and he rose to depart. But the Spaniards had no intention to suffer this. The plot was now ready for execution. The signal had been made. The entrance to the cabin was closed, and a single bold and decisive movement was alone necessary to end the game. De Ayllon had taken care silently to introduce several stout soldiers into the cabin, and these, when Chiquola took a step forward, sprang upon him and his few male companions and bore them to the floor. Chiquola struggled with a manful courage, which, equally with their forests, was the inheritance of the American Indians; but the conflict was too unequal, and it did not remain doubtful very long. De Ayllon saw that he was secure, and turned, with an air of courteous constraint, to the spot where Combahee stood. He approached her with a smile upon his countenance and with extended arms; but she bestowed upon him a single glance; and, in a mute survey, took in the entire extent of her misfortune. The whole proceeding had been the work of an instant only. That she was taken by surprise, as well as Chiquola, was sufficiently clear; but her suspicions had never been wholly quieted, and the degree of surprise which she felt did not long deprive her of her energies. If her eye betrayed the startled apprehension of the fawn of her native forests, it equally expressed the fierce indignation which flames in that of their tameless eagle. She did not speak as De Ayllon approached; and when, smiling, he pointed to the condition of Chiquola, and with extended arms seemed to indicate to her the hopelessness of any effort at escape, she hissed at him, in reply, with the keen defiance of the angry coppersnake. He advanced—his hand was stretched forth towards her person—when she drew up her queenly form to its fullest height; and, with a single word hurriedly spoken to the still struggling Chiquola, she turned, and when De Ayllon looked only to receive her submission, plunged suddenly through the stern windows of the cabin, and buried herself in the deep waters of the sea.

CHAPTER II.

Chiquola, the Captive.

"Now mounts he the ocean wave, banished, forlorn,
Like a limb from his country cast bleeding and torn."
Campbell.

The flight of Combahee, and her descent into the waters of the bay, were ominous of uproar. Instantly, the cry of rage arose from a thousand voices. The whole body of the people, as with a common instinct, seemed at once to comprehend the national calamity. A dozen canoes shot forth from every quarter, with the rapidity of arrows in their flight, to the rescue of the Queen. Like a bright mermaid, swimming at evening for her own green island, she now appeared, beating with familiar skill the swelling waters, and, with practiced hands, throwing behind her their impelling billows. Her long, glossy, black hair was spread out upon the surface of the deep, like some veil of network meant to conceal from immodest glances the feminine form below. From the window of the cabin whence she disappeared, De Ayllon beheld her progress, and looked upon the scene with such admiration as was within the nature of a soul so mercenary. He saw the fearless courage of the man in all her movements, and never did Spaniard behold such exquisite artifice in swimming on the part of any of his race. She was already in safety. She had ascended, and taken her seat in one of the canoes, a dozen contending, in loyal rivalry, for the privilege of receiving her person.

Then rose the cry of war! Then sounded that fearful whoop of hate, and rage, and defiance, the very echoes of which have made many a faint heart tremble since that day. It was probably, on this occasion, that the European, for the first time, listened to this terrible cry of war and vengeance. At the signal, the canoes upon the bay scattered themselves to surround the ships; the warriors along the shore loosened the fasts of the boats, and pushed off to join the conflict; while the hunter in the forests, stopped sudden in the eager chase, sped onward, with all the feeling of coercive duty, in the direction of those summoning sounds.

The fearless Combahee, with soul on fire, led the van. She stood erect in her canoe. Her form might be seen from ever part of the bay. The hair still streamed, unbound and dripping, from her shoulders. In her left hand she grasped a bow such as would task the ability of the strong man in our day. Her right hand was extended, as if in denunciation towards that

"—fatal bark
Built in the eclipse and rigged with curses dark,"

in which her husband and her people were held captive. Truly, hers was the form and the attitude for a high souled painter;—one, the master of the dramatic branches of his art. The flashing of her eye was a voice to her warriors;—the waving of her hand was a summons that the loyal and the brave heart sprang eager to obey! A shrill signal issued from her half parted lips, and the now numerous canoes scattered themselves on every side as if to surround the European enemy, or, at least, to make the assault on both vessels simultaneous.

The Spaniard beheld, as if by magic, the whole bay covered with boats. The light canoes were soon launched from the shore, and they shot forth from its thousand indentations as fast as the warriors poured down from the interior. Each of these warriors came armed with the bow, and a well filled quiver of arrows. These were formed from the long canes of the adjacent swamps; shafts equally tenacious and elastic, feathered with plumes from the eagle or the stork, and headed with triangular barbs of flint, broad but sharp, of which each Indian had always a plentiful supply. The vigour with which these arrows were impelled from the string was such, that, without the escaupil or cotton armour which the Spaniards generally wore, the shaft has been known to pass clean through the body of the victim. Thus armed and arranged, with numbers constantly increasing, the people of Combahee, gathering at her summons, darted boldly from shore, and, taking up positions favourable to the attack, awaited only the signal to begin.

Meanwhile, the Spanish ships began to spread forth their broad wings for flight. Anticipating some such condition of things as the present, the wily De Ayllon had made his preparations for departure at the same time that he had planned the scheme for his successful treachery. The one movement was devised to follow immediately upon the footsteps of the other. His sails were loosened and flapping in the wind. To trim them for the breeze, which, though light, was yet favourable to his departure, was the work of a moment only; and ere the word was given for the attack, on the part of the Indians, the hue fabrics of the Spaniards began to move slowly through the subject waters. Then followed the signal. First came a shaft from Combahee herself; well aimed and launched with no mean vigour; that, striking full on the bosom of De Ayllon, would have proved fatal but for the plate mail which was hidden beneath his coat of buff. A wild whoop succeeded, and the air was instantly clouded by the close flight of the Indian arrows. Nothing could have been more decided, more prompt and rapid, than this assault. The shaft had scarcely been dismissed from the string before another supplied its place; and however superior might have been the armament of the Spanish captain, however unequal the conflict from the greater size of his vessels, and the bulwarks which necessarily gave a certain degree of protection, it was a moment of no inconsiderable anxiety to the kidnappers! De Ayllon, though a base, was not a bloody-minded man. His object was spoil, not slaughter. Though his men had their firelocks in readiness, and a few pieces of cannon were already prepared and pointed, yet he hesitated to give the word, which should hurry into eternity so many ignorant fellow beings upon whom he had just inflicted so shameful an injury. He commanded his men to cover themselves behind the bulwarks, unless where the management of the ships required their unavoidable exposure, and, in such cases, the persons employed were provided with the cotton armour which had been usually found an adequate protection against arrows shot by the feebly hands of the Indians of the Lucayos.

But the vigorous savages of Combahee were a very different race. They belonged to the great family of the Muscoghees; the parent stock, without question, of those indomitable tribes which under the names of Yemassee, Stono, Muscoghee, Mickasukee, and Seminole, have made themselves remembered and feared through successive years of European experience, without having been entirely quelled or quieted to the present hour. It was soon found by De Ayllon that the escaupil was no protection against injury. It baffled the force of the shaft but could not blunt it, and one of the inferior officers, standing by the side of the commander, was pierced through his cotton gorget. The arrow penetrated his throat, and he fell, to all appearance, mortally wounded. The Indians beheld his fall. They saw the confusion that the event seemed to inspire, and their delight was manifested in a renewed shout of hostility, mingled with screams, which denoted, as clearly as language, the delight of savage triumph. Still, De Ayllon forbore to use the destructive weapons which he had in readiness. His soldiers murmured; but he answered them by pointing to the hold, and asking:

"Shall we cut our own throats in cutting theirs? I see not present enemies but future slaves in all these assailants."

It was not mercy but policy that dictated his forbearance. But it was necessary that something should be done in order to baffle and throw off the Indians. The breeze was too light and baffling, and the movements of the vessels too slow to avoid them. The light barks of the assailants, impelled by vigorous arms, in such smooth water, easily kept pace with the progress of the ships. Their cries of insult and hostility increased. Their arrows were shot,

without cessation, at every point at which an enemy was supposed to harbour himself; and, under the circumstances, it was not possible always to
take advantage of a cover in performing the necessary duties which accrued
to the seamen of the ships. The Indians had not yet heard the sound of European cannon. De Ayllon resolved to intimidate them. A small piece such as
in that day was employed for the defence of castles, called a falconet, was elevated above the canoes, so that the shot, passing over the heads of their inmates, might take effect upon the woods along the shore. As the sudden and
sullen roar of this unexpected thunder was heard, every Indian sunk upon his
knees; every paddle was dropped motionless in the water; while the uplifted
bow fell from the half-paralyzed hands of the warrior, and he paused, uncertain of safety, but incapable of flight. The effect was great, but momentary
only. To a truly brave people, there is nothing more transient than the influence of panic. When the Indian warriors looked up, they beheld one of their
people still erect—unalarmed by the strange thunder—still looking the
language,—still acting the part of defiance,—and, oh! shame to their manhood, this person was their Queen. Instead of fear, the expression upon her
countenance was that of scorn. They took fire at the expression. Every heart
gathered new warmth at the blaze shining from her eyes. Besides, they discovered that they were unharmed. The thunder was a mere sound. They had
not seen the bolt. This discovery not only relieved their fears but heightened
their audacity. Again they moved forward. Again the dart was clapt upon the
string. Singing one chorus, the burden of which, in our language, would be
equivalent to a summons to a feast of vultures, they again set their canoes
in motion; and now, not as before, simply content to get within arrow
distance, they boldly pressed forward upon the very course of the ships; behind, before, and on every side, sending their arrows through every opening, and distinguishing, by their formidable aim, every living object which
came in sight. Their skill in the management of their canoes; in swimming;
their great strength and agility, prompted them to a thousand acts of daring;
and some were found bold enough to attempt, while leaping from their
boats, beneath the very prow of the slowly advancing vessels, to grasp the
swinging ropes and thus elevate themselves to individual conflict with their
enemies. These failed, it is true, and sank into the waters; but such an event
implied no sort of risk to these fearless warriors. They were soon picked up
by their comrades, only to renew, in this or in other forms, their gallant but
unsuccessful efforts.

But these efforts might yet be successful. Ships in those days were not the
monstrous places which they are in ours. An agile form, under favouring circumstances, might easily clamber up their sides; and such was the equal activity and daring of the savages, as to make it apparent to De Ayllon that it

would need something more decisive than had yet been done, on his part, to shake himself free from their inveterate hostility. At a moment when their fury was redoubled and increased by the impunity which had attended their previous assaults—when every bow was uplifted and every arrow pointed under the eye of their Queen, as if for a full application of all their strength, and skill and courage;—her voice, now loud in frequent speech, inciting them to a last and crowning effort; and she herself, erect in her bark as before, and within less than thirty yards of the Spanish vessel;—at this moment, and to avert the storm of arrows which threatened his seamen who were then, perforce, busy with the rigging in consequence of a sudden change of wind;—De Ayllon gave a signal to bring Chiquola from below. Struggling between two Spanish officers, his arms pinioned at the elbows, the young Cassique was dragged forward to the side of the vessel and presented to the eyes of his Queen and people, threatened with the edge of the very weapon which had beguiled him to the perfidious bark.

A hollow groan arose on every hand. The points of the uplifted arrows were dropped; and, for the first time, the proud spirit passed out of the eyes of Combahee, and her head sunk forward, with an air of hopeless self-abandonment, upon her breast! A deep silence followed, broken only by the voice of Chiquola. What he said, was, of course, not understood by his captors; but they could not mistake the import of his action. Thrice, while he spoke to his people, did his hand, wresting to the utmost the cords upon his arms, smite his heart, imploring, as it were, the united arrows of his people to this conspicuous mark. But the Amazon had not courage for this. She was speechless! Every eye was turned upon her, but there was no answering response in hers; and the ships of the Spaniard proceeded on their was to the sea with a momently increasing rapidity. Still, though no longer assailing, the canoes followed close, and kept up the same relative distance between themselves and enemies, which had been observed before. Combahee now felt all her feebleness, and as the winds increased, and the waves of the bay feeling the more immediate influence of the ocean, rose into long heavy swells, the complete conviction of her whole calamity seemed to rush upon her soul. Chiquola had now been withdrawn from sight. His eager adjurations to his Queen and people, might, it was feared, prompt them to that Roman sort of sacrifice which the captive himself seemed to implore; and perceiving that the savages had suspended the assault, De Ayllon commanded his removal. But, with his disappearance, the courage of his Queen revived. Once more she gave the signal for attack in a discharge of arrows; and once more the captive was set before their eyes, with the naked sword above his head, *in terrorem,* as before. The same effect ensued. The arm of hostility hung suspended and paralyzed. The cry of anguish which the cruel spectacle extorted from the bosom of Combahee, was echoed by that of the multitude; and without a purpose or a hope, the canoes hovered around the course of the retreating ships, till the broad Atlantic, with all its mighty billows, received them.—The vigorous breath of the increasing wind, soon enabled them to shake off their hopeless pursuers. Ye still the devoted savages plied their un-remitting paddles; the poor Queen straining her eyes along the waste, until, in the grey of twilight and of distance the vessels of the robbers were com-pletely hidden from her sight.

Meanwhile, Chiquola was hurried back to the cabin, with his arms still pinioned. His feet were also fastened and a close watch was put upon him. It was a courtesy which the Spaniards considered due to his legitimacy that the cabin was made his place of imprisonment. With his withdrawal from the presence of his people, his voice, his eagerness and animation, all at once ceased. He sunk down on the cushion with the sullen, stolid indifference which distinguishes his people in all embarrassing situations. A rigid immo-bility settled upon his features; yet De Ayllon did not fail to perceive that when he or any of his officers approached the captive, his eyes gleamed upon them with the fury of his native panther;—gleamed bright, with irregular flashes, beneath his thick black eye-brows, which gloomed heavily over their arches with the collected energies of a wild and stubborn soul.

"He is dangerous," said De Ayllon, "be careful how you approach him."

But though avoided he was not neglected. De Ayllon himself proffered him food; not forgetting to tender him a draught of that potent beverage by which he had been partly overcome before. But the sense of wrong was up-permost, and completely subdued the feeling of appetite. He regarded the proffer of the Spaniard with a keen, but composed look of ineffable disdain; never lifted his hand to receive the draught, and beheld it set down within his reach without indicating, by word or look, his consciousness of what had been done. Some hours had elapsed and the wine and food remained un-touched. His captor still consoled himself with the idea that hunger would subdue his stubbornness;—but when the morning came, and the noon of the next day, and the young savage still refused to eat or drink, the case became serious; and the mercenary Spaniard began to apprehend that he should lose one of the most valuable of his captives. He approached the youth and by signs expostulated with him upon his rejection of the food; but he received no satisfaction. The Indian remained inflexible, and but a single glance of his large, bright eye, requited De Ayllon for his selfish considera-tion. That look expressed the hunger and thirst which in no other way did Chiquola deign to acknowledge; but that hunger and thirst were not for food but for blood;—revenge, the atonement for his wrongs and shame. Never had the free limbs of Indian warrior known such an indignity—never could indignity have been conceived less endurable. No words can describe, as no mind can imagine, the volume of tumultuous strife, and fiercer, maddening thoughts and feelings, boiling and burning in the brain and bosom of the gallant but inconsiderate youth;—thoughts and feelings so strangely subdued, so completely hidden in those composed muscles,—only speaking through that dilating, but fixed, keen, inveterate eye!

De Ayllon was perplexed. The remaining captives gave him little or no trouble. Plied with the liquors which had seduced them at first, they were very generally in that state of drunkenness, when a certainty of continued supply reconciles the degraded mind very readily to any condition. But with Chiquola the case was very different. Here, at least, was character—the pride of self-dependence; the feeling of moral responsibility; the ineradicable consciousness of that shame which prefers to feel itself and not to be blinded. De Ayllon had known the savage nature only under its feebler and meaner aspects. The timid islanders of the Lucayos—the spiritless and simple natives of Hayti—were of quite another class. The Indian of the North American continent, whatever his vices or his weaknesses, was yet a man. He was more. He was a conqueror—accustomed to conquer! It was his boast that where he came he stood; where he stood he remained; and where he remained, he was the only man! The people whom he found were women. He made them and kept them so.—

> "Severe the school that made them bear
> The ills of life without a tear;
> And stern the doctrine that denied
> The sachem fame, the warrior pride,
> Who, urged by nature's wants, confess'd
> The need that hunger'd in his breast:—
> Or, when beneath his foeman's knife,
> Who utter'd recreant prayer for life;—
> Or, in the chase, whose strength was spent,
> Or, in the fight, whose knee was bent;
> Or, when with tale of coming fight,
> Who sought his allies' camp by night,
> And, ere the missives well were told,
> Complain'd of hunger, wet and cold!—
> A woman, if in strife, his foe,
> Could give, yet not receive, a blow;—
> Or if, undextrously and dull,
> His hand and knife should fail to win
> The dripping warm scalp from the skull
> To trim his yellow mocasin!"

Such was the character of his race, and Chiquola was no recreant. Such was his character. He had no complaint. He looked no emotions. The marble could not have seemed less corrigible; and, but for that occasional flashing from his dark eye, whenever any of his captors drew near to the spot where he sat, none would have fancied that in his bosom lurked a single feeling of hostility or discontent. Still he ate not and drank not. It was obvious to the Spaniard that he had adopted the stern resolution to forbear all sustenance, and thus defeat the malice of his enemies. He had no fear of death, and he could not endure bonds. That he would maintain that resolution to the last, none could doubt who watched his sullen immobility—who noted the fact that he spoke nothing, neither in the language of entreaty nor complaint. He was resolved on suicide! It is an error to suppose, as has been asserted, that the Indians never commit suicide. The crime is a very common one among them in periods of great national calamity. The Cherokee warrior frequently destroyed himself when the small pox had disfigured his visage: for, it must be remembered, that an Indian warrior is, of all human beings, one of the vainest, on the score of his personal appearance. He unites, as they are usually found united even in the highest states of civilization, the strange extremes of ferocity and frivolity.

De Ayllon counselled with his officers as to what should be done with their captive. He would certainly die on their hands. Balthazar de Morla, his lieutenant—a stern fierce savage himself—proposed that they should kill him, as a way of shortening their trouble, and dismissing all farther cares upon the project.

"He is but one," said he, "and though you may call him King or Cassique, he will sell for no more than any one of his own tribe in the markets of Isabella. At worst, it will only be a loss to him, for the fellow is resolved to die. He will bring you nothing unless for the skin of his carcase, and that is not a large one."

A young officer of more humanity, Jaques Carazon, offered different counsel. He recommended that the poor Indian be taken on deck. The confinement in the cabin he thought had sickened him. The fresh air, and the sight of the sky and sea, might work a change and provoke in him a love of life. Reasoning from the European nature, such advice would most probably have realized the desired effect; and De Ayllon was struck with it.

"Let it be done," he said; and Chiquola was accordingly brought up from below, and placed on the quarter deck in a pleasant and elevated situation. At first, the effect promised to be such as the young officer had suggested. There was a sudden looking up, in all the features of the captive. His eyes were no longer cast down; and a smile seemed to pass over the lips which, of late, had been so rigidly compressed. He looked long, and with a keen expression of interest at the sky above, and the long stretch of water before and around him. But there was one object of most interest, upon which his eyes fastened with a seeming satisfaction. This was the land. The low sandy shores and island slips that skirt the Georgia coast, then known under the general name of Florida, lay on the right. The gentleness of the breeze, and smoothness of the water, enabled the ships, which were of light burthen, to pursue a course along with the land, at a small distance, varying from five to ten miles. Long and earnestly did the captive gaze upon this, to him, Elysian tract. There dwelt tribes, he well knew, which were kindred to his people. From any one of the thousand specks of shore which caught his eye, he could easily find his way back to his queen and country! What thoughts of bliss and wo, at the same moment, did these two images suggest to his struggling and agonized spirit. Suddenly, he caught the eyes of the Spanish Captain gazing upon him, with a fixed, inquiring glance; and his own eyes were instantly averted from those objects which he alone desired to see. It would seem as if he fancied that the Spaniard was able to look into his soul. His form grew more erect beneath the scrutiny of his captor, and his countenance once more put on its former expression of immobility.

De Ayllon approached, followed by a boy bringing fresh food and wine, which were once more placed within his reach. By signs, the Spaniard encouraged him to eat. The Indian returned him not the slightest glance of recognition. His eye alone spoke, and its language was still that of hate and defiance. De Ayllon left him, and commanded that none should approach or seem to observe him. He conjectured that his stubbornness derived something of its stimulus from the consciousness that eyes of strange curiosity were fixed upon him, and that Nature would assert her claims if this artificial feeling were suffered to subside without farther provocation.

But when three hours more had elapsed, and the food still remained untouched, De Ayllon was in despair. He approached Chiquola, attended by the fierce Balthazar de Morla.

"Why do you not eat, savage!" exclaimed this person, shaking his hand threateningly at the Indian, and glancing upon him with the eyes of one, only waiting and anxious for the signal to strike and slay. If the captive failed to understand the language of the Spaniard, that of his looks and action was in no wise unequivocal. Chiquola gave him glance for glance. His eye lighted up with those angry fires which it shed when going into battle; and it was sufficiently clear to both observers, that nothing more was needed than the freedom of hand and foot to have brought the unarmed but unbending savage, into the death grapple with his insulting enemy. The unsubdued tiger-like expression of the warrior, was rather increased than subdued by famine; and even De Ayllon recoiled from a look which made him momentarily forgetful of the cords which fastened the limbs and rendered impotent the anger of his captive. He reproved Balthazar for his violence, and commanded him to retire. Then, speaking gently, he endeavoured to soothe the irritated

Indian, by kind tones and persuasive action. He pointed to the food, and, by signs, endeavoured to convey to his mind the idea of the painful death which must follow his wilful abstinence much longer. For a few moments Chiquola gave no heed to these suggestions, but looking round once more to the strip of shore which lay upon his right, a sudden change passed over his features. He turned to De Ayllon, and muttering a few words in his own language, nodded his head, while his fingers pointed to the ligatures around his elbows and ancles. The action clearly denoted a willingness to take his food, provided his limbs were set free. De Ayllon proceeded to consult with his officers upon this suggestion. The elder, Balthazar de Morla, opposed the indulgence.

"He will attack you the moment he is free."

"But," replied the younger officer, by whose counsel he had already been brought upon the deck—"but of what avail would be his attack? We are armed, and he is weaponless. We are many, and he is but one. It only needs that we should be watchful, and keep in readiness."

"Well!" said Balthazar, with a sneer, "I trust that you will be permitted the privilege of undoing his bonds; for if ever savage had the devil in his eye, this savage has."

"I will do it," replied the young man, calmly, without seeming to heed the sneer. "I do not fear the savage, even if he should grapple with me. But I scarcely think it possible that he would attempt such a measure. He has evidently too much sense for that."

"Desperate men have no sense!" said the other; but the counsels of the younger officer prevailed with De Ayllon, and he was commissioned to undo the bonds of the captive. At the same time every precaution was taken, that the prisoner, when set free, should do the young man no hurt. Several soldiers were stationed at hand, to interpose in the event of danger, and De Ayllon and Balthazar, both with drawn swords, stood beside Jaques Carazon as he bent down on one knee to perform the duty of supposed danger which had been assigned him. But their apprehensions of assault proved groundless. Whether it was the Chiquola really entertained no design of mischief, or that he was restrained by prudence, on seeing the formidable preparations which had been made to baffle and punish any such attempt, he remained perfectly quiescent, and, even after his limbs had been freed, showed no disposition to use them.

"Eat!" said De Ayllon, pointing to the food. The captive looked at him in silence, but the food remained untouched.

"His pride keeps him from it," said De Ayllon. "He will not eat so long as we are looking on him. Let us withdraw to some little distance and watch him."

His orders were obeyed. The soldiers were despatched to another quarter of the vessel, though still commanded to remain under arms. De Ayllon with his two officers then withdrew, concealing themselves in different situations where they might observe all the movements of the captive. For a time, this arrangement promised to be as little productive of fruits as the previous ones. Chiquola remained immovable, and the food untouched. But, after a while, when he perceived that none was immediately near, his crouching form might be seen in motion, but so slightly, so slily, that it was scarcely perceptible to those who watched him. His head revolved slowly, and his neck turned, without any corresponding movement of his limbs, until he was able to take in all objects, which he might possibly see, on almost every part of the deck. The man at the helm, the sailor on the yard, while beholding him, scarcely saw the cat-like movement of his eyes. These, when he had concluded his unobtrusive examination of the vessel, were turned upon the shore, with the expression of an eager joy. His heart spoke out its feelings in the flashing of his dilating and kindled eyes. He was free. That was the feeling of his soul! That was the feeling which found utterance in his glance. The degrading cords were no longer on the limbs of the warrior, and was not his home almost beneath his eyes? He started to his feet erect. He looked around him; spurned the food and the wine cup from his path, and shrieking the war whoop of his tribe, with a single rush and bound, he plunged over the sides of the vessel into those blue waters which dye, with the complexion of the Gulf, the less beautiful waves of the Atlantic.

This movement, so unexpected by the captors, was quite too sudden for them to prevent. De Ayllon hurried to the side of his vessel as soon as he distinguished the proceeding. He beheld, with mingled feelings of admiration and disappointment, where the bold savage was buffeting the billows in the vain hope of reaching the distant shores. A boat was instantly let down into the sea, manned with the ablest seamen of the ship. It was very clear that Chiquola could neither make the land, nor contend very long with the powerful waters of the deep. This would have been a task beyond the powers of the strongest man, and the most skilful swimmer, and the brave captive had been without food more than twenty-four hours. Still he could be seen, striving vigorously in a course straight as an arrow for the shore; rising from billow to billow; now submerged, still ascending, and apparently without any diminution of the vigour with which he began his toils.

The rowers, meanwhile, plied their oars, with becoming energy. The Indian, though a practiced swimmer, began, at length, to show signs of exhaustion. He was seen from the ship, and with the aid of a glass, was observed to be struggling feebly. The boat was gaining rapidly upon him. He might be saved. It needed only that he should will it so. Would he but turn and employ his remaining strength in striving for the boat, instead of wasting it in an idle effort for those shores which he could never more hope to see!

"He turns!" cried De Ayllon. "He will yet be saved. The boat will reach him soon. A few strokes more, and they are up with him!"

"He turns, indeed," said Carazon, "but it is to wave his hand in defiance."

"They reach him—they are up with him!" exclaimed the former.

"Ay!" answered the latter, "but he sinks—he has gone down."

"No! they have taken him into the boat!"

"You mistake, sir, do you not see where he rises? almost a ship's length on the right of the boat. There spoke the savage soul. He will not be saved!"

This was true. Chiquola preferred death to bondage. The boat changed its course with that of the swimmer. Once more it neared him. Once more the hope of De Ayllon was excited as he beheld the scene from the ship; and once more the voice of his lieutenant cried discouragingly—

"He has gone down, and for ever. He will not suffer us to save him."

This time he spoke truly. The captive had disappeared. The boat, returning now, alone appeared above the waters, and De Ayllon turned away from the scene, wondering much at the indomitable spirit and fearless courage of the savage, but thinking much more seriously of the large number of pesos which this transaction had cost him. It was destined to cost him more, but of this hereafter.

CHAPTER III.

Combahee; or, The Last Voyage of Lucas de Ayllon.

> "—Bind him, I say;
> Make every artery and sinew crack;
> The slave that makes him give the loudest shriek,
> Shall have ten thousand drachmas! Wretch! I'll force thee
> To curse the Pow'r thou worship'st."
> Massinger—*The Virgin Martyr*.

But the losses of De Ayllon were not to end with the death of his noble captive, the unfortunate Chiquola. We are told by the historian, that "one of his vessels foundered before he reached his port, and captors and captives were swallowed up in the sea together. His own vessel survived, but many of his captives sickened and died; and he himself was reserved for the time, only to suffer a more terrible form of punishment. Though he had lost more than half of the ill-gotten fruits of his expedition, the profits which remained were still such as to encourage him to a renewal of his enterprise. To this he devoted his whole fortune, and, with three large vessels and many hundred men, he once more descended upon the coast of Carolina."

Meanwhile, the dreary destiny of Combahee was to live alone. We have heard so much of the inflexibility of the Indian character, that we are apt to forget that these people are human; having, though perhaps in a small degree, and in less activity, the same vital passions, the same susceptibilities—the hopes, the fears, the loves and the hates, which establish the humanity of the whites. They are colder and more sterile,—more characterized by individuality and self-esteem than any more social people; and these characteristics are the natural and inevitable results of their habits of wandering. But to suppose that the Indian is "a man without a tear," is to indulge in a notion equally removed from poetry and truth. At all events, such an opinion is, to say the least of it, a gross exaggeration of the fact.

Combahee, the Queen of Chiquola, had many tears. She was a young wife;—the crime of De Ayllon had made her a young widow. Of the particular fate of her husband she knew nothing; and, in the absence of any certain knowledge, she naturally feared the worst. The imagination, once excited by fear, is the darkest painter of the terrible that nature has ever known. Still, the desolate woman did not feel herself utterly hopeless. Daily she manned her little bark, and was paddled along the shores of the sea, in a vain search after that which could never more be found. At other times she sat upon, or wandered along, the headlands, in a lonely and silent watch over those vast, dark, dashing waters of the Atlantic, little dreaming that they had already long since swallowed up her chief. Wan and wretched, the sustenance which she took was simply adequate to the purposes of life. Never did city maiden more stubbornly deplore the lost object of her affections than did this single-hearted woman. But her prayers and watch were equally unavailing. Vainly did she skirt the shores in her canoe by day;—vainly did she build her fires, as a beacon, to guide him on his home return by night. His people had already given him up for ever; but love is more hopeful of the object which it loves. She did not yet despair. Still she wept, but still she watched; and when she ceased to weep, it was only at moments when the diligence of her watch made her forgetful of her tears.

The season was becoming late. The fresh and invigorating breezes of September began to warn the tribes of the necessity of seeking the shelter of the woods. The maize was already gathered and bruised for the stocks of winter. The fruits of summer had been dried, and the roots were packed away. The chiefs regarded the condition of mind under which their Queen laboured with increasing anxiety. She sat apart upon the highest hill that loomed out from the shore, along the deep. She sat beneath the loftiest palmetto. A streamer of fringed cotton was hung from its top as a signal to the wanderer, should he once more be permitted to behold the land, apprizing him where the disconsolate widow kept her watch. The tribes looked on from a distance unwilling to disturb those sorrows, which, under ordinary circumstances, they consider sacred. The veneration which they felt for their Queen increased this feeling. Yet so unremitting had been her self-abandonment—so devoted and unchangeable her daily employments, that some partial fears began to be entertained lest her reason might suffer. She had few words now for her best counsellors. These few words, it is true, were always to the purpose, yet they were spoken with impatience, amounting to severity. The once gentle and benignant woman had grown stern. There was a stony inflexibility about her glance which distressed the observer, and her cheeks had become lean and thin, and her frame feeble and languid, in singular contrast with that intense spiritual light which flashed, whenever she was addressed, from her large black eyes.

Something must be done! such was the unanimous opinion of the chiefs. Nay, two things were to be done. She was to be cured of this affection; and it was necessary that she should choose one, from among her "beloved men,"—one, who should take the place of Chiquola. They came to her, at length, with this object. Combahee was even then sitting upon the headland of St. Helena. She looked out with straining eyes upon the sea. She had seen a speck. They spoke to her, but she motioned them to be silent, while she pointed to the object. It disappeared, like a thousand others. It was some porpoise, or possible some wandering grampus, sending up his *jets d'eau* in an unfamiliar ocean. Long she looked, but profitlessly. The object of her sudden hope had already disappeared. She turned to the chiefs. They prostrated themselves before her. Then, the venerable father, Kiawah,—an old man who had witnessed the departure of an hundred and twenty summers,—rose, and seating himself before her, addressed her after the following fashion:

"Does the daughter of the great Ocketee, look into the grave of the warrior that he may come forth because she looks?"

"He sleeps, father, for Combahee. He has gone forth to hunt the deer in the blue land of Maneyto."

"Good! he has gone. Is the sea a hunting land for the brave Chiquola? Is he not also gone to the blue land of spirits?"

"Know'st thou? Who has told Kiawah, the old father? Has it come to him in a dream?"

"Chiquola has come to him."

"Ah!"

"He is a hunter for Maneyto. He stands first among the hunters in the blue forests of Maneyto. The smile of the Great Spirit beckons him to the chase. He eats of honey in the golden tents of the Great Spirit."

"He has said? Thou hast seen?"

"Even so! Shall Kiawah say to Combahee the thing which is not? Chiquola is dead!"

The woman put her hand upon her heart with an expression of sudden pain. But she recovered herself with a little effort.

"It is true what Kiawah has said. I feel it here. But Chiquola will come to Combahee?"

"Yea! He will come. Let my daughter go to the fountain and bathe thrice before night in its waters. She will bid them prepare the feast of flesh. A young deer shall be slain by the hunters. Its meat shall be dressed, of that shall she eat, while the maidens sing the song of victory, and dance the dance of rejoicing around her. For there shall be victory and rejoicing. Three days shall my daughter do this; and the night of the third day shall Chiquola come to her when she sleeps. She shall hear his voice, she shall do his bidding, and there shall be blessings. Once more shall Combahee smile among her people."

He has [was] obeyed religiously. Indeed, his was a religious authority. Kiawah was a famous priest and prophet among the tribes of the sea coast of Carolina—in their language an Iawa,—a man renowned for his supernatural powers. A human policy may be seen in the counsels of the old man; but by the Indians it was regarded as coming from a superior source. For three days did Combahee perform her lustrations, as required, and partake plentifully of the feast which had been prepared. The third night, a canopy of green bushes was reared for her by the sea side around the palmetto where she had been accustomed to watch, and from which her cotton streamer was still flying. Thither she repaired as the yellow moon was rising above the sea. It rose, bright and round, and hung above her tent, looking down with eyes of sad, sweet brilliance, like some hueless diamond, about to weep, through the green leaves, and into the yet unclosed eyes of the disconsolate widow. The great ocean all the while kept up a mournful chiding and lament along the shores. It was long before Combahee could sleep. She vainly strove to shut her eyes. She could not well do so, because of her expectation, and because of that chiding sea, and those sad eyes of the moon, big, wide, down staring upon her. At length she ceased to behold the moon and to hear the ocean; but, in place of these, towards the rising of the morning star, she heard the voice of Chiquola, and beheld the young warrior to whom her virgin heart had been given. He was habited in loose flowing robes of blue, a bunch of feathers, most like a golden sunbeam, was on his brow, bound there by a circle of little stars. He carried a bow of bended silver, and his arrows looked like darts of summer lightning. Truly, in the eyes of the young widow, Chiquola looked like a very god himself. He spoke to her in a language that was most like a song. It was a music such as the heart hears when it first loves and when hope is the companion of its affections. Never was music in the ears of Combahee so sweet.

"Why sits the woman that I love beside the cold ocean? Why does she watch the black waters for Chiquola? Chiquola is not there."

The breathing of the woman was suspended with delight. She could not speak. She could only hear.

"Arise, my beloved, and look up at Chiquola."

"Chiquola is with the Great Spirit. Chiquola is happy in the blue forests of Maneyto;" at length she found strength for utterance.

"No! Chiquola is cold. There must be fire to warm Chiquola, for he perished beneath the sea. His limbs are full of water. He would dry himself. Maneyto smiles, around him are the blue forests, he chases the brown deer, till the setting of the sun; but his limbs are cold. Combahee will build him a fire of the bones of his enemies, that the limbs of Chiquola may be made warm against the winter."

The voice ceased, the bright image was gone. In vain was it that the woman, gathering courage in his absence, implored him to return. She saw him no more, and in his place the red eye of the warrior star of morning was looking steadfastly upon her.

But where were the enemies of Chiquola? The tribes were all at peace. The war-paths upon which Chiquola had gone had been very few, and the calumet had been smoked in token of peace and amity among them all. Of whose bones then should the fire be made which was to warm the limbs of the departed warrior? This was a question to afflict the wisest heads of the nation, and upon this difficulty they met, in daily council, from the moment that the revelation of Chiquola was made known by his widow. She, meanwhile, turned not once from her watch along the waters where he had disappeared! For what did she now gaze? Chiquola was no longer there! Ah! the fierce spirit of the Indian woman had another thought. It was from that quarter that the pale warriors came by when he was borne into captivity. Perhaps, she had no fancy that they would again return. It was an instinct rather than a thought, which made her look out upon the waters and dream at moments that she had glimpses of their large white-winged canoes.

Meanwhile, the Iawas and chief men sat in council, and the difficulty about the bones of which the fire was to be made, continued as great as ever. As a respite from this difficulty they debated at intervals another and scarcely less serious question:

"Is it good for Combahee to be alone?"

This question was decided in the negative by an unanimous vote. It was observed, though no argument seemed necessary, that all the younger and more handsome chiefs made long speeches in advocacy of the marriage of their Queen. It was also observed that, immediately after the breaking up of the council, each darted off to his separate wigwam, and put on his newest mocasins, brightest leggins, his yellowest hunting shirt, and his most gorgeous belt of shells. Each disposed his plumes after the fashion of his own taste, and adjusted, with newer care, the quiver at his back; and each strove, when the opportunity offered, to leap, dance, run, climb, and shoot, in the presence of the lovely and potent woman.

Once more the venerable Iawa presented himself before the Queen.

"The cabin of my daughter has but one voice. There must be another. What sings the Coonee Latee? (mocking bird.) He says, 'though the nest be withered and broken, are there not sticks and leaves; shall I not build another? Though the mate-wing be gone to other woods, shall no other voice take up the strain which I am singing, and barter with me in the music which is love?' Daughter, the beloved men have been in council; and they say, the nest must be repaired with newer leaves; and the sad bird must sing lonely no longer. Are there not other birds? Lo! behold them, my daughter, where they run and bound, and sing and dance. Choose from these, my daughter,—choose the noblest, that the noble blood of Ocketee may not perish for ever."

"Ah!"—she said impatiently—"but have the beloved men found the enemies of Chiquola? Do they say, here are the bones?"

"The Great Spirit has sent no light to the cabin of council."

"Enough! when the beloved men shall find the bones which were the enemies of Chiquola, then will the Coonee Latee take a mate-wing to her cabin. It is not meet that Combahee should build the fire for another hunter before she has dried the water from the limbs of Chiquola!"

"The Great Spirit will smile on their search. Meanwhile, let Combahee choose one from among our youth, that he may be honoured by the tribe."

"Does my father say this to the poor heart of Combahee?"

"It is good."

"Take this," she said, "to Edelano, the tall brother of Chiquola. He is most like the chief. Bid him wear it on his breast. Make him a chief among our people. He is the choice of Combahee."

She took from her neck as she spoke, a small plate of rudely beaten native gold, upon which the hands of some native artist, had, with a pointed flint or shell, scratched uncouth presentments of the native deer, the eagle, and other objects of their frequent observation.

"Give it him—to Edelano!"—she added; "but let him not come to Combahee till the beloved men shall have said—these are the bones of the enemies of Chiquola. Make of these the fires which shall warm him."

There was something so reasonable in what was said by the mourning

Queen, that the patriarch was silenced. To a certain extent he had failed of his object. That was to direct her mind from the contemplation of her loss by the substitution of another in his place—the philosophy of those days and people, not unlike that of our own, leading people to imagine that the most judicious and successful method for consoling a widow is by making her a wife again as soon as possible. Combahee had yielded as far as could be required of her; yet still they were scarcely nearer to the object of their desire: for where were the bones of Chiquola's enemies to be found?—He who had no enemies! He, with whom all the tribes were at peace? And those whom he had slain,—where were their bodies to be found? They had long been hidden by their friends in the forests where no enemy might trace out their places of repose. As for the Spaniards—the white men—of these the Indian sages did not think. They had come from the clouds, perhaps,—but certainly, they were not supposed to have belonged to any portion of the solid world to which they were accustomed. As they knew not where to seek for the "pale faces," these were not the subjects of their expectation.

The only person to whom the proceedings, so far, had produced any results, was the young warrior, Edelano. He became a chief in compliance with the wish of Combahee, and, regarded as her betrothed, was at once admitted into the hall of council, and took his place as one of the heads and fathers of the tribe. His pleasant duty was to minister to the wants and wishes of his spouse, to provide the deer, to protect her cabin, to watch her steps—subject to the single and annoying qualification, that he was not to present himself conspicuously to her eyes. But how could youthful lover—one so brave and ardent as Edelano—submit to such interdict? It would have been a hard task to one far less brave, and young, and ardent, than Edelano. With him it was next to impossible. For a time he bore his exclusion manfully. Set apart by betrothal, he no longer found converse or association with the young women of the tribe; and his soul was accordingly taken up with the one image of his Queen and future spouse. He hung about her steps like a shadow, but she beheld him not. He darted along the beach when she was gazing forth upon the big, black ocean, but he failed to win her glance. He sang, while hidden in the forest, as she wandered through its glooms, the wildest and sweetest songs of Indian love and fancy; but her ear did not seem to note any interruption of that sacred silence which she sought. Never was sweeter or tenderer venison placed by the young maidens before her, than that which Edelano furnished; the Queen ate little and did not seem to note its obvious superiority. The devoted young chief was in despair. He knew not what to do. Unnoticed, if not utterly unseen by day, he hung around her tent by night. Here, gliding by like a midnight spectre, or crouching beneath some neighbouring oak or myrtle, he mused for hours, catching with delighted spirit every sound, however slight, which might come to his ears from within; and occasionally renewing his fond song of devoted attachment, in the hope that, amidst the silence of every other voice, his own might be better heard. But the soughing of the sad winds and the chafing of the waters against the sandy shores, as they reminded the mourner of her loss, were enough to satisfy her vacant senses, and still no token reached the unwearied lover that his devotion had awakened the attention of the object to whom it was paid.

Every day added to his sadness and his toils; until the effect began to be as clearly visible on his person as on hers; and the gravity of the sages became increased, and they renewed the inquiry, more and more frequently together, "Where can the bones of Chiquola's enemies be found?"

The answer to this question was about to be received from an unexpected quarter. The sun was revolving slowly and certainly while the affairs of the tribe seemed at a stand. The period when he should cross the line was approaching, and the usual storms of the equinox were soon to be apprehended. Of these annual periods of storm and terror, the aborigines, through long experience, were quite as well aware as a more book-wise people. To fly to the shelter of the forests was the policy of the Indians at such periods. We have already seen that they had been for some time ready for departure. But Combahee gave no heed to their suggestions. A superstitious instinct made them willing to believe that the Great Spirit would interfere in his own good time; and, at the proper juncture, bestow the necessary light for their guidance. Though anxious, therefore, they did not press their meditations upon those of their princess. They deferred, with religious veneration, to her griefs. But their anxiety was not lessened as the month of September advanced—as the days became capricious,—as the winds murmured more and more mournfully along the sandy shores, and as the waters of the sea grew more blue, and put on their whiter crests of foam. The clouds grew banked in solid columns, like the gathering wings of an invading army, on the edges of the southern and southeastern horizon. Sharp, shrill, whistling gusts, raised a warning anthem through the forests, which sounded like the wild hymn of the advancing storm. The green leaves had suddenly become yellow as in the progress of the night, and the earth was already strewn with their fallen honours. The sun himself was growing dim as with sudden age. All around, in sky, sea and land, the presentments were obvious of a natural but startling change. If the anxieties of the people were increased, what were those of Edelano? Heedless of the threatening aspects around her, the sad-hearted Combahee, whose heaviest storm was in her own bosom, still wilfully maintained her precarious lodge beneath the palmetto, on the bleak head-land which looked out most loftily upon the sea.

The wind strewed the leaves of her forest tent upon her as she slept, but she was conscious of no disturbance; and its melancholy voice, along with that of the ocean, seemed to her to increase in interest and sweetness as they increased in vigour. She heeded not that the moon was absent from the night. She saw not that black clouds had risen in her place, and looked down with visage full of terror and of frowning. It did not move her fears that the palmetto under which she lay, groaned within its tough coat of bark, as it bent to and fro beneath the increasing pressure of the winds. She was still thinking of the wet, cold form of the brave Chiquola.

The gloom thickened. It was the eve of the 23rd of September. All day the winds had been rising. The ocean poured in upon the shores. There was little light that day. All was fog, dense fog, and driving vapour, that only was not rain. The watchful Edelano added to the boughs around the lodge of the Queen. The chief men approached her with counsel to persuade her to withdraw to the cover of the stunted thickets, so that she might be secure. But her resolution seemed to have grown more firm, and duly to increase in proportion to their entreaties. She had an answer, which, as it appealed to their superstitions, was conclusive to silence them.

"I have seen him. But last night he came to me. His brow was bound about with a cloud, such as goes round the moon. From his eye shot arrows of burning fire, like those of the storm. He smiled upon me, and bade me smile. 'Soon shalt thou warm me, Combahee, with the blazing bones of mine enemies. Be of good cheer—watch well that ye behold them where they lie. Thou shalt see them soon.' Thus spoke the chief. He whispers to my heart even now. Dost thou not hear him, Kiawah? He says soon—it will be soon!"

Such an assurance was reason good why she should continue her desolate and dangerous watch. The generous determination of the tribe induced them to share it with her. But this they did not suffer her to see. Each reared his temporary lodge in the most sheltered contiguous places, under his favourite clump of trees. Where the growth was stunted, and the thicket dense, little groups of women and children were made to harbour in situations of comparative security. But the warriors and brave men of the tribe advanced along the shores to positions of such shelter as they could find, but sufficiently nigh to their Queen to give her the necessary assistance in moments of sudden peril. The more devoted Edelano, presuming upon the prospective tie which was to give him future privileges, quietly laid himself down behind the isolated lodge of the princess, with a delight at being so near to her, that made him almost forgetful of the dangers of her exposed situation.

He was not allowed to forget them, however! The storm increased with the progress of the night. Never had such an equinoctial gale been witnessed, since the memory of Kiawah. The billows roared as if with the agony of so many wild monsters under the scourge of some imperious demon. The big trees of the forest groaned, and bent, and bowed, and were snapped off, or torn up by the roots; while the seas, surcharged with the waters of the Gulf, rushed in upon the land and threatened to overwhelm and swallow it. The waves rose to the brow of the headland, and small streams came flashing around the lodge of Combahee. Her root-tree bent and cracked, but, secure in its lowliness, it still stood; but the boughs were separated and whirled away, and, at the perilous moment, the gallant Edelano, who had forborne, through a natural timidity, to come forward until the last instant, now darted in, and with a big but fast beating heart, clasped the woman of his worship to his arms and bore her, as if she had been a child, to the stunted thickets which gave a shelter to the rest. But, even while they fled—amidst all the storm—a sudden sound reached the ears of the Queen, which seemed to awaken in her a new soul of energy. A dull, booming noise, sullen, slow rolling, sluggish,—something like that of thunder, rolled to their ears, as if it came from off the seas. No thunder had fallen from the skies in the whole of the previous tempest. No lightning had illuminated to increase the gloom. "What is that sound," said the heart of Combahee, filled with its superstitious instincts, "but the thunder of the pale-faces—the sudden thunder which bellows from the sides of their big-winged canoes?"

With this conviction in her mind, it was no longer possible for Edelano to detain her. Again and again did that thunder reach their ears, slowly booming along the black precipices of the ocean. The warriors and chiefs peered along the shores, with straining eyes, seeking to discover the hidden objects; and among these, with dishevelled hair, quivering lips, eyes which dilated with the wildest fires of an excited, an inspired soul, the form of Combahee was conspicuous. Now they saw the sudden flash—now they heard the mournful roar of the minute gun—and then all was silent.

"Look closely, Kiawah—look closely, Edelano; for what said the ghost of Chiquola?—'watch well! Soon shall ye see where the bones of my enemies lie.'—And who were the enemies of Chiquola? Who but the pale-faces? It is their thunder that we hear—the thunder of their big canoes. Hark, ye hear it now,—and hear ye no cries as of men that drown and struggle? Hark! Hark! There shall be bones for the fire ere the day opens upon us."

And thus they watched for two hours, which seemed ages, running along the shores, waving their torches, straining the impatient sight, and calling to one another through the gloom. The spirit of the bravest warrior quailed when he beheld the fearless movements of Combahee, down to the very edges of the ocean gulf, defying the mounting waves, that dashed their feathery jets of foam, twenty feet above them in the air. The daylight came at last, but with it no relaxation of the storm. With its light what a picture of terror presented itself to the eyes of the warriors—what a picture of terror— what a prospect of retribution! There came, head on shore, a noble vessel, still struggling, still striving, but predestined to destruction. Her sails were flying in shreds, her principal masts were gone, her movement was like that of a drunken man—reeling to and fro—the very mockery of those winds and waters, which, at other periods, seem only to have toiled to bear her and to do her bidding. Two hundred screaming wretches clung to her sides, and clamoured for mercy to the waves and shores. Heaven flung back the ac- cents, and their screams now were those of defiance and desperation. Com- bahee heard their cries, detected their despair, distinguished their pale faces. Her eyes gleamed with the intelligence of the furies. Still beautiful, her wan, thin face,—wan and thin through long and weary watching, exposure and want of food—looked like the loveliness of some fallen angel. A spirit of beauty in the highest degree—a morning star in brightness and bril- liance,—but marked by the passions of demoniac desolation, and the livid light of some avenging hate. Her meagre arms were extended, and waved, as if in doom to the onward rushing vessel.

"Said I not," she cried to her people,—"Said I not that there should be bones for the fire, which should warm the limbs of Chiquola?—See! these are they. They come. The warrior shall be no longer cold in the blue forests of the good Maneyto."

While one ship rushed headlong among the breakers, another was seen, bearing away, at a distance, under bare poles. These were the only surviving vessels of the armament of Lucas de Ayllon. All but these had gone down in the storm, and that which was now rushing to its doom bore the ill-fated De Ayllon himself. The historian remarks—(see History of South Carolina, p. 11)—"As if the retributive Providence had been watchful of the place, no less than of the hour of justice, it so happened that, at the mouth of the very river where his crime had been committed, he was destined to meet his doom." The Indian traditions go farther. They say, that the form of Chiquola was beheld by Combahee, standing upon the prow of the vessel, guiding it to the place set apart by the fates for the final consummation of that destiny which they had allotted to the perfidious Spaniards. We will not contend for the tradition; but the coincidence between the place of crime and that of retribution, was surely singular enough to impress, not merely upon the savage, but also upon the civilized mind, the idea of an overruling and watch- ful justice. The breakers seized upon the doomed ship, as the blood-hounds seize upon and rend the expiring carcass of the stricken deer. The voice of Combahee was heard above the cries of the drowning men. She bade her people hasten with their arrows, their clubs, their weapons of whatever kind, and follow her to the beach. She herself bore a bow in her hand, with a well filled quiver at her back; and as the vessel stranded, as the winds and waves rent its planks and timbers asunder, and billows bore the struggling and drowning wretches to the shore, the arrows of Combahee were despatched, in rapid execution. Victim after victim sunk, stricken, among the waters, with a death of which he had had no fear. The warriors strode, waist deep, into the sea, and dealt with their stone hatchets upon their victims. These when despatched, were drawn ashore, and the less daring were employed to heap them up, in a vast and bloody mound, for the sacrifice of fire.

The keen eyes of Combahee distinguished the face of the perfidious De Ayllon among the struggling Spaniards. His richer dress had already drawn upon him the eyes of an hundred warriors, who only waited with their arrows until the inevitable billows should bear him within their reach.

"Spare *him!* cried the widow of Chiquola. They understood her meaning at a glance, and a simultaneous shout attested their approbation of her resolve.

"The arrows of fire!" was the cry. The arrows of reed and flint were expended upon the humble wretches from the wreck. The miserable De Ayllon little fancied the secret of this forbearance. He grasped a spar which assisted his progress, and encouraged in the hope of life, as he found himself spared by the shafts which were slaying all around him, he was whirled onward by the breakers to the shore. The knife touched *him* not—the arrow forbore *his* bosom, but all beside perished. Two hundred spirits were dismissed to eternal judgment, in that bloody hour of storm and retribution, by the hand of violence. Senseless amidst the dash of the breakers,—unconscious of present or future danger, Lucas De Ayllon came within the grasp of the fierce warriors, who rushed impatient for their prisoner neck deep into the sea. They bore him to the land. They used all the most obvious means for his restoration, and had the satisfaction to perceive that he at length opened his eyes. When sufficiently recovered to become aware of what had been done for him, and rushing to the natural conclusion that it had all been done in kindness, he smiled upon his captors, and, addressing them in his own language, endeavoured still further, by signs and sounds, to conciliate their favour.

"Enough!" said the inflexible Combahee, turning away from the criminal with an expression of strong disgust—

"Enough! wherefore should we linger? Are not the limbs of Chiquola still cold and wet? The bones of his enemies are here—let the young men build the sacrifice. The hand of Combahee will light the fire arrow!"

A dozen warriors now seized upon the form of De Ayllon. Even had he not been enfeebled by exhaustion, his struggles would have been unavailing. Equally unavailing were his prayers and promises. The Indians turned with loathing from his base supplications, and requited his entreaties and tears with taunts, and buffetings, and scorn! They bore him, under the instructions of Combahee, to that palmetto, looking out upon the sea, beneath which, for so many weary months, she had maintained her lonely watch. The storm had torn her lodge to atoms, but the tree was unhurt. They bound him to the shaft with withes of grape vines, of which the neighbouring woods had their abundance. Parcels of light-wood were heaped about him, while, interspersed with other bundles of the resinous pine, were piled the bodies of his slain companions. The only living man, he was the centre of a pile composed of two hundred, whose fate he was now prepared to envy. A dreadful mound, it rose conspicuous, like a beacon, upon the head-land of St. Helena; he, the centre, with his head alone free, and his eyes compelled to survey all the terrible preparations which were making for his doom. Layers of human carcasses, followed by layers of the most inflammable wood and brush, environed him with a wall from which, even had he not been bound to the tree, he could never have effected his own extrication. He saw them pile the successive layers, sparing the while no moment which he could give to expostulation, entreaty, tears, prayers, and promises. But the workmen with steady industry pursued their task. The pile rose,—the human pyramid was at last complete!

Combahee drew nigh with a blazing torch in her hand. She looked the image of some avenging angel. She gave but a single glance upon the face of the criminal. That face was one of an agony which no art could hope to picture. Hers was inflexible as stone, though it bore the aspect of hate, and loathing, and revenge! She applied the torch amid the increased cries of the victim, and as the flame shot up, with a dense black smoke to heaven, she turned away to the sea, and prostrated herself beside its billows. The shouts of the warriors who surrounded the blazing pile attested their delight; but, though an hundred throats set up their united clamours, the one piercing shriek of the burning man was superior, and rose above all other sounds. At length it ceased! all ceased! The sacrifice was ended. The perfidy of the Spaniard was avenged.

The sudden hush declared the truth to the Queen. She started to her feet. She exclaimed:—

"Thou art now blessed, Chiquola! Thou art no longer cold in the blue forests of Maneyto. The bones of thy enemies have warmed thee. I see thee spring gladly upon the chase;—thine eye is bright above the hills;—thy voice rings cheerfully along the woods of heaven. The heart of Combahee is very glad that thou art warm and happy."

A voice at her side addressed her. The venerable Kiawah, and the young Edelano were there.

"Now, thou hast done well, my daughter!" said the patriarch. "Chiquola is warm and happy in heaven. Let the lodge of Combahee be also warm in the coming winter."

"Ah! but there is nothing to make it warm here!" she replied, putting her hand upon her heart.

"The bird will have its mate, and build its nest, and sing a new song over its young."

"Combahee has no more song."

"The young chief will bring song into her lodge. Edelano will build a bright fire upon the hearth of Combahee. Daughter! the chief ask, 'Is the race of Ocketee to perish?'"

"Combahee is ready," answered the Queen, patiently, giving her hand to Edelano. But, even as she spoke, the muscles of her mouth began to quiver. A sudden groan escaped her, and, staggering forward, she would have fallen but for the supporting arms of the young chief. They bore her to the shade beneath a tree. They poured some of their primitive specifics into her mouth, and she revived sufficiently to bid the Patriarch unite her with Edelano in compliance with the will of the nation. But the ceremony was scarcely over, before a second and third attack shook her frame with death-like spasms. They were, indeed, the spasms of death—of a complete paralysis of mind and body. Both had been too severely tried, and the day of bridal was also that of death. Edelano was now the beloved chief of the nation, but the nation was without its Queen. The last exciting scene, following hard upon that long and lonely widow-watch which she had kept, had suddenly stopped the currents of life within her heart, as its currents of hope and happiness had been cut off before. True to Chiquola while *he* lived, to the last moment of *her* life she was true. The voice of Edelano had called her his wife, out her ears had not heard his speech, and her voice had not replied. Her hand had been put within his, but no other lips had left a kiss where those of Chiquola had been. They buried her in a lovely but lonely grove beside the Ashepoo. There, the Coonee-Latee first repairs to sing in the opening of spring, and the small blue violet peeps out from her grave as if in homage to her courage and devotion. There the dove flies for safety when the fowler pursues, and the doe finds a quiet shelter when the beagles pant on the opposite side of the stream. The partridge hides her young under the long grass which waves luxuriantly above the spot, and the eagle and hawk look down watching from the tree-tops in vain. The spirit of the beautiful Princess presides over the place as some protecting Divinity, and even the white man, though confident in a loftier and nobler faith, still finds something in the spot which renders it mysterious, and makes him an involuntary worshipper! Ah! there are deities which are common to all human kind, whatever be the faith which they maintain. Love is of this sort, and truth, and devotion; and of these the desolate Combahee had a Christian share, though the last deed of her life be not justified by the doctrine of Christian retribution. Yet, look not, traveller, as in thy bark thou sailest beside the lovely headlands of Saint Helena, at the pile of human sacrifice which thou seest consuming there. Look at the frail lodge beneath the Palmetto, or wander off to the dark groves beside the Ashepoo and think of the fidelity of that widowed heart.

"She died for him she loved—her greatest pride,
That, as for him she lived, for him she died:
Make her young grave,
Sweet fancies, where the pleasant branches lave
Their drooping tassels in some murmuring wave!"

How Sharp Snaffles Got His Capital and Wife

(1 8 7 0)

I.

The day's work was done, and a good day's work it was. We had bagged a couple of fine bucks and a fat doe; and now we lay camped at the foot of the "Balsam Range" of mountains in North Carolina, preparing for our supper. We were a right merry group of seven; four professional hunters, and three amateurs—myself among the latter. There was Jim Fisher, Aleck Wood, Sam or Sharp Snaffles, *alias* "Yaou," and Nathan Langford, *alias* the "Pious."

These were our *professional* hunters. Our *amateurs* may well continue nameless, as their achievements do not call for any present record. Enough that we had gotten up the "camp hunt," and provided all the creature comforts except the fresh meat. For this we were to look to the mountain ranges and the skill of our hunters.

These were all famous fellows with the rifle—moving at a trot along the hill-sides, and with noses quite as keen of scent as those of their hounds in rousing deer and bear from their deep recesses among the mountain laurels.

A week had passed with us among these mountain ranges, some sixty miles beyond what the conceited world calls "civilization."

Saturday night had come; and, this Saturday night closing a week of exciting labors, we were to carouse.

We were prepared for it. There stood our tent pitched at the foot of the mountains, with a beautiful cascade leaping headlong toward us, and subsiding into a mountain runnel, and finally into a little lakelet, the waters of which, edged with perpetual foam, were as clear as crystal.

Our baggage wagon, which had been sent round to meet us by trail routes through the gorges, stood near the tent, which was of stout army canvas.

That baggage wagon held a variety of luxuries. There was a barrel of the best bolted wheat flour. There were a dozen choice hams, a sack of coffee, a keg of sugar, a few thousand of cigars, and last, not least, a corpulent barrel of Western uisquebaugh,[4] vulgarly, "whisky;" to say nothing of a pair of demijohns of equal dimensions, one containing peach brandy of mountain manufacture, the other the luscious honey from the mountain hives.

Well, we had reached Saturday night. We had hunted day by day from the preceding Monday with considerable success—bagging some game daily, and camping nightly at the foot of the mountains. The season was a fine one. It was early winter, October, and the long ascent to the top of the mountains was through vast fields of green, the bushes still hanging heavy with their huckleberries.

From the summits we had looked over into Tennessee, Virginia, Georgia, North and South Carolina. In brief, to use the language of Natty Bumppo, we beheld "Creation." We had crossed the "Blue Ridge;" and the descending water-courses, no longer seeking the Atlantic, were now gushing headlong down the western slopes, and hurrying to lose themselves in the Gulf Stream and the Mississippi.

From the eyes of fountains within a few feet of each other we had blended our *eau de vie* with limpid waters which were about to part company for-ever—the one leaping to the rising, the other to the setting of the sun.

And buoyant, full of fun, with hearts of ease, limbs of health and strength, plenty of venison, and a wagon full of good things, we welcomed the coming of Saturday night as a season not simply of rest, but of a royal carouse. We were decreed to make a night of it.

But first let us see after our venison.

The deer, once slain, is, as soon after as possible, clapped upon the fire. All the professional hunters are good butchers and admirable cooks—of bear and deer meat at least. I doubt if they could spread a table to satisfy Delmonico; but even Delmonico might take some lessons from them in the preparation for the table of the peculiar game which they pursue, and the meats on which they feed. We, at least, rejoice at the supper prospect before

---

4. *WGS:* "Uisquebaugh," or the "water of life," is Irish. From the word we have dropped the last syllable. Hence we have "uisque," or, as it is commonly written, "whisky"—a very able-bodied man-servant, but terrible as a mistress or housekeeper.

us. Great collops hiss in the frying-pan, and finely cut steaks redden beautifully upon the flaming coals. Other portions of the meat are subdued to the stew, and make a very delightful dish. The head of the deer, including the brains, is put upon a flat rock in place of gridiron, and thus baked before the fire—being carefully watched and turned until every portion has duly imbibed the necessary heat, and assumed the essential hue which it should take to satisfy the eye of appetite. This portion of the deer is greatly esteemed by the hunters themselves; and the epicure of genuine stomach for the *haut gout* takes to it as an eagle to a fat mutton, and a hawk to a young turkey.

The rest of the deer—such portions of it as are not presently consumed or needed for immediate use—is cured for future sale or consumption; being smoked upon a scaffolding raised about four feet above the ground, under which for ten or twelve hours, a moderate fire will be kept up.

Meanwhile the hounds are sniffing and snuffing around, or crouched in groups, with noses pointed at the roast and broil and bake; while their great liquid eyes dilate momently while watching for the huge gobbets which they expect to be thrown to them from time to time from the hands of the hunters.

Supper over, and it is Saturday night. It is the night dedicated among the professional hunters to what is called "The Lying Camp!"

"The Lying Camp!" quoth Columbus Mills, one of our party, a wealthy mountaineer, of large estates, of whom I have been for some time the guest.

"What do you mean by the 'Lying Camp,' Columbus?"

The explanation soon followed.

Saturday night is devoted by the mountaineers engaged in a camp hunt, which sometimes contemplates a course of several weeks, to stories of their adventures—"long yarns"—chiefly relating to the objects of their chase, and the wild experiences of their professional life. The hunter who actually inclines to exaggeration is, at such a period, privileged to deal in all the extravagances of invention; nay, he is *required* to do so! To be literal, or confine himself to the bald and naked truth, is not only discreditable, but a *finable* offense! He is, in such a case, made to swallow a long, strong, and difficult potation! He can not be too extravagant in his incidents; but he is also required to exhibit a certain degree of *art*, in their use; and he thus frequently rises into a certain realm of fiction, the ingenuities of which are made to compensate for the exaggerations, as they do in the "Arabian Nights," and other Oriental romances.

This will suffice for explanation.

Nearly all our professional hunters assembled on the present occasion were tolerable *raconteurs*. They complimented Jim Fisher, by throwing the raw deer-skin over his shoulders; tying the antlers of the buck with a red handkerchief over his forehead; seating him on the biggest boulder which lay at hand; and, sprinkling him with a stoup of whisky, they christened him "The Big Lie," for the occasion. And in this character he complacently presided during the rest of the evening, till the company prepared for sleep, which was not till midnight. He was king of the feast.

It was the duty of the "Big Lie" to regulate proceedings, keep order, appoint the *raconteurs* severally, and admonish them when he found them foregoing their privileges, and narrating bald, naked, and uninteresting truth. They must deal in fiction.

Jim Fisher was seventy years old, and a veteran hunter, the most famous in all the country. He *looked* authority, and promptly began to assert it, which he did in a single word:

"Yaou!"

II.

"Yaou" was the *nom de nique* of one of the hunters, whose proper name was Sam Snaffles, but who, from his special smartness, had obtained the farther sobriquet of "*Sharp* Snaffles."

Columbus Mills whispered me that he was called "Yaou" from his frequent use of that word, which, in the Choctaw dialect, simply means "Yes." Snaffles had rambled considerably among the Choctaws, and picked up a variety of their words, which he was fond of using in preference to the vulgar English; and his common use of "*Yaou,*" for the affirmative, had prompted the substitution of it for his own name. He answered to the name.

"Ay—yee, Yaou," was the response of Sam. "I was *afeard,* 'Big Lie,' that you'd be hitching me up the very first in your team."

"And what was you afeard of? You knows as well how to take up a crooked trail as the very best man among us; so you go ahead and spin your thread a'ter the best fashion."

"What shill it be?" asked Snaffles, as he mixed a calabash full of peach and honey, preparing evidently for a long yarn.

"Give 's the history of how you got your capital, Yaou!" was the cry from two or more.

"O Lawd! I've tell'd that so often, fellows, that I'm afeard you'll sleep on it; and then agin, I've tell'd it so often I've clean forgot how it goes. Somehow it changes a leetle every time I tells it."

"Never you mind! The Jedge never haird it, I reckon, for one and I'm not sure that Columbus Mills ever did."

So the "Big Lie."

The "Jedge" was the *nom de guerre* which the hunters had conferred upon me; looking, no doubt, to my venerable aspect—for I had traveled considerably beyond my teens—and the general dignity of my bearing.

"Yaou," like other bashful beauties in oratory and singing, was disposed to hem and haw, and affect modesty and indifference, when he was brought up suddenly by the stern command of the "Big Lie," who cried out:

"Don't make yourself an etarnal fool, Sam Snaffles, by twisting your mouth out of shape, making all sorts of redickilous ixcuses. Open upon the trail at onst and give tongue, or, dern your digestion, but I'll fine you to hafe a gallon at a single swallow!"

Nearly equivalent to what Hamlet says to the conceited player:

"Leave off your damnable faces and begin."

Thus adjured with a threat, Sam Snaffles swallowed his peach and honey at a gulp, hemmed thrice lustily, put himself into an attitude, and began as follows. I shall adopt his language as closely as possible; but it is not possible, in any degree, to convey any adequate idea of his *manner,* which was admirably appropriate to the subject matter. Indeed, the fellow was a born actor.

III.

"You see, Jedge," addressing me especially as the distinguished stranger, "I'm a telling this hyar history of mine jest to please *you,* and I'll try to please you ef I kin. These fellows hyar have hearn it so often that they knows all about it jest as well as I do my own self, and they knows the truth of it all, and would swear to it a fore any hunters' court in all the county, ef so be the affidavy was to be tooken in camp and on a Saturday night.

"You see then, Jedge, it's about a dozen or fourteen years ago, when I was a young fellow without much beard on my chin, though I was full grown as I am now—strong as a horse, ef not quite so big as a buffalo. I was then jest a-beginning my 'prentice ship to the hunting business, and looking to sich persons as the 'Big Lie' thar to show me how to take the track of b'ar, buck, and painther.

"But I confess I weren't a-doing much. I hed a great deal to l'arn, and I reckon I miss'd many more bucks than I ever hit—that is, jest up to that time—"

"Look you, Yaou," said "Big Lie," interrupting him, "you're gitting too close upon the etarnal stupid truth! All you've been a-saying is jest nothing but the naked truth as I knows it. Jest crook your trail!"

"And how's a man to lie decently onless you lets him hev a bit of truth to go upon? The truth's nothing but a peg in the wall that I hangs the lie upon. A'ter a while I promise that you sha'n't see the peg."

"Worm along, Yaou!"

"Well, Jedge, I warn't a-doing much among the *bucks* yit—jest for the reason that I was quite too eager in the scent a'ter a sartin *doe*! Now, Jedge, you never seed my wife—my Merry Ann, as I calls her; and ef you was to see her *now*—though she's prime grit yit—you would never believe that, of all the womankind in all these mountains, she was the very yaller flower of the forest; with the reddest rose cheeks you ever did see, and sich a mouth, and sich bright curly hair, and so tall, and so slender, and so all over beautiful! O Lawd! when I thinks of it and them times, I don't see how 'twas possible to think of buck-hunting when thar was sich a doe, with sich eyes shining me on!

"Well, Jedge, Merry Ann was the only da'ter of Jeff Hopson and Keziah Hopson, his wife, who was the da'ter of Squire Claypole, whose wife was Margery Clough, that lived down upon Pacolet River—"

"Look you, Yaou, ain't you gitting into them derned facts agin, eh?"

"I reckon I em, 'Big Lie!' Scuse me: I'll kiver the pegs *direct-lie,* one a'ter t'other. Whar was I? Ah! Oh! Well, Jedge, poor hunter and poor man—jest, you see, a squatter on the side of a leetle bit of a mountain close on to Columbus Mills, at Mount Tryon, I was all the time on a hot trail a'ter Merry Ann Hopson. I went thar to see her a'most every night; and sometimes I carried a buck for the old people, and sometimes a doe-skin for the gal, and I do think, bad hunter as I then was, I pretty much kept the fambly in deer meat through the whole winter."

"Good for you, Yaou! You're a-coming to it! That's the only fair trail of a lie that you've struck yit!"

So the "Big Lie," from the chair.

"Glad to hyar you say so," was the answer. "I'll git on in time! Well, Jedge, though Jeff Hopson was glad enough to git my meat always, he didn't affection me, as I did his da'ter. He was a sharp, close, money-loving old fellow, who was always considerate of the main chaince; and the old lady, his wife, who hairdly dare say her soul was her own, she jest looked both ways, as I may say, for Sunday, never giving a fair look to me or my chainces, when his eyes were sot on *her*. But 'twa'n't so with my Merry Ann. She hed the eyes for me from the beginning, and soon she hed the feelings; and, you see, Jedge, we sometimes did git a chaince, when old Jeff was gone from home, to come to a sort of onderstanding about our feelings; and the long and the short of it was that Merry Ann confessed to me that she'd like nothing better than to be my wife. She liked no other man but me. Now, Jedge, a'ter that, what was a young fellow to do? That, I say, was the proper kind of in-couragement. So I said, 'I'll ax your daddy.' Then she got scary, and said, 'Oh, don't; for somehow, Sam, I'm a-thinking daddy don't like you enough *yit*. Jest hold on a bit, and come often, and bring him venison, and try to make him laugh, which you kin do, you know, and a'ter a time you kin try him.' And so I did—or rether I didn't. I put off the axing. I come constant. I brought venison all the time, and b'ar meat a plenty, a'most three days in every week."

"That's it, Yaou. You're on trail. That's as derned a lie as you've tell'd yit; for all your hunting, in them days, didn't git more meat than you could eat your one self."

"Thank you, 'Big Lie.' I hopes I'll come up in time to the right measure of the camp.

"Well, Jedge, this went on for a long time, a'most the whole winter, and spring, and summer, till the winter begun to come in agin. I carried 'em the venison, and Merry Ann meets me in the woods, and we hes sich a pleasant time when we meets on them little odd chainces that I gits hot as thunder to bring the business to a sweet honey finish.

"But Merry Ann keeps on scary, and she puts me off; ontil, one day, one a'ternoon, about sundown, she meets me in the woods, and she's all in a flusteration. And she ups and tells me how old John Grimstead, the old bach-elor (a fellow about forty years old, and the dear gal not yet twenty), how he's a'ter her, and bekaise he's got a good fairm, and mules and horses, how her daddy's giving him the open mouth incouragement.

"Then I says to Merry Ann:

"'You sees, I kain't put off no longer. I must out with it, and ax your daddy at onst.' And then her scary fit come on again, and she begs me not to—not *jist yit*. But I swears by all the Hokies that I won't put off another day; and so, as I haird the old man was in the house that very hour, I left Merry Ann in the woods, all in a trimbling, and I jist went ahead, determined to have the figure made straight, whether odd or even.

"And Merry Ann, poor gal, she wrings her hainds, and cries a smart bit, and she wouldn't go to the house, but said she'd wait for me out thar. So I gin her a kiss into her very mouth—and did it over more than onst—and I left her, and pushed headlong for the house.

"I was jubous; I was mighty oncertain, and a leetle bit scary myself; for, you see, old Jeff was a fellow of tough grit, and with big grinders; but I was so oneasy, and so tired out waiting, and so desperate, and so fearsome that old bachelor Grimstead would get the start on me, that nothing could stop me now, and I jist bolted into the house, as free and easy and bold as ef I was the very best customer that the old man wanted to see."

Here Yaou paused to renew his draught of peach and honey.

IV.

"Well, Jedge, as I tell you, I put a bold face on the business, though my hairt was gitting up into my throat, and I was almost a-gasping for my breath, when I was fairly in the big room, and standing up before the old Squaire. He was a-setting in his big squar hide-bottom'd arm-chair, looking like a jedge upon the bench, jist about to send a poor fellow to the gallows. As he seed me come in, looking queer enough, I reckon, his mouth put on a sort of grin, which showed all his grinders, and he looked for all the world as ef he guessed the business I come about. But he said, good-natured enough:

"'Well, Sam Snaffles, how goes it?'

"Says I:

"'Pretty squar, considerin'. The winter's coming on fast, and I reckon the mountains will be full of meat before long.'

"Then says he, with another ugly grin, 'Ef 'twas your smoke-house that had it all, Sam Snaffles, 'stead of the mountains, 'twould be better for you, I reckon.'

"'I 'grees with you,' says I. 'But I rether reckon I'll git my full shar' of it afore the spring of the leaf agin.'

"'Well, Sam,' says he, 'I hopes, for your sake, 'twill be a big shar'. I'm afeard you're not the pusson to go for a big shar', Sam Snaffles. Seems to me you're too easy satisfied with a small shar'; sich as the fence-squarrel carries onder his two airing, calkilating only on a small corn-crib in the chestnut-tree.'

"'Don't you be afeard, Squaire. I'll come out right. My cabin sha'n't want for nothing that a strong man with a stout hairt kin git, with good working—enough and more for himself, and perhaps another pusson.'

"'What other pusson?' says he, with another of his great grins, and showing of his grinders.

"'Well,' says I, 'Squaire Hopson, that's jest what I come to talk to you about this blessed Friday night.'

"You see 'twas Friday!

"'Well,' says he, 'go ahead, Sam Snaffles, and empty your brainbasket as soon as you kin, and I'll light my pipe while I'm a-hearing you.'

"So he lighted his pipe, and laid himself back in his chair, shet his eyes, and begin to puff like blazes.

"By this time my blood was beginning to bile in all my veins, for I seed that he was jest in the humor to tread on all my toes, and then ax a'ter my feelings. I said to myself:

"'It's jest as well to git the worst at onst, and then thar'll be an eend of the oneasiness.' So I up and told him, in pretty soft, smooth sort of speechifying, as how I was mighty fond of Merry Ann, and she, I was a-thinking, of me; and that I jest come to ax ef I might hev Merry Ann for my wife.

"Then he opened his eyes wide, as ef he never ixpected to hear sich a proposal from me.

"'What!' says he. 'You?'

"'Jest so, Squaire,' says I. 'Ef it pleases you to believe me, and to consider it reasonable, the axing.'

"He sot quiet for a minit or more, then he gits up, knocks all the fire out of his pipe on the chimney, fills it, and lights it agin, and then comes straight up to me, whar I was a-setting on the chair in front of him, and without a word he takes the collar of my coat betwixt the thumb and forefinger of his left hand, and he says:

"'Git up, Sam Snaffles. Git up, ef you please.'

"Well, I gits up, and he says:

"'Hyar! Come! Hyar!'

"And with that he leads me right across the room to a big looking-glass that hung agin the partition wall, and thar he stops before the glass, facing it and holding me by the collar all the time.

"Now that looking-glass, Jedge, was about the biggest I ever did see! It was a'most three feet high, and a'most two feet wide, and it had a bright, broad frame, shiny like gold, with a heap of leetle figgers worked all round it. I reckon thar's no sich glass now in all the mountain country. I 'member when first that glass come home. It was a great thing, and the old Squaire was mighty proud of it. He bought it at the sale of some rich man's furniter, down at Greenville, and he was jest as fond of looking into it as a young gal, and whenever he lighted his pipe, he'd walk up and down the room, seeing himself in the glass.

"Well, thar he hed me up, both on us standing in front of this glass, whar we could a'most see the whole of our full figgers, from head to foot.

"And when we hed stood thar for a minit or so, he says, quite solemn like:

"'Look in the glass, Sam Snaffles.'

"So I looked.

"'Well,' says I. 'I sees you, Squaire Hopson, and myself, Sam Snaffles.'

"'Look good,' says he, '*obzarve* well.'

"'Well,' says I, 'I'm a-looking with all my eyes. I only sees what I tells you.'

"'But you don't *obzarve*,' says he. 'Looking and seeing's one thing,' says he, 'but obzarving's another. Now *obzarve*.'

"By this time, Jedge, I was getting sort o' riled, for I could see that somehow he was jest a-trying to make me feel redickilous. So I says:

"'Look you, Squaire Hopson, ef you thinks I never seed myself in a glass afore this, you're mighty mistaken. I've got my own glass at home, and though it's but a leetle sort of a small, mean consarn, it shows me as much of my own face and figger as I cares to see at any time. I never cares to look in it 'cept when I'm brushing, and combing, and clipping off the straggling beard when it's too long for my eating.'

"'Very well,' says he; 'now obzarve! You sees your own figger, and your face, and you air obzarving as well as you know how. Now, Mr. Sam Snaffles—now that you've hed a fair look at yourself—jest now answer me, from your honest conscience, a'ter all you've seed, ef you honestly thinks you're the sort of pusson to hev *my* da'ter!'

"And with that he gin me a twist, and when I wheeled round he hed wheeled round too, and thar we stood, full facing one another.

"Lawd! how I was riled! But I answered, quick:

"'And why not, I'd like to know, Squaire Hopson? I ain't the handsomest man in the world, but I'm not the ugliest; and folks don't generally consider me at all among the uglies. I'm as tall a man as you, and as stout and strong, and as good a man o' my inches as ever stepped in shoe-leather. And it's enough to tell you, Squaire, whatever *you* may think, that Merry Ann believes in me, and she's a way of thinking that I'm jest about the very pusson that ought to hev her.'

"'Merry Ann's thinking,' says he, 'don't run all fours with her fayther's thinking. I axed you, Sam Snaffles, to *obzarve* yourself in the glass. I told you that seeing warn't edzactly obzarving. You seed only the inches; you seed that you hed eyes and mouth and nose and the airms and legs of the man. But eyes and mouth and legs and airms don't make a man!'

"'Oh, they don't!' says I.

"'No, indeed,' says he. 'I seed that you hed all them; but then I seed thar was one thing that you hedn't got.'

"'Jimini!' says I, mighty conflustered. 'What thing's a-wanting to me to make me a man?'

"'*Capital!*' says he, and he lifted himself up and looked mighty grand.

"'Capital!' says I; 'and what's that?'

"'Thar air many kinds of capital,' says he. 'Money's capital, for it kin buy every thing. House and lands is capital; cattle and horses and sheep—when thar's enough on 'em—is capital. And as I obzarved you in the glass, Sam Snaffles, I seed that *capital* was the very thing that you wanted to make a man of you! Now I don't mean that any da'ter of mine shall marry a pusson that's not a *parfect* man. I obzarved you long ago, and seed whar you was wanting. I axed about you. I axed your horse.'

"'Axed my horse!' says I, pretty nigh dumfoundered.

"'Yes; I axed your horse, and he said to me: "Look at me! I hain't got an ounce of spar' flesh on my bones. You kin count all my ribs. You kin lay the whole length of your airm betwixt any two on 'em, and it 'll lie thar as snug as a black snake betwixt two poles of a log-house." Says he, "Sam's got *no capital!* He ain't got, any time, five bushels of corn in his crib; and he's such a monstrous feeder himself that he'll eat out four bushels, and think it mighty hard upon him to give *me* the other one." Thar, now, was your horse's testimony, Sam, agin you. Then I axed about your cabin, and your way of living. I was curious, and went to see you one day when I knowed you waur at home. You hed but one chair, which you gin me to set on, and you sot on the eend of a barrel for yourself. You gin me a rasher of bacon what hedn't a streak of fat in it. You hed a poor quarter of a poor doe hanging from the rafters—a poor beast that somebody hed disabled—'

"'I shot it myself,' says I.

"'Well, it was a-dying when you shot it; and all the hunters say you was a poor shooter at any thing. You cooked our dinner yourself, and the hoe-cake was all dough, not hafe done, and the meat was all done as tough as ef you had dried it for a month of Sundays in a Flurriday sun! Your cabin had but one room, and that you slept in and ate in; and the floor was six inches deep in dirt! Then, when I looked into your garden, I found seven stalks of long collards only, every one seven foot high, with all the leaves stript off it, as ef you wanted 'em for broth; till thar waur only three top leaves left on every stalk. You hedn't a stalk of corn growing, and when I scratched at your turnip-bed I found nothing bigger than a chestnut. Then, Sam, I begun to ask about your fairm, and I found that you was nothing but a squatter on land of Columbus Mills, who let you have an old nigger pole-house, and an acre or two of land. Says I to myself, says I, "This poor fellow's got *no capital;* and he hasn't the head to git *capital;*" and from that moment, Sam Snaffles, the more I obzarved you, the more sartin 'twas that you never could be a man, ef you waur to live a thousand years. You may think, in your vanity, that you air a man; but you ain't, and never will be, onless you kin find a way to git *capital;* and I loves my gal child too much to let her marry any pusson whom I don't altogether consider a man!'

"A'ter that long speechifying, Jedge, you might ha' ground me up in a mill, biled me down in a pot, and scattered me over a manure heap, and I wouldn't ha' been able to say a word!

"I cotched up my hat, and was a-gwine, when he said to me, with his derned infernal big grin:

"'Take another look in the glass, Sam Snaffles, and obzarve well, and you'll see jest whar it is I thinks that you're wanting.'

"I didn't stop for any more. I jest bolted, like a hot shot out of a shovel, and didn't know my own self, or whatever steps I tuk, tell I got into the thick and met Merry Ann coming towards me.

"I must liquor now!"

V.

"Well, Jedge, it was a hard meeting betwixt me and Merry Ann. The poor gal come to me in a sort of run, and hairdly drawing her breath, she cried out:

"'Oh, Sam! What does he say?'

"What could I say? How tell her? I jest wrapped her up in my airms, and I cries out, making some violent remarks about the old Squire.

"Then she screamed, and I hed to squeeze her up, more close than ever, and kiss her, I reckon, more than a dozen times, jest to keep her from gwine into historical fits. I telled her all, from beginning to eend.

"I telled her that thar waur some truth in what the old man said: that I hedn't been keerful to do the thing as I ought; that the house *was* mean and dirty; that the horse was mean and poor; that I hed been thinking too much about her own self to think about other things; but that I would do better, would see to things, put things right, git corn in the crib, git 'capital,' ef I could, and make a good, comfortable home for *her*.

"'Look at me,' says I, 'Merry Ann. Does I look like a man?'

"'You're are all the man I wants,' says she.

"'That's enough,' says I. 'You shall see what I kin do, and what I *will* do! That's ef you air true to me.'

"'I'll be true to you, Sam,' says she.

"'And you won't think of nobody else?'

"'Never,' says she.

"'Well, you'll see what I kin do, and what I *will* do. You'll see that I *em* a man; and ef thar's capital to be got in all the country, by working and hunting, and fighting, ef that's needful, we shill hev it. Only you be true to me, Merry Ann.'

"And she threw herself upon my buzzom, and cried out:

"'I'll be true to you, Sam. I loves nobody in all the world so much as I loves you.'

"'And you won't marry any other man, Merry Ann, no matter what your daddy says?'

"'Never,' she says.

"'And you won't listen to this old bachelor fellow, Grimstead, that's got the "capital" already, no matter how they spurs you?'

"'Never!' she says.

"'Sw'ar it!' says I—'sw'ar it, Merry Ann—that you will be my wife, and never marry Grimstead!'

"'I sw'ars it,' she says, kissing *me,* bekaize we had no book.

"'Now,' says I, 'Merry Ann, that's not enough. Cuss him for my sake, and to make it sartin. Cuss that fellow Grimstead.'

"'Oh, Sam, I kain't cuss,' says she; 'that's wicked.'

"'Cuss him on my account,' says I—'to my credit.'

"'Oh,' says she, 'don't ax me. I kain't do that.'

"Says I, 'Merry Ann, if you don't cuss that fellow, some way, I do believe you'll go over to him a'ter all. Jest you cuss him, now. Any small cuss will do, ef you're in airnest.'

"'Well,' says she, 'ef that's your idee, then I says, "*Drot his skin,*[5] and drot *my* skin, too, ef ever I marries any body but Sam Snaffles."'

"'That 'll do, Merry Ann,' says I. 'And now I'm easy in my soul and conscience. And now, Merry Ann, I'm gwine off to try my best, and git the "capital." Ef it's the "capital" that's needful to make a man of me, I'll git it, by all the Holy Hokies, if I kin.'

"And so, after a million of squeezes and kisses, we parted; and she slipt along through the woods, the back way to the house, and I mounted my horse to go to my cabin. But, afore I mounted the beast, I gin him a dozen kicks in his ribs, jest for bearing his testimony agin me, and telling the old Squire that I hedn't 'capital' enough for a corn crib."

VI.

"I was mightily let down, as you may think, by old Squire Hopson; but I was mightily lifted up by Merry Ann.

"But when I got to my cabin, and seed how mean every thing was there, and thought how true it was, all that old Squire Hopson had said, I felt overkim, and I said to myself, 'It's all true! How kin I bring that beautiful yaller flower of the forest to live in sich a mean cabin, and with sich poor accommydations? She that had every thing comforting and nice about her.'

"Then I considered all about 'capital;' and it growed on me, ontil I begin to see that a man might hev good legs and arms and thighs, and a good face of his own, and yit not be a parfect and proper man a'ter all! I hed lived, you see, Jedge, to be twenty-three years of age, and was living no better than a three-old-year b'ar, in a sort of cave, sleeping on shuck and straw, and never looking after to-morrow.

---

5. *WGS:* "Drot," or "Drat," has been called an American vulgarism, but it is genuine old English, as ancient as the days of Ben Jonson. Originally the oath was, "God rot it;" but Puritanism, which was unwilling to take the name of God in vain, was yet not prepared to abandon the oath, so the pious preserved it in an abridged form, omitting the G from God, and using, "Od rot it." It reached its final contraction, "Drot," before it came to America. "Drot it," "Drat it," "Drot your eyes," or "Drot his skin," are so many modes of using it among the uneducated classes.

"I couldn't sleep all that night for the thinking, and obzarvations. That impudent talking of old Hopson put me on a new track. I couldn't give up hunting. I knowed no other business, and I didn't hafe know that.

"I thought to myself, 'I must l'arn my business so as to work like a master.'

"But then, when I considered how hard it was, how slow I was to git the deers and the b'ar, and what a small chaince of money it brought me, I said to myself:

"'Whar's the "capital" to come from?'

"Lawd save us! I ate up the meat pretty much as fast as I got it!

"Well, Jedge, as I said, I had a most miserable night of consideration and obzarvation and concatenation accordingly. I felt all over mean, 'cept now and then, when I thought of dear Merry Ann, and her felicities and cordialities and fidelities; and then, the cuss which she gin, onder the kiver of 'Drot,' to that dried up old bachelor Grimstead. But I got to sleep at last. And I hed a dream. And I thought I seed the prettiest woman critter in the world, next to Merry Ann, standing close by my bedside; and, at first, I thought 'twas Merry Ann, and I was gwine to kiss her agin; but she drawed back and said:

"'Scuse me! I'm not Merry Ann; but I'm her friend and your friend; so don't you be down in the mouth, but keep a good hairt, and you'll hev help, and git the "capital" whar you don't look for it now. It's only needful that you be determined on good works and making a man of yourself.'

"A'ter that dream I slept like a top, woke at day-peep, took my rifle, called up my dog, mounted my horse, and put out for the laurel hollows.

"Well, I hunted all day, made several *starts,* but got nothing; my dog ran off, the rascally pup, and, I reckon, ef Squaire Hopson had met him he'd ha' said 'twas bekaise I starved him! Fact is, we hedn't any on us much to eat that day, and the old mar's ribs stood out bigger than ever.

"All day I rode and followed the track and got nothing.

"Well, jest about sunset I come to a hollow of the hills that I hed never seed before; and in the middle of it was a great pond of water, what you call a lake; and it showed like so much purple glass in the sunset, and 'twas jest as smooth as the big looking-glass of Squaire Hopson's. Thar wa'n't a breath of wind stirring.

"I was mighty tired, so I eased down from the mar', tied up the bridle and check, and let her pick about, and laid myself down onder a tree, jest about twenty yards from the lake, and thought to rest myself ontil the moon riz, which I knowed would be about seven o'clock.

"I didn't mean to fall asleep, but I did it; and I reckon I must ha' slept a good hour, for when I woke the dark hed set in, and I could only see one or two bright stars hyar and thar, shooting out from the dark of the heavens.

But, ef I seed nothing, I haird; and jest sich a sound and noise as I hed never haird before.

"Thar was a rushing and a roaring and a screaming and a plashing, in the air and in the water, as made you think the univarsal world was coming to an eend!

"All that set me up. I was waked up out of sleep and dream, and my eyes opened to every thing that eye could see; and sich another sight I never seed before! I tell you, Jedge, ef there was one wild-goose settling down in that lake, thar was one hundred thousand of 'em! I couldn't see the eend of 'em. They come every minit, swarm a'ter swarm, in tens and twenties and fifties and hundreds; and sich a fuss as they did make! sich a gabbling, sich a splashing, sich a confusion, that I was fairly conflusterated; and I jest lay whar I was, a-watching 'em.

"You never seed beasts so happy! How they flapped their wings; how they gabbled to one another; how they swam hyar and thar, to the very middle of the lake and to the very edge of it, jest a fifty yards from whar I lay squat, never moving leg or arm! It was wonderful to see! I wondered how they could find room, for I reckon thar waur forty thousand on 'em, all scuffling in that leetle lake together!

"Well, as I watched 'em, I said to myself:

"'Now, if a fellow could only captivate all them wild-geese——fresh from Canniday, I reckon——what would they bring in the market at Spartanburg and Greenville? Walker, I knowed, would buy 'em up quick at fifty cents a head. Forty thousand geese at fifty cents a head. Thar was "capital!"'

"I could ha' fired in among 'em with my rifle, never taking aim, and killed a dozen or more, at a single shot; but what was a poor dozen geese, when thar waur forty thousand to captivate?

"What a haul 'twould be, ef a man could only get 'em all in one net! Kiver 'em all at a fling!

"The idee worked like so much fire in my brain.

"How kin it be done?

"That was the question!

"'Kin it be done?' I axed myself.

"'It kin,' I said to myself; 'and I'm the very man to do it! ' Then I begun to work away in the thinking. I thought over all the traps and nets and snares that I hed ever seen or haird of; and the leetle eends of the idee begun to come together in my head; and, watching all the time how the geese flopped and splashed and played and swum, I said to myself:

"'Oh! most beautiful critters! ef I don't make some "capital" out of you, then I'm not dezarving sich a beautiful yaller flower of the forest as my Merry Ann!'

"Well, I watched a long time, ontil dark night, and the stars begun to peep down upon me over the high hill-tops. Then I got up and tuk to my horse and rode home.

"And thar, when I hed swallowed my bit of hoe-cake and bacon and a good strong cup of coffee, and got into bed, I couldn't sleep for a long time, thinking how I was to git them geese.

"But I kept nearing the right idee every minit, and when I was fast asleep it come to me in my dream.

"I seed the same beautifulest young woman agin that hed given me the incouragement before to go ahead, and she helped me out with the idee.

"So, in the morning, I went to work. I rode off to Spartanburg, and bought all the twine and cord and hafe the plow-lines in town; and I got a lot of great fishhooks, all to help make the tanglement parfect; and I got lead for sinkers, and I got cork-wood for floaters; and I pushed for home jist as fast as my poor mar' could streak it.

"I was at work day and night, for nigh on to a week, making my net; and when 'twas done I borrowed a mule and cart from Columbus Mills, thar;—he'll tell you all about it—he kin make his affidavy to the truth of it.

"Well, off I driv with my great net, and got to the lake about noonday. I knowed 'twould take me some hours to make my fixings parfect, and git the net fairly stretched across the lake, and jest deep enough to do the tangling of every leg of the birds in the very midst of their swimming and snorting and splashing and cavorting! When I hed fixed it all fine, and jest as I wanted it, I brought the eends of my plow-lines up to where I was gwine to hide myself. This was onder a strong sapling, and my calkilation was when I hed got the beasts all hooked, forty thousand, more or less—and I could tell how that was from feeling on the line—why, then, I'd whip the line round the sapling, hitch it fast, and draw in my birds at my own ease, without axing much about their comfort.

"'Twas a most beautiful and parfect plan, and all would ha' worked beautiful well but for one leetle oversight of mine. But I won't tell you about that part of the business yit, the more pretickilarly as it all turned out for the very best, as you'll see in the eend.

"I hedn't long finished my fixings when the sun suddenly tumbled down the heights, and the dark begun to creep in upon me, and a pretty cold dark it waur! I remember it well! My teeth begun to chatter in my head, though I was boiling over with inward heat, all jest coming out of my hot eagerness to be captivating the birds.

"Well, Jedge, I hedn't to wait overlong. Soon I haird them coming, screaming fur away, and then I seed them pouring, jest like so many white clouds, straight down, I reckon, from the snow mountains off in Canniday.

"Down they come, millions upon millions, till I was sartin thar waur already pretty nigh on to forty thousand in the lake. It waur always a nice calkilation of mine that the lake could hold fully forty thousand, though onst, when I went round to measure it, stepping it off, I was jubous whether it could hold over thirty-nine thousand; but, as I tuk the measure in hot weather and in a dry spell, I concluded that some of the water along the edges hed dried up, and 'twa'n't so full as when I made my first calkilation. So I hev stuck to that first calkilation ever since.

"Well, thar they waur, forty thousand, we'll say, with, it moutbe, a few millions and hundreds over. And Lawd! how they played and splashed and screamed and dived! I calkilated on hooking a good many of them divers, in pretickilar, and so I watched and waited, ontil I thought I'd feel of my lines; and I begun, leetle by leetle, to haul in, when, Lawd love you, Jedge, sich a ripping and raging, and bouncing and flouncing, and flopping and splashing, and kicking and screaming, you never did hear in all your born days!

"By this I knowed that I hed captivated the captains of the host, and a pretty smart chaince, I reckoned, of the rigilar army, ef 'twa'n't edzactly forty thousand; for I calkilated that some few would git away—run off, jest as the cowards always does in the army, jest when the shooting and confusion begins; still, I reasonably calkilated on the main body of the rigiments; and so, gitting more and more hot and eager, and pulling and hauling, I made one big mistake, and, instid of wrapping the eends of my lines around the sapling that was standing jest behind me, what does I do but wraps 'em round my own thigh—the right thigh, you see—and some of the loops waur hitched round my left arm at the same time!

"All this come of my hurry and ixcitement, for it was burning like a hot fever in my brain, and I didn't know when or how I hed tied myself up, ontil suddenly, with an all-fired scream, all together, them forty thousand geese rose like a great black cloud in the air, all tied up, tangled up—hooked about the legs, hooked about the gills, hooked and fast in some way in the beautiful leetle twistings of my net!

"Yes, Jedge, as I'm a living hunter to-night, hyar a-talking to you, they riz up all together, as ef they hed consulted upon it, like a mighty thundercloud, and off they went, screaming and flouncing, meaning, I reckon, to take the back track to Canniday, in spite of the freezing weather.

"Before I knowed whar I was, Jedge, I was twenty feet in the air, my right thigh up and my left arm, and the other thigh and arm a-dangling useless, and feeling every minit as ef they was gwine to drop off.

"You may be sure I pulled with all my might, but that waur mighty leetle in the fix I was in, and I jest hed to hold on, and see whar the infernal beasts would carry me. I couldn't loose myself, and ef I could I was by this time quite too fur up in the air, and darsn't do so, onless I was willing to hev my brains dashed out, and my whole body mashed to a mammock!

"Oh, Jedge, jest consider my sitivation! It's sich a ricollection, Jedge, that I must rest and liquor, in order to rekiver the necessary strength to tell you what happened next."

VII.

"Yes, Jedge," said Yaou, resuming his narrative, "jest stop whar you air, and consider my sitivation!

"Thar I was dangling, like a dead weight, at the tail of that all-fired cloud of wild-geese, head downward, and gwine, the Lawd knows whar!—to Canniday, or Jericho, or some other heathen territory beyond the Massissipp, and it mout be, over the great etarnal ocean!

"When I thought of *that,* and thought of the plow-lines giving way, and that on a suddent I should come down plump into the big sea, jest in the middle of a great gathering of shirks and whales, to be dewoured and tore to bits by their bloody grinders, I was ready to die of skeer outright. I thought over all my sinnings in a moment, and I thought of my poor dear Merry Ann, and I called out her name, loud as I could, jest as ef the poor gal could hyar me or help me.

"And jest then I could see we waur a drawing nigh a great thunder-cloud. I could see the red tongues running out of its black jaws; and 'Lawd!' says I, 'ef these all-fired infarnal wild beasts of birds should carry me into that cloud to be burned to a coal, fried, and roasted, and biled alive by them tongues of red fire!'

"But the geese fought shy of the cloud, though we passed mighty nigh on to it, and I could see one red streak of lightning run out of the cloud and give us chase for a full hafe a mile; but we waur too fast for it, and, in a tearing passion bekaise it couldn't ketch us, the red streak struck its horns into a great tree jest behind us, that we hed passed over, and tore it into flinders, in the twink of a musquito.

"But by this time I was beginning to feel quite stupid. I knowed that I waur fast gitting onsensible, and it did seem to me as ef my hour waur come, and I was gwine to die—and die by rope, and dangling in the air, a thousand miles from the airth!

"But jest then I was roused up. I felt something brush agin me; then my face was scratched; and, on a suddent, thar was a stop put to my travels by that conveyance. The geese had stopped flying, and waur in a mighty great conflusteration, flopping their wings, as well as they could, and screaming with all the tongues in their jaws. It was clar to me now that we hed run agin something that brought us all up with a short hitch.

"I was shook roughly agin the obstruction, and I put out my right arm and cotched a hold of a long arm of an almighty big tree; then my legs waur cotched betwixt two other branches, and I rekivered myself, so as to set up a leetle and rest. The geese was a tumbling and flopping among the branches. The net was hooked hyar and thar; and the birds waur all about me, swinging and splurging, but onable to break loose and git away.

"By leetle and leetle I come to my clar senses, and begun to feel my sitivation. The stiffness was passing out of my limbs. I could draw up my legs, and, after some hard work, I managed to onwrap the plow-lines from my right thigh and my left arm, and I hed the sense this time to tie the eends pretty tight to a great branch of the tree which stretched clar across and about a foot over my head.

"Then I begun to consider my sitivation. I hed hed a hard riding, that was sartin; and I felt sore enough. And I hed hed a horrid bad skear, enough to make a man's wool turn white afore the night was over. But now I felt easy, bekaise I considered myself safe. With daypeep I calkilated to let myself down from the tree by my plow-lines, and thar, below, tied fast, warn't thar my forty thousand captivated geese?

"'Hurrah!' I sings out. 'Hurrah, Merry Ann; we'll hev the "capital" now, I reckon!'

"And singing out, I drawed up my legs and shifted my body so as to find an easier seat in the crutch of the tree, which was an almighty big chestnut oak, when, O Lawd! on a suddent the stump I hed been a-setting on give way onder me. 'Twas a rotten jint of the tree. It give way, Jedge, as I tell you, and down I went, my legs first and then my whole body — slipping down not on the outside, but into a great hollow of the tree, all the hairt of it being eat out by the rot; and afore I knowed whar I waur, I waur some twenty foot down, I reckon; and by the time I touched bottom, I was up to my neck in honey!

"It was an almighty big honey-tree, full of the sweet treacle; and the bees all gone and left it, I reckon, for a hundred years. And I in it up to my neck.

"I could smell it strong. I could taste it sweet. But I could see nothing.

"Lawd! Lawd! From bad to worse; buried alive in a hollow tree with never a chaince to git out! I would then ha' given all the world ef I was only sailing away with them bloody wild-geese to Canniday, and Jericho, even across the sea, with all its shirks and whales dewouring me.

"Buried alive! O Lawd! O Lawd! 'Lawd save me and help me!' I cried out from the depths. And 'Oh, my Merry Ann,' I cried, 'shill we never meet agin no more!' Scuse my weeping, Jedge, but I feels all over the sinsation, fresh as ever, of being buried alive in a beehive tree and presarved in honey. I must liquor, Jedge."

VIII.

Yaou, after a great swallow of peach and honey, and a formidable groan after it, resumed his narrative as follows:

"Only think of me, Jedge, in my sitivation! Buried alive in the hollow of a mountain chestnut oak! Up to my neck in honey, with never no more an appetite to eat than ef it waur the very gall of bitterness that we reads of in the Holy Scripters!

"All dark, all silent as the grave; 'cept for the gabbling and the cackling of the wild-geese outside, that every now and then would make a great splurging and cavorting, trying to break away from their hitch, which was jist as fast fixed as my own.

"Who would git them geese that hed cost me so much to captivate? Who would inherit my 'capital?' and who would hev Merry Ann? and what will become of the mule and cart of Mills fastened in the woods by the leetle lake?

"I cussed the leetle lake, and the geese, and all the 'capital.'

"I cussed. I couldn't help it. I cussed from the bottom of my hairt, when I ought to ha' bin saying my prayers. And thar was my poor mar' in the stable with never a morsel of feed. She had told tales upon me to Squaire Hopson, it's true, but I forgin her, and thought of her feed, and nobody to give her none. Thar waur corn in the crib and fodder, but it warn't in the stable; and onless Columbus Mills should come looking a'ter me at the cabin, thar waur no hope for me or the mar'.

"Oh, Jedge, you couldn't jedge of my sitivation in that deep hollow, that cave, I may say, of mountain oak! My head waur jest above the honey, and ef I backed it to look up, my long ha'r at the back of the neck a'most stuck fast, so thick was the honey.

"But I couldn't help looking up. The hollow was a wide one at the top, and I could see when a star was passing over. Thar they shined, bright and beautiful, as ef they waur the very eyes of the angels; and, as I seed them come and go, looking smiling in upon me as they come, I cried out to 'em, one by one:

"'Oh, sweet sperrits, blessed angels! ef so be thar's an angel sperrit, as they say, living in all them stars, come down and extricate me from this fix; for, so fur as I kin see, I've got no chaince of help from mortal man or woman. Hairdly onst a year does a human come this way; and ef they did come, how would they know I'm hyar? How could I make them hyar me? O

Lawd! O blessed, beautiful angels in them stars! O give me help! Help me out!' I knowed I prayed like a heathen sinner, but I prayed as well as I knowed how; and thar warn't a star passing over me that I didn't pray to, soon as I seed them shining over the opening of the hollow; and I prayed fast and faster as I seed them passing away and gitting out of sight.

"Well, Jedge, suddently, in the midst of my praying, and jest after one bright, big star hed gone over me without seeing my sitivation, I hed a fresh skeer.

"Suddent I haird a monstrous fluttering among my geese—my 'capital.' Then I haird a great scraping and scratching on the outside of the tree, and, suddent, as I looked up, the mouth of the hollow was shet up.

"All was dark. The stars and sky waur all gone. Something black kivered the hollow, and, in a minit a'ter, I haird something slipping down into the hollow right upon me.

"I could hairdly draw my breath. I begun to fear that I was to be siffocated alive; and as I haird the strange critter slipping down, I shoved out my hands and felt ha'r—coarse wool—and with one hand I cotched hold of the ha'ry leg of a beast, and with t'other hand I cotched hold of his tail.

"'Twas a great b'ar, one of the biggest, come to git his honey. He knowed the tree, Jedge, you see, and ef any beast in the world loves honey, 'tis a b'ar beast. He'll go his death on honey, though the hounds are tearing at his very haunches.

"You may be sure, when I onst knowed what he was, and onst got a good gripe on his hindquarters, I warn't gwine to let go in a hurry. I knowed that was my only chaince for gitting out of the hollow, and I do believe them blessed angels in the stars sent the beast, jest at the right time, to give me human help and assistance.

"Now, yer see, Jedge, thar was no chaince for him turning round upon me. He pretty much filled up the hollow. He knowed his way, and slipped down, eend foremost—the latter eend, you know. He could stand up on his hind-legs and eat all he wanted. Then, with his great sharp claws and his mighty muscle, he could work up, holding on to the sides of the tree, and git out a'most as easy as when he come down.

"Now, you see, ef he weighed five hundred pounds, and could climb like a cat, he could easy carry up a young fellow that hed no flesh to spar', and only weighed a hundred and twenty-five. So I laid my weight on him, eased him off as well as I could, but held on to tail and leg as ef all life and eternity depended upon it.

"Now I reckon, Jedge, that b'ar was pretty much more skeered than I was. He couldn't turn in his shoes, and with something fastened to his ankles, and, as he thought, I reckon, some strange beast fastened to his tail, you never seed beast more eager to git away, and git upwards. He knowed the way, and stuck his claws in the rough sides of the hollow, hand over hand, jest as a sailor pulls a rope, and up we went. We hed, howsomdever, more than one slip back; but, Lawd bless you! I never let go. Up we went, I say, at last, and I stuck jest as close to his haunches as death sticks to a dead nigger. Up we went. I felt myself moving. My neck was out of the honey. My airms were free. I could feel the sticky thing slipping off from me, and a'ter a good quarter of an hour the b'ar was on the great mouth of the hollow; and as I felt that I let go his tail, still keeping fast hold of his leg, and with one hand I cotched hold of the outside rim of the hollow; I found it fast, held on to it; and jest then the b'ar sat squat on the very edge of the hollow, taking a sort of rest a'ter his labor.

"I don't know what 'twas, Jedge, that made me do it. I warn't a-thinking at all. I was only feeling and drawing a long breath. Jest then the b'ar sort o' looked round, as ef to see what varmint it was a-troubling him, when I gin him a mighty push, strong as I could, and he lost his balance and went over outside down cl'ar to the airth, and I could hyar his neck crack, almost as loud as a pistol.

"I drawed a long breath a'ter that, and prayed a short prayer; and feeling my way all the time, so as to be sure agin rotten branches, I got a safe seat among the limbs of the tree, and sot myself down, determined to wait tell broad daylight before I tuk another step in the business."

IX.

"And thar I sot. So fur as I could see, Jedge, I was safe. I hed got out of the tie of the flying geese, and thar they all waur, spread before me, flopping now and then and trying to ixtricate themselves ; but they couldn't come it! Thar they waur, captivated, and so much 'capital' for Sam Snaffles.

"And I hed got out of the lion's den; that is, I hed got out of the honey-tree, and warn't in no present danger of being buried alive agin. Thanks to the b'ar, and to the blessed, beautiful angel sperrits in the stars, that hed sent him thar seeking honey, to be my deliverance from my captivation!

"And thar he lay, jest as quiet as ef he waur a-sleeping, though I knowed his neck was broke. And that b'ar, too, was so much 'capital.'

"And I sot in the tree making my calkilations. I could see now the meaning of that beautiful young critter that come to me in my dreams. I was to hev the 'capital,' but I was to git it through troubles and tribulations, and a mighty bad skeer for life. I never knowed the valley of 'capital' till now, and I seed the sense in all that Squaire Hopson told me, though he did tell it in a mighty spiteful sperrit.

"Well, I calkilated.

"It was cold weather, freezing, and though I had good warm clothes on, I felt monstrous like sleeping, from the cold only, though perhaps the tire and the skeer together hed something to do with it. But I was afeard to sleep. I didn't know what would happen, and a man has never his right courage on-til daylight. I fou't agin sleep by keeping on my calkilation.

"Forty thousand wild-geese!

"Thar wa'n't forty thousand, edzactly—very far from it—but thar they waur, pretty thick; and for every goose I could git from forty to sixty cents in all the villages in South Carolina.

"Thar was 'capital!'

"Then thar waur the b'ar.

"Jedging from his strength in pulling me up, and from his size and fat in filling up that great hollow in the tree, I calkilated that he couldn't weigh less than five hundred pounds. His hide, I knowed, was worth twenty dollars. Then thar was the fat and tallow, and the biled marrow out of his bones, what they makes b'ars grease out of, to make chicken whiskers grow big enough for game-cocks. Then thar waur the meat, skinned, cleaned, and all; thar couldn't be much onder four hundred and fifty pounds, and whether I sold him as fresh meat or cured, he'd bring me ten cents a pound at the least.

"Says I, 'Thar's capital!'

"'Then,' says I, 'thar's my honey-tree! I reckon thar's a matter of ten thousand gallons in this hyar same honey-tree; and if I kint git fifty to seventy cents a gallon for it thar's no alligators in Flurriday!'

"And so I calkilated through the night, fighting agin sleep, and thinking of my 'capital' and Merry Ann together.

"By morning I had calkilated all I hed to do and all I hed to make.

"Soon as I got a peep of day I was bright on the look-out.

"Thar all around me were the captivated geese critters. The b'ar laid down parfectly easy and waiting for the knife; and the geese, I reckon they waur much more tired than me, for they didn't seem to hev the hairt for a single flutter, even when they seed me swing down from the tree among 'em, holding on to my plow-lines and letting myself down easy.

"But first I must tell you, Jedge, when I seed the first signs of daylight and looked around me, Lawd bless me, what should I see but old Tryon Moun-tain, with his great head lifting itself up in the east! And beyant I could see the house and fairm of Columbus Mills; and as I turned to look a leetle south of that, thar was my own poor leetle log-cabin standing quiet, but with never a smoke streaming out from the chimbley.

"'God bless them good angel sperrits,' I said, 'I ain't two miles from home!' Before I come down from the tree I knowed edzactly whar I waur. 'Twas only four miles off from the lake and whar I hitched the mule of Columbus Mills close by the cart. Thar, too, I hed left my rifle. Yit in my miserable fix, carried through the air by them wild-geese, I did think I hed gone a'most a thousand miles towards Canniday.

"Soon as I got down from the tree I pushed off at a trot to git the mule and cart. I was pretty sure of my b'ar and geese when I come back. The cart stood quiet enough. But the mule, having nothing to eat, was sharping her teeth upon a boulder, thinking she'd hev a bite or so before long.

"I hitched her up, brought her to my bee-tree, tumbled the b'ar into the cart, wrung the necks of all the geese that waur thar—many hed got away—and counted some twenty-seven hundred that I piled away atop of the b'ar."

"Twenty-seven hundred!" cried the "Big Lie" and all the hunters at a breath. "Twenty-seven hundred! Why, Yaou, whenever you telled of this thing before you always counted them at 3150!"

"Well, ef I did, I reckon I was right. I was sartinly right then, it being all fresh in my 'membrance; and I'm not the man to go back agin his own words. No, fellows, I sticks to first words and first principles. I scorns to eat my own words. Ef I said 3150, then 3150 it waur, never a goose less. But you'll see how to 'count for all. I reckon 'twas only 2700 I fotched to market. Thar was 200 I gin to Columbus Mills. Then thar was 200 more I carried to Merry Ann; and then thar waur 50 at least, I reckon, I kep for myself. Jest you count-up, Jedge, and you'll see how to squar' it on all sides. When I said 2700 I only counted what I sold in the villages, every head of 'em at fifty cents a head ; and a'ter putting the money in my pocket I felt all over that I hed the 'capital.'

"Well, Jedge, next about the b'ar. Sold the hide and tallow for a fine market-price; sold the meat, got ten cents a pound for it fresh—'twas most beautiful meat; biled down the bones for the marrow; melted down the grease; sold fourteen pounds of it to the barbers and apothecaries; got a dollar a pound for that; sold the hide for twenty dollars; and got the cash for every thing.

"Thar warn't a fambly in all Greenville and Spartanburg and Asheville that didn't git fresh, green wild-geese from me that season, at fifty cents a head, and glad to git, too; the cheapest fresh meat they could buy ; and, I reckon, the finest. And all the people of them villages, ef they hed gone to heaven that week, in the flesh, would have carried nothing better than goose-flesh for the risurrection! Every body ate goose for a month, I reckon, as the weather was freezing cold all the time, and the beasts kept week after week, ontil they waur eaten. From the b'ar only I made a matter of full one hundred dollars. First, thar waur the hide, $20; then 450 pounds of meat, at 10 cents, was $45 ; then the grease, 14 pounds, $14; and the tallow, some $6 more; and the biled marrow, $11.

"Well, count up, Jedge; 2700 wild-geese, at 50 cents, you sees, must be more than $1350. I kin only say, that a'ter all the selling—and I driv at it day and night, with Columbus Mills's mule and cart, and went to every house in every street in all them villages. I hed a'most fifteen hundred dollars, safe stowed away onder the pillows of my bed, all in solid gould and silver.

"But I warn't done! Thar was my bee-tree. Don't you think I waur gwine to lose that honey! no, my darlint! I didn't beat the drum about nothing. I didn't let on to a soul what I was a-doing. They axed me about the wild-geese, but I sent 'em on a wild-goose chase; and 'twa'n't till I hed sold off all the b'ar meat and all the geese that I made ready to git at that honey. I reckon them bees must ha' been making that honey for a hundred years, and was then driv out by the b'ars.

"Columbus Mills will tell you; he axed me all about it; but, though he was always my good friend, I never even telled it to him. But he lent me his mule and cart, good fellow as he is, and never said nothing more; and, quiet enough, without beat of drum, I bought up all the tight-bound barrels that ever brought whisky to Spartanburg and Greenville, whar they hes the taste for that article strong; and day by day I went off carrying as many barrels as the cart could hold and the mule could draw. I tapped the old tree—which was one of the oldest and biggest chestnut oaks I ever did see—close to the bottom, and drawed off the beautiful treacle. I was more than sixteen days about it, and got something over two thousand gallons of the purest, sweetest, yellowest honey you ever did see. I could hairdly git barrels and jimmy Johns enough to hold it; and I sold it out at seventy cents a gallon, which was mighty cheap. So I got from the honey a matter of fourteen hundred dollars.

"Now, Jedge, all this time, though it went very much agin the grain, I kept away from Merry Ann and the old Squaire, her daddy. I sent him two hundred head of geese—some fresh, say one hundred, and another hundred that I hed cleaned and put in salt—and I sent him three jimmyjohns of honey, five gallons each. But I kept away and said nothing, beat no drum, and hed never a thinking but how to git in the 'capital.' And I did git it in!

"When I carried the mule and cart home to Columbus Mills I axed him about a sartin farm of one hundred and sixty acres that he hed to sell. It hed a good house on it. He selled it to me cheap. I paid him down, and put the titles in my pocket. 'Thar's capital!' says I.

"*That* waur a fixed thing for ever and ever. And when I hed moved every thing from the old cabin to the new farm, Columbus let me hev a fine milch cow that gin eleven quarts a day, with a beautiful young caif. Jest about that time thar was a great sale of the furniter of the Ashmore family down at Spartanburg, and I remembered I hed no decent bedstead, or any thing rightly sarving for a young woman's chamber; so I went to the sale, and bought a fine strong mahogany bedstead, a dozen chairs, a chist of drawers, and some other things that ain't quite mentionable, Jedge, but all proper for a lady's chamber; and I soon hed the house fixed up ready for any thing. And up to this time I never let on to any body what I was a-thinking about or what I was a-doing, ontil I could stand up in my own doorway and look about me, and say to myself—this is my 'capital,' I reckon; and when I hed got all that I thought a needcessity to git, I took 'count of every thing.

"I spread the title-deeds of my fairm out on the table. I read 'em over three times to see ef 'twaur all right. Thar was my name several times in big letters, 'to hev and to hold.'

"Then I fixed the furniter. Then I brought out into the stable-yard the old mar'—you couldn't count her ribs *now,* and she was spry as ef she hed got a new conceit of herself.

"Then thar was my beautiful cow and caif, sealing fat, both on 'em, and sleek as a doe in autumn.

"Then thar waur a fine young mule that I bought in Spartanburg; my cart, and a strong second-hand buggy, that could carry two pussons convenient of two different sexes. And I felt big, like a man of consekence and capital.

"That warn't all.

"I had the shiners, Jedge, besides—all in gould and silver—none of your dirty rags and blotty spotty paper. That was the time of Old Hickory—General Jackson, you know—when he kicked over Nick Biddle's consarn, and gin us the beautiful Benton Mint Drops, in place of rotten paper. You could git the gould and silver jest for the axing, in them days, you know.

"I hed a grand count of my money, Jedge. I hed it in a dozen or twenty little bags of leather—the gould—and the silver I hed in shot-bags. It took me a whole morning to count it up and git the figgers right. Then I stuffed it in my pockets, hyar and thar, every whar, wherever I could stow a bag; and the silver I stuffed away in my saddle-bags, and clapped it on the mar'.

"Then I mounted myself, and sot the mar's nose straight in bee-line for the fairm of Squaire Hopson.

"I was a-gwine, you see, to supprise him with my 'capital;' but, fust, I meant to give him a mighty grand skeer.

"You see, when I was a-trading with Columbus Mills about the fairm and cattle and other things, I ups and tells him about my courting of Merry Ann; and when I told him about Squaire Hopson's talk about 'capital,' he says:

"'The old skunk! What right hes he to be talking big so, when he kain't pay his own debts. He's been owing me three hundred and fifty dollars now gwine on three years, and I kain't git even the *intrust* out of him. I've got a mortgage on his fairm for the whole, and ef he won't let you hev his da'ter, jest you come to me, and I'll clap the screws to him in short order.'

"Says I, 'Columbus, won't you sell me that mortgage?'

"'You shill hev it for the face of the debt,' says he, 'not considerin' the intrust.'

"'It's a bargin,' says I; and I paid him down the money, and he signed the mortgage over to me for a vallyable consideration.

"I hed that beautiful paper in my breast pocket, and felt strong to face the Squaire in his own house, knowing how I could turn him out of it! And I mustn't forget to tell you how I got myself a new rig of clothing, with a mighty fine over-coat, and a new fur cap; and as I looked in the glass I felt my consekence all over at every for'a'd step I tuk; and I felt my inches growing with every pace of the mar' on the high-road to Merry Ann and her beautiful daddy!"

X.

"Well, Jedge, before I quite got to the Squaire's farm, who should come out to meet me in the road but Merry Ann, her own self! She hed spied me, I reckon, as I crossed the bald ridge a quarter of a mile away. I do reckon the dear gal hed been looking out for me every day the whole eleven days in the week, counting in all the Sundays. In the mountains, you know, Jedge, that the weeks sometimes run to twelve, and even fourteen days, specially when we're on a long camp-hunt!

"Well, Merry Ann cried and laughed together, she was so tarnation glad to see me agin. Says she:

"'Oh, Sam! I'm so glad to see you! I was afeard you had clean gin me up. And thar's that fusty old bachelor Grimstead, he's a coming here a'most every day; and daddy, he sw'ars that I shill marry him, and nobody else; and mammy, she's at me too, all the time, telling me how fine a fairm he's got, and what a nice carriage, and all that; and mammy says as how daddy'll be sure to beat me ef I don't hev him. But I kain't bear to look at him, the old griesly!'

"'Cuss him!' says I. 'Cuss him, Merry Ann!'

"And she did, but onder her breath——the old cuss.

"'Drot him!' says she; and she said louder, 'and drot me, too, Sam, ef I ever marries any body but you.'

"By this time I hed got down and gin her a long strong hug, and a'most twenty or a dozen kisses, and I says:

"'You sha'n't marry nobody but me, Merry Ann; and we'll hev the marriage this very night, ef you says so!'

"'Oh! psho, Sam! How you does talk!'

"'Ef I don't marry you to-night, Merry Ann, I'm a holy mortar, and a sinner not to be saved by any salting, though you puts the petre with the salt. I'm come for that very thing. Don't you see my new clothes?'

"'Well, you hev got a beautiful coat, Sam; all so blue, and with sich shiny buttons.'

"'Look at my waistcoat, Merry Ann! What do you think of that?'

"'Why, it's a most beautiful blue welvet!'

"'That's the very article,' says I. 'And see the breeches, Merry Ann; and the boots!'

"'Well,' says she, 'I'm fair astonished, Sam! Why whar, Sam, did you find all the money for these fine things?'

"'A beautiful young woman, a'most as beautiful as you, Merry Ann, come to me the very night of that day when your daddy driv me off with a flea in my ear. She come to me to my bed at midnight—'

"'Oh, Sam! *ain't* you ashamed!'

"' 'Twas in a dream, Merry Ann; and she tells me something to incourage me to go for'a'd, and I went for'a'd, bright and airly next morning, and I picked up three sarvants that hev been working for me ever sence.'

"'What sarvants?' says she.

"'One was a goose, one was a b'ar, and t'other was a bee!'

"'Now you're a-fooling me, Sam.'

"'You'll see! Only you git yourself ready, for, by the eternal Hokies, I marries you this very night, and takes you home to *my* fairm bright and airly to-morrow morning.'

"'I do think, Sam, you must be downright crazy.'

"'You'll see and believe! Do you go home and git yourself fixed up for the wedding. Old Parson Stovall lives only two miles from your daddy, and I'll hev him hyar by sundown. You'll see!'

"'But ef I waur to b'lieve you, Sam—'

"'I've got on my wedding-clothes o' purpose, Merry Ann.'

"'But *I* hain't got no clothes fit for a gal to be married in,' says she.

"'I'll marry you this very night, Merry Ann,' says I, 'though you hedn't a stitch of clothing at all!'

"'Git out, you sassy Sam,' says she, slapping my face. Then I kissed her in her very mouth, and a'ter that we walked on together, I leading the mar'.

"Says she, as we neared the house, 'Sam, let me go before, or stay hyar in the thick, and you go in by yourself. Daddy's in the hall, smoking his pipe and reading the newspapers.'

"'We'll walk in together,' says I, quite consekential.

"Says she, 'I'm so afeard.'

"'Don't you be afeard, Merry Ann,' says I; 'you'll see that all will come out jest as I tells you. We'll be hitched to-night, ef Parson Stovall, or any other parson, kin be got to tie us up!'

"Says she, suddenly, 'Sam, you're a-walking lame, I'm a-thinking. What's the matter? Hev you hurt yourself any way?'

"Says I, 'It's only owing to my not balancing my accounts even in my pockets. You see I feel so much like flying in the air with the idee of marrying you to-night that I filled my pockets with rocks, jest to keep me down.'

"'I do think, Sam, you're a leetle cracked in the upper story.'

"'Well,' says I, 'ef so, the crack has let in a blessed chaince of the beautifulest sunlight! You'll see! Cracked, indeed! Ha, ha, ha! Wait till I've done with your daddy! I'm gwine to square accounts with *him,* and, I reckon, when I'm done with him, you'll guess that the crack's in *his* skull, and not in mine.'

"'What! you wouldn't knock my father, Sam!' says she, drawing off from me and looking skeary.

"'Don't you be afeard; but it's very sartin, ef our heads don't come together, Merry Ann, you won't hev me for your husband to-night. And that's what I've swore upon. Hyar we air!'

"When we got to the yard I led in the mar', and Merry Ann she ran away from me and dodged round the house. I hitched the mar' to the post, took off the saddle-bags, which was mighty heavy, and walked into the house stiff enough I tell you, though the gould in my pockets pretty much weighed me down as I walked.

"Well, in I walked, and thar sat the old Squire smoking his pipe and reading the newspaper. He looked at me through his specs over the newspaper, and when he seed who 'twas his mouth put on that same conceited sort of grin and smile that he ginerally hed when he spoke to me.

"'Well,' says he, gruffly enough, 'it's you, Sam Snaffles, is it?' Then he seems to diskiver my new clothes and boots, and he sings out, 'Heigh! you're tip-toe fine to-day! What fool of a shop-keeper in Spartanburg have you tuk in this time, Sam?'

"Says I, cool enough, 'I'll answer all them iligant questions a'ter a while, Squaire ; but would prefar to see to business fust.'

"'Business!' says he; 'and what business kin you hev with me, I wants to know?'

"'You shill know, Squaire, soon enough; and I only hopes it will be to your liking a'ter you l'arn it.'

"So I laid my saddle-bags down at my feet and tuk a chair quite at my ease; and I could see that he was all astare in wonderment at what he thought my sassiness. As I felt I had my hook in his gills, though he didn't know it yit, I felt in the humor to tickle him and play him as we does a trout.

"Says I, 'Squaire Hopson, you owes a sartin amount of money, say $350, with intrust on it for now three years, to Dr. Columbus Mills.'

"At this he squares round, looks me full in the face, and says:

"'What the old Harry's that to you?'

"Says I, gwine on cool and straight, 'You gin him a mortgage on this fairm for security.'

"'What's that to you?' says he.

"'The mortgage is over-due by two years, Squaire,' says I.

"'What the old Harry's all that to you, I say?' he fairly roared out.

"'Well, nothing much, I reckon. The $350, with three years' intrust at seven per cent., making it now—I've calkelated it all without compound-ing—something over $425—well, Squaire, that's not much to *you,* I reckon, with your large capital. But it's something to me.'

"'But I ask you again, Sir,' he says, 'what is all this to you?'

"'Jist about what I tells you—say $425; and I've come hyar this morning, bright and airly, in hope you'll be able to square up and satisfy the mortgage. Hyar's the dockyment.'

"And I drawed the paper from my breast pocket.

"'And you tell me that Dr. Mills sent you hyar,' says he, 'to collect this money?'

"'No; I come myself on my own hook.'

"'Well,' says he, 'you shill hev your answer at onst. Take that paper back to Dr. Mills and tell him that I'll take an airly opportunity to call and arrange the business with him. You hev your answer, Sir,' he says, quite grand, 'and the sooner you makes yourself scarce the better.'

"'Much obleeged to you, Squaire, for your ceveelity,' says I; 'but I ain't quite satisfied with that answer. I've come for the money due on this paper, and must hev it, Squaire, or thar will be what the lawyers call *four closures* upon it!'

"'Enough! Tell Dr. Mills I will answer his demand in person.'

"'You needn't trouble yourself, Squaire; for ef you'll jest look at the back of that paper, and read the 'signmeant, you'll see that you've got to settle with Sam Snaffles, and not with Columbus Mills!'

"Then he snatches up the dockyment, turns it over, and reads the rigilar 'signmeant, writ in Columbus Mills's own handwrite.

"Then the Squaire looks at me with a great stare, and he says, to him-self like:

"'It's a *bonny fodder* 'signmeant.'

"'Yes,' says I, 'it's *bonny fodder*—rigilar in law—and the titles all made out complete to me, Sam Snaffles; signed, sealed, and delivered, as the law-yers says it.'

"'And how the old Harry come you by this paper?' says he.

"I was gitting riled, and I was determined, this time, to gin my hook a pretty sharp jerk in his gills; so I says:

"'What the old Harry's that to *you,* Squaire? Thar's but one question 'twixt us two—air you ready to pay that money down on the hub, at onst, to me, Sam Snaffles?'

"'No, Sir, I am not.'

"'How long a time will you ax from me, by way of marciful indulgence?'

"'It must be some time yit,' says he, quite sulky; and then he goes on agin:

"'I'd like to know how you come by that 'signmeant, Mr. Snaffles.'

"Mr. Snaffles! Ah! ha!

"'I don't see any neecessity,' says I, 'for answering any questions. Thar's the dockyment to speak for itself. You see that Columbus Mills 'signs to me for full *con*sideration. That means I paid him!'

"'And why did you buy this mortgage?'

"'You might as well ax me how I come by the money to buy any thing,' says I.

"'Well, I do ax you,' says he.

"'And I answers you,' says I, 'in the very words from your own mouth, What the old Harry's that to you?'

"'This is hardly 'spectful, Mr. Snaffles,' says he.

"Says I, ''Spectful gits only what 'spectful gives! Ef any man but you, Squaire, hed been so onrespectful in his talk to me as you hev been I'd ha' mashed his muzzle! But I don't wish to be onrespectful. All I axes is the civil answer. I wants to know when you kin pay this money?'

"'I kain't say, Sir.'

"'Well, you see, I thought as how you couldn't pay, spite of all your "capital," as you hedn't paid even the *intrust* on it for three years; and, to tell you the truth, I was in hopes you couldn't pay, as I hed a liking for this fairm always ; and as I am jest about to git married, you see—'

"'Who the old Harry air you gwine to marry?' says he.

"'What the old Harry's that to you?' says I, giving him as good as he sent. But I went on:

"'You may be sure it's one of the woman kind. I don't hanker a'ter a wife with a beard; and I expects—God willing, weather premitting, and the parson being sober—to be married this very night!'

"'To-night!' says he, not knowing well what to say.

"'Yes; you see I've got my wedding-breeches on. I'm to be married to-night, and I wants to take my wife to her own fairm as soon as I kin. Now, you see, Squaire, I all along set my hairt on this fairm of yourn, and I detarmined, ef ever I could git the "capital," to git hold of it; and that was the idee I hed when I bought the 'signmeant of the mortgage from Columbus Mills. So, you see, ef you kain't pay a'ter three years, you never kin pay, I reckon; and ef I don't git my money this day, why—I kain't help it—the lawyers will hev to see to the *four closures* to-morrow!'

"'Great God, Sir!' says he, rising out of his chair, and crossing the room up and down, 'do you coolly propose to turn me and my family headlong out of my house?'

"'Well now,' says I, 'Squaire, that's not edzactly the way to put it. As I reads this dockyment'—and I tuk up and put the mortgage in my pocket— 'the house and fairm are *mine* by law. They onst was yourn; but it wants nothing now but the *four closures* to make 'em mine.'

"'And would you force the sale of property worth $2000 and more for a miserable $400?'

"'It must sell for what it'll bring, Squaire; and I stands ready to buy it for my wife, you see, ef it costs me twice as much as the mortgage.'

"'Your wife!' says he; 'who the old Harry is she? You once pertended to have an affection for my da'ter.'

"'So I hed; but you hedn't the proper affection for your da'ter that I hed. You prefar'd money to her affections, and you driv me off to git "capital!" Well, I tuk your advice, and I've got the capital.'

"'And whar the old Harry,' said he, 'did you git it?'

"'Well, I made good tairms with the old devil for a hundred years, and he found me in the money.'

"'It must hev been so,' said he. 'You waur not the man to git capital in any other way.'

"Then he goes on: 'But what becomes of your pertended affection for my da'ter?'

"''Twa'n't pertended; but you throwed yourself betwixt us with all your force, and broke the gal's hairt, and broke mine, so far as you could; and as I couldn't live without company, I hed to look out for myself and find a wife as I could. I tell you, as I'm to be married to-night, and as I've swore a most etarnal oath to hev this fairm, you'll hev to raise the wind to-day, and square off with me, or the lawyers will be at you with the *four closures* to-morrow, bright and airly.'

"'Dod tern you!' he cries out. 'Does you want to drive me mad!'

"'By no manner of means,' says I, jest about as cool and quiet as a cowcumber.

"But he was at biling heat. He was all over in a stew and a fever. He filled his pipe and lighted it, and then smashed it over the chimbly. Then he crammed the newspaper in the fire, and crushed it into the blaze with his boot. Then he turned to me, suddent, and said:

"'Yes, you pertended to love my da'ter, and now you are pushing her father to desperation. Now ef you ever did love Merry Ann honestly, raally, truly, and *bonny fodder,* you couldn't help loving her yit. And yit, hyar you're gwine to marry another woman, that, prehaps, you don't affection at all.'

"'It's quite a sensible view you takes of the subject,' says I; 'the only pity is that you didn't take the same squint at it long ago, when I axed you to let me hev Merry Ann. *Then* you didn't valley her affections or mine. You hed no thought of nothing but the "capital" then, and the affections might all go to Jericho, for what you keered! I'd ha' married Merry Ann, and she me, and we'd ha' got on for a spell in a log-cabin, for, though I was poor, I hed the genwine grit of a man, and would come to something, and we'd ha' got on; and yit, without any "capital" your own self, and kivered up with debt as with a winter over-coat, hyar, you waur positive that I shouldn't hev your da'ter, and you waur a-preparing to sell her hyar to an old sour-tempered bachelor, more than double her age. Dern the capital! A man's best capital for any woman, ef so be he *is* a man. Bekaise, ef he be a man, he'll work out cl'ar, though he may hev a long straining for it through the sieve. Dern the capital! You've as good as sold that gal child to old Grimstead, jest from your love of money!'

"'But she won't hev him,' says he.

"'The wiser gal child,' says I. 'Ef you only hed onderstood me and that poor child, I hed it in me to make the "capital"—dern the capital!—and now you've ruined her, and yourself, and me, and all; and dern my buttons but I must be married to-night, and jest as soon a'ter as the lawyers kin fix it I must hev this fairm for my wife. My hairt's set on it, and I've swore it a dozen o' times on the Holy Hokies!'

"The poor old Squire fairly sweated; but he couldn't say much. He'd come up to me and say:

"'Ef you only did love Merry Ann!'

"'Oh,' says I, 'what's the use of your talking that? Ef you only hed ha' loved your own da'ter!'

"Then the old chap begun to cry, and as I seed that I jest kicked over my saddle-bags lying at my feet, and the silver Mexicans rolled out—a bushel on 'em, I reckon—and, O Lawd! how the old fellow jumped, staring with all his eyes at me and the dollars!

"'It's money!' says he.

"'Yes,' says I, 'jest a few hundreds of thousands of *my* "capital."' I didn't stop at the figgers, you see.

"Then he turns to me and says, 'Sam Snaffles, you're a most wonderful man. You're a mystery to me. Whar, in the name of God, hev you been? and what hev you been doing? and whar did you git all this power of capital?'

"I jest laughed, and went to the door and called Merry Ann. She come mighty quick. I reckon she was watching and waiting.

"Says I, 'Merry Ann, that's money. Pick it up and put it back in the saddle-bags, ef you please.'

"Then says I, turning to the old man, 'Thar's that whole bushel of Mexicans, I reckon. Thar monstrous heavy. My old mar'—ax her about her ribs now!—she fairly squelched onder the weight of me and that money. And I'm pretty heavy loaded myself. I must lighten; with your leave, Squaire.'

"And I pulled out a leetle doeskin bag of gould half eagles from my right-hand pocket and poured them out upon the table; then I emptied my left-hand pocket, then the side pockets of the coat, then the skairt pockets, and jist spread the shiners out upon the table.

"Merry Ann was fairly frightened, and run out of the room; then the old woman she come in, and as the old Squaire seed her, he tuk her by the shoulder and said:

"'Jest you look at that thar.'

"And when she looked and seed, the poor old hypercritical scamp sinner turned round to me and flung her airms round my neck, and said:

"'I always said you waur the only right man for Merry Ann.'

"The old spooney!

"Well, when I hed let 'em look enough, and wonder enough, I jest turned Merry Ann and her mother out of the room.

"The old Squaire, he waur a-setting down agin in his airm-chair, not edzactly knowing what to say or what to do, but watching all my motions, jest as sharp as a cat watches a mouse when she is hafe hungry.

"Thar was all the Mexicans put back in the saddle-bags, but he hed seen 'em, and thar was all the leetle bags of gould spread upon the table; the gould—hafe and quarter eagles—jest lying out of the mouths of the leetle bags as ef wanting to creep back agin.

"And thar sot the old Squaire, looking at 'em all as greedy as a fish-hawk down upon a pairch in the river. And, betwixt a whine and a cry and a talk, he says:

"'Ah, Sam Snaffles, ef you ever did love my leetle Merry Ann, you would never marry any other woman.'

"Then you ought to ha' seed me. I felt myself sixteen feet high, and jest as solid as a chestnut oak. I walked up to the old man, and I tuk him quiet by the collar of his coat, with my thumb and forefinger, and I said:

"'Git up, Squaire, for a bit.'

"And up he got.

"Then I marched him to the big glass agin the wall, and I said to him: 'Look, ef you please.'

"And he said, 'I'm looking.'

"And I said, 'What does you see?'

"He answered, 'I sees you and me.'

"I says, 'Look agin, and tell me what you *obzarves*.'

"'Well,' says he, 'I obzarves.'

"And says I, 'What does your *obzarving* amount to? That's the how.'

"And says he, 'I sees a man alongside of me, as good-looking and hand-some a young man as ever I seed in all my life.'

"'Well,' says I, 'that's a correct obzarvation. But,' says I, 'what does you see of *your own self?*'

"'Well, I kain't edzackly say.'

"'Look good!' says I. 'Obzarve.'

"Says he, 'Don't ax me.'

"'Now,' says I, 'that won't edzactly do. I tell you now, look good, and ax yourself ef you're the sawt of looking man that hes any right to be a feyther-in-law to a fine, young, handsome-looking fellow like me, what's got the "capital?"'

"Then he laughed out at the humor of the sitivation; and he says, 'Well, Sam Snaffles, you've got me dead this time. You're a different man from what I thought you. But, Sam, you'll confess, I reckon, that ef I hedn't sent you off with a flea in your ear when I hed you up afore the looking-glass, you'd never ha' gone to work to git in the "capital."'

"'I don't know *that*, Squiaire,' says I. 'Sarcumstances sarve to make a man take one road when he mout take another; but when you meets a man what has the hairt to love a woman strong as a lion, and to fight an inimy big as a buffalo, he's got the raal grit in him. You knowed I was young, and I was poor, and you knowed the business of a hunter is a mighty poor business ef the man ain't born to it. Well, I didn't do much at it jest bekaise my hairt was so full of Merry Ann; and you should ha' made a calkilation and allowed for *that*. But you poked your fun at me and riled me consumedly; but I was de-tarmined that you shouldn't break *my* hairt or the hairt of Merry Ann. Well, you hed your humors, and I've tried to take the change out of you. And now, ef you raally thinks, a'ter that obzarvation in the glass, that you kin make a respectable feyther-in-law to sich a fine-looking fellow as me, what's got the "capital," jest say the word, and we'll call Merry Ann in to bind the bargin. And you must talk out quick, for the wedding's to take place this very night. I've swore it by the etarnal Hokies.'

"'To-night!' says he.

"'Look at the "capital"' says I; and I pinted to the gould on the table and the silver in the saddle-bags.

"'But, Lawd love you, Sam,' says he, 'it's so suddent, and we kain't make the preparations in time.'

"Says I, 'look at the "capital," Squaire, and dern the preparations!'

"'But,' says he, 'we hain't time to ax the company.'

"'Dern the company!' says I; 'I don't b'lieve in company the very night a man gits married. His new wife's company enough for him ef he's sensible.'

"'But, Sam,' says he, 'it's not possible to git up a supper by tonight.'

"Says I, 'Look you, Squire, the very last thing a man wants on his wedding night is supper.'

"Then he said something about the old woman, his wife.

"Says I, 'Jest you call her in and show her the "capital."'"

"So he called in the old woman, and then in come Merry Ann, and thar was great hemmings and hawings; and the old woman she said:

"'I've only got the one da'ter, Sam, and we must hev a big wedding! We *must* spread ourselves. We've got a smart chaince of friends and acquaintances, you see, and 'twon't be decent onless we axes them, and they won't like it! We *must* make a big show for the honor and 'spectability of the family.'

"Says I, 'Look you, old lady! I've swore a most tremendous oath, by the Holy Hokies, that Merry Ann and me air to be married this very night, and I kain't break sich an oath as that! Merry Ann,' says I, 'you wouldn't hev me break sich a tremendous oath as that?'

"And, all in a trimble, she says, 'Never, Sam! No!'

"'You hyar that, old lady!' says I. 'We marries to-night, by the Holy Hokies! and we'll hev no company but old Parson Stovall, to make the hitch; and Merry Ann and me go off by sunrise to-morrow morning—you hyar?—to my own fairm, whar thar's a great deal of furniter fixing for her to do. A'ter that you kin advertise the whole county to come in, ef you please, and eat all the supper you kin spread! Now hurry up,' says I, 'and git as ready as you kin, for I'm gwine to ride over to Parson Stovall's this minit. I'll be back to dinner in hafe an hour. Merry Ann, you gether up that gould and silver, and lock it up. It's *our* "capital!" As for you, Squaire, thar's the mortgage on your fairm, which Merry Ann shill give you, to do as you please with it, as soon as the parson has done the hitch, and I kin call Merry Ann, Mrs. Snaffles— Madam Merry Ann Snaffles, and so forth, and aforesaid.'

"I laid down the law that time for all parties, and showed the old Squaire sich a picter of himself, and me standing aside him, looking seven foot high, at the least, that I jest worked the business 'cording to my own pleasure. When neither the daddy nor the mammy hed any thing more to say, I jumped on my mar' and rode over to old Parson Stovall.

"Says I, 'Parson, thar's to be a hitch to-night, and you're to see a'ter the right knot. You knows what I means. I wants you over at Squaire Hopson's. Me and Merry Ann, his da'ter, mean to hop the twig to-night, and you're to see that we hop squar', and that all's even, 'cording to the law, Moses, and the profits! I stand treat, Parson, and you won't be the worse for your riding. I pays in gould!'

"So he promised to come by dusk; and come he did. The old lady hed got some supper, and tried her best to do what she could at sich short notice. The venison ham was mighty fine, I reckon, for Parson Stovall played a great stick at it; and ef they hedn't cooked up four of my wild-geese, then the devil's an angel of light, and Sam Snaffles no better than a sinner! And thar was any quantity of jimmyjohns, peach and honey considered. Parson Stovall was a great feeder, and I begun to think he never would be done. But at last he wiped his mouth, swallowed his fifth cup of coffee, washed it down with a stiff dram of peach and honey, wiped his mouth agin, and pulled out his prayer-book, psalmody, and Holy Scrip—three volumes in all—and he hemmed three times, and begun to look out for the marriage text, but begun with giving out the 100th Psalm.

"'With one consent, let's all unite—'

"'No,' says I, 'Parson; not all! It's only Merry Ann and me what's to unite to-night!'

"Jest then, afore he could answer, who should pop in but old bachelor Grimstead! and he looked round 'bout him, specially upon me and the parson, as ef to say:

"'What the old Harry's they doing hyar!'

"And I could see that the old Squaire was oneasy. But the blessed old Parson Stovall, he gin 'em no time for ixplanation or palaver; but he gits up, stands up squar', looks solemn as a meat-axe, and he says:

"'Let the parties which I'm to bind together in the holy bonds of wedlock stand up before me!'

"And, Lawd bless you, as he says the words, what should that old skunk of a bachelor do, but he gits up, stately as an old buck in spring time, and he marches over to my Merry Ann! But I was too much and too spry for him. I puts in betwixt 'em, and I takes the old bachelor by his coat-collar, 'twixt my thumb and forefinger, and afore he knows whar he is, I marches him up to the big looking-glass, and I says:

"'Look!'

"'Well,' says he, 'what?'

"'Look good,' says I.

"'I'm looking,' says he. 'But what do you mean, Sir?'

"Says I, 'Obzarve! Do you see yourself? Obzarve!'

"'I reckon I do,' says he.

"'Then,' says I, 'ax yourself the question, ef you're the sawt of looking man to marry my Merry Ann.'

"Then the old Squaire burst out a-laughing. He couldn't help it.

"'Capital!' says he.

"'It's capital,' says I. 'But hyar we air, Parson. Put on the hitch, jest as quick as you kin clinch it; for thar's no telling how many slips thar may be 'twixt the cup and the lips when these hungry old bachelors air about.'

"'Who gives away this young woman?' axes the parson; and the Squire stands up and does the thing needful. I hed the ring ready, and before the parson had quite got through, old Grimstead vamoosed.

"He waur a leetle slow in understanding that he warn't wanted, and warn't, nohow, any party to the business. But he and the Squire hed a mighty quarrel a'terwards, and ef 't hedn't been for me, he'd ha' licked the Squire. He was able to do it; but I jest cocked my cap at him one day, and, says I, in the Injin language:

"'Yaou!' And he didn't know what I meant; but I looked tomahawks at him, so he gin ground; and he's getting old so fast that you kin see him growing downwards all the time.

"All that, Jedge, is jest thirteen years ago; and me and Merry Ann git on famously, and thar's no eend to the capital! Gould breeds like the cows, and it's only needful to squeeze the bags now and then to make Merry Ann happy as a tomtit. Thirteen years of married life, and look at me! You see for yourself, Jedge, that I'm not much the worse for wear; and I kin answer for Merry Ann, too, though, Jedge, we hev hed thirty-six children."

"What!" says I, "thirty-six children in thirteen years!"

The "Big Lie" roared aloud.

"Hurrah, Sharp! Go it! You're making it spread! That last shot will make the Jedge know that you're a right truthful sinner, of a Saturday night, and in the 'Lying Camp.'"

"To be sure! You see, Merry Ann keeps on. But you've only got to do the ciphering for yourself. Here, now, Jedge, look at it. Count for yourself. First we had *three* gal children, you see. Very well! Put down three. Then we had *six* boys, one every year for four years; and then, the fifth year, Merry Ann throwed deuce. Now put down the six boys a'ter the three gals, and ef that don't make thirty-six, thar's no snakes in all Flurriday!

"Now, men," says Sam, "let's liquor all round, and drink the health of Mrs. Merry Ann Snaffles and the thirty-six children, all alive and kicking; and glad to see you, Jedge, and the rest of the company. We're doing right well; but I hes, every now and then, to put my thumb and forefinger on the Squire's collar, and show him his face in the big glass, and call on him for an *obzarvation*—for he's mighty fond of *going shar's* in my 'capital.'"

Nonfiction

Notes of a Small Tourist—No. 10

[April or May 1831]
From Mobile, after a day's delay, I proceeded, in the stage to Pascagoula, a
distance from that city, over a rough road, of about thirty miles. From the
Bay of Pascagoula, a steamboat in waiting, took us, in something like twenty
hours, through the Lakes Bergne and Pontchartrain, and the Rigolets; (somewhat notorious during the last war, for the loss of our gunboat armament in
that quarter) on to the city of New-Orleans.—At the entrance of the Lake
Pontchartrain, we passed the beautiful Island and Fort of *Petit Coquille,* (Little Shell) which graces and overlooks the pass into this wrothy little Bay. The
Island was green with a herbage interspersed with trees of luxuriant foliage,
and relieved handsomely by the rather elegant quarters of the officers and
men of the station. The Fort is, in most general particulars, not unlike our
own Castle Pinckney.

Our next point made, was the light house and pickets (piques?) of the
petty harbor, canal and Bayou of St. John, the private and backdoor entrance
to New-Orleans. From the light house to the city, is from five to seven miles.
This distance you are carried in a pirogue (so called)—a couple of cause bot-
toms, lashed together, and overlaid with a plain deck and railing something
like a ferry boat, having a mast in the fore, to the top of which is attached
a rope, which in turn, is tackled to a horse on shore, mounted by an urchin of some twelve or fifteen years, who trots him on at the rate of four or
five miles an hour, sometimes increasing and sometimes lessening the speed,
according to the indentions of the shore, and the obstructions arising from

collision with other craft travelling in a like manner, until you are safely deposited at the reservoir in the rear of the town, called the Basin. This is a kind of roadstead for the little navigators who trade to Mobile, Biloxi, Pearlington, Madisonville and the contiguous rivers.

New-Orleans has grown prodigiously—perhaps its increase in wealth, population and business generally, since 1825, is without parallel in these United States. Its population, in that year, was, I believe about 10,000. I should not hesitate now, to consider it, at the least calculation, 65,000. By some, it is estimated, including transients at 70 and 75,000. It is destined probably, in the period of twenty years hence to become the greatest city, in a commercial and trading point of view, in our country—New-York, not excepted. The resources of the Mississippi are incomputable—population, without limit to its increase; and its advantages, over any other single section of territory, without any comparison or rivalship. In size, it has grown two-fold. The Fauxbourg St. Marie, (the American portion) is larger or as large as the City Proper. The buildings, by law, are made only of brick, and they run along in solid masses, that give them an air of durability, proportioned to what one conceives the destiny the city. The American population is daily and rapidly increasing, as well in number, as in respectability. A further and more scrupulous attention to the police regulations and general cleanliness of the city has greatly added to its order and salubrity, and the improvement in society, consequent thereto, is evident to the most indifferent spectator. I shall not have time to speak at large of many topics of interest, which presented themselves to my view during my stay in Orleans, from the press of business and the little time left me, before I commence my return journey—which I propose to do in a week hence. But, I visited the French and American Theatres—with the order, neatness and elegance of the former, so different from the confusion, bungling and noise, which so interfere with the scene, in ours—not to speak of the general respectability and ease of the acting, I was highly delighted. They have at this Theatre one *reputed* able Tragedian Aristippe—but, him I had not the pleasure to see in character. Caldwell's American Theatre is very respectable—but the fact is, we Americans, are rather too indifferent to genuine *politeness,* properly to appreciate this most elevated among the Fine Arts. Here I saw Clara, the Fisher—clever and fascinating as ever, and Kean the younger. He tells me, he shall visit us professionally during the season ensuing. His person is small and well made—his features amiable, and, in conversation, rather intelligent. As an actor, I do not estimate his pretensions highly. I saw him in Othello and Reuben Glenroy. I think him better calculated to succeed in melo-dramatic heroes and in genteel comedy generally, than in the more arduous and absorbing labors of the tragic muse. He is respectable however, and does not blunder. His Reuben Glenroy was excellent. His voice is low, hoarse and unpleasing upon the ear. The consonant S he pronounces, as if written Sh. His accentuation, I did not relish—I find it broken and unmusical. A dash of Cooperism would do him no harm.

Glover, of the Ship Tallahassee, brought forward during my stay in Orleans, a new melo-drama, called the "Rake-hellies" and founded upon Cooper's novel of Lionel Lincoln. It went off with infinite success and was repeated. He has done more, towards effect, with Job Pray than the original author. I think his two pieces, the "Last of the Mohicans" and the "Rakehellies," their nationality considered, among the very best of our minor American *acted* drama, and in point of scenic effect, much better than ever Major Noah, made out to execute. Caldwell's Theatre is lit with gas—thereby much smoke is lost—much bad odor from lamp oil avoided, and the eyes of the audience considerably the better for wear.

From Orleans, I proceeded across Lake Ponchartrain to Madisonville, a little village on the river Chifuncta, of some 10 or 12 families; whence I took horse for Columbia, on Pearl River, Mississippi, passing through quite a respectable looking settlement called Covington. This was a two day's ride. Columbia holds a population of one hundred or more inhabitants and is on the decline. I have just returned from a journey on horseback, of seventeen days into the Yazoo purchase, over and through swamps and creeks and bayous, half the time swimming and wading through mud and water waist deep. We passed through several little townships and country seats, of little note, and not calculated to interest you. Innumerable little villages are springing up in every quarter, averaging in population about three hundred, and stagnating at that. The great rage at this time in Mississippi, is the possession of the new Indian purchase, the Choctaw lands. Many of the Choctaws have already gone to the Arkansas, and more are upon the go. I cannot but think the possession of so much territory, greatly inimical to the well being of this country. It not only conflicts with, and prevents the formation of society, but it destroys that which is already well established. It makes our borderers mere Ishmaelites, and keeps our frontiers perpetually so. Scarcely have they squatted down in one place, and built up their little "improvements," than they hear of a new purchase, where corn grows without planting, and cotton comes up five bales to the acre, ready picked and packed—they pull up stakes and boom off for the new Canaan, until they hear of some still better, when they commence the same game—death not unfrequently stopping them on the road before they have had time to hew their burial stone from the quarries which surrounded them. When this reaches you, I shall be on my way home. Adieu.

Copy-text: *Letters* 1 : 34–38.

Advertisement, *The Yemassee:*
A Romance of Carolina

(1 8 3 5)

I have entitled this story a romance, and not a novel—the reader will permit me to insist upon the distinction. I am unwilling that "THE YEMASSEE" should be examined by any other than those standards which have governed me in its composition; and unless the critic is willing to adopt with me, those leading principles, in accordance with which the materials of my book have been selected, the less we have to say to one another the better.

Supported by the authority of common sense and justice, not to speak of Pope—

> "In every work regard the writer's end,
> Since none can compass more than they intend"—

I have surely a right to insist upon this particular. It is only when an author departs from his own standards, that he offends against propriety and deserves punishment. Reviewing "Atalantis," a fairy tale, full of machinery, and without a purpose save the imbodiment to the mind's eye of some of those

> "Gay creatures of the element,
> That in the colours of the rainbow live,
> And play i' the plighted clouds"—

a distinguished writer of this country gravely remarks, in a leading periodical,—"Magic is now beyond the credulity of eight years"—and yet, the author set out to make a story of the supernatural, and never contemplated, for a moment, the deception of any good citizen!

The question briefly is, what are the standards of the modern romance— what is the modern romance itself? The reply is instant. Modern romance is the substitute which the people of to-day offer for the ancient epic. Its standards are the same. The reader, who, reading Ivanhoe, keeps Fielding and Richardson beside him, will be at fault in every step of his progress. The domestic novel of those writers, confined to the felicitous narration of common and daily occurring events, is altogether a different sort of composition; and if such a reader happens to pin his faith, in a strange simplicity and singleness of spirit, to such writers alone, the works of Maturin, of Scott, of Bulwer, and the rest, are only so much incoherent nonsense.

The modern romance is a poem in every sense of the word. It is only with those who insist upon poetry as rhyme, and rhyme as poetry, that the identity fails to be perceptible. Its standards are precisely those of the epic. It invests individuals with an absorbing interest—it hurries them through crowding events in a narrow space of time—it requires the same unities of plan, of purpose, and harmony of parts, and it seeks for its adventures among the wild and wonderful. It does not insist upon what is known, or even what is probable. It grasps at the possible; and, placing a human agent in hitherto untried situations, it exercises its ingenuity in extricating him from them, while describing his feelings and his fortunes in their progress. The task has been well or ill done, in proportion to the degree of ingenuity and knowledge which the romancer exhibits in carrying out the details, according to such proprieties as are called for by the circumstances of the story. These proprieties are the standards set up at his starting, and to which he is required religiously to confine himself.

The Yemassee is proposed as an American romance. It is so styled, as much of the material could have been furnished by no other country. Something to much of extravagance—so some may think,—even beyond the usual license of fiction—may enter into certain parts of the narrative. On this subject, it is enough for me to say, that the popular faith yields abundant authority for the wildest of its incidents. The natural romance of our country has been my object, and I have not dared beyond it. For the rest—for the general peculiarities of the Indians, in their undegraded condition—my authorities are numerous in all the writers who have written from their own experience. My chief difficulty, I may add, has arisen rather from the discrimination necessary in picking and choosing, than from any deficiency of the material itself. It is needless to add that the leading events are strictly true, and that the outline is to be found in the several histories devoted to the region of country in which the scene is laid. A slight anachronism occurs in the first volume, but it has little bearing upon the story, and is altogether unimportant.

New-York, April 3, 1835

Copy-text: *The Yemassee* (1835), v–vii.

Advertisement, *The Partisan:*
A Tale of the Revolution

(1 8 3 5)

Spending a few weeks, some eighteen months ago, with a friend,[1] in the neighbourhood of the once beautiful, but now utterly decayed, town of Dorchester, South Carolina, I availed myself of the occasion to revisit the old, and, at one time, familiar ruins. When a boy, I had frequently rambled over the ground, and listened to its chronicles from the lips of one—now no more—who had been conversant with all its history. Many of its little legends were known to me, and the story of more than one of its inhabitants, of whom nothing now remains but the record in the burial-place, had been long since registered in my mind. These,—together with its own sad transition by repeated disasters, from the busy bustle of the crowded thorough-fare, to the silence and the desolation of the tombs—were well adapted to inspire in me a sentiment of veneration; and, with the revival of many old time feelings and associations, I strolled through the solemn ruins—the dismantled church—the frowning fortress, now almost hidden in the ac-cumulating forests—reading and musing as I went, among the mouldering tombstones, and finding food for sweet thoughts and a busy fancy at every step in my ramble. The walls of the fort, built of the shell and mortar, or ta-pia work, and still in tolerable preservation—the old church, tottering, but

---

1. *WGS:* Mr. John W. Sommers, of St. Paul's Parish—a gentleman whose fine con-versational powers and elegant hospitality need no eulogy from me for their proper ap-preciation among all those who know him.

still erect, and the grassy hillocks marking the dwelling-places of the dead—are all that now remain in proof of its sometime existence, as the abiding-place of living man.

In this ramble, the restless imagination grew active in the contemplation of objects so well calculated to stimulate its exercise. Memory came warmly and vividly to its aid, and recalled a series of little events, carefully treasured up by the local tradition, which, unconsciously, my mind began to throw together, and to combine in form. Some of these had long before ministered to my own pleasurable emotions—why should they not yield similar pleasure to others? I revolved them over, thoughtfully, with this idea. The Revolutionary history of the colony was full of references to the neighbourhood; and numberless incidents, of a nature purely domestic, were yet so associated with some of the public occurrences of that period, that I could not well resist the desire to link them more closely together. The design grew more familiar and more feasible, the more I contemplated it; and though intervening difficulties, and other labours, have hitherto prevented my prosecution of the purpose, I have still continued to revolve it over as some unavoidable and favourite topic. To these circumstances, and to this desire, "The Partisan" owes its origin.

The work was originally contemplated as one of a series, to be devoted to our War of Independence. With this object, I laid the foundation more broadly and deeply than I should have done had I purposed merely the single work. Several of the persons employed were destined to be the property of the series;—that part of it, at least, which belonged to the locality. Three of these works were to have been devoted to South Carolina, and to comprise three distinct periods of the war of the Revolution in that state. One, and the first of these, is the story now submitted to the reader. I know not that I shall complete, or even continue the series. Much will depend upon the reception of the present narrative. I will not bind myself to the prosecution of an experiment, hazardous in many respects, and the success of which, is, at present, so problematical.

The "Partisan" comprises the leading events from the fall of Charlestown, to the close of 1780; and is proposed as a fair picture of the province—its condition, resources, and prospects—pending the struggle of Gates with Cornwallis, and immediately after the disastrous close of that campaign, in the complete defeat of the southern defending army. In the narrative, the various and very copious histories of the time have been continually before me. I have drawn from one, or from the other, as it seemed most to answer my purpose, or to accord with the truth. The work, indeed, is chiefly historical.

Even where the written history has not been found, tradition, and the local chronicles, preserved as family records, have contributed the rest.

The story of Frampton, for example, greatly modified, indeed, in many respects, was one which I had heard in childhood. That of Col. Walton is a familiar one in Carolina domestic history—recorded and unrecorded. The minor events—the little ambuscade and sortie—the plans of fight—of forage—of flight and safety—are all familiar features of the partisan warfare; and the title of the work, indeed, will persuade the reader to look rather for a true description of that mode of warfare, than for any consecutive story comprising the fortunes of a single personage. This, he is solicited to keep in mind, as one of my leading objects has been to give a picture, not only of the form and pressure of the time itself, but of the thousand scattered events making up its history. The very title should imply something desultory in the progress and arrangement of the tale; and my aim has been to give a story of events, rather than of persons. The one, of course, could not well have been done without the other; yet it has been my object to make myself as greatly independent as possible of the necessity which would combine them. A sober desire for history—the unwritten, the unconsidered, but veracious history—has been with me, in this labour, a sort of principle. The phases of a time of errors and of wrongs—of fierce courage—tenacious patriotism—yielding, but struggling virtue, not equal to the pressure of circumstances, and falling for a time, Antæus-like, only for a renewal and recovery of its strength—it has been my aim to delineate, with all the rapidity of one, who, with the mystic lantern, runs his uncouth shapes and varying shadows along the gloomy wall, startling the imagination and enkindling curiosity. The medium through which we now look at these events, is, in some respects, that of a glass darkened. The characters rise up before us grimly or indistinctly. We scarcely believe, yet we cannot doubt. The evidence is closed—the testimony now irrefutable—and imagination, however audacious in her own province, only ventures to imbody and model those features of the past, which the sober truth has left indistinct, as not within her notice, or unworthy her regard.

I have entitled the "Partisan" a tale of the Revolution—it was intended to be particularly such. The characters, many of them, are names in the nation, familiar as our thoughts. Gates, Marion, De Kalb, and the rest, are all the property of our country. In the illustrations which I have presumed to give of these personages, I have followed the best authorities. The severity with which I have visited the errors of the former general, is sustained by all the writers—by Otho Williams, by Lee, by Johnson, and the current histories. There can be little doubt, I believe, of the truth, in his case, of my drawing. It may be insisted on, as of questionable propriety, thus to revive these facts, and to dwell upon the faults and foibles of a man conspicuous in our history, and one, who, in a single leading event, contributed so largely to the glory of its pages. But, on this point, I am decided, that a nation gains only, in glory and in greatness, as it is resolute to behold and to pursue the truth. I would paint the disasters of my country, where they arose from the obvious error of her sons, in the strongest possible colours. We should then know—our sons and servants, alike, should then know—how best to avoid them. The rock which has wrecked us once, should become the beacon for our heirs hereafter. It is only by making it so, that the vicissitudes of life—its follies or misfortunes—can be made tributary to its triumphs. For this reason I have dwelt earnestly upon our disasters; and, with a view to the moral, I have somewhat departed from the absolute plan of the story, to dilate upon the dangerous errors of the leading personages in the events drawn upon. The history of the march of Gates' army, I have carefully elaborated with this object; and the reflecting mind will see the parallel position of cause and effect which I have studiously sought to make obvious, wherever it seemed to me necessary for the purposes of instruction. It is in this way, only, that the novel may be made useful, when it ministers to morals, to mankind, and to society.

Copy-text: *The Partisan* (1835), vii–xii.

From *Slavery in America,*
Being a Brief Review of
Miss Martineau on That Subject

(1 8 3 8)

A friend, with whom I travelled last summer, reading the late work of Miss Martineau, entitled 'Society in America,' drew my attention to certain portions of her remarks upon South Carolina. As I have the honor to be a native of that state, and the fortune to have been, for the better part of my life, a resident within it, he referred to me as one likely to know how far she was correct in her facts;—her deductions from them,—we were mutually agreed,—were after matters. I complied with his desire, so far as I was able, and we looked over the volumes together. In this hasty manner, I notched with my pencil, here and there, a few passages, as we turned the pages, which I noted, either for general incorrectness in the premises, or for an unfair and erroneous conclusion from them. When I had done this, and dwelt somewhat at length upon the various incidental topics which the matter necessarily suggested, he observed, that it might be well, if in every state through which the lady travelled, and upon which she has elaborated notes equally partial and unjust, some citizen who knew better, would come forward and correct her. By this means, the public, as well at home as abroad, for which the book was prepared, would not only be better able to determine upon its own accuracy, but would be materially assisted in arriving at a knowledge — which at this day seems so difficult, yet so very necessary — of region so barbarous as ours. [. . .]

On the subject of American slavery, her detestation is avowed as being entertained long before entering the slave states; and so cordial is this detestation, that it is fed and fattened by everything which she sees, and in sundry cases, we are sorry to add, at the expense of truth. I do not mean to say that she has wilfully related falsehoods. Not so;—I think the book of Miss Martineau written in good faith throughout. But she was biassed and bigoted on this subject to the last degree; and could neither believe the truth when it spoke in behalf of the slaveholder; nor doubt the falsehood, however gross, when it told in favor, or fell from the lips of the abolitionist. Thus, for example, in proof, not less of this unhappy bias, than of the dogmatism of the writer, we are told that the abolitionists sent no incendiary tracts among the slaves, and that they use no direct means towards promoting their objects in the slave states. "It is wholly untrue that they insinuate their publications into the south." Such is her bold assertion; yet, "Mr. Madison made the charge, so did Mr. Clay, so did every slaveholder and merchant with whom I conversed. I chose afterwards to hear the other side of the whole question; and I found, to my amazement, that this charge was wholly groundless." Here the lady undertakes to decide a question of veracity . . . with singular composure, in favor of her friends, and at the expense of the first names in our country.

"Nor did it occur to me," she writes, "that as slaves cannot read," &c. This is one of her facts, which is notoriously false, and which may be proved to be so, in every southern city. Thousands of slaves do read; and, if this were wanting to their information, the slaveholders assert,—though the abolitionists may deny,—that gross prints are employed in these abolition newspapers to help the understanding where it may lack, and that these prints are sometimes put upon manufactured cottons, such as are employed entirely for negroes, and insinuated here and there, at decent intervals, among the bales intended for the southern market. Such bales were discovered in a merchant's collection in Charleston, to the knowledge of the writer, but a few years ago. "*Slavery of a very mild kind,* has been abolished in the northern parts of the union," &c. Another of Miss Martineau's facts, which may call for a remark. What knowledge had Miss M., except from parties interested, that this slavery was of a mild kind;—and did she ask whether the slavery was abolished from principle, or because it was more profitable to work the slaves in a richer soil than that of New-England? Did she inquire how long a time was granted to slaveholders to dispose of their slaves to the south, before the act of abolition went into operation; and did she farther inquire, from what colonies the vessels and crews were fitted out which brought the African to America, and sold him to the south? A little more inquiry might have resulted in her hearing,—to her surprise, no doubt,—that the province of Carolina, was the very first from which a prayer ever arose to the British government, that this trade should be abolished, and no more slaves be permitted to enter within its territories. [. . .]

[. . . T]here is one painful chapter in these two volumes, under the head of "Morals of Slavery." It is painful, because it is full of truth. It is devoted to the abuses among slaveholders of the institution of slavery; and it gives a collection of statements, which, I fear, are in too many cases founded upon fact, of the illicit and foul conduct of many among us, who make their slaves the victims and the instruments alike of the most licentious passions. Regarding our slaves as a dependant and inferior people, we are their natural and only guardians; and to treat them brutally, whether by wanton physical injuries, by a neglect, or perversion of their morals, is not more impolitic than it is dishonorable. We cannot blame Miss Martineau for this chapter. The truth—though it is not all truth—is quite enough to sustain her and it; and we trust that its utterance may have that beneficial effect upon the relations of master and slave in our country, which the truth is at all times most likely to have every where. Still we are not satisfied with the spirit with which Miss M. records the grossness which fills this chapter:—she has exhibited a zest in searching into the secrets of our prison-house in the slave states, which she does not seem to have shown in any other quarter. The female prostitution of the south, is studiously looked after, as if it were the peculiar result of slavery—she makes no corresponding inquiry into the prostitution of the north. She picks up no tales of vice in that quarter—no rapes—no murders—no robberies—no poisoning—no stabbing. She has addressed her whole mind to the search after these things in the slave states; and with a strange singleness of vision, she has entirely forborne the haunts of the negro at the north, and the degraded classes in the free states. She says nothing whatsoever about them. [. . .]

Still there have been crimes and outrages which are without their excuse, and I do not seek to excuse them. I look upon all violence and all injustice as brutal. [. . .]

Democracy is not levelling—it is, properly defined, the harmony of the moral world. It insists upon inequalities, as its law declares, that all men should hold the place to which they are properly entitled. The definition of true liberty, is the undisturbed possession of that place in society to which our moral and intellectual merits entitle us. *He is a freeman, whatever his condition, who fills his proper place. He is a slave only, who is forced into a position in society below the claims of his intellect. He cannot but be a tyrant who is found in a position for which his mind is unprepared, and to which it is inferior.* [. . .]

[. . . I]ndeed, the slaveholders of the south, having the moral and animal guardianship of an ignorant and irresponsible people under their control, are the great moral conservators, in one powerful interest, of the entire world. Assuming slavery to be a denial of justice to the negro, there is no sort of propriety in the application of the name of slave to the servile of the south.

He is under no despotic power. There are laws which protect him, *in his place,* as inflexible as those which his proprietor is required to obey, *in his place. Providence has placed him in our hands, for his good, and has paid us from his labor for our guardianship.* The question with us is simply as to the manner in which we have fulfilled our trust. How have we employed the talents which were given us—how have we discharged the duties of our guardianship? What is the condition of the dependant? Have we been careful to graduate his labors to his capacities? Have we bestowed upon him a fair proportion of the fruits of his industry? Have we sought to improve his mind in correspondence with his condition? Have we raised his condition to the level of his improved mind? Have we duly taught him his moral duties—his duties to God and man? And have we, in obedience to a scrutinizing conscience, been careful to punish only in compliance with his deserts, and never in brutality or wantonness? These are the grand questions for the tribunal of each slaveholder's conscience. He must answer them to his God.

Copy-text: *Slavery in America* (1838), 9–10, 18–20, 38–39, 42, 65, 82–83.

From *A Letter to the Editor,*
by the Author of
"The Loves of the Driver"

To P. C. Pendleton, Esq.   [August 12, 1841]
Dear Sir: I perceive that you have been censured for the publication in your
pages of an article of mine, and no doubt you are quite as much astonished
as myself, that such should be the case. Were the affair mine only—were
you not indirectly involved in this censure—I should suffer it to pass
without notice. [. . .] As I should be very loth, however, that your journal
should suffer in the estimation of your readers by any of my effusions, I will
endeavor to account for my stubbornness in persisting to see nothing in "The
Loves of the Driver," that can, in the slightest degree, prove hurtful to the
delicacy of the purest mind. For the impure minds I say nothing. To them all
things are impure. All things receive their type and color from the innate
qualities and conceptions of the individual.

Let me premise by saying that it must be sufficiently clear to every thinking person, that neither you nor I could have any deliberate purpose to put
forth an immoral publication. Even if we had no higher motives, the ordinary policy of selfishness, would prevent us [. . .] from the commission of
such a policy. We have both something to lose—something more to gain. It
is not our cue to offend our readers. It is clear, therefore, that if we have
done wrong, we have done so unwittingly. We have had no malice in the
business. It is because of a lack of wisdom and sagacity, of which our neighbours have so much, that we have offended. What we have done has been
done ignorantly, not wilfully; and the language of censure must therefore be

somewhat modified with that of pity. This is equally the law of Christianity and wisdom. Moreover, it is a duty with the Judge, while he condemns, to designate, especially, the subject matter of his censure—to show the sore spots—describe the offence in unequivocal terms, and not in vague generalities. Have these particulars been observed in our case?

Very far from it. The paper in question is decried as immoral, but the exception is not sustained by particulars; and I find some difficulty in knowing exactly where to answer. I certainly did not set out to write an immoral story. I can assure your readers of this fact. I have read the paper twice, and confess myself still at a loss. It is a tale of low life—very low life—that is true. Elegant people,—very elegant people, I mean—revolt, I very well know, at mere human interests when they do not relate to the fortunes and movements of other elegant people. There is nothing surely very attractive in Negroes and Indians; but something is conceded to intellectual curiosity; and the desire is human, and a very natural one, to know how our fellow beings fare in other aspects than our own, and under other forms of humanity, however inferior. No race is so very low, as to deprive them of the power of exciting this interest in the breasts of men;—unless in the case of very elegant people—people to whom the moral Poet refers, when he warns the Preacher, never to "mention hell to ears polite." I take it for granted that there can be no substantial moral objection to the mere agents in the narrative. Their modes of life, passions, pursuits, capacities and interests, are as legitimately the objects of the analyst, as those of the best bred people at the fashionable end of London; and possibly, considering their superior wants, are more obviously the objects of a higher moral and Christian interest.

Well then, for the moral of the material. Now, upon inquiry, you will find that this is very much the same with that of Shakspeare's Othello; one of the most noble of all dramatic moralities. The same passions are in exercise precisely—the same pursuit of lust;—passions the most demoniac; lusts the least qualified and scrupulous. It so happens that a work of Lady Blessington, recently published, and which I suppose has been very well thumbed by every fair reader of the Magnolia, ("The Governess,") contains similar material;—deprived of its grossness however, as the events are related of very fine and fashionable people—people in high life; who, as they are in high life and fashionable people, are to be justified, we suppose, in the exercise and indulgence of passions, which, however natural to red skins and black equally, are still not to be permitted them. Certainly, there is some presumption in imitating the vices of their betters. We are apt to get angry, and to resent as an impertinence, the mimicry below stairs of the faults and follies which are so elegant and so popular above. This is natural too; but, may there not be some moral benefit from this sort of exposition of such vices? Stripped of their silks and fine manners, how gross shows the moral depravity which never troubled us before! I am afraid your critics found no fault, with my Lady Blessington's "Governess," who dealt, however, in the same materials with my "Driver."

In this country we are very much the victims of what is plainly, but expressively called, "mock modesty." A modern writer, who does not always speak either so very truly or forcibly, says that "very nice people are those who are apt to have very nasty ideas." The truth is so. There is an ugly consciousness in the mind which makes the lips fear to speak. We are reluctant, in very nice society, to call things by their proper names. We dare not speak of legs, or thighs, in the presence of many very nice ladies; and the young damsel who would be shocked beyond recovery, if you craved permission to embrace her, had no sort of objection if you will only substitute the word "waltz," for that of embrace. The act is very much the same, and like the "rose" of Shakespeare, equally sweet under any name. I really cannot see that there is any thing immoral in our material. Do you see it, Mr. Pendleton? Look closely, and take care only to speak after due deliberation.

But, says the critic, and very wisely, the material may be very innocent and very becoming, but the treatment of it is the thing. He is right. The best porridge in the world may be spoiled by the cooking. Let us see to this point, Mr. Pendleton. You are to ask, if, in the management of the "Driver," the author has depicted evil passions in such a manner as to make them attractive to the reader? You are to see if any one scene is such as to whet appetite, and stimulate, by its luscious exhibitions, the always watchful and eager passions of the young. You are to ask if the names of things and their qualities are falsely represented; if the truth is disguised, or blurred, or obliterated; if, in the comment, a false gloss is put upon vice so as to make it seem virtue,—if the author seeks to excuse, or to screen the criminal;—if the criminal is made successful—made to triumph,—and is shown to the reader as superior to the stings of law, or conscience, or such other retribution as seems to be imperatively demanded by his offences? Is virtue made the subject of scorn, or sneer,—is she humbled beneath her pursuing enemy, or does she rise superior to circumstances, and finally triumph at and over injustice and persecution?

In these questions are embodied the whole of these tests by which the morals of a story are to be determined. Now, what is the fact in relation to our Driver? Do you perceive any thing in the carriage and fortunes of Mingo calculated to put him in any but an odious and revolting light? Are his lusts likely to become winning examples to the incipient *roue* of Savannah? Are they so elegant, so enticing, so attractive? [. . .] As for our Indian friend

Knuckles—surely blind jealousy never took a form more likely to bring into contempt with the reader—and the Indian woman, Caloya—pardon me the egotism Mr. Editor, but I am forced to declare my belief, that as a pattern of natural and human morality, her carriage and conduct might well be studied with respect and sympathy, by the purest daughter in the land. She is as true to duty—the highest idea of virtue that we have—as if she had been taught in the temple; and she fulfills all its requisitions in spite of scorn, and wrong, and ill-treatment, with a spirit as unyielding and patient as if Earth had never known sorrow, and the peace of Eden, with all its privileges, was yet within her allotment. She bears her burden without faltering and complaint, endures the buffets and abuse of the very person to whom she had a right to look for love, honor, and protection; scorns the artifices of the seducer; spurns his temptations; and in the most trying event of her life, manages her conduct in such a manner, as, finally, while maintaining her virtue, to prevent strife and murder. I am incapable, I confess, of conceiving a higher idea of mere morality apart from manners, and intellect, than I have embodied in this Indian woman.

The story, pursuing the natural course of its details, results in the constant defeat of the wrong-doer; the escape of the innocent from his snares; his final punishment; and the complete freedom from thraldom of the prisoner and the persecuted! The means employed are believed to be natural and ordinary; the penalties are adapted to the offence. It is believed that moral justice has been obeyed in all its requisitions; that no offences have been winked at, and none forgiven that demanded punishment. I deceive myself very much if, upon a critical and manly examination, you do not concur with me in this summary.

There is something very lackadaisical in much of the tone of modern criticism. Its cant, on the subject of morality, is as senseless as it is hypocritical. It lacks all discrimination. It never analyses motives; still less does it look to effects. The brief question to be asked, in determining upon the morality of a work of art, and one which puts it within the power of the humblest intellect in the community to answer for himself, is simply—what is the moral effect upon the individual? Does he feel himself to be a better or a worse man, after the perusal of a tale of crime? Do its details attract or repel him? Does he long to employ the same passions in the same manner, or does he revolt with loathing at their unwholesome exhibition? However strange it may seem to some of your readers, I have really succeeded and without much difficulty, in persuading myself, that the 'Driver,' is quite a moral story. I doubt if any body, male or female—not absolutely too far gone in morbid sentiment—will not rise from the perusal of it, hating the offenders, and admiring, if not loving, the poor Indian woman, Caloya!

But the truth is, too many of our critics draw their rules of judgment, not from their thoughts, but from their tastes. This is a very important distinction. Such people are diseased with fastidiousness. They are always afflictingly nice. They seldom use appropriate language. They look through the dictionary for the bad words, only to blame Dr. Johnson for putting them there. The very idea of strong passions, in exercise, revolts them; overlooking the truth, that where there are no passions in exercise, there can be no trial of the virtues—no proof of their presence—no triumph over their continual foes. Active virtues can only live in the heart which is filled with active passions. It is because of this fact, that nearly all of the great writers that ever survive their day, employ this very material. Your Homers, your Shakspeares, your Chaucers, your Beaumonts, your Fletchers, your Shirleys; your Massingers, your Scotts, your Byrons—the whole tribe of great names, employ the deadly sins of man, as so many foils to his living virtues and whether he falls or triumphs, the end of the moralist is attained, if he takes care to speak the truth, the whole truth and nothing but the truth! In this, in fact, lies the whole secret of his art. *A writer is moral only in proportion to his truthfulness.* He is and cannot but be, immoral, whose truth is partial and one-sided; who shows the sweets of vice, without their bitterness; who depicts the successes, while he hides or softens the defeats, the shame and the suffering of the criminal.

Enough.—My purpose was not my defence, but your justification. Conscious of no wrong intention, and believing, so far as my poor judgment enables me to see, that there has been no wrong performance, I should have been satisfied, for my part, to leave the matter to time and to the consideration of reflecting men. I have neither the leisure nor the inclination to engage in controversy with my critics. I have usually yielded to them the satisfaction of cracking the nuts at liberty. Your readers will acquit us both, whatever they may think of our judgment, of any deliberate design to disturb their moral sense or assay their feelings. Of this, I give them my full assurance, and sincerely trust that they will be satisfied with you. If they harbour any remaining hostility, I beg that it will be confined to the true offender. If you have erred at all, it can only have been in so frequently and urgently soliciting my contributions to a work, to do justice to which, I have so little leisure and perhaps ability. Still I had tried my best to please, and am sincerely sorry that my ability has not kept pace with my desires.

It is something singular that another South Carolinian has offended in similar respects with myself. My worthy brother, from the sweet springs of Pickens, has also, it would seem, though for what reason I cannot well perceive, fallen under the ban of the moralist. There must be something in our atmosphere that is unfavorable to the development of a sufficiently delicate taste. It is very evident that the Savannah river is a line of demarcation, which must be regarded now as establishing a moral as well as a political difference between our sections. I must confess myself much more sorry to suspect this, than even to incur the dangers of unfriendly criticism. I am afraid that our literature is somewhat retarded by an unhappy sectionality among our people. We are quite too individual,—too much the creatures of bounds and land-marks,—to effect many of those great national achievements which require the hearty co-operation of all the minds of a country. Unless we can rid ourselves of these narrow prejudices of place, I am afraid, Mr. Pendleton, that your Magnolia, like our laurels, will be of short life and small stature. Do me the justice to think that I have not spared my endeavor,—rate the ability as you will—that it should be otherwise.

Faithfully yours,
W. G. S.

[*In a postscript Simms added important commentary:*]
   [. . .]
   It would do our people, as well as our critics, a great good, if they would study the old writers, the great men of British Literature. They would then cease to confound substances and shadows, names and things. They would then discover an important distinction, which is not often made, between morality intrinsically considered, and conventional tastes. The one by no means implies the other. There is marrow and passion, and feeling; human nature, and consequently truthfulness in these writers, which makes them always prefer the direct way, and the properest terms to express a subject. They belong to the same class of gigantic moralists, by whom the Holy Bible was translated—a volume, that, in every page, offends against the petty tastes of petty people, and yet a volume, the darkest and the most unseeming pages of which are full of startling truths, and moralities the most tremendous and exacting. There is no work, more abounding in tales of crime, expressed in the clearest colors; more vivid, more to the life; and yet whoever learned a guilty lesson from that inspired volume? The great crime of David is the lustful pursuit of another's wife—the murder of that other in the prosecution of his cruel purpose—and what makes the narrative there, a moral narrative, accompanied with a moral lesson to mankind? It is because we are made to see that in the very success of his crime, he is compelled to endure the punishments of the criminal. We are made to see, and almost to share, in his shame; to hear his groans, to behold his agonies; to witness, in scalding tears, his deep and heartfelt penitence! It is from guilt that the moral lessons are adduced which strengthen innocence; and I am disposed to think that when we seek to disguise these agonies, and to cloak strong passions and

base deeds under very nice and namby-pamby characteristics, we invite to crime. The tenderness with which we speak of such offences—the smooth, lackadaisical forms of descriptions which we employ when the object spoke of is a deed of blood, or of lust, or of shame and abject prostitution—diminishes the awful proportions of the offence—takes from its disgustful appearances, and makes it less difficult for the moral sense to be reconciled to its indulgence. To be truthful, a true writer—an earnest man, full of his subject and having no sinister, and only the direct object, must lay it as bare as possible. He must roll up his sleeves to it, and not heed the blushes of the sophisticated damsel, who is shocked at the bare, brawny arms. Convention is always the foe to truth; and the literature of a country, and the literary men thereof, if they wish to live, and do good to their fellows, must stick to nature and scorn the small requisitions of little cliques and classes. They have higher responsibilities than those of fashion. Fashionable Society requires them to lie; to say they are not at home when they are; to embrace and smile with those whom they hate, and despise, and vilify; permits them to seek embraces in a ball room which they would exclaim against in a private parlor on a morning visit; and while blushing at the bare arms of a man, to lay bare all the bosom of a woman. Now, my statement of these facts is much more shocking to conventions than the facts themselves. Thousands of ladies go to look at Dubufe's picture of the naked bodies of Adam and Eve, who would denounce you as guilty of a grossness in offering to discuss the symmetry of leg, or thigh, or bosom! The same pictures, if called Mars or Venus, would be seized by the moral police, and consigned to the hands of the executioner.

It is the literature of a country which preserves the language and represents the morality of a period. It is not your delicate people. They criticise; nothing more. [. . .] With these people we have but little to do. Let them grumble if it does them good. Our responsibilities, fortunately, are not to them; and if we respect ourselves, [. . .] we must pursue the even tenor of our way—first having assured ourselves that we hold the mirror truly up to nature. The authors of a country are its true authorities. The name denotes as much. They preserve all that is preserved. Our legislation is a small matter in comparison. Even in our country, where letters have not reached their true point of elevation, it is yet the men of letters who govern. Very few of your people who go to Congress, or to the State Legislature, originate those views of public affairs which they yet bring forward. [. . .] *Apropos* to our original subject. Any reader who is curious will find a very strong case of parallelism in the materials of the 'Loves of the Driver'-that very immoral story—and Shakspeare's 'Merry Wives of Windsor'—Falstaff pursues the same course with Mingo, and the same results happen precisely. The virtue of the woman goes thro' the furnace unsmerched. Falstaff gets pinched and tumbled into the Thames——'slighted into the river with as little remorse as they would have drowned a bitch's blind puppies, fifteen i' the litter,'——and Mingo gets the horse-whip and a broken head, not to speak of degradation from his high place of authority. The language quoted in inverted commas is Shakspeare's. Let your people of very nice moral nerves make the most of it. Had it been ours, Mr. Pendleton, we should have been in the stocks ere this. We should, at least, have had to soften one of the words used into 'female dog,' 'feminine dog,' or something equally inoffensive and equally stupid; but while it would be perfectly moral to say 'bitch,' where the sense called for it, it would be a proof of an immodest thought, in the mind of the speaker, who should say 'female dog!' But one swallow makes no summer, and I trust for your sake and their own, that there is but one of your subscribers whose stomach has been turned by my immoralities. [. . .] The South has been too slow, sadly slow, in asserting its literary claims in the great circle of the creation. I trust that such men as these [leading writers of the South], will not suffer its slow coming, and necessarily its imperfect effort to be trodden down in the beginning, by dillettantism, by petty tastes and frivolous notions of social mora[l]ity. Suppose it does offend; suppose it commits some excesses in that generous ardor which belongs to its very nature? What then? If England had denounced and destroyed every writer for her stage or firesides, who had offended against morals in some respects, scarce one of them would have escaped the halter. Her Shakspeare would have been the first to burn; and what a glorious array of great spirits would have suffered in the same unholy blaze. There is no end to the catalogue, and the fag end alone would have been left us. [. . .] I spare your ears the mortification of such a list. Enough to speak of the spirit which we would have lost, without lingering over the *caput mortuum,* which would have remained.——VALE!

W. G. S.

Copy-text: *Letters* 1 : 254–66.

From *The Social Principle:*
The True Source of National Permanence

(1 8 4 3)

It is now nearly twenty years, my friends, since the individual who addresses you, first made his acquaintance with your city; and that glance at our mutual past which the present visit has occasioned, discovers a strange similitude in our common fortunes. What I am in the regards of my friends and countrymen,—whether well or ill-deserved,—is sufficiently attested by my presence here,—in the midst of such an assembly,—engaged in the honorable duty which your gracious opinion has confided to my hands. But, in the proud fortunes of the community by which I am surrounded,—remembering what she was in that day of my obscurity,—I am forcibly impressed with those wondrous effects of time, which we never so clearly understand as when they are somewhat associated with our individual experience. Little did I imagine that the rude and scattered hamlet which I then surveyed,—a fragmentary form, not half made up,—was, in so short a space of time, to become so eminent a city;—her dwellings informed by intellect and enlivened by society;—her sons refined by education,—her daughters ennobled by sentiment;—Learning at home, with an allotted and noble mansion in her high places, and Taste secure in her dominions of equal peace and prosperity. Still less was it in my thought, that, in that same little space of time, the unknown and obscure boy who then beheld her in that unimproved condition, was to be summoned from his distant home in Carolina, to minister at her most sacred anniversary,—to prepare the altar for the offerings of her infant literature,—and to join with her sons in the holy sacrifice to that Genius, equally proud and pure, in whose honor the song of the bard, and the voice of the orator, "never *should* be mute."

Then—a decapitated Colossus—the forest tree lay prostrate before her threshold,—the wild vine swung luxuriantly across her pathway,—and, at the close of evening, the long howl of the wolf might be heard, as he hungered upon the edges of the forest for the prey that lay within her tents. Scarcely less wild, in its unpruned, uncultivated condition, was the mind of that youthful spectator,—cumbered by fragmentary materials of thought,— choked by the tangled vines of erroneous speculation, and haunted by passions, which, like so many wolves, lurked, in ready waiting, for their unsuspecting prey.

The egotism of this comparison will be forgiven for its truth. We are now, both of us, to a certain extent, free from these incumbrances and enemies. The danger is withdrawn from our immediate neighborhood,—the pathway is open for our present footsteps. The security which waits on social order, has rendered your avenues peaceful; and the passions in my bosom, if not entirely overcome, are, I trust, kept in subjection to those ordinances of God and society, which alone preserve in freedom the community and the man. We have both succeeded to that condition of prosperity, which enables us sometimes to rise from the immediate struggle, and to look around us with the eye of a well-satisfied contemplation; and it becomes us to inquire, as a matter of equal duty and acknowledgment, by what agency we have triumphed,—what means have effected our successes,—and why, indeed, we are now assembled here. The inquiry is not one of very serious difficulty. The answer in one case will naturally be suggestive of the other. To account for the successes of individual mind, will go far to account for those of the community; and the history of a community, will, in turn, measurably illustrate the progress of its individual minds. Your prosperity is the due result of whatsoever degree of thought has been expended upon your progress, and whatever measure of energy has been concentrated upon the plans and purposes of your intellect. The same causes which lead to prosperity will secure permanence. Unhappily, for great cities and great nations, they do not always perceive, or do not always regard, with sufficient respect, a truth so equally valuable and obvious. It is only by venerating the mind which had made, that the works of mind may be preserved, unimpaired, for posterity.

This glance at our mutual past awakens many reflections, the principal of which, as it relates to that strange philosophical romance, the progress of society, may well enchain our attention, and constitute the legitimate topic of our present essay. Traversing the then dreary wastes of this south-western region,—contemplating with a superior sense of awe the numerous cities of her solitude,—the recollections of her European history rushed through my thoughts, and in recalling the course of French, Spanish and British invasion, through the then spacious empire called Florida, I was struck with the remarkable fact, that, of the efforts of these three powerful nations, to establish the banner of Civilization within this wondrous province, two of them should so utterly have failed. That a nation, in that day of such gigantic powers,—endued with such superhuman energies, as Spain,—grasping at the acquisition of territory, with a tenacity which looked less like policy than passion;—that a people of such constitutional ardor as the French,—so capable of endurance in the prosecution of a favorite purpose,—so full of resource in finding means of progress, and in providing against defeat;—that neither of these should have been able to secure themselves in the homes which they overrun,—and that it should be left to a race of traders—fewer in number—poorer in purse and spirit—less practised in war—less fervent in zeal—to achieve the conquest in which they found nothing but defeat,—would seem a difficult problem for the solution of the philosopher. And yet, I fancy, that a just survey of the true objects of these several nations, and of the usual progress of society among them, will lessen, if not entirely remove, this difficulty. The solution may be found in a single sentence. While the Spaniards and the French, in the new world, sought either for gold, for slaves, or for conquest, the English sought for nothing but a home. While Ponce de Leon, in the decline of life,—when the place of his abode should have been already endeared to him, close almost as the human affections which Time had consecrated to his need,—abandons all in a wild and visionary search after delusive waters, which are to reverse the usual destiny of man, and lift him to the condition of immortality;—while De Soto,— blest with those ties which love should have rivetted to his soul, dear as its own vital springs,—abandons wife, family, friends and security,—those very things for which man is alone justified in departing from his birthplace;—while similar purposes, in like manner, invite to the new world the arms of thousands more, French and Spanish,—we are constrained to perceive, in the aims and objects of the British colonists, nothing wild, nothing irrational—no purposes not plausible, no plans not feasible—no design not comprehended within the well-recognized wants of a free and wholesome state of society. They came to colonize and not to conquer, though, in effecting the one object, they necessarily secured the other. In this simple fact consists the great secret of their success. [. . .]

[. . . W]e, in America, have lost, in a great degree, the benefits of this lesson. The quantity of land before us, deprives us of that veneration for the soil, to which the Englishman owes so many of his proudest virtues. The intrinsic value of his paternal estate, great in itself, is heightened by the recollection, that it has constituted the inheritance of his fathers, and is endowed with the numerous improvements of successive generations. Every race has striven in the same grateful employment of adding to its beauties. No spot is left unhallowed by the all-endowing hands of love and veneration. Every tree has its appropriate name and history; and if affection has not been able to keep from decay, these memorable fathers of the forest, she has, at least, decorated their hoary brows with the ivied green which mantles their desolation. It may seem something of an absurdity, in the eyes of a freeman, to assume as important, even to Liberty itself, these little concerns of life,—these domestic additaments,—the small interests which make physical comfort, and address themselves somewhat to the sensuous nature. Doubtlessly, Liberty is the greatest social good,—nay, without such liberty as becomes one's moral condition, there is no social good. But that sort of liberty which is entertained without human comforts,—which neither knows nor desires them,—is the liberty of the savage, which, insisting upon its freedom, returns only to is wallow. Now, the Englishman, with liberty, possesses a thousand other social goods, and those of the domestic hearth, of which we have spoken, are the greatest. They make his comforts, they endear his home,—they couple his freehold with his freedom, and making his very selfishness a patriotism, the love which he maintains for both, secures him in their mutual possession.

How much of this passion for the family homestead—how much of this social principle—did the Briton bring with him to America? How much of it, when his authority over the soul was broken, did he transmit to his successors? Have we preserved the household virtues of the Englishman? Do we maintain his tastes in this particular;—do we honor those humanities which every lesson of our common ancestry should teach us to revere? Do we sustain the gentle—do we venerate the old? Are we, like them, solicitous always of the decencies of life and society? Do we bow to intellect? Seek we to promote, by letters, religion and the arts, the altars of a high civilization? Are our freeholds so identified, in our regards, with our freedom, that the abandonment or decay of the one, makes us tremble for the safety of the other? Where are we in the social world? What is our rank, compared with other nations, in the estimates of the civilized? Where are the proofs that we are nobler, gentler, purer, wiser than our ancestors,—for, let me remark,—no civilized people can continue stationary! The law of civilization is a law of progress; to fail in reporting which is a sure sign of retrograde, fatal to all our pretensions, and terrible in its consequences to posterity! These are questions to be answered,—not easy of answer. [. . .]

[*Simms has spoken of "the ravages of sword and flame" in the Revolutionary War.*] [. . .] Even pecuniary prosperity, in a progress of years, may be restored to a nation;—but what can re-unite affections which have been sundered by the sword—bring back the sweet peace which made the homestead lovely—re-awaken the often-banished confidence in man—rekindle the fires of mutual zeal in the common cause of society—subdue those wild spirits whom a seven years war, suddenly ended, had cast loose, without employment, upon the country—of habits, reckless and dissolute, formed to idleness, incapable of a patient and slow-advancing industry? It need not be said that the return of peace was followed by little social improvement. The *lares familiares,* overthrown by hands of violence, were not soon reinstated by hands of peace. We do not find the American citizen pursuing the spoiler into the wilderness, as in the case of the Pagan father, of whom we read in Scripture, for the recovery of his teraphim. On the contrary, we are constrained to see in the history of our social progress, for the last fifty years, but few signs of that sober-thoughted love of home, the absence of which we regard as among the most alarming evils of our present social condition. Undoubtedly, as we have endeavoured to show, the Revolutionary struggle threw us back in this respect—how much we need not say, but to this cause we attribute the first impelling direction in this downward progress,—covered as was the face of the land with an impoverished soldiery—impatient of control, ready for strife, and reckless, under the pressure of necessity, of all human consequences.—For, it will be remembered, that, in the South at least, the whole body of the people had been in arms on one side or the other:—the citizen was the soldier, and nowhere was there a community, preserved from over-throw, sufficiently large and imposing to overawe the insubordinate, or subdue the brutal nature. What this domestic calamity may have spared to society, was more than usurped by the prevalent warfares of the frontier—the desperate assaults of outlawed men, leagued with the savage, who, once stimulated to phrenzy by British arts, could not be quieted by British exhortation—if, indeed, such exhortation was ever attempted among them. The interregnum of peace which followed, was simply a rest from war. But thirty years had elapsed from the peace of '83, when the doors of Janus were again thrown violently open, and we were again summoned to contend, for the liberties of society, in another bloody passage with our foreign brother. Old feuds were to be revived—old war-cries of the savage to be re-sounded, and the maternal love which now insists so much upon our inferior civilization, was once-more busy in the endeavour to help it forward by shot and sabre. Now,—the blessings of a superior civilization, are blessings which flow almost entirely from the reign of peace. A nation kept constantly at war, within its own borders, is necessarily demoralized. With but few intervals, and those of short duration, the people of America, from the first Colonial settlements, whether at Jamestown, Massachusetts Bay or Ashley River, were in continual conflict—now with the French and Spaniards, now with the savages, and finally, and worst of all,—a conflict not yet ended—with the mother country. It would be something wonderful, indeed, judging by the histories of other nations, if there should be a perfect state of civilization among us—if there should be no violence,—no strife,—no absence, in frequent regions, of just principles,—no social disquiets, discomforts, wild dwellings and wilder men. Immunity from such evils, under such circumstances, would be miraculous. There are no such immunities for mortals in the stores of providence, and with the help of our mother country, the curse is at our doors!

But I should regard it as a mistaken patriotism, however legitimate the plea, to endeavor to extenuate the faults, the follies or ferocities of our people, by showing how much they were occasioned by the ambition of Great Britain. We claim to be a sensible and Christian people—and the plea will not avail us any farther than to show the difficulties in the way of our virtue. It will not excuse us for having fallen in the struggle, for we need not to have fallen. It is enough to render sure our responsibility to show that we are not now ignorant of the claims of society—of what is due to ourselves, our children and our ancestors. It is not for us, speaking the language of Milton and Shakspeare, and claiming their writings as in part our heritage, to plead ignorance of what we owe to the humanities, to the arts, to the pure, the true, the beautiful and intellectual. Our responsibility is strictly proportioned to our knowledge. What *we know,* pronounces the judgment upon what *we are.* Nay, even evasion will not serve us, else how easy to show, from our British censors themselves, that they too have fallen—that they share in our shame—that they no longer maintain the virtues of their ancestors, and that the same vices which are conspicuous in ourselves, are of no mean prominence in them. [. . .]

[. . .] Certainly, it is a curious coincidence, that, just now, the very evils which the British find in us, they should denounce among themselves; vanity, ostentation, the worship of wealth, selfishness and want of manners. It would be a becoming study with the philosophical mind to trace the source of this coincidence. Doubtless, it is a result due to some defect in the character of both—something in the common customs or principles—some lamentable want in the popular education—the domestic policy,—all to be found, embodied among the constituents of the social principle. But our aim is less discursive—our limits too confined for such an examination. That we owe, however, many of our social vices to a miserable and servile imitation of the English, in their vain displays and boyish affectations, is beyond all question. It is this wretched love of show, this absence of plain living and high thinking, which is making us all bankrupt,—hurrying us on, with gamester phrenzy, in change and speculation; and, placing before us ever the dazzling forms of unsubstantial and fraudulent desires, is momently beguiling us from that

―――"Good old cause,
And pure religion breathing household Laws."

But I note other causes among us, superior to these, for promoting this deteriorating social tendency. The first and most important is the wandering habit of our people. Now, the first requisite to the civilization of any people, is to make them stationary. To become stationary implies the necessity of labor, and this necessity is the origin of agriculture. With the increase of the community, a farther necessity arises for diversifying the objects of labor, and with this necessity spring the arts, mechanical and fine. I need not pursue this suggestion. A wandering people is more or less a barbarous one. We see in the fate of the North American savage, that of every nomadic nation. What is true of them, is true in degree of every civilized people that adopts, in whatever degree, their habits. Every remove, of whatever kind, is injurious to social progress; and every remove into the wilderness, lessens the hold which refinement and society have hitherto held upon the individual man. One of the securities of the Englishman, from a danger of this sort, was his moral and social inflexibility. It was his boast that he maintained his authority over the savage―that he made no concessions to the inferior nature; but, as we have already said, set up his household Gods, in whatever wilderness he sought abode. In this he differed from the Frenchman, who, when he built his lodge among the Hurons, with the levity of his character, surrendered in part his own, while adopting the habits of the Indians. He was won by the novelty, which the intense self-esteem of the Englishman made him treat with loathing. The latter surrendered nothing,―lost nothing of his original claim to moral authority,―preserved the superior organization of the society in which he had been taught, and, by this alone, maintained his foothold in the forest. [. . .]

[. . .] One, [. . .] being less of the seer than Franklin, might have supposed, that, in his day, lessons of thrift were unnecessary in New-England. An ordinary mind, not regarding the emulative nature of the American, in all parts of the country, would have assumed that, in his neighbourhood, similar necessities to those which had tutored him, would have forced like maxims of economy on every citizen. But, even then, they might have been properly addressed to the South, where a more genial climate and a more productive industry, had already sown, broad cast, the seeds of a lavish and profligate expenditure. But the passion for gain grew with the expenditure. It was necessary to it. Hence, in great part, the devotion of our people to staple culture, or to the production of that one commodity only which could find a market.

The whole labor of the Planter was expended,—not in the cultivation of the soil,—for the proper cultivation of a soil improves it,—but in extorting by violence from its bosom, seed and stalk, alike, of the wealth which it contained. He slew the goose that he might grasp, at one moment, its whole golden treasure. A cultivation like this, by exhausting his land, left it valueless, and led to its abandonment;—and, unhappily, there was nothing in the circumstances of his progress, to make him reluctant to do so, and studious, by every means, to avert this necessity. His insatiate rage for gain had rendered him regardless of all other considerations. In few instances had he built the stately mansion, the solid walls and sweet manifold comforts of which would have prompted him to repeated toils and experiments, ere he had been persuaded to abandon it. He laid out no gardens, the gravelled walks and tropical beauties of which would have fastened, as with the spells of an Armida, his reluctant footsteps—planted no favorite trees, whose mellowing shade, covering the graves of father, mother or favorite child—would have seemed too sacred for desertion—would have seemed like venerated relatives whom it would be cruel to abandon in their declining years. These, are the substantial marks of civilization, by which we distinguish an improving people. Regardless of these, we find him regardless of still more sacred obligations. What is the condition of the homestead in moral respects? Do we find his daughters nourished with the food of thought, lofty sentiment, and the graces of such an education as becomes the position of their sex? How worthless is their education,—limited to what servile objects, and how commonly meant only for the purposes of a vain and selfish display of superficial accomplishments;—"plain living and high thinking"—those noblest of all the essentials of social life, being utterly set at naught! And, for the sons! In the prosecution of that same feverish, phrenzied passion for gain,—he has sent them forth, while their sinews were yet unhardened— their minds yet untaught—their tempers untuned—at the very time when, in their mental gristle, none other than the parental dwelling should be entrusted with their care—he has sent them forth in the same mad, pitiful thirst for gold—for the sordid traffic—the petty salary—the cogging, cunning world of speculation. The poor boy, thoughtless, but hopeful of the world—simple and confident, but oh! how vain, how rash, how impatient of the time and the truth—ere he has yet gone through his accidence—ere he has learned the lesson, most sacred and necessary of all, to honor his father and mother in the day of his youth;—is dispatched in the morning of that day from their controlling presence,—thrust among strangers, who care not for father or mother—care not for the boy,—care not that he has learned any but the one commandment—'thou shalt not steal!' This is the custom, worse than death, in the history of our American career—the most misery-bringing custom that prevails among us. Nothing can be so fatal to discipline—and without discipline all is lost—there is nothing worth remaining—power, wealth, talent, all are worse than useless, without this most necessary, soul-bracing, body-strengthening ordeal, which we call discipline.—Nothing is so fatal to this discipline as the emancipation of the boy, in his tender years, from the restraints of the maternal household—from the guidance of the parental hand and eye—from the pure and sobering influences—the regular habits and the cheering smiles of the domestic hearth and habitation. Nothing so soon prompts the boy to throw off his allegiance to years, to station, to worth and virtue, as the capacity of earning money for himself. Money is the sign, among us, unhappily, of the highest social power,—and the possessor of it soon learns to exercise it as a means of authority. It is new doctrine, certainly, in our country—but not the less true for that—to teach that the longer a boy is kept from earning money for himself, the better for himself—for his real manhood—for his morals— his own, and the happiness of those who love him. Unhappily, the infatuated parent beholds with delight the exercise of this capacity, though it might not be difficult, at the same time, to show, that, with this exercise comes presumption, insubordination and insolence—looseness of principle—recklessness of conduct—levity of manners, excess in indulgence, brutality in habit, drunkenness and debauchery, beastliness the most loathsome, and, frequently, crimes the most atrocious. What dreadful penalties are paid, by child and parent, for this premature exposure of the infant mind to the rank resort of the stranger, to the enslaving tyrannies of trade, to the crude admixtures of a heartless foreign society, and the absence of all those holy, love-compelling influences which are seldom or never to be found out of the sacred circle of family and home.

I have said nothing here of the effect upon the social world of this malappropriation of the mind by which it is to be governed. Yet of this appropriation you may predicate all the pernicious effects which are to follow. The domestic hearth will be without its attractions,—the domestic altar without its worshipper. Fireside and altar will be equally outraged by the narrowing concerns of trade. There will be but one topic, and that will be the how, the when and where of the successful speculation. There will be but one chaunt, and the chorus of that will be the eternal dollar.—There will be but one care wrinkling our souls as it wrinkles prematurely our cheeks, and that will be for the miserable secret, which shall turn our baser metals into gold, or at least, into a currency, which shall serve a present purpose. This is the only concern of newspaper and statesman. The schemes of the politician and the philosopher, are equally addressed to this one necessity. Even the government it is now assumed, must be made subservient to trade; and to hearken to the universal language of orator and press, it would seem as if the

popular enterprise were the only consideration which deserved our esteem.
—An improvement in Rail-roads or Steam Engines, is spoken of as a great
moral improvement—a discovery in physical science, which may increase
the powers of machinery, wins all the palinodes of the press, and we constantly deceive ourselves in this way by confounding the idea of a cunning or
an ingenious with a great people. We hear *ad nauseam,* the applause of those
toils or inventions which may be applied to the acquisition or the preservation of property, and this seems to be the whole amount of our national idea
of progress. To morals, letters and the fine arts,—to the pure, reserved and
delicate forms of taste and fancy—which to be won are to be worshipped,
we are as profoundly indifferent as if we were no longer human, or as if there
was no world beside to reproach us with our shame. How should such things
deserve our regard? They can only minister to the affections—they can
only elevate the soul—they can only tame the savage—they can only give
birth to such stale virtues as veneration, filial love, meekness, charity, gentle moods and hallowing household graces. And what are these to him
who wants money only—who knows no other want—whose heart seeks
no other affections—whose taste demands no other objects of delight—
whose soul is perfectly satisfied having no other God!

With impatient spirit, a heart swelling with diseased desires, a hope that
knows no measure in modesty or reason—our country, at this moment,
through its inappreciation of the social virtues, presents a deplorable picture
to the eye and mind. It is a nation free from beggary. Never was nation so
free at all times from this saddest of all conditions. No man lacks in food
or clothing. Never was nation, in the whole broad eye of the sun, so well fed
and habited,—with such various food—with such fine raiment. Plenty covers the land, and the God who has been thus bountiful in blessings, has withheld the arm of punishment. There is no pestilence in our cities—there is
no savage at riot along our borders. Yet we clamor—we complain! Never
was mouth so loud as the American in the language of complaint! Of what
do we complain? That the Arts avoid our shores—that the Graces fly from
our habitations—that we have lost

> "Our peace, our fearful innocence,"

that we are selfish men—that we have no Literature worthy of the name—
that our desires are base—that brutality stalks among us with a rare impudence—that crime is rising with hideous dimensions throughout the land?
Is it of these things we clamour? No! No! These are matters of small significance—these call for no complaints—offend no feelings—alarm no virtues—occasion no lamentations. Our clamor is for something better,
sweeter, dearer,—more necessary to our souls—for gold, for silver, or,
more specious delusion still, though more harmless, for good current paper

of banks not yet absolutely broken. The national appetite rages—is still un-satisfied—will never be satisfied. We are torn with the greed that works within us—our want, not our need,—raving that "promises to pay," will no longer enable us to fleece the poor of our own, and defraud the rich of a for-eign nation!

This is a terrible picture! Is it not a true one? Where are we as a people? What is our moral rank among the nations? We cannot shut our eyes to the melancholy truth. We cannot close our ears to the accents of scornful de-nunciation. We are sunk, lamentably sunk in character—not our Govern-ment—do not delude yourselves,—but our people,—you, and I, and all of us. The Government of State and Nation is a name—the mere creature of the people, drawing breath at our will, dependant wholly upon our decree, and moving this way or that, at our ordinance. The sin is ours, and the shame, and we must face its consequences, with what courage is left us.—And yet, hear our orators—read our newspapers! Unless when dealing in the grate-ful toil of defaming a rival party, their language is that of the happiest self-complacency.—Their skirts, they fancy,—at least they allege,—are clear of the dishonor, and, if they allow themselves to speak at all of our foreign dis-credit, it is only to lament that the loss of fame will be a loss of money—will prevent us from getting new loans. I, for one, rejoice that the nation can procure no new loans. It is necessary for the national virtue that we should be humbled. We have run a long career of profligacy, and the humiliation which is due to our vices is necessary to our regeneration. We must be made to feel the want and the shame together. We must be made to see that while the foreign creditor points one finger at our violated obligations, he keeps the other tenaciously upon his money-bags.

Gentlemen of the Erosophic Society:

The vices which have degraded the nation first had their beginning in the household. The character of a popular Government is that of its society;—and this consideration brings us back to our starting place.—Our reform must begin where our virtues faltered—at home—in each home—in all homes—by the hearths which we are too prone to abandon,—and pros-trate before those family altars which we do not sufficiently venerate. We must endeavor, as rapidly as we can, to recal the domestic virtues of our ancestors—those which made them triumph over French and Spaniard—which enabled them to give you permanent seisin of this noble State and City—that profound reverence for the social tie, which is at the very root of all our human obligations, and, without which, no nation ever perpetu-ates its conquests. In this maternal virtue, (for such I consider it,) I have endeavored to show the good old English excellence. To the decline of this virtue among us, I ascribe our present feebleness, distress and discontent. There is distress among us, because there is discontent, and this distress and discontent are the more dangerous because they are without cause. They show that something is wrong in our morals, in our affections, in our hopes, in our economy. But it is our religion, not our fortune, which is at fault. We have need to pray rather than complain. [. . .]

[. . .T]he powers of steam—the facilities of railroads—the capacity to overcome time and space, are wonderful things,—but they are not virtues, nor duties, nor laws, nor affections. I do not believe that all the steam power in the world can bring happiness to one poor human heart. Still less can I believe that all the railroads in the world can carry one poor soul to heaven. And these are the real objects of life—to live well, and do well, in preparation for the future. By keeping these objects in mind, you will patiently submit to the conviction that labor is the law of life, and that labor is not only honorable in itself, but ennobling to him who adopts it as his law. You will discard all thoughts of fortune-making. This is not the business of man,—nay, its pursuit is usually fatal to all his proper performances. On this subject we have a conclusive authority. What is it that we are authorized to ask for, in our morning prayer to God? "Give us this day our daily bread." No more,—Yet this is much—much more than any of us deserve. Millions rise every morning in Europe, with an overpowering apprehension, that day, that they shall get no bread,—neither for themselves nor for their little ones. Nobody contents himself, in America, with so humble a desire;—and were we to form any idea of our prayers, in this country, from our complaints, we should be seen, morning and night, before the throne of God, supplicating, not for bread, but fortune. The mere bread of life seems but a sorry object of prayer; and yet, without this prayer, no better future awaits us. Certainly, peace, security, happiness, are not ours, with all our toils, and with all our prayers to fortune. Gentlemen, we must pray to God, and not to fortune!

Copy-text: *The Social Principle,* 5—53.

From *Caloya, or,*
The Loves of the Driver

(1 8 4 5)

To those who insist that the working classes in the South should enjoy the good things of this world in as bountiful a measure as the wealthy proprietors of the soil, it would be very shocking to see that they lived poorly, in dwellings which, though rather better than those of the Russian boor, are yet very mean in comparison with those built by Stephen Girard, John Jacob Astor, and persons of that calibre. Nay, it would be monstrous painful to perceive that the poor negroes are constantly subjected to the danger of ophthalmic and other diseases, from the continued smokes in which they live, the fruit of those liberal fires which they keep up at all seasons, and which the more fortunate condition of the poor in the free States, does not often compel them to endure at any. It would not greatly lessen the evil of this cruel destiny, to know that each had his house to himself, exclusively; that he had his little garden plat around it, and that his cabbages, turnips, corn and potatoes, not to speak of his celery, his salad, &c., are, in half the number of cases, quite as fine as those which appear on his master's table. Then, his poultry-yard, and pig-pen—are they not there also?—but then, it must be confessed that his stock is not quite so large as his owner's, and there, of course, the parallel must fail. He has one immunity, however, which is denied to the owner. The hawk, (to whose unhappy door most disasters of the poultry yard are referred,) seldom troubles his chickens—his hens lay more numerously than his master's, and the dogs always prefer to suck the eggs of a white rather than those of a black proprietor. These, it is confessed, are very curious facts, inscrutable of course, to the uninitiated; and, in which the irreverent and sceptical alone refuse to perceive any legitimate cause of wonder.

You may see in his hovel and about it, many little additaments which, among the poor of the South, are vulgarly considered comforts; with the poor of other countries, however, as they are seldom known to possess them, they are no doubt regarded as burthens, which it might be annoying to take care of and oppressive to endure. A negro slave not only has his own dwelling, but he keeps a plentiful fire within it for which he pays no taxes. That he lives upon the fat of the land you may readily believe, since he is proverbially much fatter himself than the people of any other class. He has his own grounds for cultivation, and, having a taste for field sports, he keeps his own dog for the chase—an animal always of very peculiar characteristics, some of which we shall endeavour one day to analyse and develope. He is as hardy and cheerful as he is fat, and, but for one thing, it might be concluded safely that his condition was very far before that of the North American Indian—his race is more prolific, and, by increasing rather than diminishing, multiply necessarily, and unhappily the great sinfulness of mankind. This, it is true, is sometimes urged as a proof of improving civilization, but then, every justly-minded person must agree with Miss Martineau, that it is dreadfully immoral. We suspect we have been digressing.

Copy-text: *The Wigwam and the Cabin* (Redfield, 1856), 410–11.

On Poe's *Tales*

(*1 8 4 5*)

We have read with delight the fine artistic stories of Mr. Edgar A. Poe,—a writer of rare imaginative excellence, great intensity of mood, and a singularly mathematic directness of purpose, and searching analysis, by which the moral and spiritual are evolved with a progress as symmetrical, and as duly dependent in their data and criteria, as any subject matter however inevitable, belonging to the fixed sciences. Certainly, nothing more original, of their kind, has ever been given to the American reader. Mr. Poe is a mystic, and rises constantly into an atmosphere which as continually loses him the sympathy of the unimaginative reader. But, with those who can go with him without scruple to the elevation to which his visions are summoned, and from which they may all be beheld, he is an acknowledged master,—a Prospero, whose wand is one of wonderful properties. That he has faults, are beyond question, and some very serious ones, but these are such only as will be insisted upon by those who regard mere popularity as the leading object of art and fiction. At a period of greater space and leisure, we propose to subject the writings of Mr. Poe, with which we have been more or less familiar for several years, to a close and searching criticism. He is one of those writers of peculiar idiosyncracies, strongly marked and singularly original, whom it must be of general service to analyze with justice and circumspection.

Copy-text: *SWMMR* 2 (Dec. 1845): 426.

Americanism in Literature

(1845)

Americanism in Literature: An Oration before the Phi Kappa and Demosthenean Societies of the University of Georgia, at Athens, August 8, 1844. By Alexander B. Meek, of Alabama. Charleston: Burges & James. 1844.

This is the right title. It indicates the becoming object of our aim. Americanism in our Literature is scarcely implied by the usual phraseology. American Literature seems to be a thing, certainly,—but it is not the thing exactly. To put Americanism in our letters, is to do a something much more important. The phrase has a peculiar signification which is worth our consideration. By a liberal extension of the courtesies of criticism, we are already in possession of a due amount of American authorship; but of such as is individual, and properly peculiar to ourselves, we cannot be said to enjoy much. Our writers are numerous—quite as many, perhaps, in proportion to our years, our circumstances and necessities, as might be looked for among any people. But, with very few exceptions, their writings might as well be European. They are European. The writers think after European models, draw their stimulus and provocation from European books, fashion themselves to European tastes, and look chiefly to the awards of European criticism. This is to denationalize the American mind. This is to enslave the national heart—to place ourselves at the mercy of the foreigner, and to yield all that is individual, in our character and hope, to the paralyzing influence of his will, and frequently hostile purposes.

There is a season, perhaps, when such a condition of dependence is natural enough in the history of every youthful nation. It is in the national infancy that such must be the case. The early lab ours of a newly established people, in all the intellectual arts, must necessarily be imitative. They advance, by regular steps, from the necessary to the intellectual—from the satisfaction of vulgar cravings, to a desire for the gratification of moral and spiritual tastes;—and, in this progress, they can only advance through the assistance of other nations. This condition is inevitable in the history of a people wanting in homogeneousness at first, and but recently segregated from their several patriarchal trees. Time must be allowed to such a people—time to combine—to exchange thoughts and sympathies—and to learn the difficult, but absolutely necessary duty, of working together, as a community, in harmonious and mutually relying action. Generations must pass away, and other generations take their places, before they shall utterly lose the impressions made upon their plastic infancy by arbitrary models—before they shall begin to look around them, and within themselves, for those characteristics which are peculiar to their condition, and which distinguish the country of their present fortunes. It is idle to say, as has been urged by the British Reviewers in their reply to Mr. Jefferson, that the Anglo-Americans were of full age at the very birth of their country. This is scarcely true, even in physical respects. They did not represent the intellect of the nation which they left, though they did its moral and its temperament. They represented neither its tastes, nor its acquisitions, nor its luxuries. The eminence upon which the superior characteristics of the British nation stood, had never been reached by the footsteps of the Pilgrims. They were in possession of the AngloNorman genius, no doubt—upon this it will be the duty of the Americans to insist;—but its great attainments—its cherished acquisitions—its tastes, its refinements, its polish, were not theirs. In all these essentials, the founders of the Anglo-American States were in their infancy. And so they were kept for a century, by the novel necessities, the trying hardships, the perilous wars which followed upon their new condition. The conquest of a savage empire—the conflict with barbarian enemies,—kept them back from the natural acquisitions, which were due to their origin and genius. Great Britain herself is fairly chargeable, by her tyrannous exactions and the bloody wars with which she sought us out in the new homes so perilously won in the wilderness, with having withstood our people in their progress to the attainment of those objects the lack of which she this day makes our reproach.

But these excuses can be urged no longer, nor is it necessary that they should. Europe must cease to taunt us because of our prolonged servility to the imperious genius of the Old World. We must set ourselves free from the tyranny of this genius, and the time has come when we must do so. We have our own national mission to perform—a mission commensurate to the extent of our country,—its resources and possessions,—and the numerous nations, foreign and inferior, all about us, over whom we are required to extend our sway and guardianship. We are now equal to this sway and guardianship. The inferior necessities of our condition have been overcome. The national mind is now free to rise to the consideration of its superior wants and more elevated aims; and individuals, here and there, are starting out from the ranks of the multitude, ready and able to lead out, from the bondage of foreign guidance, the genius which, hitherto, because of its timidity, knew nothing of its own resources for flight and conquest.

If the time for this movement has not yet arrived, it is certainly very near at hand. This conviction grows out of the fact that we now daily taunt ourselves with our protracted servility to the European. We feel that we are still too humbly imitative, wanting in the courage to strike out boldly, hewing out from our own forests the paths which should lead us to their treasures, and from the giant masses around us the characteristic forms and aspects of native art. This reproach has been hitherto but too much deserved, qualified only by a reference to the circumstances in our condition at which we have been able to glance only for a moment. We have done little that may properly be called our own; and this failure, due to influences which still, in some degree, continue, is one which nothing but a high and stimulating sense of nationality will enable us to remedy. It is so easy, speaking the English language, to draw our inspiration from the mother country, and to seek our audience in her halls and temples, that, but for the passionate appeals of patriotic censure, it may be yet long years before we throw off the patient servility of our dependence. With a daily influx of thousands from foreign shores, seeking to share our political securities and the blessings of the generous skies and rich soil which we possess, Europe sends us her thoughts, her fashions, and her tastes. These have their influence in keeping us in bondage, and we shall require all the activity of our native mind to resist the influence which she thus exercises upon our national institutions and education. Besides, our very wealth of territory, and the ease with which we live, are obstacles in the way of our improvement. The temptations of our vast interior keep our society in a constant state of transition. The social disruptions occasioned by the wandering habits of the citizen, result invariably in moral loss to the whole. Standards of judgment fluctuate, sensibilities become blunted, principles impaired, with increasing insecurity at each additional remove; and this obstacle in the way of our literary progress must continue, until the great interior shall react, because of its own overflow, upon the Atlantic cities.

There is nothing really to distress us in this survey, unless,—either because of a supineness of character which is not our reproach in merely every-day pursuits, or because of an intrinsic deficiency of the higher intellectual resources,—we continue to yield ourselves to our European teachers. Our literature, so far, has been English in its character. We have briefly striven to show why. Glad are we that we can make some exceptions to this admission—that we can point, here and there throughout the country, to some individuals, and say, here stands a true scion of young America,—this is a plant of our own raising—true to the spirit of the country,—to its genuine heart—a man to represent and speak for the nature which we acknowledge, and of which time shall make us proud. In these instances we find our hope. It is thus that we feel ourselves encouraged to say to our people, and to the workers in the mind of Europe, that we too are making a beginning in a purely individual progress—evolving, however slowly, a national aim and idea, out of the fulness and overflow of the national heart. We are rejoiced to behold symptoms of this independent intellectual working, simultaneously, in remote regions of the country; and flatter ourselves with the vision of a generous growth in art and letters, of which tokens begin to make themselves felt from the Aroostook to the Rio Brave. This evidence needs but sympathy and encouragement to grow powerful, and to challenge a living rank among the great spirits of other lands and periods. As yet, perhaps, the shows are faint and feeble. Few of the hurrying multitude have leisure to behold them,—our progress declaring itself, as it now does, rather by its anxieties and cravings,—its discontents with itself, and its feverish impatience at the advance of other communities—than by its own proper performances. But such a condition of the popular mind is the precursor of performance. The wish to do, is the forerunner of the way. Let us only take something for granted. Let the nation but yield a day's faith to its own genius, and that day will suffice for triumph. We do not yet believe in ourselves,—unless in the meaner respects which prove our capacity for acquisition only in concerns the most inferior—in the mechanical arts,—in pursuits regarded as simply useful,—in selfish desires, and such as are necessary to our physical condition merely. This scepticism is the great barrier to be overcome. Our development depends upon our faith in what we are, and in our independence of foreign judgment. A resolute will, a bold aim, and a spirit that courageously looks within for its encouragements and standards,—these are our securities for intellectual independence. To these acquisitions our labours must be addressed. To the want of these, and the necessity for them, the attention of our people must be drawn. The popular mind scarcely yet seems to perceive that there is a vast and vital difference between the *selfspeaking* among our people, and that numerous herd, which, though born, living and walking in our midst, speak never *for* our hearts, and seldom *from* their own—whose thoughts, no less than language, are wholly

English, and who, in all general characteristics—so far as the native progress and development are effected—might as well have been born, dwelling and dilating in Middlesex or London. It is but to see these things as we
should—to understand the world-wide difference between writing for, and
writing *from* one's people. This difference is the whole,—but *what* a difference! To write *from* a people, is *to write* a people—to make them live—to
endow them with a life and a name—to preserve them with a history forever. Whether the poet shall frame his song according to custom, or according to the peculiar nature and the need of those for whom it is made, is, in
other words, to ask whether he shall be a poet at all or not. It was by properly understanding this difference in ancient days that he grew into the stature of the poet, and won his reputation; and it was through the proper comprehension of this *difference* and this *duty,* on the part of the Poet, that the
genius and the history of the great nations have survived all the political disasters which have bowed their pillars in the dust.

Up to the present day—the signs whereof encourage us with better
hopes—the question might properly have been asked, how should objects,
such as these, be to us of any consideration?—we who live not for the morrow but the day—whose plans are conceived for temporary not eternal refuge—who hurry forward as if we had no children, and who rear them as if
we loved them not! Such is the profligacy of every people who show themselves indifferent to the developments of native art. It is by the exhibition
of the constructive faculty that the intellectual nature of a people is distinguished. In proportion to the possession and exercise of this faculty, which
embodies all the elements of the imagination, will be the moral rank of the
nation. We have been very heedless of this matter. Our people have taken too
little interest in the productions of the American mind, considered purely as
American, whether in art or letters. In all that relates to the higher aims of
the social and spiritual nature, England, and what she is pleased to give us,
sufficiently satisfies our moral cravings. Yet we have an idea of independence
in some respects which tends to show how wretchedly limited has been our
ambition. Parties are formed among us to compel the manufacture of our
own pots and kettles, our woollens and window glass; parties ready to revo-
lutionize the country, and make all chaos again, if these things be not of our
own making:—made too,—such is the peculiar excellence of the jest, at our
own heavy cost and pecuniary injury;—but never a word is said, whether
by good sense or patriotism, touching the grievous imposition upon us of
foreign opinion and foreign laws, foreign tastes and foreign appetites, taught
us through the medium of a foreign, and perhaps hostile and insulting
teacher. These, say these profound haberdashers in the wares of patriotism,
are really matters of slight concern. Thoughts are common, say the paper

manufacturers, and though we insist upon supplying the paper from domestic mills, upon which such thoughts are to be printed, yet these are quite as properly brought from abroad, as conceived and put in proper utterance at home. The European may as well do our thinking. The matter is not worth a struggle. English literature is good enough for us for many hundred years to come.[2] So, for that matter, are English woollens.

But this will not suffice. The question is one which concerns equally our duties and our pride. Are we to aim and arrive at all the essentials of nationality—to rise into first rank and position as a people—to lift our heads, unabashed, among the great communities of Europe—plant ourselves on the perfect eminence of a proud national will, and show ourselves not degenerate from the powerful and noble stocks from which we take our origin? This is a question not to be answered by the selfishness of the individual nature, unless it be in that generous sort of selfishness which is moved only by the highest promptings of ambition. It is an argument addressed to all that is hopeful and proud in the hearts of an ardent and growing people. It is not addressed to the tradesman but to the man. We take it for granted, that we are not—in the scornful language of the European press,—a mere nation of shop-keepers:[3]—that we have qualities of soul and genius, which if not yet developed in our moral constitution, are struggling to make themselves heard and felt;—that we have a pride of character,—growing stronger (as we trust) with the progress of each succeeding day,—which makes us anxious to realize for ourselves that position of independence, in all other departments, which we have secured by arms and in politics. Mere political security—the fact that we drink freely of the air around us, and at our own choosing partake of the fruits of the earth—is not enough,—constitutes but a small portion of the triumphs, and the objects of a rational nature. Nay, even political security is temporary, always inferior if not wholly uncertain,

---

2. *WGS:* This language was actually employed by one of the American reviews of highest rank. Yet these reviews, themselves are anticipated by foreign criticism, as, in most cases, they expend their analysis, upon foreign publications. I have heard an American author speak with wholesale scorn of all American art, and an American painter, of superior distinction, declare that he never allowed himself to read an American book. Neither of these unfortunate persons seemed to perceive, that, in thus disparaging the native genius, they were effectually sealing their own condemnation.

3. *WGS:* This language, originally applied by Napoleon to the English nation, at the very time when his highest ambition was to transfer to France a portion of that commerce upon which the great distinction and power of the rival country was built up,— has been transferred, by the latter, in a sense still more scornful, to our own. It is, perhaps, no bad sign of our successful progress as a nation, that our national enemy shows herself more angry with us than ever.

unless it be firmly based upon the certain and constant vigilance of the intellectual moral. A nation, properly to boast itself and to take and maintain its
position with other States, must prove itself in possession of self-evolving attributes. Its character must be as individual as that of the noblest citizen that
dwells within its limits. It must do its own thinking as well as its own fighting, for, as truly as all history has shown that the people who rely for their
defence in battle upon foreign mercenaries inevitably become their prey, so
the nation falls a victim to that genius of another, to which she passively de-
fers. She must make, and not borrow or beg, her laws. Her institutions must
grow out of her own condition and necessities, and not be arbitrarily framed
upon those of other countries. Her poets and artists, to feel her wants, her
hopes, her triumphs, must be born of the soil, and ardently devoted to its
claims. To live, in fact, and secure the freedom of her children, a nation must
live through them, in them, and by them,—by the strength of their arms,
the purity of their morals, the vigour of their industry, and the wisdom of
their minds. These are the essentials of a great nation, and no one of these
qualities is perfectly available without the co-operation of the rest. And, as
we adapt our warfare to the peculiarities of the country, and our industry to
our climate, our resources and our soil, so the operations of the national
mind must be suited to our characteristics. The genius of our people is required to declare itself after a fashion of its own—must be influenced by its
skies, and by those natural objects which familiarly address themselves to the
senses from boyhood, and colour the fancies, and urge the thoughts, and
shape the growing affections of the child to a something kindred with the
things which he beholds. His whole soul must be imbued with sympathies
caught from surrounding aspects within his infant horizon. The heart must
be moulded to an intense appreciation of our woods and streams, our dense
forests and deep swamps, our vast immeasurable mountains, our volumi-
nous and tumbling waters. It must receive its higher moral tone from the
exigencies of society, its traditions and its histories. Tutored at the knee of
the grand-dame, the boy must grasp, as subjects of familiar and frequent
consideration, the broken chronicles of senility, and shape them, as he grows
older, into coherence and effect. He must learn to dwell often upon the
narratives of the brave fathers who first broke ground in the wilderness, who
fought or treated with the red men, and who, finally, girded themselves up
for the great conflict with the imperious mother who had sent them forth.
These histories, making vivid impressions upon the pliant fancies of childhood, are the source of those vigorous shoots, of thought and imagination,
which make a nation proud of its sons in turn, and which save her from becoming a by-word and reproach to other nations. In this, and from such impressions, the simplest records of a domestic history, expand into the most

ravishing treasures of romance. But upon this subject let us hearken to the writer of the eloquent discourse before us.

> Literature, in its essence, is a spiritual immortality, no more than religion a creation of man; but, like the human soul, while enduring the mystery of its incarnation, is subject to the action of the elements, is the slave of circumstance. In the sense in which we would now view it, it is the expression of the spiritual part of our nature, in its intellectual action, whether taking form in philosophy, history, poetry, eloquence, or some other branch of thought. The sum of all this, in any nation, is what constitutes her literature, and it is always modified and coloured by the peculiarities about it. As the river, sliding under the sunset, imbibes for the time, the hues of the heavens, so the stream of literature receives, from the people through which it passes, not only the images and shadows of their condition, but the very force and direction of its current. Every literature, Greek or Roman, Arabic or English, French, Persian or German, acquired its qualities and impression from the circumstances of the time and people. The philosophic eye can readily detect the key, cause and secret of each, and expose the seminal principle from which they grew into their particular shape and fashion. The same scrutinizing analysis will enable us to determine the influences among ourselves, which are to operate in the formation of our literature, as well as to decide whether it will comport with those high spiritual requisitions which I have already avowed, should be demanded from it. Let us then attempt to see how Americanism will develop itself in Literature. pp. 11, 12.

There is something equally thoughtful and fanciful in the passage which follows. It betrays a mind as sensible to the picturesque, as it is searching and speculative. The writer proceeds to illustrate his proposition by glimpses of the physical material which our own country affords for the uses of the native poet.

> The physical atributes of our country are all partial to the loftiest manifestations of mind. Nature here presents her loveliest, sublimest aspects. For vastness of extent, grandeur of scenery, genial diversities of climate, and all that can minister to the comforts and tastes of man, this heritage of ours is without a parallel. In its mountains of stone and iron, its gigantic and far-reaching rivers, its inland seas, its forests of all woods, its picturesque and undulating prairies, in all its properties and proportions, it might well be considered, in comparison with the eastern hemisphere, the work of a more perfect and beneficent artist. To the eyes of the Genoese mariner, the wildest dreams of Diodorus and Plato were more than realized. Seneca sang,—

Venient Annis
Saecula series, quibus oceanus
Vincula rerum laxet, et ingens
Pateat tellus, Typhisque novos
Detegat orbes:

Yet, not even in the mirror of his prophetic fancy were these more than Elysian fields glossed with all their beauty and sublimity. Even the bilious British satirist, who could see no good in all our institutions, was compelled to confess that here

————Nature showed
The last ascending footsteps of the God!

Well nigh all this vast expanse of fruitfulness and beauty, too, has been subject to the control of civilized man. Our country has extended her jurisdiction over the fairest and most fertile regions. The rich bounty is poured into her lap, and breathes its influence upon her population. Their capacities are not pent and thwarted by the narrow limits which restrict the citizens of other countries. No spec[u]lative theorist, a Malthus, Stultz or Liceto, has cause here to apprehend the dangers of over-population. Room, bountiful room, is all about us, for humanity to breathe freely in, and to go on expanding in a long future. Do these things afford no promise of intellectual improvement? Are they no incitements to a lofty and expanded literature? Do they furnish no *matériel* for active, generous, elevated thought? Is there no voice coming out from all this fragrance and beauty and sublimity, appealing to the heart and fancy of man, for sympathy, utterance, embodiment? Why, it was once said, that the sky of Attica would make a Boeotian a poet; and we have seen even 'the red old hills of Georgia' draw inspiring melody from the heart of patriotic genius. Physical causes have always operated in the formation and fashioning of literature. In all the higher productions of mind, ancient and modern, we can easily recognize the influence of the climate and natural objects among which they were developed. The sunsets of Italy coloured the songs of Tasso and Petrarch; the vine-embowered fields of beautiful France are visible in all the pictures of Rousseau and La Martine, you may hear the solemn rustling of the Hartz forest, and the shrill horn of the wild huntsman throughout the creations of Schiller and Goethe; the sweet streamlets and sunny lakes of England smile upon you from the graceful verses of Spenser and Wordsworth, and the mist-robed hills of Scotland loom out in magnificence through the pages of Ossian, and the loftier visions of Marmion and Waverly.

Our country, then, must receive much of the character of her literature from her physical properties. If our minds are only original, if they be not base copyists, and servile echoes of foreign masters; if we can assert an intellectual as well as political independence; if we dare to think for ourselves, and faithfully picture forth, in our own styles of utterance, the impressions our minds shall receive from this great fresh continent of beauty and sublimity; we can render to the world the most vigorous and picturesque literature it has ever beheld. Never had imagination nobler stimulants; never did nature look more encouragingly upon her genuine children. In poetry, romance, history and eloquence, what glorious objects, sights and sounds, for illustration and ornament! I have stood, down in Florida, beneath the overarching groves of magnolia, orange and myrtle, blending their fair flowers and voluptuous fragrance, and opening long vistas between their slender shafts, to where the green waters of the Mexican Gulf lapsed upon the silversanded beach, flinging up their light spray into the crimson beams of the declining sun, and I have thought that, for poetic beauty, for delicate inspiration, the scene was as sweet as ever wooed the eyes of a Grecian minstrel on the slopes of Parnassus, or around the fountains of Castaly.

Again: I have stood upon a lofty summit of the Alleghanies, among the splintered crags and vast gorges, where the eagle and the thunder make their home; and looked down upon an empire spread out in the long distance below. Far as the eye could reach, the broad forests swept away over territories of unexampled productiveness and beauty. At intervals, through the wide champaign, the domes and steeples of some fair town, which had sprung up with magical suddenness among the trees, would come out to the eye, giving evidence of the presence of a busy, thriving population. Winding away through the centre too, like a great artery of life to the scene, I could behold a noble branch of the Ohio, bearing upon its bosom the already active commerce of the region, and linking that spot with a thousand others, similar in their condition and character. As I thus stood, and thought of all that was being enacted in this glorious land of ours, and saw, in imagination the stately centuries as they passed across the scene, diffusing wealth, prosperity and refinement, I could not but believe that it presented a nobler theatre, with sublimer accompaniments and inspirations, than ever rose upon the eve of a gazer from the summits of the Alps or the Appenines.

Such are some of the physical aspects of our country, and such the influence they are destined to have upon our national mind. Very evidently they constitute noble sources of inspiration, illustration and description. For all that part of literature which is drawn from the phases of nature, from the varying moods and phenomena of the outward world, the elements and the seasons, they will be more valuable than all the beauties of the Troad or Campania Felix. Rightly used, they would bring a freshness and spirit into the domain of high thought, which would revive it like a spring-time return, and we might take up, in a better hope, the exultation of Virgil,—

> Jam ultima aetas Cumali carmidis venit,
> Magnus ordo saeclorum nascitur abintegro,
> Et jam virgo redit Saturnia regna redeunt! pp. 12–17.

This is a long extract, but we have no apologies to make for it. Its pictures will interest, its grace, glow and eloquence, delight the reader, until he forgets its length. No one can question the fact that the scenery of a country has always entered largely into the inspiration of the native genius. The heart of the poet is apt to dwell frequently and fondly upon the regions on which the eyes of his youth first opened, with a rare acuteness of delight, even though these were wholly wanting in natural beauty and grossly barren of all the accessories of art. What then must be the effect upon the young genius where the scenery is beautiful or imposing in itself—distinguished by sweetness, grace and loveliness, or stirring deeper and sublimer sentiments by its wild and awe-compelling attributes. That our scenery has not yet found its painter on canvas or in fiction, is due to other than its own deficiencies. It must be our care to prove that it is not because the genius itself is not among us.

One remark may be offered here. In all probability, the merely descriptive poet will be among the latest productions of our land. Britain herself has not produced many poets of this order, nor do they rank, with the single exception of Thomson, among the very noble of her train. Bloomfield was a driveller, and the rank of Somerville is low. The genius of the Anglo-Saxon would seem to be too earnest, too intensely moral in its objects, for the consideration of still life except as subordinate to the action. He puts it in his story, as the painter upon his canvas, as a sort of back-ground, and he usually hurries from this sort of painting to that which better tasks his more exacting powers. In this characteristic the genius of the American is naturally like,—with this difference, that the circumstances of his career tends still more to increase his love of action and his disregard of mere adjuncts and dependencies. He has an aim, and, eager in its attainment, he pauses not to see how lovely is the lake and valley—how vast the mountain—how wild the gorge, how impetuous the foaming rush of the unbridled waters. If he sees or feels, it is but for an instant,—and he is driven forward, even as the ataract beneath his gaze, by a power of which he is himself unconscious, and in a direction, the goal of which he is not permitted to behold. Our orator has already, adequately and sufficiently, instanced the various charms of scenery which our country possesses. These will make themselves felt in due season, when the national mind is permitted to pause in its career of conflict—for such is the nature of its progress now—for a survey of its conquests and itself. We pass, with him, to other considerations of still more importance, as essential to Americanism in our Letters. The extract which we make is brief:

These pleasant anticipations are also justified in part, by the excellent and diversified character of the population of our country. Herein will reside one of the strong modifying influences of Americanism upon literature. Though our population is composed principally of the several varieties of the Anglo-Saxon stock, yet every other race of Europe, and some from the other continents, have contributed to swell the motley and singular combination. Coming from every quarter of the globe, they have brought with them their diverse manners, feelings, sentiments, and modes of thought, and fused them in the great American alembic. The stern, clear-headed, faith-abiding Puritan, the frank, chivalrous, imaginative Huguenot, the patient, deep-thoughted, contemplative German,—pilgrims from every clime, creed, and literature—are to be found in contact and intercourse here. They interact upon each other to fashion all the manifestations of society, in thought or deed. The contrasts and coincidences, they present under our institutions, afford new and graceful themes for the poet, the novelist and the philosopher; and the historian will have to give us pictures of life and humanity here, such as are found not elsewhere. I need but allude, in this connection, to the existence of three distinct races of men upon our continent, with their strongly marked peculiarities of condition, colour and history. The immense rapidity with which our numbers are increasing—well nigh doubling in every fifteen years!—will produce an unexampled demand for knowledge, and act as a powerful impetus to its elevation. Already has the great and fluctuating intermixture of our population had an influence upon the English language. In no part of the world is our mother tongue spoken with such general purity of pronunciation as in our country. The constant tide of internal emigration tends to rectify the provincialisms into which stationary communities so frequently fall. Otherwise is it even in England. The whole kingdom is broken up into dialects as numerous as her counties; and the respective inhabitants are almost as unintelligible to each other, as if they spoke languages radically distinct. Is it Utopian to expect the proudest results, when one common language shall be employed by the many millions who are to occupy this almost illimitable republic?—But it is in the strong, industrious and wholesome character of our population, that the best hope for our national mind depends. Their habits of life will generate a *muscularity* of intellect, becoming their position and destiny. No effeminacy of thought or feeling will be tolerated among a people, composed of the choicest varieties of every race, stimulating each other to mental exertion, and accumulating wealth and power with almost miraculous rapidity and extent. Such a people, if they should have no powerful impediments, are better fitted than any other to render the world an intellectual illumination, and to bring round in reality the poetic vision of the golden age. pp. 17–19.

But the most imposing considerations arrayed by our author in this discussion, as indicative of the future resources of Americanism in our Literature, are to be found in those passages in which he considers the influence of our political institutions upon the mind of the country. It would afford us great pleasure did our limits suffice to give these passages, but we must content ourselves with a bare glance at their prominent suggestions. Mr. Meek justly draws our attention to the fact, that, of all the ancient tyrannies, but very few of them have contributed to the advancement of letters. He exhibits the baldness in literature of Chaldea, Babylon, Assyria and Phoenicia, and hurriedly compares their performances with the more glorious showings of the free states of the past. And he argues justly that this result is in the very nature of things;—that, as liberty of opinion is favourable to thought and provocative of discussion, so almost must it favour the general development of intellect in all departments. The deduction is absolutely inevitable. Tyranny, on the other hand, always trembling for its sceptre, and jealous of every antagonist influence, watches with sleepless solicitude to impose every fetter upon the free speech of orator and poet. It would seem almost impertinent to insist upon these points, were it not that there really exists among thinking men a considerable difference of opinion upon them, and this difference of opinion is the natural fruit of a too hasty glance only at the surfaces. The friends of aristocracy, lingering fondly over those bright but unfrequent pages in literary history, as associated with a despotism, which are adorned by the works of genius, hurriedly conclude that they are the issues of that despotism itself. They point with confidence to such periods as those of Augustus Caesar and Leo the Tenth. The courtly sway of the one, and the magnificent ambition of the other, are sufficient to delude the imagination, and hurry the reason aside from a consideration of the true analysis. They overlook the important fact that, in all these cases, it has so happened that men of literary tastes were themselves the despots. It was not that the despotism was itself favourable to such persons, but that the despotism, wielded by a particular hand, was not unwilling to smile with indulgence upon the obsequious poet, and the flattering painter. It so happened that an absolute tyrant was yet possessed of some of the higher sensibilities of the intellectual nature, and had almost as strong a passion for letters and the arts, as for political dominion. Thus feeling, he rendered the one passion in some degree subservient to the other. If it could be shown that his tastes were transmitted with his robes, to his successor, there might be some reason in the faith which we are required to have in the benignant literary influences of such a government; but the sufficient fact that, in the histories of despotism, these brief and beautiful periods shine out alone, and rest like green spots, at remote stages, through a long and lamentable wilderness, would seem to conclude the question.

It was the wealth and taste of the despot that made him a patron, and not because he held the reins of government with a rigorous or easy hand. The peculiar sort of rule in Rome and Italy had no part in making the poet or historian; and, for the patronage itself, accorded by the despot, let the reader turn to the histories of denied and defrauded genius, and see what a scorned and wretched beggar it has ever been in the courts of Aristocracy. Let him look to the history of Tasso for example—let him turn to that curious book of Benvenuto Cellini,—if he would see what sort of countenance is that which mere power is apt to bestow upon the labours of the man of letters or of art. Great wealth,—that of private persons—has done for them much more in every nation. Spenser owed much more to Sydney, and Shakspeare to Southhampton, than either of them ever owed to Elizabeth. We need not multiply examples. The man of genius, in all departments, has achieved his triumphs rather in despite and defiance of despotism than because of its benign and genial atmosphere. The true patron of letters is the lover of them, and where are these persons likely to be more numerous, than in regions where the great body of the people are lifted by the political institutions of the country into a responsibility which tasks the intellect, and requires a certain amount of knowledge in every department. The despotism is apt to absorb in itself all the taste and intellect where it governs. Democracy naturally diffuses them. At first, the diffusion would seem to lessen the amount of the whole,—to subtract from its spirit—reduce its volume, and, by too minute division of its parts, to render it feeble and inert for active purposes. But the constant attrition of rival minds in a country where the great body of the people are forced into consideration, strengthens and informs, with a peculiar and quickening vigour, each several share of that capacity with which the genius of the nation was at first endowed. The genius of the nation does not the less act together, because it acts through many rather than through one; and, by insensible transitions, the whole multitude rise to the same elevated platform, upon which, at the beginning, we may have beheld but one leading mind, and that, possibly, borrowed from a rival nation. It is a wondrous impulse to the individual, to his hope, his exertions and his final success, to be taught that there is nothing in his way, in the nature of the society in which he lives;—that he is not to be denied because of his birth or poverty, because of his wealth or his family;—that he stands fair with his comrades, on the same great arena,—with no social if no natural impediments,—and that the prize is always certain for the fleetest in the race.

This must be the natural influence of the democratic principle upon the minds of a people by whose political institutions its supremacy is recognized. Let no man deceive himself by a glance confined only to the actual condition of things around him. No doubt that, in the beginning of a democracy, in that first wild transition state, which follows upon the overthrow of favourite and long acknowledged authorities, art and literature, alarmed at the coil and clamour, will shroud themselves in their cells, venturing abroad only in those dim hours of dusk and twilight, in which a comparative silence promises comparative security. But this is also the history of nearly all of the arts of peace. Commerce and trade, mechanical and mercantile adventure, show themselves nearly equally timid. True, they are the first to recover from their panic, but this is solely because they belong to the more servile and earthly necessities of our nature. They are followed by the gradual steps of art and science, and these in turn by the lovelier and gentler offspring of united grace and muse. It is the error of persons of taste that, shrinking themselves from the uproar of this transition period, they regard its effects as likely to continue, as being not temporary only, and as destined to perpetuate the commotion which, in our notion, is nothing more than that natural outbreak of elements in the moral, which, in the natural world, almost always harbingers a clear sky and pure, salubrious and settled weather. Such, when the time comes,—when the first rude necessities of a new condition are pacified, and the machine begins to turn evenly and smoothly upon its axis,—such will be the working of democracy. This is not less our faith than our hope. The natural conclusions of reason led us directly to this confidence, even if the history of the past did not afford us sufficient guaranties for the future.

Our orator next instances, with effect, the wholesome influences in our government of the "let alone" principle. This, by the way, is an important matter to be understood. Democracy goes into society, with scarcely any farther desire than that men should be protected from one another—left free to the pursuit of happiness, each in the form and manner most agreeable to himself, so long as he does not trespass upon a solitary right of his neighbour. This is the principle. We do not tolerate any interference of government with those employments of its citizens which violate none of the rights of others, and which do not offend against the sense of a Christian country. To protect or to disparage that occupation of the individual or the community, which, in itself, is regarded as legitimate, is a power which, according to our construction of the social contract in America, is wholly unwarranted by our laws. Something is due certainly to the necessities of the whole; but, for the "general welfare" principle, we insist that the "general necessity and exigency" is the true standard by which we impose restraints, or hold out encouragements. Mr. Meek properly insists upon the value of this "let alone" practice, on the part of government, as vastly promotive of the interests of literature; and particularly dwells upon the advantages, in this regard, which grow out of our system of confederated sovereignties. The very inequalities of things in moral respects, in employments, in climate, soil and circumstance, which we find in these severalties, is at once calculated to provoke the mind in each to exertion, and to endow it with originality. There is none of that even tenor of aspect, in the genius of the country, which somewhat monotonously distinguishes an empire the whole energies of which spring from centralization. A natural rivalry and emulation are the consequence of a form of political independence, which, in all domestic subjects, leaves us utterly free to our own pursuits. We watch the progress of our neighbour, and strive rather to surpass than to follow. There is none of that servile, blind adhesion to a superior, which, in Europe, invariably brings the popular intellect, even in the most remote dependencies of the nation, to the beaten tracks which conduct them to the centre. The very divergencies of our paths are favourable to the boldness, the freedom and the flights of the national intellect. We make our own paths—we trace out our own progress—and, just in due degree as we turn aside from the dictation of those great cities, which, among us, are more immediately allied with the marts of Europe, so do we discover marks of the most certain freshness and originality, though coupled with rudeness and irregularity—a harshness which offends and a wilderness which, we are encouraged to believe, it is not beyond the power of time and training to subdue to equable and noble exercises. To any one who looks into the character of our people,—who passes below the surface, and sees in what way the great popular heart beats in the several States of the confederacy,—with what calm, consistent resolve in some—with what impatient heat in others—how cold but how clear in this region,—how fiery, but how clouded in that;—there will be ample promise for the future, not only in the value of the material, but in its exquisite and rich variety. And, even on the surface, how these varieties speak out for themselves, so that it shall not be difficult for a shrewd observer of men to distinguish at a glance, and to declare from what quarter of America the stranger comes,— whether from the banks of the Charles or the Hudson, the Savannah or the Mississippi.

Our orator justly reminds us, while treating of this part of his subject, that, by our compact, the interests of education and literature are left entirely in the control of the States. This vital matter is in our own hands, and nothing but our lachesse or our wilfulness, can possibly lose us the power of moulding the temper of our people in due compliance with our peculiar circumstances, whether moral or physical. We may make our literature what we please if we do not neglect the interests of education. We should confer upon it all the becoming characteristics of our section — our social sympathies, our political temper, and those moral hues and forms which the intellectual nature so happily imbibes from the aspects which surround us in the natural world. The airy structures of our imagination, born of a like sky and atmosphere with that of Greece, should not shrink from comparison with those of Dodona and Hymettus. Our Olympus rises at our will, and the divine spirits which we summon to make sacred its high abodes, clothed in a political freedom superior to that of Athens, with less danger of having their supremacy disputed and their rites disturbed, should surely bring to their altars a priesthood no less great and glorious.

Copy-text: *VRAH,* 7–29.

The Four Periods of American History

(1 8 4 5)

We have passed over many topics, illustrative of our subject, suggestively, and without seeking to discuss them. Our limits would not suffer more. Having intimated to you that the poet and romancer are only strong where the historian is weak, and can alone walk boldly and with entire confidence in those dim and insecure avenues of time which all others tremble when they penetrate; having arrived at the conclusion that, in the employment of historical events, for the purposes of art in fiction, a condition of partial obscurity and doubt in history being that which leaves genius most free to its proper inventions, is the one which is most suitable for its exercise;—it becomes necessary, if possible, to ascertain and to define those periods in our history which are most distinguished by this palpable obscurity—which are the most coupled with this condition of picturesque doubt and uncertainty—and which, hereafter, or even now, may be found most eligible for the uses of the muse. This susceptibility of the *matériel* of fiction, is, of course, a matter of degree. The real genius wants but little of the absolute in fact upon which to work. It is his rare endowment to subject the most stubborn events to his purposes—to mould the most incorrigible forms, and, out of truths the most ungracious and little promising, to evolve the most imposing and delightful fabrics. A happy thought, an inspired fancy, brings out to his mind the form and the colour in the mass, and teaches him to throw off the incumbrance, and in what way to relieve from its impediments, the exquisite ideal that his imagination has pictured in the rock. But, even for him the way may be made smooth, as the French and Italian novelists opened paths for Shakspeare. The grosser difficulties of the work may be overcome, and some of the barriers thrown down, though by the rudest workman, for the uses of the mightiest master.

To facilitate our examination of this subject, we propose to divide the history of our country into four unequal periods. This division, however arbitrary it may seem, is one that belongs naturally to our modes of progress, and would suggest itself to the most casual inquirer into the moral steps by which we attain the several successive epochs in our national career. The first period should comprise the frequent and unsuccessful attempts at colonization in our country by the various people of Europe—the English, French, and Spaniard—from the first voyage of the Cabots, under Henry the Seventh,—and should include all subsequent discovery and exploration, by whatever people, down to the permanent settlement of the English in Virginia. This period involves a term of seventy-five years, and abounds in romantic detail and interesting adventure. This was a time when the fountains of the marvellous seemed every where to be opened upon mankind—when, on the eve of wonderful discoveries in the natural, the people of Christendom lent a greedy ear to every sort of legend which held out similar assurances in the spiritual world—when popular faith reposed without a doubt upon the very bosom of fancy, and sucked in the wildest superstitions from the breast of the most prolific invention;—when the search after the improbable and the impossible prompted a singular disregard to the wonders that were real and every where growing, broad cast, around the very footsteps of adventure. All the pulses of mortal imagination seemed to have quickened at this period under a like maternal influence. Man was alive and eager in the thirst after great truths, and his progress was in due correspondence with the ambitious and restless nature of his desires. If he found not exactly what he sought, he yet laid his hand upon treasures which time has shown him were inappreciable in value. The real advantages of printing were then for the first time beginning to display themselves. The great but degraded masses were slowly realizing its fruits, and the popular imagination seemed to expand with new wings and eyes, dilating in the far survey of its newly opened possessions, in all the provinces of art and office. It will be sufficient to illustrate from one department for the rest—to show, by the achievements of the muse—as we well may—how active, on a sudden, had grown that impatient genius of uprising Europe (in England at least) to which the present owes so many trophies and delights. The period we have indicated was the great period in the literary history of Great Britain—vulgarly and improperly called the Elizabethan period. We have but to name the masters of that day—to point to Marlowe, Ben Jonson and Shakspeare;—to Spenser and to Sidney; to Bacon, and to him—a genius no less noble than hapless—whom Spenser has so felicitously called the "Ocean Shepherd." Never was era, in any country, more rich than this, in the one designated—

in the abundant variety, the matchless beauty, the masculine pathos, the grace, the strength and the originality of its productions. Nay, never was period half so rich. What was true of its poetry, was scarcely less true in other respects. In fact, it is usually a period most rich in poetry, that is most prolific in progress and discovery. The offices of the imagination are much more various than men ordinarily suppose. It is her eye and her wing that guide and impel genius in all of her departments. It is her sensibilities that quicken the impatient pulses of all adventure—her yearnings that prompt the hopes, and warm the courage of the builder and the battler, whether his province be the conquest of empires, or the more humble desire which contents itself with the planting of towns and the rearing of shrubs and gardens. The spirit therefore which constitutes the soul of poetry, and urges the unwearied labours of the poet, is shared in some degree by all who work, in all the branches of human industry. The labour which is undertaken *con amore,* is a take but an imperfect view of the European mind, as exhibited in what may be termed the more national progress of the age indicated, if we fail to see in it the strong proofs of sympathy with that more ethereal working of spirit, in the same nation, to which we are indebted for its poetry and art. Kindred with the poetry of a race is its religion; and this also was a period when, in England, under the impulse of a fresher spiritual yearning, the religion of the age, taking its direction from the unregulated passions of the popular mind, grew more than usually active in the great struggle with the inner world—when, the same imagination, unschooled and untutored in the popular mood, grew wild with misdirected enthusiasm—when, accordingly, the dark spirits seemed to receive a call to new exertions in consequence of the dangers from this very passionate activity of the common mind—when there were witches in the land—sorcerers needing to be baffled—devils to be cast forth—all angrily striving for continued possession of their ancient strong-holds in the troubled heart of man. A transition state, in a people, is thus always one of excited imagination. All the waters become turbid. But their commotion, though in storm, is the proof of a new and more hopeful life. It is the sign of a new spirit abroad. There are clouds—there is blackness—gloom in the sky—error on the face of the land—but the winds and the waters sweeten themselves by progress, and the thunderbolt which rends the spire, purifies the atmosphere which envelopes the stagnant city. In the history of the being whose law of life is eternal progress—from province to province, and from empire to empire—it is the calm alone that we have any need to fear.

The vigorous wing put on by the mind of Europe in the sixteenth century, might well lead the nation into cloud and frequent obscurity. And thus it is that we find King James—a sovereign who shared the excursive imagination of his age, without its judgment—writing with equal enthusiasm against witches and tobacco. His superstitions were those of wiser men who did not share in his antipathies. Thus, and then it was, that Bacon had his superstitions also — that Columbus meditated the restoration of the Holy City, and dreamed of the Golden Chersonesus — when Marco Polo was the popular authority — when Sir John Mandeville was the very ideal of the traveller — when Raleigh asserted the existence of the Anthropophagi, and told of a people who wore their eyes in their shoulders, and carried their heads under their arms.

Every working age and people must have their superstitions. Their superstitions are at the bottom of the work and impel it. But for the exaggerations of the imagination, we should lose the chief incentives to endeavour. It is by these that we are deluded to achievement. The objects which reward our toil, are not those which provoke it. The chemist was first a seeker after the philosopher's stone. It was pursuing Raphael that he met with Hermes. We must be careful then, in all our studies of the actual, in the history of the past, not to forget the apparent, by which it was enveloped as in a luminous garment, dazzling the eye from afar, and inviting the enterprise. The superstition is not the less a part of the religion, because, when we have attained to the real, we can separate it from the luminous atmosphere by which it was made to loom out upon the imagination. The faith of a time, by which a people works, is a truth, though it teaches many falsehoods. The artist who would employ the materials of American history for his purposes, must be an earnest student of the lore — must warmly sympathize with the spirit — by which all Europe was governed at the same corresponding period. There are no absurdities in a time, when a people is alive and in action, which the true philosopher can despise. The absurdity which moves the national heart, has always a real foundation, and, to the writer of fiction, it affords the best material by which to work upon the hearts, and lessen the superstitions of other periods and people. He must seek deeply to imbue himself with all the workings of our spiritual nature — what they hoped and what they dreaded — how deep were their terrors, how high their anticipations. It is in the god and the devil of a race that you can behold the truest picture of themselves. Here you may see the extent of their ambition, the degree of purity in their hearts, the things that they are, and the things which are dearest to their pursuit. These subjects, in English history, from the time of the Eighth Henry to the First Stuart, will be best read in the records of the courts, and in the dramatic literature of the same period. They should be studied by him who seeks to turn to account our first American period in history. The analysis of the properties, of the constituents and causes of national character, belongs to the first duties of the philosophical poet, and is absolutely essential to the successful labours of any architect who would build his fabric out of the materials of history. This analysis of the time of which we speak, will lead, as we have already said, to those wonders, crude and shapeless, which embodied in the faith of the past, may become, made symmetrical by the hands of imaginative art, a wondrous study for the future. The popular credulity is so much fairy-land itself—a land of twilight and uncertain shadows—to every shooting star of which a name and office may be given, and whose phosphorescent *ignes fatui,* may each, in turn, be translated to a star.

Our second period should comprise the history and progress of British settlement down to the accession of George the Third, and to the beginning of those aggressions upon the popular liberties in America, which ended in the revolutionary conflict. It will be readily seen what a marked difference of characteristic is that of this period in comparison with the preceding. The discovery of the country has been made, and there is an end to speculation on the subject of those wonders which the popular credulity of Europe was prepared to see. America was no longer El Dorado!—or, if it was recognized as substantially possessing a claim to be considered a land of golden treasure, it was only among that sober, secondthoughted few, whose expectations were based upon the effects of sturdy labour and industrious enterprise. The idle exploration which set forth on adventures in the vain hope to realize its own dreams, had given way to a cooler and more reasonable pioneer; and the steel which had been employed by the one for the slaughter of the savage, was employed by the other in laying their forests bare to cultivation. The truth remained—a great truth—but freed from its superstition. The romance which gave impulse to the wing of adventure was happily diminished, and what remained, though of a character which might still excite in a subdued period, was of far more phlegmatic character. But it still possessed the features of romance, was still full of aspects highly novel, persuasive and interesting, to the European. Adventure was no longer a phrenzy. It had become a duty. The explorer did not so much seek for gold, but he sought for that which was still more precious—freedom. It was not the conquest of a mighty empire that was in his aim—it was a home—a secure and happy homestead that won his hopes and stimulated his enterprises. If he no longer went forth glittering in armour, and to the sound of the trumpet, there was yet a stateliness in his simplicity, a nobleness and a majesty in his firm aspect—a glory in his strength and hardihood—a brightness in his hope and a beauty in his faith—such as might well beseem the classical simplicity of subject as chosen by the old Grecian masters—such as might well be chosen to adorn and give dignity to the choicest annals of future song. His career will be found not without its attractions. The adventure of a life in the wilderness—the lonely travel through unbroken forests—the musing upon the tumulus of ancient and unbroken tribes—the conflict with the wolf, and the midnight whoop of the savage—these are all incidents, which, however hacknied they may seem, shall yet be grouped in happiest combination by the hand of genius. The period of which we now speak was full of incident—a rare life, teeming in animation and exertion, derived from sources of this character—from the inevitable progress of the Anglo-Norman—from the inevitable fate of the Indian—a fate as relentless as that of the victim in the Grecian drama, and which, coupled with the history of his own gods, may be wrought into forms as nobly statuesque as any that drew a nation's homage to the splintered summits of Olympus. Following this almost individual struggle of the white man with the red, a larger field opens upon us. The conflict is no longer individual. New interests have arisen, and Christian Europe finds it politic to send her rival armies across the waters, in search of battle grounds, upon the soil of heathen America. How strange the sight to the savage—that of war to the knife, waged for supremacy between opposing nations in a realm so remote from their own several empires, and upon which they have scarce won foothold. Beneath the same sign of mercy and of blessing, he sees them encounter with hate and curses. He sees, but is not suffered to look on unemployed. He is marshalled in the opposing ranks, and, under the banners of the Cross, the singular and sad spectacle is presented to our eyes of the Christian employing the savage for the murder of his brother Christian. Those old French and Spanish wars, involving the fine trials of strength between Wolfe and Montcalm, the feebler warfare in which Braddock fell, and, nearer home, the frequent conflicts of Virginia, Carolina and Georgia, with the Apalachian tribes, influenced to hostility by the machinations of French and Spanish leaders—are all so many vast treasure-stores of art—stores which you may work upon for ages, yet leave still unexhausted to the workmen of succeeding ages. This period, dating from the settlement of Virginia to the beginning of the popular discontents in the reign of George the Third, will be found to comprise a term of nearly two hundred years.

A third division would cover the preliminaries to the revolutionary war—preliminaries which are not always to be found originating in the aggressions of the British parliament, but will be traced to the increasing power of the colonies, and their reluctance at being officered from abroad—the sentiment of independence growing in their feelings long ere it ripened into thought, and making them jealous of, and hostile to, their foreign governors and officers, long before the popular will had conceived any certain desire of separation. The same period would carry us through the war of the revolution, and include our brief passages of arms with the Barbary powers and with France under the Directory. For the merits of this period, in serving the purposes of art, we have but to refer you to the partisan conflict in the South—the wars of riflemen and cavalry, the sharp shooter and the hunter, and the terrible civil conflicts of whig and tory, which, for wild incident and daring ferocity, have been surpassed by no events in history.

SIMMS'S "THE FOUR PERIODS OF AMERICAN HISTORY" (1845)

This chart demonstrates how Simms made use of "The Four Periods of American History" in his epic fictional portrayal of America through more than four centuries.

Period	Dates	Fictional Representation
First: "The first period should comprise the frequent and unsuccessful attempts at colonization in our country by the various people of Europe—the English, French, and Spaniard—from the first voyage of the Cabots, under Henry the Seventh,—and should include all subsequent discovery and exploration, by whatever people, down to the permanent settlement of the English in Virginia."	c. 1497—c. 1607	*Vasconselos* (1853): Spanish in Florida and Mississippi Valley, 1538—42 *The Lily and the Totem* (1850): French in Florida and the Southeast, 1562—70
Second: "Our second period should comprise the history and progress of British settlement down to the accession of George the Third, and to the beginning of those aggressions upon the popular liberties in America, which ended in the revolutionary conflict."	c. 1608—1763	*The Cassique of Kiawah* (1859): colonial South Carolina, 1684 *The Yemassee* (1835): colonial South Carolina, 1715
Third: "A third division would cover the preliminaries to the revolutionary war . . . through the war of the revolution. . . . For the merits of this period, in serving the purposes of art, we have but to refer you to the partisan conflict in the South—the wars of riflemen and cavalry, the sharp shooter and the hunter, and the terrible civil conflicts of whig and tory, which, for wild incident and daring ferocity, have been surpassed by no events in history."	1764—82	*Joscelyn* (1867): Augusta, Georgia, and South Carolina backcountry, 1775 *The Partisan* (1835): events of the summer of 1780 (battle of Camden) *Mellichampe* (1836): guerrilla warfare on Santee following the battle of Camden *Katharine Walton* (1851): British occupation of Charleston, late 1780—81 *The Scout* (1841): May 1781 to the British evacuation of Ninety-Six, June 1781

Period	Dates	Fictional Representation
Third (*continued*)	1764–82	*The Forayers* (1855): events around Orangeburg before the battle of Eutaw Springs
		Eutaw (1856): battle of Eutaw Springs in September 1781; British defeated in South Carolina
		Woodcraft (1852): postwar problems after English evacuation in 1782
Fourth: "A fourth and last period would bring us to the present time, include our transition experience from the colonial to republican condition, illustrate the progress of interior discovery and settlement, comprise our Indian wars, the settlement of Kentucky and Ohio, the acquisition of Louisiana and Florida, the war of 1812 with Great Britain; the conquest of Texas, and the final and complete conversion to the purposes of civilized man, of that vast wild tract, that 'Boundless contiguity of shade,' spreading away from Altamaha to the Rio Bravo!"	1783 to mid-19th century	[Border Romances and other frontier writings]
		Guy Rivers (1834): Georgia
		Richard Hurdis (1838): Alabama
		Border Beagles (1840): Mississippi
		Confession (1841): South Carolina, Alabama, Texas
		Charlemont (1842): Kentucky
		Beauchampe (1845): Kentucky
		Helen Halsey (1845): Louisiana and Mississippi
		The Wigwam and the Cabin (1845): frontier stories
		Norman Maurice (poetic drama; 1851): Missouri
		Michael Bonham (poetic drama; 1852): Texas
		As Good as Comedy (1852): Georgia
		Paddy McGann (1863): South Carolina
		The Cub of the Panther (1869): North Carolina
		Voltmeier (1869): North Carolina
		"Sharp Snaffles" (1870) and "Bald-Head Bill Bauldy" (1870): tall tales in dialect

A fourth and last period would bring us to the present time, include our transition experience from the colonial to the republican condition, illustrate the progress of interior discovery and settlement, comprise our Indian wars, the settlement of Kentucky and Ohio, the acquisition of Louisiana and Florida, the war of 1812 with Great Britain; the conquest of Texas, and the final and complete conversion to the purposes of civilized man, of that vast wild tract, that "Boundless contiguity of shade," spreading away from the Altamaha to the Rio Bravo!

These tracts of time, indicated according to these divisions, may not be equally fruitful and diversified. The materials differ in character, but are in all sufficiently abundant. The future romancer will find them so. With the future Homer, the thousand barbarian tribes by which these woods and wilds were traversed before the coming of our ancestors—their petty wars, their various fortunes, their capricious passions, their dark-eyed women, their favourite warriors—will, like those of Greece, be made immortal on the lips of eternal song. Their dark and gloomy mythologies—not gloomier nor less pleasing than those of the Scandinavian—will receive some softening lights, some subduing touches, from the all-endowing spells of genius, which shall make them quite as imposing, if not so graceful and ethereal, as those of the people who prostrated themselves in worship along the banks of the Peneus. The future descendants of our line, stretching along the great blue heights of the Alleghanies, may be persuaded and fond to believe that they sprang from the loins of two mighty and rival races—the one, the fierce Viking of the northern ocean,—and not less fierce but less adventurous, some haughty Mico or Cassique of Apalachy—the Powhatan, the Pontiac, or the Tecumseh of future romance.[4]

We leave these speculations for another time. Having indicated our separate eras, as suggestive, each of separate resources, and suitable, severally, for distinct kinds of illustration, we will devote the rest of our essay to a brief examination of such specimens, from these materials, as occur to us, passingly, as proper subjects for the exercise of art. These are by no means limited during the first of our epochs. We consider the whole history of discovery, as commenced by the Northmen, as pursued by Columbus, and followed by the Portuguese and Spanish nations with a religious sort of

---

4. *WGS:* To those who read and confide in the claims set up by Professor Rafn, and others to the first discovery and partial settlement of America by the Northmen, long before the voyages of Columbus, there is nothing extravagant in this conjecture. On the contrary, the traditions of the northern *savans* are exceedingly plausible, and the poet will make no scruple of insisting upon them if his scheme and genius leads him to their use. The material is susceptible of admirable handling.

enthusiasm that partook of the aspects of a sacred fury, to be, in itself, a long and wonderful romance—furnishing resources the most ample, events the most startling—sometimes grand, frequently pathetic and always pictur-esque and new:—in almost all of their details, suitable for the poet, and re-quiring for successful elaboration less of genius than of taste. The artist will need to study the events of this period, not as a narrow student of the events themselves, but in all their connections. The collateral histories must be familiar to his mind. He must exercise the philosophic vision which looks deeply down, for the sources of mere facts, into the hearts of the people whom they concern. A profound inquiry into the moral and social char-acteristics of the several nations engaged in these discoveries—the English, French, Spanish and Portuguese—is an absolutely indispensable prelimi-nary. Above all, he must *feel* their religious characteristics, in his own spirit, before he can boldly enter upon the delineation of the spirit of their time! This, alone, can lead to a just comprehension of their various motives—their strange phrenzies—their implicit faith—their sleepless jealousies—their fanatic enthusiasm—their curious inconsistency of performance—and the singular union, so frequently found in the same personage, of so much that is base and bloody, with so much that is magnanimous and great! With this preparatory knowledge, the artist possesses that *"open sesames"* of character, without which, as he could not comprehend himself, he could never make his readers feel, the truth or the propriety of those anomalies which would otherwise be crowded in his story. For there is yet a latent probability at the bottom of all that is extravagant among the absolute performances of man; and it becomes a first duty of the philosophical artist to search out, and to find, this latent probability, as a key positively essential to the analysis of his subject.

Copy-text: *VRAH,* 75–86.

From *The Writings of James Fenimore Cooper*

(1 8 4 5)

We are among those who regard Mr. Cooper as a wronged and persecuted man. We conceive that his countrymen have done him gross injustice—that they have not only shown themselves ungenerous but ungrateful, and that, in lending a greedy ear to the numerous malicious aspersions which have assailed his person and his reputation, they have only given confirmation and strength to the proverbial reproach, of irreverence and ingratitude, to which countries, distinguished by popular governments, have usually been thought obnoxious. We do not mean to regard him as wholly faultless—on the contrary, we look upon Mr. Cooper as a very imprudent person; one whose determined will, impetuous temperament, and great self-esteem, continually hurry forward into acts and expressions of error and impatience. We propose to compare sides in this question:—to put the case fairly between himself and countrymen, and show where the balance of justice lies.

Of Mr. Cooper, little or nothing was known, by the American people at large, until the publication of "the Spy." To a few, perhaps, the novel of "Precaution" had brought him acquainted. That was a very feeble work—coldly correct, elaborately tame—a second or third rate imitation of a very inferior school of writings, known as the social life novel. In works of this class, the imagination can have little play. The exercise of the creative faculty is almost entirely denied. The field of speculation is limited; and the analysis of minute shades of character, is all the privilege which taste and philosophy possess, for lifting the narrative above the province of mere lively dialogue, and sweet and fanciful sentiment. The ordinary events of the household, or of the snug family circle, suggest the only materials; and a large gathering of the set, at ball or dinner, affords incident of which the novelist is required to make the highest use. Writers of much earnestness of mood, originality of thought, or intensity of imagination, seldom engage in this class of writing. Scott attempted it in St. Ronan's Well, and failed;—rising only into the rank of Scott, in such portions of the story as, by a very violent transition, brought him once more into the bolder displays of wild and stirring romance. He consoled himself with the reflection that male writers were not good at these things. His conclusion, that such writings were best handled by the other sex, may be, or not, construed into a sarcasm.

Mr. Cooper failed egregiously in "Precaution." So far as we know, and as we believe, that work fell still-born from the press. But for the success of "the Spy," and the succeeding works, it never would have been heard of. But "the Spy" was an event. It was the boldest and best attempt at the historical romance which had ever been made in America. It is somewhat the practice, at this day, to disparage that story. This is in very bad taste. The book is a good one,—full of faults, perhaps, and blunders; but full also of decided merits, and marked by a boldness of conception, and a courage in progress, which clearly showed the confidence of genius in its own resources. The conception of the Spy, as a character, was a very noble one. A patriot in the humblest condition of life,—almost wholly motiveless unless for his country—enduring the persecutions of friends, the hate of enemies—the doomed by both parties to the gallows—enduring all in secret, without a murmur,—without a word, when a word might have saved him,—all for his country; and all, under the palsying conviction, not only that his country never could reward him, but that, in all probability, the secret of his patriotism must perish with him, and nothing survive but that obloquy under which he was still content to live and labour.

It does not lessen the value of such a novel, nor the ideal truth of such a conception, that such a character is not often to be found. It is sufficiently true if it wins our sympathies and commands our respect. This is always the purpose of the ideal, which, if it can effect such results, becomes at once a model and a reality. The character of the "Spy" was not the only good one of the book. Lawton and Sitgreaves were both good conceptions, though rather exaggerated ones. Lawton was a somewhat too burly Virginian; and his appetite was too strong an ingredient in his chivalry. But, as his origin was British, this may have been due to the truthfulness of portraiture.

The defect of the story was rather in its action than its characters. This is the usual and grand defect in all Mr. Cooper's stories. In truth, there is very little story. He seems to exercise none of his genius in the invention of his fable. There is none of that careful grouping of means to ends, and all, to the one end of the denouement, which so remarkably distinguished the genius of Scott, and made all the parts of his story fit as compactly as the work of the joiner,—but he seems to hurry forward in the delineation of scene after scene, as if wholly indifferent to the catastrophe. [. . .]

[. . .T]he success of the "Spy" was very great, and it at once gave Mr. Cooper reputation in Europe. It may be said to have occasioned a greater sensation in Europe than at home;—and there were good reasons for this. At that period America had no literature. Just before this time, or about this time, it was the favourite sarcasm of the British Reviewers that such a thing as an American book was never read. Mr. Irving, it is true, was writing his sweet and delicate essays; but he was not accounted in England an American writer, and he himself,—no doubt with a sufficient policy—his own fortunes alone being the subject of consideration—took no pains to assert his paternity. The publication of the "Spy" may be assumed to have been the first practical reply to a sarcasm, which, since that day, has found its ample refutation. It was immediately republished in England, and soon after, we believe, found its way into half the languages of Europe. Its farther and more important effect was upon the intellect of our own country. It at once opened the eyes of our people to their own resources. It was something of a wonder, to ourselves, that we should be able—(strange, self-destroying humility in a people springing directly from the Anglo-Norman stock)—to produce a writer who should so suddenly, and in his very first work ("Precaution" was not known and scarcely named in that day) rise to such an eminence—equalling most, excelling most, and second to but one, of the great historical romance writers of Britain. This itself was an important achievement—a step gained, without which, no other step could possibly have been taken. It need scarcely be said, that the efforts of a nation at performance,—particularly in letters and the arts,—must first be preceded by a certain consciousness of the necessary resources. This consciousness, in the case of America, was wanting. Our colonial relation to Great Britain had filled us with a feeling of intellectual dependence, of which our success in shaking off her political dominion had in no respect relieved us. We had not then, and, indeed, have not entirely to this day, arrived at any just idea of the inevitable connexion between an ability to maintain ourselves in arts as well as in arms—the ability in both cases arising only from our intellectual resources, and a manly reliance upon the just origin of national strength,—Self-dependence! To Mr. Cooper the merit is due, of having first awakened us to this self-reference,—to this consciousness of mental resources, of which our provincialism dealt, not only in constant doubts, but in constant denials. The first step is half the march, as in ordinary cases, the first blow is half the battle. With what rapidity after that did the American press operate.

How many new writers rose up suddenly, the moment that their neighbours had made the discovery that there were such writers—that such writers should be. Every form of fiction, the legend, tale, novel and romance—the poem, narrative and dramatic—were poured out with a prolific abundance, which proved the possession, not only of large resources of thought, but of fancy, and of an imagination equal to every department of creative fiction. It will not matter to show that a great deal of this was crude, faulty, un-digested—contracted and narrow in design, and spasmodic in execution. The demand of the country called for no more. The wonder was that, so suddenly, and at such short notice, such resources could be found as had not before been imagined. The sudden rise and progress of German literature seems to have been equally surprising and sudden—equally the result of a national impulse, newly moved in a novel and unexpected direction. The wonderful birth and progress of American letters in the last twenty years—and in every department of thought, art and science, so far from discourag-ing, because of its imperfections, holds forth the most signal encouragement to industry and hope—showing most clearly, that the deficiency was not in the resource but in the demand, not in the inferior quality, or limited quantity, but in the utter indifference of our people to the possession of the material.

Having struck the vein, and convinced the people not only that there was gold in the land, but that the gold of the land was good, Mr. Cooper pro-ceeded with proper industry to supply the demand which his own genius had occasioned in the markets, as well of Europe as his own country, for his pro-ductions. "The Spy" was followed by Lionel Lincoln, the Pioneers, the Last of the Mohicans, the Pilot, Red Rover, Prairie, Water Witch, &c. We speak from memory—we are not so sure that we name these writings in their proper order, nor is this important to us in the plan of this paper, which does not contemplate their examination in detail. All these works were more or less interesting. [. . .]

To these succeeded a satirical work entitled the Monikins which was followed by a "Letter to his Countrymen." These performances, which are among the least popular of the numerous writings of our author, are among those which have contributed in latter days to lessen his popularity and subtract, whether justly or not, from his well earned claims to pre-eminence, as among the first writers of his age. For the proper understand-ing of Mr. C.'s position we must rise to a consideration of other subjects.

Mr. Cooper is a man, as we have already indicated, very much given to intensify every subject which affects his mind;—a man of that earnest, and not easily satisfied temper, who resolutely perseveres in what he undertakes, and in the prosecution of inquiry or argument, is very apt to probe a matter to the bottom, without giving much heed to the sensibility he wounds. Such men are necessary in every age for the progress of truth, and they incur always the penalties of the reformer. If not crucified or stoned, they are pelted by missiles of one sort or another, the principal of which, in our day, are defamation and slander. In Europe, Mr. Cooper was soon made aware of the humble, and even contemptuous estimate, which was every where put upon the American character. We, at home, urged by our own vanities, and miserably be mocked by the spurious flatteries of false prophets,—school-boy orators and selfish demagogues,—are really of opinion that we not only are, but are universally regarded as, one of the greatest people on the face of the earth. Of this folly and falsehood Mr. Cooper undertakes to disabuse us. He discovered, very soon after being in Europe, that we were thought a very small people. Our national and narrow economy seldom permitted any proper displays abroad of our national power, and such as were made were supposed to be rather discreditable than otherwise. The people of the Continent knew us chiefly by British opinions, which were, usually, not merely unfavourable, but scornful in the last degree. This opinion found its expression in a thousand ways. It was the habitual language of the Englishman when the name of American was spoken; and Mr. Cooper records it as a fact, known to himself as to every body that ever travelled on the Continent, that nothing was more common than the practice of the British traveller, to write, on the books kept at the public houses in the chief cities, the most contemptuous comments, on himself and country, in connection with the recorded name of every American. The people of the Continent could easily believe the propriety and justice of this scorn; for, as the Englishman himself was odious among them, by reason of his bad manners, and as they just knew enough of our history to know that we are sprung from the same stocks with him, it was not difficult to arrive at the conclusion, that, what he himself said of his descendant was likely to be true enough. There were other reasons why they should be easy of faith on this subject. Certain young Americans had been behaving badly among them thrusting themselves by various arts upon society; begging and borrowing money, and indulging in other practices, scarcely less dishonourable, which naturally cast a stigma upon the nation with which they were identified. Mr. Cooper, a proud man, felt this condition of things like a pang:—an impetuous man, he undertook, in some measure, to correct them. He spoke out his defiance to the English, by whom his nation was slandered; and freely denounced the spurious Americans, by whom the country was disgraced. After this, it did not need that he should publish satirical books in order to make enemies and meet denunciation. His hostility to the English secured it to him in sufficient abundance from the British press; and his unsparing reproof of the young Americans, provoking not only their anger, but that of their friends, was quite enough to engage against him the active hostility of numberless enemies among the newspapers, and even the literary journals, in this country. Our readers need not be told, that, in such a torrent of news and literary papers (so called) with which the American world is flooded, it is not possible for many among them to possess a tone or character of their own. In opinion, as in action, a few lead the way and the rest follow. It was enough that the British press denounced Mr. Cooper, for the American press, very generally, to denounce him likewise. It would be a day of independence, truly, when we should throw off our servile faith in the justice of British judgment, and the superiority of British opinion. To this, the virulence of personal and party antipathy gave additional tongues, and the consequence was, that, while Mr. Cooper was most busy in asserting our character and defending our institutions abroad, the press at home was equally busy in denouncing him for his pains. [. . .]

Mr. Cooper was not the man for this. He was not the man to make improper and unbecoming concessions, either on his own part, or on the part of his country. His nature led him to defiance, to resistance, to the unmeasured language of his resentment. We do not say that he was altogether wise in this. It is one thing to submit to indignity—it is another to be forever on the look-out, as if expecting to meet it. We are not so sure that Mr. Cooper was not wrong sometimes in his impetuosity—in his violence of tone and manner. There are some things in his deportment, as shown in his own travels, which we are constrained to disapprove and censure; and we are apprehensive that he sometimes mistook the burly defiance of the backwoodsman for the calm, manly tone of gentlemanly independence. This charge has been made against him. We do not make it. We are afraid, however, that the inference may be drawn fairly from some passages of his own writings, in his book of travels in England. His game, while in that country, for the proper defence of his own, was to "carry the war into Africa." To retort upon them their own charges,—to show them the mirror for self-reflection,—and to prove that they, too, were made of penetrable stuff. Mr. Cooper, of all our literary men abroad, seems to have been almost the only one who did not sink his Americanism—who strove to maintain it, and employed his cudgel, whenever his country was defamed, with the able hand and the hearty good-will and courage of a sailor. Whatever his errors may have been, they are more than redeemed in our eyes by his sturdy, uncompromising attachment to his country. And who can prescribe to the wronged and the indignant, what shall be the measure of his anger?—who shall say, in such and such terms only shall you speak out your feelings? It is for the greatly injured to determine for themselves what shall be their measure of redress. At all events, it was the unkindest fortune, that, while Mr. Cooper was thus doing battle for his countrymen, abroad,—whatever may have been the propriety of his course,—he should not only not find sympathy at home, but, on the contrary, rebuke. At that time, several of our newspapers were either wholly, or in part, conducted by foreigners. These naturally had sympathies only with the countries from which they came. They naturally watched the progress of the foreign controversy, and took sides with their own countrymen. Communications from abroad appeared in our literary and other journals, furnishing accounts of the affair, as may be supposed, hostile to Mr. Cooper. Among a class of our literary papers, such communications were particularly acceptable. No matter whom they disparaged, in what degree of defamation—no matter what prurient displays of vice were made,—what morals suffered here, or what character was defamed or slandered in Europe. It was taken for granted—and was, indeed, a truth too little to be questioned—that there was a morbid hungering, on the part of a large class of American pretenders, to be duly apprized of the doings abroad, particularly of the excesses of the English fashionable world; and some of the most atrocious revelations, fatal to female character, and garnished with the most brutal details of vice, were made by anonymous foreign correspondents, in publications which were especially addressed to American ladies. With foreign editors and foreign correspondents, each having, it would seem, *carte blanche,* Mr. Cooper, like every other subject of notoriety or distinction, had the usual risk of defamation to encounter. To these, in his case, is to be added the hostility of party, which he had provoked by an imprudent pamphlet, the "Letter to his Countrymen." This performance took the republican or democratic side with the Jackson dynasty, at the time of its fierce conflict with the old United States Bank. It was not wanting in ability. Some portions of the writer's argument were new and ingenious, and much of it was interesting. But the performance, as a whole, was in bad taste. It lacked congruity. It mixed up various matters of examination and complaint,—an olla podrida of literary, personal and political grievance; which, however well enough discussed, if separate, were yet oddly put together, in such a manner as to impair the value and the force of all. The superior egotism of one which pervaded it, was not its least misfortune and defect. This brought into the field a new and more bitter host of enemies—unscrupulous as the first, and with interests more actively involved in the pressing concerns of party,—such as never suffer any restraints of justice or veneration to impede them in their utterance. Nobody thought much of combating Mr. Cooper's opinions, but all seemed at once impressed with the impertinence of a literary man presuming to entertain a political opinion at all. Even those who concurred with the views of Mr. Cooper, seemed equally to concur with his assailants, in the absurd notion that his literary pursuits effectually excluded him from any right to give them utterance. Of his prudence in doing so, as a selfish man, thinking only of the success of his forthcoming publication, we, of course, offer no opinion. Enough, in this place, to add, that it is to be regretted, not that our literary men do not more frequently engage in Politics but that our politicians are not more generally literary men—at all events, not so very illiterate. Some increase of political decency might be the fruit of their improvement in this respect.

The warfare waged against Mr. Cooper was neither just nor generous. Envy loves always a shining mark. Dulness hates distinction. He had offended party, which is the most brutal of all assailants—a gross, blind savage, equally curbless, pitiless and conscienceless. He had offended some small Americans abroad, who were eager, under the cover of patriotism, or any other cover, to revenge their petty personal grievances. [. . .] But he put them into his books, and this was quite a compliment, which, however unintended by him, was very undeserved by them. Besides, of what avail to show up one of these creatures in his proper light, when the country is so full of them, that they are sufficiently numerous and strong to give one another support and countenance. This, by the way, is one of the greatest evils to which our American literature is exposed. The pretender-critics are so numerous and so noisy, that it is no wonder they succeed so frequently, and for so long a time, in imposing false standards upon the several circles which look to the current press for all the supplies of literary aliment which they crave. It is a question with many on which side to look for their authorities. With a poor people, now for the first time beginning to have a hankering after letters, nothing can be more natural than that they should turn to those who, while selling their wares at the most moderate price, are, at the same time, the most clamorous on the subject of their merits. Quack literature resorts to the same arts with quack medicine, and quacks of all sorts have been, from all times, the most pompous and presuming. They making up in mouthing what they lack in merit; in insolence what they lack in strength; and are hostile to the really honest and intellectual, in due degree with the consciousness of their own lamentable deficiencies. [. . .]

Mr. Cooper committed two errors when he wrote his satires—the one much more decided than the other. He wrote them at the wrong time, and he wrote them in the wrong spirit. Vanity listens to no homily in the full sunshine of its day. Pride hears no warning, when the homage of vulgar admiration fills its ears. Trade hearkens to no admonitions of prudence, or of principle, in the full tide of a seemingly successful speculation. Mr. Cooper wrote the books which proved so offensive to the American people, at a time when an angel from heaven would have spoken to them in vain,—when, besotted with the boldest dreams of fortune that ever diseased the imagination of avarice, they seemed to have lost the usual faculties of thought, prudence and observation—when, they appeared to think they had but to will, and *presto,* they won—to lift a finger, and, as at the wand of a magician, the waters flowed with sparkling treasures, and the sands glittered with the precious metal. The Spaniards in Peru or Mexico were never half so bedevilled with their own imaginings, as were the people of our trading cities within our recent remembrance. Our merchants assumed the port of princes, and the Merchant-Princes of the Adriatic never loomed out with a more dazzling and determined ostentation.

Was it likely, that, swollen with pride, gloating over their imaginary treasures, and swaggering with the affectations of fashion, borrowed from the old fools—and young ones—of older countries, they should listen to any censor, receive any counsel, tolerate with patience any rebuke? The attempt of Mr. Cooper was unseasonable, and only vexed them. They wished praise only,—nothing more,—praise from any quarter,—they had stomachs for no stronger aliment. They had flattered the foreigner to secure this praise. They had run with headlong speed to hail the advent of English Lord and English Lady,—had spread their dinner cloths, and thrown wide their saloons and ball-rooms and theatres—asking only for praise. That their own countrymen should withold the precious condiment—should, like the foreigner, find fault only—was an offence not to be forgiven. Nay, there was some reason for their anger. The censure of Mr. Cooper was not expressed in the right spirit. The tone of "Homeward Bound," and "Home as Found," was bad. It expressed the language of querulousness and distaste, if not disgust. It was written less in sorrow than in anger, as if the writer took a malicious delight in singling out the sore spots, which it had been the better purpose of the patriot to hide if he could not heal. He showed himself more disposed to revenge his own hurts and injuries than to amend the faults of his countrymen. Besides, as we have already said, he was unjust because too sweeping in his condemnation. This was the consequence of writing in his anger. Passion has no powers of discrimination, and the wilful mind will exercise none. But if Mr. Cooper's censure had been just in all respects, and in its entire application, it must have failed of any good result at the time of its utterance. It was unseasonable, and therefore impolitic and unwise.

We give Mr. Cooper credit for good motives in spite of this imprudence. We regard the promptings as patriotic which drove him to his task. These, no doubt, were farther stimulated by his personal feelings. But this does not alter the case. In the instance of the sanguine temperament, the personal man always enters actively into the principles. The heart co-operates with the head, the blood impels the intellect, and hence the rare energy with which such persons commence and carry on their works. The patriotism of Mr. Cooper has always been a striking trait in this character and writings. It is conspicuous in all his performances. How fondly he dwells, even in his foreign books, while discussing their institutions, on the superiority of our own. How ready he is to do battle in their behalf. This very readiness was one of the first occasions of offence which he gave to those cold-blooded Americans, who were content to truckle abroad for their porridge, silent when their nation was openly scorned, and snatching their miserable pittance of bread and society from the very hands that were lifted in reprobation of their country. As we have already said, the Americanism of Mr. Cooper would move us to forgive him all his faults, were they twice as many. That he should come home to censure ours, was equally the proof, though an unwise one, of his honest and fearless patriotism. [. . .]

We see with satisfaction that we are soon to have another story from his pen. We are glad of this for two reasons. We always read his books with great pleasure; and we rejoice at this annunciation, as it affords another proof that the terms of relation between this favourite author and his countrymen, are becoming every day more and more grateful to the amenities, equally of patriotism and letters.

Copy-text: *VRAH,* 258–92.

From *The Life of the Chevalier Bayard*

(1 8 4 7)

CHAPTER 1

It was at a time when chivalry was at its lowest condition in Christian Europe; when the fine affectations of the order, erring always on the side of generosity and virtue—its strained courtesies, its overwrought delicacies, its extravagant and reckless valor—every thing, in short, of that grace and magnanimity which had constituted its essential spirit and made of it a peculiar institution—had given way to less imposing and less worthy characteristics; when, ceasing to be the distinguishing boast of courtliness and noble blood, it had yielded on every hand, in Spain, in France, England, Italy and Germany, to a growth of the grossest passions, a disregard of the point of honor and of those pledges of faith which it had been the great end of chivalry to maintain, at every hazard, as the first tests of courtesy and manhood,—it was even at such a time that the now decaying institution was destined to furnish to the world the happiest illustration, in a single great example, of its ancient pride and character, and of those virtues which had made it fruitful of good to humanity, in spite of many curious anomalies. The name of the Chevalier Bayard has grown into proverbial identification, in modern times, with all that is pure and noble in manhood, and all that is great and excellent in the soldier. It is not that he ranks among brave men as one wholly without fear in battle. This character would scarcely afford him, in a period wholly given up to war, and remarkable for its sanguinary conflicts, any very peculiar distinction. That he had the virtue of a rare courage, in its utmost perfection, is undeniable; but the equally distinguishing and more beautiful qualities of his heart, accord him an eminence among his contemporaries which none has ever presumed to question. He was not only the Chevalier *sans peur,* but *sans reproche* also; so equally good and brave that his character furnishes the most admirable model to the generous ambition of the young that we find in all the pages of history. His valor he shared, in a great measure, with his associates; but his truth and fidelity were singularly his own. His period was one distinguished for its small possession of faith and virtue. It was a time exemplary for its treacheries, particularly among the great. To deceive and to betray, were practices too common among nobles and princes, to make these offences against virtue any longer odious in the sight of men; and the perfidy which was taught to Italy, not less by her seeming necessities than by the subtle studies of her statesmen, had become widespread lessons for the misdirection of the whole civilized world. Breathing this very atmosphere for a considerable period of his life, the nature of Bayard imbibed none of its unwholesome influences. He still kept the whiteness of his soul free from spot, in spite of the contagion in which he lived. His fidelity and truth soon grew to be as remarkable as his valor, and his talents for war were no less conspicuous than these. Yet these talents never urged him to any of that undue self-esteem which makes the highly endowed person recoil from the command of others. His possessions were tempered by a wonderful modesty, which taught him to propriety of submission to his superiors. Obedience, indeed, as the first duty of the soldier, was a lesson which he had happily learned when alone it can be properly acquired—in the days of his youth. This lesson gave stability to the native virtues of his character, and forms one of the distinguishing traits in his high reputation. Never was hero more unselfish. His generosity and disinterestedness, struggling steadily against his successful valor, left him always poor while in the constant acquisition of money. He gave as rapidly as he gained, and, in conferring favors upon his friends and followers, he frequently denied himself the means for encountering his own necessities. True to his word, his enemies, equally with his friends, yielded every where the most ready faith to all his assurances. He was scarcely less liberal to the one than the other. His captive, whom he always treated with kindness and courtesy, went forth frequently without ransom, while his acquisitions were made the means for serving his companions, and for exhibitions of chivalrous pageants, which drew together all young and ambitious cavaliers, emulous of gallant trophies to be distributed by the hands of beauty. And, in all these relations, nothing could exceed the sweetness and nobleness of manner for which Bayard was remarkable. His successes, his high fame, never made him regardless of the claims of others. He never haughtily presumed upon his superiority nor abused its advantages, but, deferring gently to the inferior, he made his way to all hearts, and, which the virtues of a Scipio blended the graces of an

Alcibiades. Admirable in council, his opinions won their way to the under-standings of his hearers by their native justness, urged without presumption, and enforced by the modest deference with which he first listened to the thoughts of others. Always solicitous of gallant undertakings, he betrayed no disquiet if their results enured to the renown of rivals. His moral sense was singularly sound and reflective. He often said, "The best lordship is the com-munion with virtuous persons; the greatest evil to a lord is in the counsels of ignorant and vicious men, as there is nothing more dangerous than audacity when unsustained by wisdom." A gentleman once asked him, "What goods a noble man should leave to his children?" "Those," he answered, "which fear neither rain nor storm, nor human injustice, nor all the power of man— wisdom and virtue." His maxims were illustrated by his life. His respect and admiration for the sex prompted him to the frequent tournament. The lady whose colors he wore might safely repose as well upon his loyalty as his valor and skill. Modesty and innocence never looked to him in vain. It will be our province, in the course of this history, to give one curious example of his generosity in this respect. His sympathies were always given to the good; his succor gladly sustained the weak; his bounty helped the indigent. He allevi-ated, where he could, the miseries of war, over which he mourned with ear-nest commiseration. To complete the beauties of his character, his piety was deep and unaffected. He enjoyed, without any of the enfeebling supersti-tions of his age, a profound sense of his obligations to the Deity, and an abid-ing confidence in the saving mercies of Jesus Christ. His morning began, and his evening closed, with prayer. He prepared himself for battle by becoming devotions, recommending his soul to God, and invoking the pardon of his sins. His life, indeed, furnishes an admirable example to the soldier, of a ca-reer in which the most heroic valor may be blended with the most gentle virtues, with mildness of temper, sweetness of demeanor, generosity with-out display, and the most humble submission to human and Divine author-ity. True to his God, his country, and his duty, he found it no ways arduous to share in the vicissitudes of war and the incongruous associations of the camp, without yielding to the brutalities of the one, or partaking of the ex-cesses of the other. As a partisan warrior, he was, perhaps, one of the great-est captains that France has ever produced—eager and watchful, observant every where, always secure against surprise himself, and always prompt to seize upon the error of his enemy. Considered in every point of view, we are constrained to affirm the spontaneous judgment of his contemporaries, who knew him proverbially as the "Good Knight," and in the comprehensive sur-name of the *Chevalier, sans peur et sans reproche,* have left to us the model of a perfect character, with which none among themselves could presume to compare. It is for us now, from the too meagre chronicles, to procure the proofs upon which this noble reputation rests.

The House of Terrail, to which Bayard owes his origin, was one of the most ancient in the province of Dauphiny. It was well placed at the extremity of the beautiful valley of Grésivaudan, which Louis XI. used to call the *Garden of Dauphiny,* and his *fourth wonder.* The lords of Terrail had been distinguished from the earliest periods by their valor and intrepidity. His grandsire of the fifth remove, Aubert, was mortally wounded at the battle of Varces; Robert, the son of Aubert, was killed in the service of the Dauphin; Humbert the First, in an action with the Savoyards; Philip, the grandfather of Bayard in the third remove, perished at the feet of King John, at the fatal battle of Poictiers; Pierre, his great-grandfather, was killed at Agincourt; the brother of this Pierre perished in the fight of Vermeuil, in 1224, where no less than three hundred of the Dauphinese gentry—called by way of honorable distinction, "The Scarlet of France"—lost their lives. His grandfather, who was called Pierre also, maintained the military distinction of the family, and acquiring great credit in the wars with the English, gained the surname of L'Epée Terrail—the sword of the House of Terrail. He was honored with the respect and friendship of Charles VII., whom he served with tried fidelity. He contributed more than any other individual to the defeat of Louis of Chalons, Prince of Orange, at the battle of Auton; and when the Dauphin, afterward Louis XI., presumed to claim his independence, and to assert the rights of a sovereign in Dauphiny, our Lord of Terrail, having no fear of the future, adhered faithfully to the monarch, and was fortunate, by this manly fidelity, not to forfeit the respect and confidence of the young prince, whom it was not always safe to offend. This brave chieftain shared the fate of his ancestors, and died on the field of battle at Montlhéry. Aymond, his son, and the father of him whose biography we write, followed the example of his house, and in good season took the profession of the soldier. At the mature term of sixty-five we find him in the battle of Guinegate, disabled from all future conflicts by four wounds, by which he lost the use of his arms.

Hélene des Allemans, the mother of Bayard, is described as exceedingly small of person, but of great heart and intrepid spirit. In one respect she differed largely from her husband, who is represented as of great stature and vigorous frame. Our hero shared the characteristics of both. Honorably descended, and with an unbroken series of good examples before him, of courage, conduct, and fidelity, his own nature seemed destined, even at an early period, to embody and to perfect all the virtues of his race. If it is greatly honorable to found an illustrious family, it is no less meritorious to maintain its character, and finish nobly its career. This destiny was reserved for Bayard. He was born, the second of four sons, in 1476, in the castle the name of which he bears. His father, at the mature age of eighty, and when Bayard was only thirteen, finding his end approaching, called his children to his bedside, and examined them as to their choice of vocation. While two of the brothers declared for the church, and one of them for the homestead, Bayard boldly avowed his passion for the camp. He was a lively lad, of playful disposition, gay as a lark, and with an open, laughing countenance. But the face and manner of the boy served only to conceal, not to impair, the wisdom of a far maturer period. His answer was expressed with sufficient gravity. "I should like to remain with you, my father, to the end of your days; but your own discourses, daily, in my hearing, of the noble men by whom our house has been distinguished in times past, leads me to desire, with your permission, that I may also embrace the profession of arms. This is the pursuit which I most affect, and I hope, with the grace of God, to do you no dishonor."

The tears of the old man followed his speech. It probably met all his expectations, and may have been the anticipated fruit of his own training. "God grant that it may be so, my son. Already in face and figure thou lookest like thy grandsire, who was one of the best knights in Christendom. I will put thee in the way of obtaining thy desire."

We need not linger for the answers of the remaining brothers. They did not share in the military tastes of Bayard. These, in him, were quite too decidedly expressed to be mistaken. It is true he had shown nothing of that fierce, unrestrainable temper, which is supposed to mark the character of those who incline to arms at an early period. Though eager, his moods were mild—though firm, his bearing was always gentle. He was the slave to no reckless passions, and his will, except in this one respect, was prompt in submission to that of his superiors. It was fortunate that the views of his father seem to have kept pace with his own; or, with so strong a desire for arms, he might, for the first time in his life, have shown himself insubordinate. In the direction his infant mind had taken, he was fully resolved. He obeyed an instinct. It was not that he chose war as his vocation—the vocation had chosen him. His natural endowments required him to go and be a soldier, and the stories which he daily heard of the achievements of his ancestors but strengthened his desire for the performance of his ancestors but strengthened his desire for the performance of his duties. His father did not hesitate. He sent for the Bishop of Grenoble, the uncle of the boy, and gathered the gentry of the neighborhood around him. The affair was one of solemn import. It was no less than the dedication of his son to the country, and the matter needed deliberation. The aged man sat like a patriarch, with his friends and children grouped around him. Dinner was served to the guests, and Bayard officiated as a waiter. This custom, which would in our day equally offend the father and the son, was, in that, one of the essential features in the training of the young man ambitious of distinction. It was no bad way, we may add, for securing the object of desire. It taught obedience to authority, veneration for age and superiority, and a patient submission to the will of others. These are the great and necessary lessons by which the otherwise imperious nature is rendered methodical and endued with the requisite strength for the due endurance of the unavoidable evils of life.

When dinner was over, the patriarch declared the business which had led to the assembling of his guests. "You are all," said he, "my relatives and friends. Give me your counsel as to the disposition of my children. Pierre, my second, has given me inexpressible delight, in declaring his preference for arms. In whose house shall I place him—to what noble prince or lord shall I confide him, in order that he should acquire a proper deportment, and prepare himself for this profession?"

Various was the counsel. One was for sending him to the King of France; another, to the House of Bourbon. But the Bishop of Grenoble recommended the Duke of Savoy, who had always been a friend of the family, and who was then in the neighborhood, at Chambery. It was though that the duke would not hesitate to adopt him as one of his pages. The advice was taken, and the tailor was kept busy with velvet and silks all night to make our young page ready in the morning. There were no long delays in that period; and the moment breakfast was over, the next day, the horse was brought, and all the company went forth into the court of the castle, to see what sort of figure Bayard would make in appearing before the duke. The horse was one which he had never crossed before;—but the boy was fearless. He leapt boldly upon the steed, which, accustomed to a weightier burden, and suddenly pricked by the spurs of his new rider, dashed away with an impatience of spirit which alarmed the family for the safety of the youth. But it was with the spirit of an Alexander that our Bucephalus of Dauphiny had to contend. While the company were looking to hear the boy cry out in apprehension, he bestrode the animal, not only without fear, but with such a triumphant courage as to change their doubts into delight and admiration. He struck the rowel into the flanks of the beast, set him off in rage, and brought him back in docility and foam, as effectually mastered as if he had been his rider for twenty years.

The old father was happy beyond expression. "What! you are not afraid?" he said to his son, when he had returned from his gallop. "I hope," said the boy, "before six years be gone, to make him, or another, bestir himself in a more dangerous place. Here I am among friends. I shall then probably find myself among the enemies of my master." At parting, the father gave him his blessing, and, in few words, exhorted him to be faithful to the prince he served, never to forget that his natural sovereign was the King of France, and never to bear arms against him or against his country. His pride kept down all other feelings. But there was no restraint of this sort upon his mother, who did not seek to conceal her tears. Not that she had any misgivings, or felt any dislike to the profession he had chosen. She was proud of the boy, and not unwilling that he should engage in a career, of which his youthful promise showed such grateful auguries, and which had already been so honorable to his ancestors. But, in spite of these feelings and connections, the mother declared herself warmly in the tenderness with which her parting charge was given him. "Pierre, my son," she said, "you are going into the service of a noble prince: now, as much as a mother can command her child, look, there are three things which I commend to you. First, you love and serve God in all things without offending him; night and morning you recommend yourself to him. He gave us all that we have, and without him we can do nothing. He will aid you. Second.——Be you mild and courteous to all, casting away pride. Be humble and obliging. Be not a liar nor a slanderer. Be temperate in eating and drinking. Avoid envy——it is a mean excess. Be neither talebearer nor flatterer——such people never excel. Be loyal in word and deed. Keep your promise. Succor the widow and orphan, and look for your reward to God. The third is, be bountiful to the poor and needy. To give for the honor of God makes no man poor——your alms will profit your body and soul. Go now, my son, this is all with which I have to charge you. Your father and I shall not live long, but God grant that while we do live we may hear nothing but good of you."

The answer of Bayard was appropriate, but brief. The farewell was soon over, and, with a change of linen, and a little purse containing six crowns in gold, which his mother at the close of her advice bestowed upon him, our hero departed, in the company of his uncle, "thinking himself," in the language of one of his early biographers, "in Paradise, while on the back of his good steed."

Copy-text: *Bayard,* 1–10.

On Walter Scott

(1 8 4 9)

Let it suffice, that the great or successful writer in prose fiction, must be, taking Scott for our example, a person of equal imagination and cool common sense; of lively sensibilities; of great tact—which is another word for admirable taste—and of equal vigilance and courage. He must observe without effort;—so endowed by nature, and so trained by practice, as to achieve, as it were, by the simple out-pouring of his customary thoughts. Carrying the materials which he thus realizes, by a corresponding and simultaneous movement of his thoughts, to the alembic of his mind, he must extract from them, by a process which goes on without respite, and almost without his own consciousness, all the sublimated essences which, thus resolved, become aggregated within himself, and constitute the means and expedients of his own genius.

To attain these results, and to acquire such materials, no mere fagging, with a purpose, can possibly avail. No sort of drudgery will answer to provide these means. There can be no cramming. There must be,—to employ the idiom of a contemporary nation—a nature for it. It is very clear, that of the thousand fine issues which belong to every action in the progress of a story, the trials of the heart, the displays of passion, the subtle combinations of wit, the logical results of judgment, the repose which happily relieves the actors in the proper place, and the vivacity which keeps interest astir;—it must be very clear, we say, that there are very few of these, about which, as the necessity for their use occurs, the author could deliberately sit down and reason. It would be morally impossible, were this necessity to exist, that his labors should ever arrive at the honors of a single volume. His mental constitution, on the contrary, must be that of the poet. He is born, not fashioned, to his task. He works by intuition, quite as much as by calculation and common reasoning. He leaps to his conclusions on a wing, which is one of equal certainty and fleetness; and all that he is required to do, at the beginning, is so to choose his ground, with such regard to his peculiar tastes, studies and experience, as to give free play to whatever is individual in his character and genius. Great readiness of resource, a quick and keen perception of the differing shades and degrees, in quality, of human character; a nice sense of what is just and delicate, the lofty and the low, the sublime and the ridiculous; an eye always eager for the picturesque; a facility in the employment of details, and a flexibility of utterance, by which he may readily individualize the various dialects of his *dramatis personae* — dialects which as completely distinguish the individual from his fellows, as do the particular traits of his countenance; — these are all, in greater or less degree, — the essentials of the novelist and romance writer. If held generally, and in large endowment, he will be an artist of the highest order — a universalist in art, — remarkable for his *many sidedness,* as the Germans have it — a poet, a dramatist; a philosopher, a painter; a seer and a prophet. His words will flow from him like those of inspiration. His creations will seem like those of a god. His voice will possess a natural authority in every ear.

Copy-text: *SQR* 15 (April 1849): 46–47.

From *The Southern Convention*

(1 8 5 0)

The Northern people take counsel from no other teachers than their own; and these teachers, by the same growing influence of popular vanity, are false prophets, who gloze in the ears of their people the most lying histories. In New-England, the popular belief, engendered by their orators and historians, teaches that the establishment of American independence was wholly due to that section. The vulgar notion is, that their statesmen furnished all the thought, and their soldiers all the valour of the country. They claim the wisdom of the nation, and assert a right to all the battle-fields. We need not state that all this claim is absurd, false and impertinent, and that the New-England States did far less than their share in the great drama of the American Revolution. But the falsehood serves the purposes of those whose egregious vanity needs a daily supply of this treacherous aliment. They have learned, by repetition, to believe the falsehood which they themselves have manufactured; and assume, accordingly, the possession of resources, in wisdom and weight of arms, which precludes any thought of successful resistance to their objects. Another of the falsehoods which have grown into a faith among them, is that the South is too weak, in consequence of her slave institutions, for her own defence. They actually believe that they have assisted us in our battles for liberty before, and that, in the moment of emergency, they would be required to assist us again. All this is equally false and foolish. Their ignorance of their own deficiencies, and of our resources in the South, is partly the secret of that insolence which is hurrying them on to extremities, which must test both in such a manner as shall effectually seal all the frauds of future history.

It is another misfortune of the Northern people to be really ignorant of politics. The great masses by which their society is every where controlled, have no leisure to study; and their politicians are not the persons, from principle, to teach them any better. The vulgar notion is that our policy is to be swayed always by majorities; and a reference to the constitution, as an arbitrary pact which precludes the will of the majority, is almost a matter of offence, in reasoning with a people who derive all their strength, courage and information from the conviction that they belong to the masses. Where this ignorance does not exist, the morals of the persons better informed, are not sufficiently strong to resist the force of numbers. If they struggle, they are overwhelmed, and they make the temporary necessity a sufficient excuse for an habitual deference to a power which they despair of successfully resisting. The difficulty of resistance is annually increased by an influx of two hundred thousand foreigners. These crowd to the Northern States especially, as being the best theatres for the exercise of their peculiar virtues. Of the merits of our revolution, they know nothing; of the intricate doctrine of State Rights, and a sovreignty reserved to the separate States, over which the General Government has no authority, you can teach them nothing; and it is their special policy to insist upon a doctrine which resents every principle that seems to stand in conflict with a self-esteem suddenly brought into existence, and a lust for power which is duly precious from the fact that it has never been enjoyed before.

They have brought the country to a fearful peril. The fate of the Union hangs upon a hair. One rash step, one fearful collision, one overt act which shall force the trial of strength, between any portion of the separate sections and there is an end to the confederacy. There is a blind confidence in the integrity of the Union, which makes thousands unwilling to believe in this peril. Still more reluctant are these hostile sections to believe in an event which shall cut them off from the pleasant pastures in which they have so long fattened. The worshipper who cried "Great is Diana of the Ephesians," at the very moment when the image of the goddess, her shrines and temples, were about to perish by storm and fire, was not a whit more blind and deaf to the signs of danger—not a whit more loth to believe in such danger— than is that blatant priesthood at the altars of the Union, whose ministry is chiefly shown by their appropriation, to their own purposes, of all the rich gifts and treasure of its worshippers. If, by insisting the more earnestly upon the preservation of the temple—if, by cries of sacrilege against all those who denounce its abuses and their selfish spoliations—they can, not only avert its fate, but its reform, they will not, we may be assured, be sparing of their voices. They cry aloud when they behold the besom spread which would only purge the shrine of its pollution. It is to them much more important that they should still spoil the altars than that the temple should continue in existence.

Such is the Union to the Northern States. It is their place of pleasant pasturage. There they feed and fatten free of charge. The labours of the South, through this medium, are made to enure almost wholly to their advantage. Our fruits pass into their granaries. The toll which is assessed upon Southern productions, pays their taxes, builds their fortresses, crowds their marts with shipping, and clothes their barren hills with marble cities. Will they peril these goodly spoils, gathered at the shrine of Union? Not if they know it. That they do not believe in the peril, is only the natural result of that assurance which springs from habitual successes, which belongs to minds rioting in power, and wholly forgetful of the vicissitudes of earthly things. If, in moments of calm and reflection, they apprehend a danger, they do not seek to avert if by doing justice, for that would be a surrender of the privilege of spoliation. They prefer to alarm the fears of the discontented sections— they prefer to appeal to the superstitions of the people. They throw up their hands and eyes in holy horror, as they insist upon the sacredness of the Union; precisely as the gambling Jews in the temple must have done, when our Saviour cast down the table of the money changers, denouncing the crime which had converted the altar of the Father into a den of thieves.

To make and preserve the Union, the South has done many things at her own grievous charge and loss, and has made a thousand concessions. In the original acts of confederation, there were no social affinities which brought the two sections together. They were by no means of congenial temper. The Union contemplated the mutual weaknesses as of the parties, and their protection against common dangers from without. The dread was still of Great Britain, her power, her ambition, and her natural resentments. Had there been a sufficient degree of sympathy between the sections, the confederacy would have been the act of a single people. But a prudent jealousy insisted upon maintaining the individuality and independence of the several States. The bond of Union was one designed for the common safety against foreign pressure, rather than the promotion of any common objects of interest at home. The more perfect union, contemplated by our ancestors, was one which regarded their securities simply. It was the error of the South, at that season, to undervalue her natural securities, and, through this self-disparagement, to show quite too much anxiety for the formation of the confederacy. She was too heedless of the proper conditions of the Union. It was, perhaps, natural enough that such should be the case. Sparsely settled, recovering slowly and painfully from the exhausting effects of the war with Great Britain, which, for the last three years of the conflict, had fallen almost exclusively upon her unassisted shoulders,—the most perilous period of the war—marked with the most bloody battlefields—when the resources of the country were mostly exhausted, and when the enemy, concentrating all his strength for a last effort, was urging his assaults with greatly increased ferocity and earnestness—she exaggerated the dangers from without, and made a disparaging estimate of her own resources in the encounter with them. This same feeling, to a greater or lesser extent, prevailed with all the sections. But, in the South, it was naturally increased by what was there supposed to be an especial element of weakness—her slave population. Her Statesmen overlooked their own experience of seven years war, which should have taught them that African slavery, in the hands of the Anglo-American people, was really an element of strength rather than of weakness. They preferred to reason from the histories of slavery in ancient nations, where the subject race was one fully equal in natural intellect with the conqueror, and without any distinctive marks of colour; rather than to look at their own facts, occurring beneath their own eyes, during a conflict in which all the circumstances were against them. This was a natural error, since men, in general, reason rather from habit, and from principles imbibed in memory, than from the absolute facts in their own experience. The South underrated its own strength and its own resources, exaggerated its own weaknesses, and included, in the category of the causes of apprehension, certain speculative dangers, which time has shown to be wholly imaginary. It was thus prepared, from the outset, to make sacrifices for the establishment of the Union, referring to the importance of the tie, in a conflict with external pressure. It did not perceive as it might have done, that all expectation of support from the New-England States, in the event of war, was utterly futile. Their course, in the war of 1812, in that of Florida and Mexico, might well have been anticipated by a reference to their history in the war of the revolution. From the moment when the troops of Great Britain were withdrawn from the absolute territory of New-England, the people of that region lost all interest in the struggle, and left their Southern brethren to get through the conflict as they might. Their regiments were unfilled, and the hosts which they had on paper were only known to the country through means of the pension list.

Thus selfish from the beginning, they have continued selfish to the end. They have never made, as a section, a single concession to the confederacy for which they have not exacted ample and direct recompense; while they have grasped tenaciously at every concession of the South, without according any thing like a return. In this business of concession, the South has been as spontaneous and frank as if they had fashioned their public policy wholly upon the individual and personal character of their people. Governed by a sincere desire, which has sometimes looked like an absolute passion, for the general welfare, and the dignity and glory of the Union, they have yielded rights, lands and securities, without pausing to consider consequences. Their earnest wish to establish the confederacy, too precipitately indulged in action, led to the commission of the first great error, that of suffering the Northern States to class our population for us,—degrading a certain portion of our numbers to a rank in representation greatly inferior to that which was asserted for the corresponding race living in Northern territory. This exaction of the North was sufficiently significant of what we might expect from their tender mercies, whenever the power to compel and control should pass into their hands. By what right did they presume to look into our domestic arrangements, and reject from representation altogether, two-fifths of our servile population? What was it to them, in what manner, for local purposes, we classed our people; and how did it affect our foreign relations, that we insisted on keeping in a condition of minority, and under guardianship, even as we did our women and children, a certain portion of our population, whom we could not but see were inadequate to the duties of their own government? In what moral or human respect was our negro of the South inferior to the same race in New-England and New York, that he should have been denied like recognition with them, man for man. In moral respects, indeed, as more fully complying with God's first law of labour, his claim was essentially far superior, and he was more legitimately a human being. Here was the first grand error of our Southern Statesmen, conducting to all the rest. It yielded up a vital portion of our political strength without any equivalent,—the loss necessarily increasing annually with the due increase of the population whose claims to representation were thus degraded. We should have made their recognition the *sine quâ non,* and have better struggled on alone, than have yielded on a point so dangerous in its probably results to our safety and independence. That we did not exhibit sufficient tenacity on this point, arose chiefly from the fact, that too many of our Southern Statesmen were morbidly diseased in opinion touching the institution of slavery. Mr. Jefferson was inoculated with French opinion on this subject; and, even to a later day, it has been the unhappy distinction of our sister State of Virginia, to have furnished from her own armory of debate, most of the arguments which the abolitionists have so desperately wielded since. Had our Statesmen, at the formation of the confederacy, been as sound and sagacious in regard to the morals of slavery, as the people of the South have since become—had they examined the question *per se,* according to intrinsic standards, and to the exclusion of all the formulas and pet phrases of French fraternization and equality—they would have become fortified in its behalf, regarding it, indeed, as the great medium through which all inferior nations have been raised from barbarism to civilization, and the only means for the exaltation of the African, to a christian, from a savage condition. Any events which shall render necessary a revision of the American Constitution, will find the people of the South prepared to insist, as an absolute preliminary essential to any Union, upon the recognition of the Southern slave, without qualification, according him a representation, man for man, on equal terms with any other people of the confederacy.

Another of the great evils to the South, constituting one of the causes of her present disparagement and lack of strength, arose again from the liberality of her own concessions. Virginia voluntarily ceded to the United States, without equivalent, the whole of that immense territory, out of which Ohio and Indiana, Illinois, Michigan, Wisconsin and Minnesota, have been erected into States. Here she planted the teeth which were to spring up dragons, seeking to devour the generous mother to whom they owed their birth. Even this liberal grant has been openly abused. The absolute condition of her grant required that no more than five States should be framed out of this territory. They have contrived to manufacture six; which having covered them with a New-England population—restless, envious, exacting and insolent—they have converted into vast instruments of annoyance to the maternal State, which has so unwisely surrendered her soil to the possession of her enemies.

In like manner, South-Carolina and Georgia yielded up the territories of Alabama and Mississippi, without equivalent, for the formation of these States. Very far different, if we remember rightly, was the conduct of Connecticut. She, it appears, had some territorial rights to surrender also; but she required and received two hundred thousand dollars for the cession. This we believe to be the fact, but we speak now from memory, and cannot lay hands upon the proper authority. The contrast will illustrate fully the degree of attachment which the two sections have uniformly shown in respect to the Union. The war of 1812, a strictly national necessity, was treacherously and bitterly opposed by New-England, who refused her succour to the Union, and gave her sympathies to the enemy. It was the South from which came the declaration that flung out our flag in defiance to the insolent foe; and her patriotic sacrifices were accompanied by the exhibitions of a spirit that never once faltered or failed throughout the struggle. In the war with the Indians of Florida, the North, which had cut off her domestic savages with a tomahawk as ruthless as their own, interposed for the protection of ours—encouraged them in resistance to the Southern people, and fomented the ill temper which made them refuse all the efforts of Government at conciliation, and finally beguiled them into the attitude of hostility. The same spirit was manifested by the North upon the proposed annexation of the State of Texas. The North which had eagerly grasped at all acquisitions of territory, which has been long lusting after Canada, encouraging insurrection among the people of that foreign country, strenuously toiled to defeat the alliance of the South with a kindred people, and prevent our possession of a territory which otherwise must have fallen into the hands of a hostile power. The war with Mexico was but another chapter in the same history. The volunteers from the South numbered twice as many as those from the free States. New-England denounced the war, denounced the few troops that offered from her own borders, refused them all sympathy and assistance, and dealt in terms of moral rebuke in regard to the conflict, worthy of that saintly period in her history, when Puritanism, with the Bible in one hand and sword and scourge in the other, robbed the Indians of their soil, slaughtered them without mercy, and scourged the Quaker and the imputed witch, with the same instruments of torture. Yet, thus saintly in denouncing the war with Mexico, her people were the first, the conquest made, to rush in, seize upon and monopolize the golden spoils of California. The virtues that were proof against all temptations to the conflict, yields, without scruple, when the division of the spoils is to be made! And throughout the whole history of the confederacy, every page is thus distinguished by a base and slavish selfishness, which makes no sacrifices itself, yet continually exacts them at the hands of its neighbors. The revenues of the country, two-thirds of which are drawn from the Southern exports, are three-fourths consumed in the Northern States. In possession of the majority, the North is wholly unrestrained by principle, moderation, justice or the constitution, in the exercise of it. Taxes are raised for the two-fold object of appropriation among themselves, and for the stimulation of their domestic manufactures. In the adoption of tariff laws, their simple rule, if less bold than that of Rob Roy, the outlaw—

> "That they should take, who have the power,
> And they should keep who can—"

is not more barefaced and unscrupulous. Not content with these spoliations, they deny protection to the very regions from which they make their levies. Instead of protecting us, the government becomes the instrument of our degradation and ruin. Our institutions are threatened with continual overthrow; and, too feeble for our protection, the Government of the United States is made the medium through which to destroy our securities, prejudice our property, and deprive us of all the benefits which the constitution was expected to afford. No one in the South can blind himself to the fact that we have no worse enemies *without,* than those which assail us from within;— that the States, professing to be sisters, which appeal to us continually in behalf of the Union for our detriment—organizing schemes and parties by which to rob us of our property, abridge our provinces, and cut us off from all the advantages and all the securities of our government,—the government itself, being too little able, or too little willing, to interpose its ægis for our shelter.

Our space will not suffer us to go into details; nor is this necessary. The facts from which we draw our conclusions, are already the convictions of the great body of the Southern people. They have been arrayed, time after time, by our first Statesmen, equally before the eyes of North and South; and here we have but to pursue the parallels of history, to show how equally do all nations receive the warning, which, failing to heed, they rush headlong on their own ruin. So far, the history of our relations with the Northern States is a precise counterpart of the case of the whole of the colonies of Great Britain, prior to 1776, with the mother country. In both cases, through means of unjust legislation and continual encroachment, the more powerful States endeavoured to rob and to oppress the weak. Vainly did the colonies appeal to the constitution, and implore the sense of justice in the superior power. Appeal and entreaty were alike scorned, until the colonies began to look to one another. It was a common cause, forced upon them against their own will, by the foreign oppressor. They took counsel together; they met in convention; and, for the first time, began to comprehend their own resources, their own power of resistance and defence. In the first conference of the colonies together, was the germ of the future Congress. In the first moment in which they compared notes, and took the hands of each other in friendly grasp, the independence of the country was determined!

The South, after long years of argument, appeal, entreaty and expostulation, have been brought to the necessity of a convention of the threatened and the injured States. They have been as slow to this meeting as were their fathers during the long interval from 1756 to 1776. In South-Carolina, a convention of the Southern States was urged in 1830. In 1850 it is obtained; twenty years of gestation, just about the same period of time occupied by our fathers in opposing the pretensions of Great Britain, before the sense of wrong ripened to a sense of the necessity of resistance. Is the parallel to be pursued? Will the wisdom of the North take counsel from the experience of the past, shown in this parallel passage from our own history; or must the future chronicler, mourning over the downfall and complete defeat of one of the most glorious political experiments in the history of humanity, pursue the gloomy record through other chapters, distinguished by the disruption of all the ties of States, and marked in characters of strife, captivity, of blood and desolation? Fortunately, the action of the Southern Convention has been so moderate, so reluctant to precipitate events, so full of forbearance as well as firmness, so willing to afford an opportunity to the assailing States to return to the paths of peace and justice, that, unless utterly deaf to the counsels of wisdom, to the appeals of kindred, to the experience of seventy years of a prosperity utterly unexampled, to all the parallels of history, the North has still the power to avert the omens of evil that threaten her future progress. She may avoid the catastrophe that belongs to the parallel we have employed; and the perilous and fearful chapters that seem now unavoidably to belong to the close of the history, may yet remain unwritten! [. . .]

[The delegates to the Nashville convention] have declared their ultimatum in regard to the boundary line which separates the territories North and South. Will the Southern States sustain this ultimatum? Will the Congress of the United States give any heed to this decision? We can more easily respond to the last than the first question. But we have no hope that the North will show more moderation, or a better sense of justice, than has hitherto marked her career. In the supposed possession of all the power for aggression, we do not see the proofs of a wisdom which should shape her action safely. And

> "What is strength, without a double share
> Of wisdom!—Vast, unwieldy, burdensome,
> Proudly secure, yet liable to fall,
> By weakest subtleties."

Her course is destined to be reckless. She will provoke all the fatal parallels which marked the career of Great Britain, in respect to her colonies. And she will provoke these results without any such relative superiority as Great Britain possessed. It was said in England, in 1775, by way of warning, "Three millions of freemen, with arms in their hands, are not to be enslaved." Five millions of Southrons, not only with arms in their hands, but practised in their use, and with a host of gifted warriors to lead them, the sons of the soil, will never submit to such tremendous acts of legislation, as will make a blank of their prosperity, and convert their country into a desert. The hand-writing is upon the wall, where the North, in her high places, may read it if she will. Unfortunately, her Daniel is not the man to decypher it, with that peculiar sense of the truth, that asks only what God wills, and not what man requires. It is the most melancholy history in the progress of the nations, that their Clays and Websters, commissioned by heaven with endowments for a great work, will yet waste themselves upon petty work— will forever substitute man for God, in the objects of their solicitude; and will narrow the province, which they might control, to the base and little ends of vulgar and temporary power. It is in the falsehood of such men to their high trusts—it is in their selfishness, or their cowardice—their fear of men and factions—that they lost themselves and mislead their people,— so that a judicial blindness overspreads the faculty, that, kept clear, and purged by constant and humble reference to the Great Master, in whose hands lie all the destinies of empire, would enable them, with unscaled eyes, to decypher, in season for the safety of their people, the terrible denunciations of an outraged deity, and the fiery warnings, which the benevolence of God still vouchsafes to the offender, so that, seeing, he may repent and live. The signs of warning are before them,—the writing is luminous upon their walls, and they still have time for safety. But————!

Copy-text: *SQR*, n.s. 2 (Sept. 1850): 199–208, 231–32.

From *Poetry and the Practical*

(1 8 5 4)

The world rarely does justice, even when it recognizes, the wonderful sympathy which exists between the most remote agencies which the bounty of God bestows upon the necessities of man; and though the obvious in all things is born of the occult, yet nothing is more certain than that the source of it is usually hidden from the narrowly selfish of pursuit. The connection of Poetry with the practical is such that most persons think that it will need a rare metaphysics to detect their latent sympathies. I think otherwise, and do not despair of showing you that God has assigned us no faculties, however uncommon, *without an eye to the absolute uses of the race.* That we do not at once make the recognition for ourselves, is our misfortune if not our fault;—our grievous loss always, since it too frequently results in the rejection of our most precious possessions. That I speak of Poetry, at all, knowing as I do, the vulgar notion of its barrenness, is due entirely to my purpose of addressing the popular want, rather than its wish. That the faith is wanting, of its uses, is yet the very motive to its inculcation; and, once in a way, my friends, you may well listen to one who teaches such a novel doctrine. You will never lack teachers of the simply useful. You will have science unveiling for you all her stars; chemistry will subdue for you the elements, and steam will enable you to girdle the earth with iron chains of empire. You will always be well supplied with material teachers. The danger is that such teachers will confirm the too popular lesson which finds the useful only in the material. The philosophies which promote our physical strength and comfort, are not indeed to be disparaged. On the contrary, within certain limits, it is wisdom to insist upon them. The acquisition of wealth is, in fact, a moral duty, since our very capacity for virtuous usefulness depends much upon the extent and variety of our resources. The instincts of man all lead to acquisition. But the very fact that such are his instincts, lessens greatly the necessity of insisting upon them. It is easy to obey the instincts; and gravely to teach that we should do, that which it is very certain we will do, is something worse than wasteful exhortation. The better policy is to teach *against* the instincts, lest they rise into dominion over the reason, and usurp all the better possessions of the soul. It is from this very struggle of the soul against the instincts that virtue takes her birth. To strengthen virtue, we must humble the instincts, lest they grow beyond our human need, beyond our capacity to control them, and depress and devour our virtues. Actual life tutors these instincts hourly, in all the highways, in spite of all that is taught elsewhere; and it is this wretched schooling, natural enough to the necessities and training of our race, which has done so much towards making the national character so hardfavoured, so grasping, so hostile to the refining influences of society and art, and so ready to regard as frivolous all pursuits which promise neither wealth nor aggrandisement. [. . .] The narrowly worldly nature which rejects the Fine Arts as unproductive, must equally, and for the same reason, reject all spiritual teachers. Among merely practical people the whole course of life shows itself hostile to the lessons which religion teaches,—all their faculties are addressed only to toils and desires which contemplate nothing but the lowest attributes of humanity, the vanities, the sensuous pleasures, the gratification of the animal. Yet—"Man doth not live by bread alone." What does this mean? This living, this *human* living, makes the vital question. What is the life in man? The whole subject lies in the answer to this question. Were he a dog the answer might be easy; but being a man, the case is very different. Living, in his case, means something more than daily bread and drink, fine linen and other luxuries, which he owes to the meanest, but too frequently the strongest of his moral urgencies. These do not suffice; and the consequence is that there is a perpetual thirst and hunger pleading from within, which he knows not how to pacify. The true nature in man, can be nourished only by such food as proceeds from the mouth of God,—soul sentiment—and for this food we must acquire a taste and appetite before we are summoned to abodes where there shall be no other. [. . .] The Divine Master himself implores you to put the world behind you, teaching against the instincts, as if the true life were elsewhere. All teachers of pure and noble genius echo the same counsel. The poets, a natural priesthood, take up the lesson, in songs of equal sweetness and significance. "The world is too much with us," is their melancholy chaunt. Their instincts, by the way, peculiar to their gifts, have always made them, more or less willingly, so many moral teachers. Even Byron is unconsciously a moral teacher. What is his prolonged cry of torture, but that of a struggling soul, harnessed by a Demon, and writhing, and raging, to break away and escape to holier and happier pastures.

Now, my friends, Religion is the vital necessity of man, or it is nothing. The Deity is surely not a mere idea to be adopted or rejected by Convention. There is surely a wonderful significance in that craving after spiritual things, which, in however feeble degree, all nations have shown, in all periods. These cravings are not to be satisfied by the utilitarian. He does not trouble himself about such foreign matters. He does not see their necessity. He has not taken the first step towards the recognition of the soul itself, and his daily life ignores all its desires. We can get nothing from him. Are our cravings to be denied utterly. Surely, there must be a Divine utility somewhere, in other arts and teachers, to bring us to the aliment we seek. Our faith, born equally of revelation and instinct, has a living need which no extent of mere material performance can satisfy. Prove that you possess the ability to conquer all the nations—exhibit the longest stretch of railways and electric wires—show the most splendid cities—still, you have done little, in all this, to meet the wants of the true life in man. We may be all minds—yet have not a truly living soul among us. And we are daily working this mind at the cost of this soul. The faith that aspires above the reason—above humanity itself, which involves much more than reason,— must live wholly in sentiments and affections, such as tend to ennoble the aims and desires, and in the good fruits of performance which flow from sentiments and affections. That faith grows, and glows with hopes and aspirations which promote subtler and more magnanimous attributes than can be brought into exercise by the simply mortal energies of man. It is by these spiritual hopes and fancies that we must endow his soul with its necessary wings. [. . .] If we are really to associate hereafter with angelic natures and sublime intelligences, we must surely undergo a lifelong preparatory training, day by day, for this association. It so happens, as we are also taught, that this training presents the only condition upon which we can hope to merit this elevation. Such being the case, and this our elevation being, as we are told, the earnest desire of the Deity himself, it follows that he must have done, for the promotion of this object, all that could be done, consistently with our individual free agency. His justice and benevolence must not be disparaged by a supposition so terrible as that he has left any people without such necessary light and guidance as will suffice for their spiritual no less than mortal necessities. The difficulty lies in finding these guides; but this would be no difficulty if we did not resolutely shut our eyes against the lights they carry. We are too apt to demand the truth without waiting for the answer.

Now, were we only content to suppose that God has appointed that nothing shall exist in vain,—that all creatures, however humble, all talents, however profitless in trade—have their decreed uses, we should be at no loss for these necessary ministers. The Poet looks for them in all created things—in objects which your practical man rarely sees, and still more rarely studies. When we speak of ministers, in moral things, we are apt to assume that reference is made simply to the Holy Volume, to the Prophets and Apostles, to the existing churches, and to those who officiate in stole and surplus, at consecrated altars. [. . .] But these are rather authorities than ministries, and the distinction is somewhat important to our object. Besides, even these, as they are taught us, do not entirely suffice—were, perhaps, not intended to suffice, with a nature so habitually hard and self hardening, as that of man! [. . .] When rival churches array their hosts for conflict, the very identity of truth grows questionable, and we know not well what to believe unless we call in the help of other teachers. It is, therefore, with no lack of reverence for these, that I declare the conviction that God has not confided us to these only. He has not left himself without other witnesses, thronging earth and air, thronging your common highway, all of whom cooperate for his glory, and as dutiful ministers to the eternal needs of man. We are, in fact, apostles to one another, and the recognition of our brotherhood, with a human sympathy, as opposed to a human selfishness, endows each of us with a faculty, as a spiritual teacher. And we are not alone. Nature, through which we behold God himself every where about us, is full of her ministries. The Deity too well knew the weak, vain, unstable, easily perverted head and heart of man, to rely, for his guidance upon any one class of teachers. He had endowed him with too many hungry instincts and blind passions, not to feel the necessity of coupling these with daily monitors, within and without, perpetually appealing, with voices of tenderness and love, to his better nature in opposition to his instincts. [. . .] Earth, ocean, sky, all speak to him in turn, with ceaseless varieties of aspect, compel his admiration, awaken his curiosity, inspire him with wonder, with awe and with affection. Day and night thus equally contribute to the latent sympathies within his soul, its large desires and exquisite sensibilities. And he feels them all, if these sensibilities have not been made callous, by the gross growth of his baser instincts. The daily rising of the sun—the birth of light with every dawn,—what a glorious miracle still! It has staled upon our senses by familiarity, but that we may concieve its full and marvellous effect, let us suppose the case of a people for the first time put in possession of his glories. You can surely concieve of such a case, since you well remember what were the sensations inspired among the enlightened nations of the earth, no less than the ignorant, when, recently, all the stars of Heaven seemed to be raining down upon us, and science knew not, and knows not yet, how to account for the phenomenon. Concieve then the case of a people, wholly ignorant, who, for the first time, behold the advent of the sun! [. . .] The terrors inspired in the souls of his people, by the loss of that sun, which they have for the first time beheld, were unquestionably inspired everywhere by the first known eclipse. But he is not, though a heathen, suffered to sink beneath his terrors. Even while his people, with shuddering souls, and troubled faces, brood over the disappearance of that warrior God, so lately known and lost, what a delicious surprise comes to relieve them, in that softer glory, suddenly gliding upward along the pathway which has been irradiated by the passage of the sun. It is the Queen of Nature in fond pursuit of her flying Lord. Such is the solution of the mystery, and it grows into a faith and becomes the vital beauty of tradition, whence it passes into song and story. With the birth of Light, the Poet is thus also born. He is coeval with the light. He provides his people with the first grand ideas which unseal their spiritual senses. Under his tuition, the Moon hath her moral ministries also,—not simply to give us light by night, as the Utilitarian, who is always a materialist, would teach,—but to soothe, and harmonize and sweeten; to fling over life a spiritual atmosphere, which is to sink, like dews upon the earth, into the spirit of man, and to attune the soul, with its own music, by means of such influences as sing in the stars and blossom in the breeze. In the fiercely bright orb of day, the Heathen beholds,—and not mistakenly,—the model, as the miracle, of strength and power. In the moon, he sees the miracle of Love and Beauty. From the one, he gathers his lesson of toil, exercise, performance; from the other, he finds counsel to repose, to tenderness, to reverie—while a secret influence winds through all his nature, under whose subtle power, he grows fond and fanciful,—his soul asserting itself through this medium, and bringling back his thought, from that stirring, striving world in which it toils with lowly necessities, to refreshing hopes, beguiling fancies and exhilarating dreams, the potency of which lies in the very fact that they are vague and shadowy. Their uses grow from their equal mystery and beauty.

Such is the poet's philosophy! Let us contrast it with that of the practical man. One of our philosophers greatly renowned for his shrewd *Common* Sense, which always took care of itself,— once gravely concieved of the sun, as a very good substitute for farthing candles,—by which conception he taught the virtues of early rising, early couching and house-wifely economy. In its way, the lesson was a good homely one, particularly applicable at a period when Gas was not, and when the Civilization of the country had not learned to reject tallow for wax. There can be no objections to his practical philosophy, if, in accepting his lessons you forfeit none of higher value; but it speaks doubtfully for the moral, where one degrades the object in order to use it, as we should all feel in the case of one who should see in rapids, only an admirable water power, by which to turn a mill. Need I say that I regard the erring faith of the simple Heathen, who beheld the God himself in the blazing creation of his hands, as arguing more sublimely, and so more usefully and profitably; the one who beheld in the sun the visible form of that majesty and grandeur which filled his soul with awe and abundance, rather than the other who saw in the great luminary of the day only the means by which to save a sixpence. What was erring in the faith of the simple savage was soon repaired by his increasing knowledge of the truth, while that which was elevating in his superstition, remained with him to cheer and encourage. Sun, moon and stars had their educational value as representatives, when they were no longer to be esteemed as Gods. They were creatures only, but they argued for a power, which was to be known as much through their media as any other; at whose secret bidding, each of these ministers fulfilled his mission of light, and love, and beauty, for the earth. That such glorious creatures should be made tributary to his daily use, naturally elevated the man in his own consciousness,—elevated him to heights of prospect, no less than of possession, while filling his soul with godlike desires, and working upon it subtly, with the most mysterious impulses. They were revelations from the Divine Sources when written Revelation was not; and the wild Arab, watching nightly from the bosom of the trackless desert, was drawn upward insensibly by the beckoning eyes which he learned to study with desire,— until he grew wiser, equally in his mystic as his mortal meditations. The inferior uses of these nightly studies to himself, gave to the world its first lessons in astronomy. But how far wiser, than all that was in his mind, did he grow from the spell of their silvery voices stealing into his simple heart.

The earth itself—air and ocean, share also in this unobtrusive ministry to the soul of man. The winds that rage in storm,—the zephyr that whispers to affection; the seasons that glide, each with its own music into the bosom of the other;—these exercise our sensibilities, beguile our thoughts, and wait upon and soothe our passions. What crowds of moral teachers gather about us in our daily walks, if we will but deign to look down upon them, and listen to their modest voices. Lo! now, on the very bankside where the snows slept but a night ago; you detect the small blue flower of the springtime silently unveiling its jewelled bosom—a form perfect in its simple beauty and exquisite in the delicacy of its hues. Hath it no eye for your eye—no beauty for your taste, no sweetness for any of your senses—no still small whisper for your soul in its solitude? Has it really no uses? None, surely, save in its ministry of the Beautiful—in its ministry to the musing mood, the gentle sensibilities, and the Fancies that wait, like loving Pages, upon Thought and Feeling. What are its virtues, why it gives us pleasure to behold it, we know not; unless it be that it warms the hope; for we do not forget that it reappears upon the very spot which made its grave but a little year ago. What a wondrous mystery then lurks in that silent earth, which harbours such curious abodes for life. There is no death in its silence. The work of Nature is perpetually going on within; and her myriad pulses are evermore beating harmoniously with the toils of reproduction—and she gives out no murmur all the while, and we hear no cries from her multitudinous operatives, clamoring of their toils and praying escape from their bonds. Yet there, in impenetrable caverns, her central furnaces are kept alive—unseen spirits feed their quenchless fires; unknown workmen are busy at her forges, and season after season, she sends forth a thousand tribes, innumerable hosts, sweet, beautiful and perfect of their kind, which, in our insolent ignorance, we assume to be made without a purpose. How should we concieve the immeasurable absurdity of such a notion, when all earth is the workshop in which they grow to form, and where such perpetual fires are maintained solely for their reproduction? Still they reappear with the seasons—they meet us where we go—they welcome us when we return—and are always beside us with their gentle ministries:—their smiles, their songs; the innocent sweetness of their lives, the perfect loveliness of their aspects. We have only to find out their ministries, and be wise! How significant this ceaseless and certain reproduction of their great hope that is the life in revelation,—nay, which the history of the humblest flowret might sufficiently reveal. Decay shall throw off her wither'd branches; age shall reclothe himself anew, in all the glory and the strength of youth. If the flower so frail and evanescent— so inferiorly conscious of life,—is thus assured of renovation, and of seasons, endlessly successive of birth and beauty, what may not Hope anticipate for man—he, the favorite creature of Heaven—preferred over all the rest—endowed beyond all the rest—only a little lower than the angels,— to whom Revelation speaks—to whom all things bring revelations, and for whose daily help and happiness, God is daily working miracles.—We ask ourselves, half assured only, in consequence of our utilitarianism,—Have these things no uses? Estimated by the laws of trade, and by the habitual thought and practice of society—none whatever! "They toil not, neither do they spin." What then, have they to do with us? We demand toil of all that live? For what then were they made? Unless our sensibilities have been kept alive somehow, there is no answer to the question. [. . .]

If the only proper human purposes were limited to those which we vulgarly describe as the *useful,* we might well question God's wisdom in the creation of beings so very frail and valueless. But the objects of Divine Wisdom are not to be determined by the estimates of the grain and cotton market. Here the Poets interpose as our best teachers. Their faith assures them that

"Every flower
Enjoys the air it breathes."

and this should be our sufficient answer, since we are not to limit the blessings of existence to our own race merely. Their uses are moral. They were made for man, though they add nothing to his stock in trade, or his weight on 'Change. Their value is found in their ministry to his merest fancies—his dreams—his sense of the simply Beautiful. And the sense of the Beautiful is something. The Greeks accounted it a virtue. They deified it. They honored it with rapturous devotion; with the noblest offices of art; and, through it, they taught lessons of virtue to their young. Was this a mistake of the Greeks? *Our* practical men rarely show much sense of the Beautiful. They are Greeks only in the Market Place! The old Greeks were accordingly in error! And yet,—are we insensible to the fact that the element of Beauty enters, as a vital essential, into all the works of God's creation? We see it in the meanest of his insects, in the most inferior forms of vegetable life, as conspicuously present as in sun, and sky, and star and rainbow. There is a meaning in all this. Beauty implies the most exquisite symmetry, and the most perfect organization. It thus represents the highest law—the perfection of moral in the Being who creates,—and thus establishes an absolute Law for the nature of him who beholds. That we should duly esteem this law, it was made to appeal, through every possible variety of form and aspect, to our tastes and senses; and Beauty is thus decreed to be the visible representative of a principle and a virtue—involving models which govern our invention, refine our tastes, elevate our genius, and conciliate our affections. There is not a bud that blows—not a bird that flies, not an insect that chirrups beside us on the winter hearth, but fully displays its uses to the soul that can see—in the fancies which they inspire, the tastes which they awaken, and the moralities, which, unconsciously to ourselves, perhaps, they serve to teach. But we need not, in our philosophies, go below the obvious, and a single example will suffice. I have pointed you to a flower at your feet—such as the spring flings everywhere along the common highways—one of those insignificant forms—not finger high from earth,—with four little leaves of violet, five perhaps, and a tiny bright eye in the centre. Well! it is in your path. You tread upon it—you are about to do so,—for what are its uses. But you pause! Something arrests your footstep. There is some little nimble Fancy, waiting upon your thoughts, which, at that moment, whispers you and checks your movement. Meanwhile, other fancies start into activity, and what a crowd of human associations suddenly occupy the mind—strange, silly fancies, no doubt, which Common Sense,—if you let her speak— which she is very apt to do—will rate with ridicule, if not with indignation. But, for once, she is silent, and your fancies have their way. You feel that you are under the dominion of a spell. You dream, in short, and look back over a tract of years, and recal a thousand memories, all of which have been awakened by the simple eye of that little flower, looking upward, pleadingly, to your own. And you think of your own innocent childhood, when you had no fear of being trodden upon,—when your only craving was to be loved—your only care how to consume the sunshine and be happy along the highways;—and, even as you brood thus in present forgetfulness, your soul,—now permitted to look forth from your eyes—you catch glimpses of human forms and faces,—the well remembered aspects of your youthful playmates. They seem to fill the places of all the little violets that gather about you; and magically quick, you behold, rising in the midst of them, one pale, sweet, sad looking damsel—so real, so near, that you feel that you can take her to your bosom, by simply stretching out your arms. You know her, on the instant, as the one dear sister—the one who shared all your boyhood's sports, and helped soothe your childish sorrows. You have seen these little violets strewing her grave with sweetness,—and the vivid fancy is due to this simple association. And when the vision disappears, you turn carefully aside from the innocent blossom you were about to bruize,—you walk away with slow and heedful steps, so that you shall not graze a single leaflet. The flower and the Fancy have done their work, and the pitying and the loving moods are active: and your heart grows softened within you; and your soul grows lifted;—and you feel,—God grant that you *do* feel!—that you are a better man that day—that the world has not stript you of all your sensibilities—that the innocent affections of youth still linger in your heart—that your heart itself is still youthful in some degree;—that you are still human, though it may be somewhat practical in your notions—and, in time, perhaps, may be made to understand that God provides for the tastes and the affections, as certainly as for the appetites and passions.

Thus, in like manner, and with examples forever varying, to meet, as it were, and to satisfy, every change of mood in man, do the leaves and trees, the winds and waves, and all earth's tributary things and creatures, appeal to latent sensibilities, which were given to us as so many antagonist agencies, to our simply animal instincts. Let us beware how we reject any, the meanest of these unobtrusive ministries. Let us rather welcome them always as the truest friends of the heart—such as we can never suspect, even though we may despise—which entertain no selfish designs upon us, and claim only, modestly to serve, and soothe and chasten; to recal grateful memories, and encourage precious Hopes. Our animal tendencies are necessarily very powerful, as they enforce the appetites. But we need not be wholly animal. If we are *Isaacs* under his daily burdens, we may yet nightly possess ourselves of the ladder of Jacob. The appetites, unless met and modified by other powers of the soul and mind, would soon become utterly overwhelming and defiling passions, fatal to all the faculties. They become so, in the case of thousands, every day. The drunkard, for example, is a case where the beastly appetite has totally expelled all the corrective resources of heart and fancy. We may curb his excess, but by what process shall we reanimate the compensative faculties, without the due exercise of which, the degradation is inevitable. To prevent this degradation we are provided with a thousand natural tastes and pure sensibilities, which call to us for better aliment, and work upon us with redeeming power; and in proportion as we despise and discourage these from our association, do we deliver our young up to the power of the debasing passions. To combat these, there is the play of fancy in our minds; the gay caprice of mental impulses, which coerce the blood to enthusiastic sports, none of which need be hurtful; the soothing and inspiriting influence of music; the grateful in the innocent breath of flowers; the seductive charms of wood and landscape. Hence too, the subtle and mysterious influence of reverie and dream, which perpetually lead us out, from ourselves, into unknown and wondrous regions; showing us faint shadows of a Past or of a Future, the worlds that we may have lost, and those which we may be yet destined to inhabit. Hence our visionary Hopes, which are sometimes so extravagant as to mock all our calculations;—but which raise us infinitely above them;— our fears, which grow vivid without any sensible provocation,—making us feel, like Job, that a spirit, wrapt in midnight, is passing before us, compelling every instinct of the soul into a terrible consciousness, while the limbs grow numbed, and the hair starts up in bristles upon the clammy forehead! These influences—aye, powers—a countless multitude, for which we have neither name nor definition—for which, certainly, few of us attempt to conjecture the use—hang about our lives, keeping us forever sensible of a *nature,* without us and within, whose subtle associations are wholly beyond our control—teaching a condition far more profound and mysterious than any thing which lies within the ordinary provinces of Nature. They are subject to no common laws of earth—mere Common Sense cannot sit in judgement upon them—they are inscrutable to ordinary Reason. Shall we dismiss them from our thoughts as mere Illusions? We cannot, if we would! Nay, as mere Illusions, have they not their uses? Are we not bound to assume that their uses are commensurate with their effects, and are justified by wisdom in due degree with our sensibility to their influence? And this precious sensibility, it enshrines all flowers, and makes all fruits innocent; in its warmth, and youth, and happy freedom, the soul enjoys its being unafraid. Yet it is this flower of immortality that you crush with scorn, in obedience to the brutal appetites; even as the iron legions of the Roman, and the swarming archers and horsemen of the Assyrian, marched over the living hearts of innocent humanity. What hope is there for the nations that thus trample on the Beautiful. The worship of the Beautiful had saved them——will save you,——when horse and rider are overthrown. But we must learn to love before we worship; and the idol of the vulgar superstition must be torn down from its high places in our hearts, before the true God can find his shrine!

Copy-text: Lecture 1, "Poetry and the Practical," Charles Carroll Simms Collection, South Caroliniana Library.

From Advertisement,
Richard Hurdis: A Tale of Alabama

(1 8 5 5)

"RICHARD HURDIS" was singularly successful with the public in spite of much hostile criticism. It was objected, to the story, that it was of too gloomy and savage a character. But the entire aspect of a sparsely-settled forest, or mountain country, is grave and saddening, even where society is stationary and consistent; and, where society is only in process of formation the saddening and the grave in its aspect are but too apt to take on even sterner features, and to grow into the gloomy and ferocious. It is quite enough, in answer to the objection, to say that the general portraiture is not only a truthful one, in the present case, but that the materials are really of historical character. The story is a genuine chronicle of the border region where the scene is laid, and of the period when the date is fixed. Its action, throughout, is founded on well-known facts. Its personages were real, living men; being, doing, and suffering, as here reported. Nothing has been "extenuate," nothing has been "set down in malice." A softer coloring might have been employed, and, more frequently, scenes of repose might have been introduced for relieving the intense and fierce aspects of the story; but these would have been out of place in a narrative so dramatic of cast, and where the action is so rapid. [. . .]

Copy-text: *Richard Hurdis* (Redfield, 1855), 10.

From Dedication,

The Wigwam and The Cabin

(1 8 5 6)

One word for the material of these legends. It is local, sectional——and to be *national* in literature, one must needs be *sectional*. No one mind can fully or fairly illustrate the characteristics of any great country; and he who shall depict *one section* faithfully, has made his proper and sufficient contribution to the great work of *national* illustration. I can answer for it, confidently, that these legends represent, in large degree, the border history of the south. I can speak with confidence of the general truthfulness of its treatment. I have seen the life——have *lived* it——and much of my material is the result of a very early personal experience. The life of the planter, the squatter, the Indian, and the negro——the bold and hardy pioneer, the vigorous yeoman——these are the subjects. In their delineation I have mostly drawn from living portraits, and, in frequent instances, from actual scenes and circumstances within the memories of men. More need not be said. I need not apologize for the endeavor to cast over the actual that atmosphere from the realms of the ideal, which, while it constitutes the very element of fiction, is neither inconsistent with intellectual truthfulness, nor unfriendly to the great policies of human society.

Copy-text: *The Wigwam and the Cabin* (Redfield, 1856), 4–5.

From *South Carolina in the Revolution:*
A Lecture

(1 8 5 6)

For eighty years, my friends, the people of South Carolina have reposed securely in the faith that the fame of their ancestors was beyond reproach;—that they had no reason to dread the comparison of their deeds with those of any other people in this confederacy;—that their contributions to the national capital, of mind, moral and manhood, were of a sort to establish for them a perfect claim to the respect of all good men;—that they had given some, and not a few, of the greatest men in the country, to its several struggles for liberty & honorable renown;—that nothing, in brief, could take away, cloud or diminish, the glories of their Past, whatever might be thought of their performances in the Present. The Past, they were confident, was secure—safe equally against the dull hoof of the ass, and the slimy trail of the reptile!

But the history, it would seem, must undergo revision. The old chronicles are to be ignored—the grateful traditions of three quarters of a century, are pronounced to be mere delusions; and there have been those to proclaim that the ancestors of whom we were so loud in boast, were in fact, false to their duties & their country;—recreant to their trusts—heedless of their honour—faithless to their bretheren—traitors in the cabinet and cowards in the field!

These are substantially the allegations, made by a Senator in the Senate House; in sight and hearing of the assembled States—while the Representatives from South Carolina, upon the same floor, assembled for grave deliberation upon the affairs of the whole country, are regaled with the cruel history, as it is poured forth with a malignant satisfaction, seemingly with no other purpose than to goad and mortify the natural pride and sensibility of a hated party! What other motive? South Carolina-her conduct in the Past, at least,—was in no respect the subject of present deliberation. Whether true or not, in substance, the assault was gratuitously wanton,—hostile to all the ends of council, and grossly subversive of all the parliamentary & social proprieties.

Was it true? If so, how happens it that South Carolina is identified with so many glorious passages in our history;—with so many of the brightest deeds;—with so many fields of battle;—with so many names of deathless men, which, in the National records, are the recognized representatives of the noblest heroism—in fact, the recieved models of heroism whenever the song or story of the Revolution is the subject? How is it that she has acquired a spurious military and patriotic reputation, so distinguished in spite of the chronicle? How is it that it has been left to the present day to make discoveries of her shortcomings in the past, of which the Past, itself, knew nothing? Is it, indeed, true, that Marion, and Sumter, and Moultrie and Pickens— the very greatest among the revolutionary partizans—were simulacra, myths —mere men of straw & vapor;— or did they stand alone, fighting & achieving victories single handed, and without any glorious array of followers? Is it true that Gadsden & Rutledge, Laurens and the Pinckneys,— to whom we owe some of the very first revolutionary movements, were common men;-worthless—mere makeweights in a struggle, to which they could accord neither soul nor intellect? Verily, if this be so, there was no Revolution;—the whole History is an invention.

But suppose these charges be untrue? Suppose the same malignity which made the assault upon South Carolina so wholly gratuitous, to have darkened the moral vision of the assailant;—obscured his perceptions;—made obtuse his faculty for discrimination between fact and falsehood;—making him ready to bear false witness in the case, and only too happy to do so? What then should be the atonement to that people from whose history he would tear away so many of their most brilliant records?—Do not mistake me, my friends. Do not suppose that I am about to engage in any review of the miserable politics of today. I know no subject so little calculated to provoke my consideration, as the small traffic of politics, in the hands of hireling partisans. It is an outrage upon sacred histories which I resent. It is the memories of a grand national epic, which I would protect from the assailant—the fame of great Sages and Statesmen—great Patriots and Warriors—that chronicle of Pride, upon which a whole people brood with satisfaction, & to which they refer their sons, when they would train them to honorable aims and a generous ambition. The blow is aimed, alike, at the Dead and the Living—the past, present & future;—robbing the one of laurels made sacred; consecrated forever by their tears and blood;—the other of all those monuments by which the future generations are to be taught becoming lessons & examples. The crime of the Incendiary who should penetrate your sanctuaries and burn your archives, is nothing to this, since the memories of men may still cherish all the essential histories. But to tear away from the hearts of men their loving faith in the virtues of their sires—this is to slay the very hopes of a people, along with all their honest pride and most prolific impulses. This is to deprive them of all the most noble stimulants which goad a people to great performance. What must be the malice of a spirit which shall strive at such an object?—What the desperate necessities of that party Hate which shall justify a policy so profane and Barbarous!

It will be permitted to a son of Carolina to assert her character;—to reassert her history;—and endeavour to maintain her argument; and every just and magnanimous nature, will not only accord to him this privilege, but will rejoice, with a becoming satisfaction, if he shall do so successfully. None but the base of soul can possibly feel pleasure in raking up, from foul & obscure sources, those proofs of lapse or shame, which shall go to detract from what is honorable in the history of any people. And such may somewhere be found in the progress of every people. There will be a momentary weakness of resolve;—a momentary sinking of the soul; among all nations; the wisest, the bravest, the best; in a long and trying conflict. Here and there, in all histories—even in yours—there shall be a failure among individual men, high in station. What nation is free from blot, cast upon its chronicles, by the feeble or the erring citizen? But, because of an Arnold, shall we decry a people? Because of an occasional lapse from virtue, or honorable courage, shall we insist upon the obscuration, or obliteration of annals otherwise glorious? What fool will insist upon such logic? Who but a malignant will shut his eyes against the noble performances of a race, while dilating with a base complacency, upon the occasional stain upon its 'scutcheon? In the case of States, such as ours, is it not the duty of the Philosophic Statesmen to take them in their entirety—the general course which they pursued—the virtues which preponderated—the great, and the good, & the valiant, whom they produced, & if need be to refer to a weakness, a fault, an error or a vice, to do so with sorrow, & not with exultation;—to do so, simply because of the requisitions of the truth, and not with the foul and malicious aim to make the failure tell against the unquestionable virtue. South Carolina asks only to be tried by the standards which are applied to other States. She asks no favour, but she demands justice. She requires, that, while you expose her faults, you do not suppress her virtues. Be sure of this, that if there be stains upon her shield, they are of virgin whiteness in comparison with those, which a diligent delver in the sewers of history, may discover, on many others, which now most loudly vaunt their purity! [. . .]

Enough that I repeat, in the briefest summary the true history which the chronicles must every where sustain. The closing struggles of the war were in South Carolina mostly; the bloody frequency of her fields of fight, declare the superior earnestness of the contending parties; the final events made the most fearful impression; the venom & virulence of the war were reserved, as usual, for the last acts of this fierce tragedy, and South Carolina, where the last blood of the Revolution, and almost the first, was shed, was compelled to endure them all. Those who read the History, as they should, with no malignant determination to rake up the evil and suppress the good; to expose the base, and deny the noble; will soon be forced to admit that the exertions of South Carolina were unexampled in the case of so feeble a State; that she was one of the most self-sacrificing of the whole Confederacy; that her spirit was always greater than her strength; and so prompted friend and foe equally to overrate her ability! A few more words, my friends, and I have done. South Carolina was the first colony to second Massachusetts. She had no such interests at stake—no such causes of complaint, and plunged headlong into the conflict. Her battles followed close upon those of Lexington & Bunker. She defeated the first British fleet—is the only power that ever did defeat a British fleet. In those days it was no part of the policy of Massachusetts to deny or decry her services. It does not become her that she should do so now. The Past of both regions ought to be secure. Let the strifes of the Present be what they may, neither party gains by the brutal defamation of the other. If there is to be strife between our respective countries—if the future is to witness a conflict among ourselves—and this great empire be doomed to the convulsions of Civil War,—let the issues be unmixed; simple, single, unconfounded! If South Carolina, imbecile in the Past—be *now* imbecile— no matter from what cause—there need be no effort to prove the fact by argument. It will prove itself, in action! If imbecile, past and present, how absurd for the brave to go into the discussion! We scorn the imbecile; we do not contend with them! We crush them under foot, and feel that, while we do so, we do nothing. We argue with those only who can coerce our respect. Massachusetts gains nothing by showing that South Carolina is faithless as a friend, & worthless as a foe! Let her establish the fact in either case, & what follows? Is the argument meant to persuade the imbecile that she should yield without struggle?—submit,—that she may escape from blows & bondage? Ah! my friends, what *real* power, confident in itself, and noble in its courage, ever descends to such an artifice? Better, braver, nobler, the short process, of the mailed hand, & the biting weapon. Better for both parties—for the honor of the one, and the due conviction of the other. Standing, here, before you, on a purely Literary Mission,—with all my tastes, feelings, sentiments, habits, opposed to brutality & violence,—I yet deprecate no wrath—no censure; appeal to no sympathies; ask no forbearance. I demand, of a just and conscientious people; in a moment of comparative calm; in a hall sacred to peace, letters and the arts; I demand justice for my Mother Country. She has been more faithful to you,—more submissive— than she ever was to Britain; more true to *your* cause than she has ever been to her own! If she is now to perish,—if she is to be isolated by odium, that she may be more easily offered up at the altar, without sympathy or succour—be it so! Let the Future declare itself in its grimmest aspect, I shall not fear for her deportment in the worst of seasons. As neither Massachusetts, nor any other State, will gain any thing of honour when they lend a too eager [hand] to the defamation of the Past of South Carolina, so, be sure, the profit will be quite as small from her contemplated destruction in the future. If her doom is written, be equally sure, that she will fall no easy victim. With her lithe and sinewy limbs & muscles, she will twine herself around the giant caryatides which sustain the anchor of the great Confederacy, and falling like the strong man of Israel, will bring down with her, in a common ruin, the vast and wondrous fabric, which her own prowess has so much helped to raise. Then, if there shall be one surviving sister, sitting solitary in the desolation, she will remain a monument more significant of ruin than all the wreck which grows around her—the trophy of a moral desolation, which, by perversity and wrong, by a base selfishness which knew not how to be just, or how to be human, has with fratricidal hand, destroyed all its own securities and hopes—a moral suicide.—Forgive me, my friends, if I have spoken warmly; but you would not, surely, have me speak coldly in the assertion of a Mother's honour!

Copy-text: *Letters* 3 : 5 2 1 – 24, 547 – 49.

From *Sack and Destruction of the City of Columbia, S.C.*

(1 8 6 5)

CHAPTER VIII.

Evacuation of Columbia by the Confederate Troops—Terrible Explosion at the South Carolina Railroad Depot—The Commissary and Quartermaster Stores Thrown Open—The Surrender of the City by the Mayor—The Mayor's Letter—Assurances of Protection by the Federal Officers.

The end was rapidly approaching. The guns were resounding at the gates. Defence was impossible. At a late hour on Thursday night, the Governor, with his suite and a large train of officials, departed. The Confederate army began its evacuation, and by daylight few remained who were not resigned to the necessity of seeing the tragedy played out. After all the depletion, the city contained, according to our estimate, at least twenty thousand inhabitants, the larger proportion being females and children and negroes. Hampton's cavalry, as we have already mentioned, lingered till near 1 0 o'clock the next day, and scattered groups of Wheeler's command hovered about the Federal army at their entrance into the town.

The inhabitants were startled at daylight, on Friday morning, by a heavy explosion. This was the South Carolina Railroad Depot. It was accidentally blown up. Broken open by a band of plunderers, among whom were many females and negroes, their reckless greed precipitated their fate. This building had been made the receptacle of supplies from sundry quarters, and was crowded with stores of merchants and planters, trunks of treasure, innumerable wares and goods of fugitives—all of great value. It appears that, among its contents, were some kegs of powder. The plunderers paid, and suddenly, the penalties of their crime. Using their lights freely and hurriedly, the better to pick, they fired a train of powder leading to the kegs. The explosion followed, and the number of persons destroyed is variously estimated, from seventeen to fifty. It is probable that not more than thirty-five suffered, but the actual number perishing is unascertained.

At an early hour on Friday, the commissary and quartermaster stores were thrown wide, the contents cast out in to the streets and given to the people. The negroes especially loaded themselves with plunder. All this might have been saved, had the officers been duly warned by the military authorities of the probable issue of the struggle. Wheeler's cavalry also shared largely of this plunder, and several of them might be seen, bearing off huge bales upon their saddles.

It was proposed that the white flag should be displayed from the tower of the City Hall. But General Hampton, whose command had not yet left the city, and who was still eager to do battle in its defence, indignantly declared that if displayed, he should have it torn down.

The following letter from the Mayor to General Sherman was the initiation of the surrender:

MAYOR'S OFFICE

COLUMBIA, S. C., February 17, 1865.

TO MAJOR-GENERAL SHERMAN: The Confederate forces having evacuated Columbia, I deem it my duty, as Mayor and representative of the city, to ask for its citizens the treatment accorded by the usages of civilized warfare. I therefore respectfully request that you will send a sufficient guard in advance of the army, to maintain order in the city and protect the persons and property of the citizens.

Very respectfully, your obedient servant,

T. J. GOODWYN, Mayor.

At 9 o'clock, on the painfully memorable morning of the 17th February, (Friday,) a deputation from the City Council, consisting of the Mayor, Aldermen McKenzie, Bates and Stork in a carriage bearing a white flag, proceeded towards the Broad River Bridge Road. Arriving at the forks of the Winnsboro Road, they discovered that the Confederate skirmishers were still busy with their guns, playing upon the advance of the Federals. These were troops of General Wheeler. This conflict was continued simply to afford the main army all possible advantages of a start in their retreat. General Wheeler apprised the deputation that his men would now be withdrawn, and instructed them in what manner to proceed. The deputation met the column of the Federals, under Captain Platt, who sent them forward to

Colonel Stone, who finally took his seat with them in the carriage. The advance belonged to the 15th corps.

The Mayor reports that on surrendering the city to Colonel Stone, the latter assured him of the safety of the citizens and of the protection of their property, *while under his command.* He could not answer for General Sherman who was in the rear, but he expressed the conviction that he would fully confirm the assurances which he (Colonel Stone) had given. Subsequently, General Sherman did confirm them, and that night, seeing that the Mayor was exhausted by his labors of the day, he counselled him to retire to rest, saying, "Not a finger's breadth, Mr. Mayor, of your city shall be harmed. You may lie down to sleep, satisfied that your town shall be as safe in my hands as if wholly in your own." Such was very nearly the language in which he spoke; such was the substance of it. He added: "It will become my duty to destroy some of the public or Government buildings: but I will reserve this performance to another day. It shall be done to-morrow, provided the day be calm." And the Mayor retired with this solemnly asserted and repeated assurances.

CHAPTER IX.

Occupation of Columbia by the Federal Army—The Advance Guard Fired Upon—Plundering Private Property—The Jail Fired—Burning Cotton—The "Raid" On Watches—The Convent—Clergymen Abused by the Soldiers.

About 11 o'clock, the head of the column, following the deputation—the flag of the United States surmounting the carriage—reached Market Hall, on Main street, while that of the corps was carried in the rear. On their way to the city, the carriage was stopped, and the officer was informed that a large body of Confederate cavalry was flanking them. Colonel Stone said to the Mayor, "We shall hold you responsible for this." The Mayor explained, that the road leading to Winnsboro, by which the Confederates were retreating, ran nearly parallel for a short distance with the river road, which accounted for the apparent flanking. Two officers, who arrived in Columbia ahead of the deputation, (having crossed the river at a point directly opposite the city,) were fired upon by one of Wheeler's cavalry. We are particular in mentioning this fact, as we learn that, subsequently, the incident was urged as a justification of the sack and burning of the city.

Hardly had the troops reached the head of Main street, when the work of pillage was begun. Stores were broken open within the first hour after their arrival, and gold, silver, jewels and liquors, eagerly sought. The authorities, officers, soldiers, all, seemed to consider it a matter of course. And woe to him who carried a watch with gold chain pendant; or who wore a choice hat, or overcoat, or boots or shoes. He was stripped in the twinkling of an eye. It is computed that, from first to last, twelve hundred watches were transferred from the pockets of their owners to those of the soldiers. Purses shared the same fate; nor was the Confederate currency repudiated. But of all these things hereafter, in more detail.

At about 12 o'clock, the jail was discovered to be on fire from within. This building was immediately in rear of the Market, or City Hall, and in a densely built portion of the city. The supposition is that it was fired by some of the prisoners—all of whom were released and subsequently followed the army. The fire of the jail had been preceded by that of some cotton piled in the streets. Both fires were soon subdued by the firemen. At about half-past 1 P. M., that of the jail was rekindled, and was again extinguished. Some of the prisoners, who had been confined at the Asylum, had made their escape, in some instances, a few days before, and were secreted and protected by citizens.

No one felt safe in his own dwelling; and, in the faith that General Sherman would respect the Convent, and have it properly guarded, numbers of young ladies were confided to the care of the Mother Superior, and even trunks of clothes and treasure were sent thither, in full confidence that they would find safety. Vain illusions! The Irish Catholic troops, it appears, were not brought into the city at all; were kept on the other side of the river. But a few Catholics were collected among the corps which occupied the city, and of the conduct of these, a favorable account is given. One of them rescued a silver goblet of the church, used as a drinking cup by a soldier, and restored it to the Rev. Dr. O'Connell. This priest, by the way, was severely handled by the soldiers. Such, also, was the fortune of the Rev. Mr. Shand, of Trinity (the Episcopal) Church, who sought in vain to save a trunk containing the sacred vessels of his church. It was violently wrested from his keeping, and his struggle to save it only provoked the rougher usage. We are since told that, on reaching Camden, General Sherman restored what he believed were these vessels to Bishop Davis. It has since been discovered that the plate belonged to St. Peter's Church in Charleston.

And here it may be well to mention, as suggestive of many clues, an incident which presented a sad commentary on that confidence in the security of the Convent, which was entertained by the great portion of the people. This establishment, under the charge of the sister of the Right Rev. Bishop Lynch, was at once a convent and an academy of the highest class. Hither were sent for education the daughters of Protestants, of the most wealthy classes throughout the State; and these, with the nuns and those young ladies sent thither on the emergency, probably exceeded one hundred. The Lady Superior herself entertained the fullest confidence in the immunities of the

establishment. But her confidence was clouded, after she had enjoyed a conference with a certain major of the Yankee army, who described himself as
an editor, from Detroit. He visited her at an early hour in the day, and announced his friendly sympathies with the Lady Superior and the sisterhood;
professed his anxiety for their safety—his purpose to do all that he could to
insure it—declared that he would instantly go to Sherman and secure a
chosen guard; and, altogether, made such professions of love and service, as
to disarm those suspicions, which his bad looks and bad manners, inflated
speech and pompous carriage, might otherwise have provoked. The Lady
superior with such a charge in her hands, was naturally glad to welcome
all shows and prospects of support, and expressed her gratitude. He disappeared, and soon after re-appeared, bringing with him no less than eight or
ten men—none of them, as he admitted, being Catholics. He had some specious argument to show that, perhaps, her guard had better be one of Protestants. This suggestion staggered the lady a little, but he seemed to convey a
more potent reason, when he added, in a whisper: "*For I must tell you, my sister, that Columbia is a doomed city!*" Terrible doom! This officer, leaving his
men behind him, disappeared, to show himself no more. The guards so left
behind were finally among the most busy as plunderers. The moment that
the inmates, driven out by the fire, were forced to abandon their house, they
began to revel in its contents.

Quis custodiet ipsos custodes?—who shall guard the guards?—asks the prov-
erb. In a number of cases, the guards provided for the citizens were among
the most active plunderers; were quick to betray their trusts, abandon their
posts, and bring their comrades in to join in the general pillage. The most
dextrous and adroit of these, it is the opinion of most persons, were chiefly
Eastern men, or men of immediate Eastern origin. The Western men, including the Indiana, a p[o]rtion of the Illinois and Iowa, were neither so dextrous nor unscrupulous—were frequently faithful and respectful; and, perhaps, it would be safe to assert that many of the houses which escaped the
sack and fire, owed their safety to the presence or the contiguity of some of
these men. But we must retrace our steps.

CHAPTER X.

*Firing the City by Sherman's Troops—The Discipline of the Men—Citizens
Applying for a Guard—"A Reign of Terror"—The Firemen Interrupted—A
Terrible Sight—Soldiers Burnt to Death—The City Clock Gives Its Last Sound.*

It may be well to remark that the discipline of the soldiers, upon their first
entry into the city, was perfect and most admirable. There was no disorder or

irregularity on the line of march, showing that their officers had them completely in hand. They were a fine looking body of men, mostly young and of vigorous formation, well clad and well shod, seemingly wanting in nothing. Their arms and accoutrements were in bright order. The negroes accompanying them were not numerous, and seemed mostly to act as drudges and body servants. They groomed horses, waited, carried burdens, and, in almost every instance under our eyes, appeared in a purely servile, and not a military, capacity. The men of the West treated them generally with scorn or indifference, sometimes harshly, and not unfrequently with blows.

But, if the entrance into town and while on duty, was indicative of admirable drill and discipline, such ceased to be the case the moment the troops were dismissed. Then, whether by tacit permission or direct command, their whole deportment underwent a sudden and rapid change. The saturnalia soon began. We have shown that the robbery of the persons of the citizens and the plunder of their homes commenced within one hour after they had reached the Market Hall. It continued without interruption throughout the day. Sherman, at the head of his cavalry, traversed the streets everywhere—so did his officers. Subsequently, these officers were everywhere on foot, yet beheld nothing which required the interposition of authority. And yet robbery was going on at every corner—in nearly every house. Citizens generally applied for a guard at their several houses, and, for a time, these guards were allotted them. These might be faithful or not. In some cases, as already stated, they were, and civil and respectful; considerate of the claims of women, and never trespassing upon the privacy of the family; but, in numbers of cases, they were intrusive, insulting and treacherous— leaving no privacy undisturbed, passing without a word into the chambers and prying into every crevice and corner.

But the reign of terror did not fairly begin till night. In some instances, where parties complained of the misrule and robbery, their guards said to them, with a chuckle: "This is nothing. Wait till to-night, and you'll see h—ll."

Among the first fires at evening was one about dark, which broke out in a filthy purlieu of low houses, of wood, on Gervais street, occupied mostly as brothels. Almost at the same time, a body of the soldiers scattered over the Eastern outskirts of the city, fired severally the dwellings of Mr. Secretary Trenholm, General Wade Hampton, Dr. John Wallace, J. U. Adams, Mrs. Starke, Mr. Latta, Mrs. English, and many others. There were then some twenty fires in full blast, in as many different quarters, and while the alarm sounded from these quarters a similar alarm was sent up almost simultaneously from Cotton Town, the Norther[n]most limit of the city, and from Main street in its very centre, at the several stores or houses of O. Z. Bates, C. D. Eberhardt, and some others, in the heart of the most densely settled portion of the town; thus enveloping in flames almost every section of the devoted city. At this period, thus early in the evening, there were few shows of that drunkenness which prevailed at a late hour in the night, and only after all the grocery shops on Main street had been rifled. The men engaged in this were well prepared with all the appliances essential to their work. They did not need the torch. They carried with them, from house to house, pots and vessels containing combustible liquids, composed probably of phosphorous and other similar agents, turpentine, &c.; and, with balls of cotton saturated in this liquid, with which they also overspread floors and walls, they conveyed the flames with wonderful rapidity from dwelling to dwelling. Each had his ready box of Lucifer matches, and, with a scrape upon the walls, the flames began to rage. Where houses were closely contiguous, a brand from one was the means of conveying destruction to the other.

The winds favored. They had been high throughout the day, and steadily prevailed from South-west by West, and bore the flames Eastward. To this fact we owe the preservation of the portions of the city lying West of Assembly street.

The work, begun thus vigorously, went on without impediment and with hourly increase throughout the night. Engines and hose were brought out by the firemen, but these were soon driven from their labors—which were indeed idle against such a storm of fire—by the pertinacious hostility of the soldiers; the hose was hewn to pieces, and the firemen, dreading worse usage to themselves, left the field in despair. Meanwhile, the flames spread from side to side, from front to rear, from street to street, and where their natural and inevitable progress was too slow for those who had kindled them, they helped them on by the application of fresh combustibles and more rapid agencies of conflagration. By midnight, Main street, from its Northern to its Southern extremity, was a solid wall of fire. By 12 o'clock, the great blocks, which included the banking houses and the Treasury buildings, were consumed; Janney's (Congaree) and Nickerson's Hotels; the magnificent manufactories of Evans & Cogswell—indeed every large block in the business portion of the city; the old Capitol and all the adjacent buildings were in ruins. The range called the "Granite" was beginning to flame at 12, and might have been saved by ten vigorous men, resolutely working.

At 1 o'clock, the hour was struck by the clock of the Market Hall, which was even then illuminated from within. It was its own last hour which it sounded, and its tongue was silenced forevermore. In less than five minutes after, its spire went down with a crash, and, by this time, almost all the buildings within the precinct were a mass of ruins.

Very grand, and terrible, beyond description, was the awful spectacle. It was a scene for the painter of the terrible. It was the blending of a range of burning mountains stretched in a continuous series of more than a mile.

Here was Aetna, sending up its spouts of flaming lava; Vesuvius, emulous of like display, shooting up with loftier torrents, and Stromboli, struggling, with awful throes, to shame both by its superior volumes of fluid flame. The winds were tributary to these convulsive efforts, and tossed the volcanic torrents of sulphurous cloud—wreaths of sable, edged with sheeted lightnings, wrapped the skies, and, at short intervals, the falling tower and the tottering wall, avalanche-like, went down with thunderous sound, sending up at every crash great billowy showers of glowing fiery embers.

Throughout the whole of this terrible scene the soldiers continued their search after spoil. The houses were severally and soon gutted of their contents. Hundreds of iron safes, warranted "impenetrable to fire and the burglar," it was soon satisfactorily demonstrated, were not "Yankee proof." They were split open and robbed, yielding, in some cases, very largely of Confederate money and bonds, if not of gold and silver. Jewelry and plate in abundance was found. Men could be seen staggering off with huge waiters, vases, candelabra, to say nothing of cups, goblets and smaller vessels, all of solid silver. Clothes and shoes, when new, were appropriated— the rest left to burn. Liquors were drank with such avidity as to astonish the veteran Bacchanals of Columbia; nor did the parties thus distinguishing themselves hesitate about the vintage. There was no idle discrimination in the matter of taste, from that vulgar liquor, which Judge Burke used to say always provoked within him "an inordinate propensity to sthale," to the choiciest red wines of the ancient cellars. In one vault on Main street, seventeen casks of wine were stored away, which, an eye-witness tells us, barely sufficed, once broken into, for the draughts of a single hour—such were the appetites at work and the numbers in possession of them. Rye, corn, claret and Madeira all found their way into the same channels, and we are not to wonder, when told that no less than one hundred and fifty of the drunken creatures perished miserably among the flames kindled by their own comrades, and from which they were unable to escape. The estimate will not be thought extravagant by those who saw the condition of hundreds after 1 o'clock A. M. By others, however, the estimate is reduced to thirty; but the number will never be known. Sherman's officers themselves are reported to have said that they lost more men in the sack and burning of the city (including certain explosions) than in all their fights while approaching it. It is also suggested that the orders which Sherman issued at daylight, on Saturday morning, for the arrest of the fire, were issued in consequence of the loss of men which he had thus sustained.

One or more of his men were shot, by parties unknown, in some dark passages or alleys—it is supposed in consequence of some attempted outrages which humanity could not endure; the assassin taking advantage of the obscurity of the situation and adroitly mingling with the crowd without. And while these scenes were at their worst—while the flames were at their highest and most extensively raging—groups might be seen at the several corners of the streets, drinking, roaring, revelling—while the fiddle and accordeon were playing their popular airs among them. There was no cessation of the work till 5 A. M. on Saturday.

CHAPTER XII.

Scenes and Incidents—The Soldiers and the Ladies—
"Pluck" of the South Carolina Ladies—The Poor French Lady with
the Soldiers—What Occurred in the Houses—"Swapping" Guns—
An Officer Protects a House—Singular Incident.

Within the dwellings, the scenes were of more harsh and tragical character, rarely softened by any ludicrous aspects, as they were screened by the privacy of the apartment, with but few eyes to witness. The pistol to the bosom or the head of woman, the patient mother, the trembling daughter, was the ordinary introduction to the demand. "Your gold, silver, watch, jewels." They gave no time, allowed no pause or hesitation. It was in vain that the woman offered her keys, or proceeded to open drawer, or wardrobe, or cabinet, or trunk. It was dashed to pieces by axe or gun-butt, with the cry, "We have a shorter way than that!" It was in vain that she pleaded to spare her furniture, and she would give up all its contents.

All the precious things of a family, such as the heart loves to pore on in quiet hours when alone with memory—the dear miniature, the photograph, the portrait—these were dashed to pieces, crushed under foot, and the more the trembler pleaded for the object so precious, the more violent the rage which destroyed it. Nothing was sacred in their eyes, save the gold and silver which they bore away. Nor were these acts those of common soldiers. Commissioned officers, of rank so high as that of a colonel, were frequently among the most active in spoliation, and not always the most tender or considerate in the manner and acting of their crimes. And, after glutting themselves with spoil, would often utter the foulest speeches, coupled with oaths as condiment, dealing in what they assumed, besides, to be bitter sarcasms upon the cause and country.

"And what do you think of the Yankees now?" was a frequent question. "Do you not fear us, now," "What do you think of secession?" &c., &c. "We mean to wipe you out! We'll burn the very stones of South Carolina." Even

General Howard, who is said to have been once a pious parson, is reported to have made this reply to a citizen who had expostulated with him on the monstrous crime of which his army had been guilty: "It is only what the country deserves. It is her fit punishment; and if this does not quiet rebellion, and we have to return, we will do this work thoroughly. We will not leave woman or child."

Almost universally, the women of Columbia behaved themselves nobly under their insults. They preserved that patient, calm demeanor, that simple, almost masculine firmness, which so becomes humanity in the hour of trial, when nothing can be opposed to the tempest but the virtue of inflexible endurance. They rarely replied to these insults; but looking coldly into the faces of the assailants, heard them in silence and with unblenching cheeks. When forced to answer, they did so in monosyllables only, or in brief, stern language, avowed their confidence in the cause of their country, the principles and rights for which their brothers and sons fought, and their faith in the ultimate favor and protection of God. One or two of many of these dialogues—if they may be called such, where one of the parties can urge his speech with all the agencies of power for its enforcement, and with all his instruments of terror in sight, while the other stands exposed to the worst terrors which maddened passions, insolent in the consciousness of strength—may suffice as a sample of many:

"Well, what do you think of the Yankees now?"

"Do you expect a favorable opinion?"

"No! d——n it! But you fear us, and that's enough."

"No—we do not fear you."

"What! not yet?"

"Not yet!"

"But you shall fear us."

"Never!"

"We'll make you."

"You may inflict, we can endure; but fear—never! Anything but that."

"We'll make you fear us!" clapping a revolver to the lady's head.

Her eye never faltered. Her cheek never changed its color. Her lips were firmly compressed. Her arms folded on her bosom. The eye of the assassin glared into her own. She met the encounter without flinching, and he lowered the implement of murder, with an oath: "D——n it! You have pluck enough for a whole regiment!"

In a great many cases the guard behaved themselves well, using their utmost endeavors to protect the property under their charge, even to the use of the bayonet.

An officer, Lieutenant McQueen, stopped with Dr. Wm. Reynolds, and during the fire, worked manfully, and was the means of saving the residence from destruction. His gentlemanly manners won the respect and confidence of the family, and when he was on the point of leaving, the doctor gave him a letter, signed by several gentlemen, acknowledging his grateful feelings for the manner in which he had been treated; saying that the fortunes of war might some time place him in a position that the letter might be of use to him. This proved to be the case. At the skirmish near Lynch's Creek, this officer was wounded and captured. On showing the letter to a friend of Dr. Reynolds, who happened to be in the hospital, he was removed to a private house, every attention shown him, and when he was able to move, a special parole was obtained for him, and he returned to his home.

The "pluck" of our women was especially a subject of acknowledgment. They could admire a quality with which they had not soul to sympathize— or rather the paramount passion for greed and plunder kept in subjection all other qualities, without absolutely extinguishing them from their minds and thoughts. To inspire terror in the weak, strange to say, seemed to them a sort of heroism. To extort fear and awe appeared to their inordinate vanity a tribute more grateful than any other, and a curious conflict was sometimes carried on in their minds between their vanity and cupidity. Occasionally they gave with one hand, while they robbed with another.

Several curious instances of this nature took place, one of which must suffice. A certain Yankee officer happened to hear that an old acquaintance of his, whom he had known intimately at West Point and Louisiana, was residing in Columbia. He went to see him after the fire, and ascertained that his losses had been very heavy, exceeding two hundred thousand dollars. The parties had not separated for an hour, when a messenger came from the Yankee, bringing a box; which contained one hundred thousand dollars in Confederate notes. This the Yankee begged his Southern friend to accept, as helping to make up his losses. The latter declined the gift, not being altogether satisfied in conscience with regard to it. In many cases, Confederate money by the handfull was bestowed by the officers and soldiers upon parties from whom they had robbed the last particles of clothing, and even General Sherman could give to parties, whom he knew, the flour and bacon which had been taken from starving widows and orphans. So he left with the people of Columbia a hundred old muskets for their protection, while emptying their arsenals of a choice collection of beautiful Enfield rifles. And so the starving citizens of Columbia owe to him a few hundred starving cattle, which he had taken from the starving people of Beaufort, Barnwell, Orangeburg and Lexington—cattle left without food, and for which food could not be found, and dying of exhaustion at the rate of fifteen to twenty head per diem.

In this connection and this section, in which we need to devote so much of our space to the cruel treatment of our women, we think it proper to include a communication from the venerable Dr. Sill, one of the most esteemed and well-known citizens of Columbia. It is from his own pen, and the facts occurred under his own eyes. We give this as one of a thousand like cases, witnessed by a thousand eyes, and taking place at the same time in every quarter of the city, almost from the hour of the arrival of the army to that of its departure. He writes as follows:

"On Thursday, the day before the evacuation of the city by the Confederate forces, I invited a very poor French lady, (Madame Pelletier,) with her child, refugees from Charleston, to take shelter in my house, where they might, at least, have such protection as I could give her, shelter and food for herself and child. She was poor, indeed, having very little clothing, and only one or two implements—a sewing machine and a crimping apparatus—by means of which she obtained a precarious support. My own family (happily) and servants being all absent, and being myself wholly incapacitated by years of sickness from making any exertion, all that the poor widow woman and myself could remove from my house, besides the few things of hers, consisted of two bags of flour, a peck of meal, and about the same of grist, and about thirty pounds of bacon and a little sugar. These few things we managed to get out of the house, and, by the aid of a wheelbarrow, removed about fifty yards from the burning buildings. Waiting then and there, waiting anxiously the progress and direction of the fire, we soon found that we had been robbed of one bag of flour and a trunk of valuable books of account and papers. The fire continuing to advance on us, we found it necessary to remove again. About this time, there came up a stalwart soldier, about six feet high, accoutred with pistols, Bowie-knife, &c., and stooping down over the remaining bag of flour, demanded of the poor French lady what the bag contained. Having lost, but a few moments before, almost everything she had in the way of provisions, she seemed most deeply and keenly alive to her destitute situation, in the event she should lose the remaining bag of flour; the last and only hope of escape from starvation of her child and herself. She fell upon her knees, with hands uplifted, in a supplicating manner, and most piteously and imploringly set forth her situation—an appeal which, under the circumstances, it would be impossible to conceive, more touching or heartrending. She told him she was not here of her own choice; that herself and husband had come to Charleston in 1860 to better their fortunes; that they had been domiciled in New Jersey, where her husband had taken the necessary steps to become a citizen of the United States. She had in her hands his papers vouching the truth of her statement; that her husband had died of yellow fever in Charleston; that being unable, from want of the means, to return to New Jersey, she had been driven from Charleston to Columbia, (a refugee, flying from the enemy's shells,) to try to make an honest support for herself and child. To all this, he not only turned a deaf ear, but deliberately drew from his breast a huge shining Bowie-knife, brandished it in her face, rudely pushed her aside, using, at the same time, the most menacing and obscene language; shouldered the bag of flour, and marched off, leaving the poor starving creature, with her helpless child, overwhelmed with grief and despair.

E. SILL."

This is surely very piteous to hear, and were the case an isolated one, it would probably move compassion in every heart; but where the miseries of like and worse sort, of a whole community of twenty thousand, are massed, as it were, together before the eyes, the sensibilities become obtuse, and the universal suffering seems to destroy the sensibilities in all. We shall not seek to multiply instances like the foregoing, which would be an endless work and little profit.

CHAPTER XIII.

General Sherman on Foraging.

General Sherman tells General Hampton that, could he find any civil authority, and could they provide him with forage and provisions, he would suffer no foraging upon the people. His logic and memory are equally deficient. Was there no Mayor and Council in Columbia? They had formally surrendered the city into his hands. They constituted the civil authority; but he made no requisition upon them for provisions for his troops. He did not say to them, "Supply me with twenty thousand rations in so many hours." Had he done so, the rations would have been forthcoming. The citizens would have been only too glad, by yielding up one-half of their stores, to have saved the other half, and to have preserved their dwellings from the presence of the soldiers. Nay, did not the in-dwellers of every house—we will say five thousand houses—seek at his hands a special guard—which usually consisted of two men—and were not these fed wholly by the families where they lodged during the whole time of their stay? Here, by a very simple computation, we find that ten thousand soldiers were thus voluntarily provided with rations; and a requisition for twenty thousand men might easily and would probably have been provided, had any such been made; for the supplies in the city were abundant of every sort—the population generally having laid in largely, and without stint or limit, anticipating a period of general scarcity from the march of the enemy.

But, even had the people been unable to supply these provisions—even had the Council failed to respond to these requisitions—at whose doors should the blame be laid? The failure would have been the direct consequences of General Sherman's own proceedings. Had he not ravaged and swept, with a bosom of fire, all the tracts of country upon which the people of Columbia depended for their supplies? Had he not, himself, cut off all means of transportation, in the destruction, not only of the railways, but of every wagon, cart, vehicle, on all the plantations through which he had passed—carrying off all the beasts of burden of any value, and cutting the throats of the remainder? He cuts off the feet and arms of a people, and then demands that they shall bring him food and forage!

But even this pretext, if well grounded, can avail him nothing. He was suffering from no sort of necessity. It was the boast of every officer and soldier in his army, that he had *fed* fat upon the country through which he had passed; everywhere finding abundance, and had not once felt the necessity of lifting the cover from his own wagons, and feeding from his own accumulated stores. But the complaint of Hampton, and of our people at large, is not that he fed his followers upon the country, but that he destroyed what he did not need for food, and tore the bread from the famishing mouths of a hundred thousand women and children—feeble infancy and decrepit age.

CHAPTER XIX.

Proffered Assistance—The Lady's Plume and Riding Whip.

It was one almost invariable feature of the numerous melancholy processions of fugitive women and children and old men escaping from their burning houses, to be escorted by Federal officers or soldiers—as frequently by the one as by the other—who sometimes pretended civility, and mixed it up with jeering or offensive remarks upon their situation. These civilities had an ulterior object. To accept them, under the notion that they were tendered in good faith, was to be robbed or insulted. The young girl carrying work-box or bundle, who could be persuaded to trust it to the charge of one of the men, very often lost possession of it wholly.

"That trunk is small, but it seems heavy," quoth one to a young lady, who, in the procession of the nuns, was carrying off her mother's silver.

"What's in it, I wonder? Let me carry it."

"No thank you. My object is to save it, if I can."

"Well, I'll save it for you; let me help you."

"No; I need no help of yours, and wish you to understand that I mean to save it, if I can."

"You are too proud, miss! but we'll humble you yet. You have been living in clover all your life——we'll bring you down to the wash-tub. Those white hands shall be done brown in the sun before we're done with you.

Officers, even ranking as high as colonels, were found as active in the work of insults and plunder as any of their common men. One of these colonels came into the presence of a young girl, a pupil at the Convent, and the daughter of a distinguished public man. He wore in his hat her riding plume, attached by a small golden ornament, and in his hands he carried her riding whip. She calmly addressed him thus:

"I have been robbed, sir, of every article of clothing and ornaments; even the dress I wear is borrowed. I am resigned to their loss. But there are some things that I would not willingly lose. You have in your cap the plume from my riding hat——you carry in your hand my riding whip. They were gifts to me from a precious friend. I demand them from you."

"Oh! these cannot be yours——I have had them a long time."

"You never had them before last night. It was then I lost them. They are mine, and the gold ornament of the feather engraved with the initials of the giver. Once more I demand them of you."

"Well, I'm willing to *give* them to you, if you'll accept them as a keepsake."

"No, sir; I wish no keep-sake of your's; I shall have sufficiently painful memories to remind me of those whom I could never willingly see again—— whom I have never wished to see."

"Oh! I rather guess you're right there," with a grin.

"Will you restore me my whip and feather?"

"As a keep-sake! Yes."

"No, sir; as my property——which you can only wear as stolen property."

"I tell you, if you'll take them as a keep-sake from me, you shall have them."

"You must then keep them, sir——happy, perhaps, that you cannot blush whenever you sport the plume or flourish the whip."

And he bore off the treasures of the damsel.

In these connections, oaths of the most blasphemous kind were rarely foreborne, even when their talk was had with females. The troops had a large faith in Sherman's generalship. One of their lieutenants is reported to have said: "He's all hell at flanking. He'd flank God Almighty out of Heaven and the devil into hell."

CHAPTER XX.

The Cathedral——"The War upon Women"——
Curious House——Building——The Stays in the Wrong Place.

But this is enough on this topic, and we must plead the exactions of truth and the necessities of historical evidence, to justify us in repeating and recording such monstrous blasphemies. We shall hereafter, from other hands, be able to report some additional dialogues held with the women of Columbia, by some of the Federal officers. Of their *temper,* one or two more brief anecdotes will suffice.

The Convent, among its other possessions, had a very beautiful model of the Cathedral, of Charleston. This occupied a place in the Convent ground. It was believed to have been destroyed by the soldiers. One of the nuns lamented its fate to the Mother Superior, in the presence of Colonel Ewell, (?) an aid of one of the generals. He muttered bitterly, "Yes; it is rightly served; and I could wish the same fate to befall every cathedral in which *Te Deum* has been performed at the downfall of our glorious flag."

A gentleman was expressing to one of the Federal generals the fate of the Convent, and speaking of the losses, especially of the Lady Superior, he replied dryly: "It is not forgotten that this lady is the sister of Bishop Lynch, who had *Te Deum* performed in his cathedral at the fall of Fort Sumter."

A lady of this city spoke indignantly to General Atkins, of Sherman's army, and said of that general, "He wars upon women."

"Yes," said Atkins, "and justly. It is the women of the South who keep up this cursed rebellion. It gave us the greatest satisfaction to see those proud Georgia women begging crumbs from Yankee leavings; and this will soon be the fate of all you Carolina women."

Escorting a sad procession of fugitives from the burning dwellings, one of the soldiers said:

"What a glorious sight!"

"Terribly so," said one of the ladies.

"Grand!" said he.

"Very pitiful," was the reply.

The lady added:

"How, as men, you can behold the horrors of this scene, and behold the sufferings of these innocents, without terrible pangs of self-condemnation and self-loathing, it is difficult to conceive."

"We glory in it!" was the answer. "I tell you, madam, that when the people of the North hear of the vengeance we have meted out to your city, there will be one universal shout of rejoicing from man, woman and child, from Maine to Maryland."

"You are, then, sir, only a fitting representative of your people."

Another, who had forced himself as an escort upon a party, on the morning of Saturday, said, pointing to the thousand stacks of chimneys, "You are a curious people here in house building. You run up your chimneys before you build the house."

One who had been similarly impudent, said to a mother, who was bearing a child in her arms:

"Let me carry the baby, madam."

"Do not touch him for your life," was the reply. "I would sooner hurl him into the flames and plunge in after him than that he should be polluted by your touch. Nor shall a child of mine ever have even the show of obligation to a Yankee!"

"Well, that's going it strong, by——; but I like your pluck. We like it d——e; and you'll see us coming back after the war—every man of us—to get a Carolina wife. We hate your men like h——l, but we love your women!"

"We much prefer your hate, even though it comes in fire. Will you leave us, sir?"

It was not always, however, that our women were able to preserve their coolness and firmness under the assaults. We have quite an amusing story of a luckless wife, who was confronted by a stalwart soldier, with a horrid oath and a cocked revolver at her head.

"Your watch! your money! you d——d rebel b——h!"

The horrid oaths, the sudden demand, fierce look and rapid action, so terrified her that she cried out, "Oh! my G——d! I have no watch, no money, except what's tied round my waist!"

We need not say how deftly the Bowie-knife was applied to loose the stays of the lady.

She was then taught, for the first time in her life, that the stays were wrongly placed. They should have been upon her tongue.

In all their conversation, the officers exhibited a very bombastic manner, and their exaggerations of their strength and performances great and frequent. On their first arrival they claimed generally to have sixty thousand men; in a few hours after, the number was swollen to seventy-five thousand;

by night, it had reached one hundred thousand; and on Saturday, the day after, they claimed to have one hundred and twenty-five thousand. We have already estimated the real number at forty thousand—total cavalry, infantry and artillery.

CHAPTER XXIII.

Another Day of Horrors—When Will It End?—
The Bugles—Blackened Walls—Sympathizing Soldiers.

The morning of Saturday, the 18th of February, opened still with its horrors and terrors, though somewhat diminished in their intensity. A lady said to an officer at her house, somewhere about 4 o'clock that morning:

"In the name of God, sir, when is this work of hell to be ended?"

He replied: "You will hear the bugles at sunrise, when a guard will enter the town and withdraw these troops. It will then cease, and not before."

Sure enough, with the bugle's sound, and the entrance of fresh bodies of troops, there was an instantaneous arrest of incendiarism. You could see the rioters carried off in groups and squads, from the several precincts they had ravaged, and those which they still meditated to destroy.

The tap of the drum, the sound of the signal cannon, could not have been more decisive in its effect, more prompt and complete. But two fires were *set,* among private dwellings, after sunrise; and the flames only went up from a few places, where the fire had been last applied; and these were rapidly expiring.

The best and most beautiful portion of Columbia lay in ruins. Never was ruin more complete; and the sun rose with a wan countenance, peering dimly through the dense vapors which seemed wholly to overspread the firmament. Very miserable was the spectacle. On every side ruins, and smoking masses of blackened walls, and towers of grim, ghastly chimneys, and between, in desolate groups, reclining on mattress, or bed, or earth, were wretched women and children, gazing vacantly on the site of a once blessed abode of home and innocence.

Roving detachments of the soldiers passed around and among them. There were those who looked and lingered nigh, with taunt and sarcasm. Others there were, in whom humanity did not seem wholly extinguished; and others again, to their credit, be it said, who were truly sorrowful and sympathizing, who had labored for the safety of family and property, and who openly deplored the dreadful crime, which threatened the lives and honors of the one, and destroyed so completely the other.

CHAPTER XXV.

*Treatment of the Negroes—General Sherman and
the Dead Negro—Who Caused the War.*

Something should be said in respect to the manner in which the negroes were treated by the Federals while in Columbia, and as regards the influences employed by which to beguile or take them from their owners. We have already adverted to the fact that there was a vast difference between the feelings and performances of the men from the West, and those coming, or directly emanating, from the Eastern States. The former were adverse to a connection with them; but few negroes were to be seen among these, and they were simply used as drudges, grooming horses, bearing burdens, humble of demeanor and rewarded with kicks, cuffs and curses, frequently without provocation. They despised and disliked the negro; openly professed their scorn or hatred, declared their unwillingness to have them as companions in arms or in company at all.

Several instances have been given us of their modes of repelling the association of the negro, usually with blow of the fist, butt of the musket, slash of the sword or prick of the bayonet.

Sherman himself looked on these things indifferently, if we are to reason from a single fact afforded us by Mayor Goodwyn. This gentleman, while walking with the general, heard the report of a gun. Both heard it, and immediately proceeded to the spot. There they found a group of soldiers, with a stalwart young negro fellow lying dead before them on the street, the body yet warm and bleeding. Pushing it with his feet, Sherman said, in his quick, hasty manner:

"What does this mean, boys?"

The reply was sufficiently cool and careless. "The d——d black rascal gave us his impudence, and we shot him."

"Well, bury him at once! Get him out of sight!"

As they passed on, one of the party remarked:

"Is that the way, General, you treat such a case?"

"Oh!" said he, "we have no time now for courts martial and things of that sort!"

A lady showed us a coverlet, with huge holes burned in it, which she said had covered a sleeping negro woman, when the Yankees threw their torches into her bed, from which she was narrowly extricated with life.

Of the recklessness of these soldiers, especially when sharpened by cupidity, an instance is given where they thrust their bayonets into a bed, where they fancied money to be hidden, between two sleeping children—being, it is admitted, somewhat careful not to strike through the bodies of the children.

The treatment of the negroes in their houses was, in the larger proportion of cases, quite as harsh as that which was shown to the whites. They were robbed in like manner, frequently stripped of every article of clothing and provisions, and where the wigwam was not destroyed, it was effectually gutted. Few negroes having a good hat, good pair of shoes, good overcoat, but were incontinently deprived of them, and roughly handled when they remonstrated. These acts, we believe, were mostly ascribed to Western men. They were repeatedly heard to say: "We are Western men, and don't want your d——d black faces among us."

When addressing the negro, they frequently charged him with being the cause of the war. In speaking to the whites on this subject, especially to South Carolinians, the cause was ascribed to them. In more than one instance, we were told:

"We are going to burn this d——d town. We've begun and we'll go through. *This thing began here,* and we'll stack the houses and burn the town."

A different *role* was assigned to, or self-assumed by, the Eastern men. They hob-a-nobbed with the negro, walked with him, and smoked and joked with him. Filled his ears with all sorts of blarney; lured him, not only with hopes of freedom, but all manner of license. They hovered about the premises of the citizens, seeking all occasion to converse with the negroes. They would elude the guards, slip into the kitchens, if the gates were open, or climb over the rear fence and converse with all who would listen. No doubt they succeeded in beguiling many, since nothing is more easy than to seduce, with promises of prosperity, ease and influence, the laboring classes of any people, white or black. To teach them that they are badly governed and suffering wrong, is the favorite method of demagogueism in all countries, and is that sort of influence which will always prevail with a people at once vain, sensual and ignorant. But, as far as we have been able to see and learn, a large proportion of the negroes were carried away forcibly. When the beguiler failed to seduce, he resorted to violence.

The soldiers, in several cases which have been reported to us, pursued the slaves with the tenacity of blood-hounds; were at their elbows when they went forth, and hunted them up, at all hours, on the premises of the owner. Very frequent are instances where the negro, thus hotly pursued, besought protection of his master or mistress, sometimes voluntarily seeking a hiding place along the swamps of the river; at other times, finding it under the bed of the owner; and not leaving these places of refuge till long after the troops had departed.

For fully a month after they had gone, the negroes, singly or in squads, were daily making their way back to Columbia, having escaped from the Federals by dint of great perseverance and cunning, generally in wretched plight, half-starved and with little clothing. They represented the difficulties in the way of their escape to be very great, the officers placing them finally under guards at night, and that they could only succeed in flight at the peril of life or limb. Many of these were negroes of Columbia, but the larger proportion seemed to hail from Barnwell. They all sought passports to return to their owners and plantations.

CHAPTER XXVII.

Conclusion.

The reader will have seen that we have brought to a close our narrative of the most conspicuous events, in the "capture, sack, and burning of the city of Columbia." We have been at great pains to make the statements ample, and to justify them by reference to the best authorities and witnesses to be found. We believe that the facts are substantially complete, and so, true in all respects. The incidents given are selected as typical of large groups of facts, representative anecdotes, uniform in their variety, and quite too numerous for separate consideration. But the very uniformity, amidst such a numerous collection, is in confirmation of the general authenticity of the whole; and we repeat the conviction that the narrative is wholly true withal, and to be relied on as a history.

We have seen, with surprise, some attempts, in sundry quarters, to account for the destruction of Columbia by ascribing it to accident, to the drunkenness of straggling parties, to our negroes, and, indeed, to any but the proper cause. It is evidently the design of these writers, without inquiring into the motives by which they were governed, to relieve General Sherman and his army from the imputation. If it could be shown that one half of the army were not actually engaged in firing the houses in twenty places at once, while the other half were not quiet spectators, indifferently looking on, there might be some shrewdness in this suggestion. If it could be shown that the whiskey found its way out of stores and cellars, grappled with the soldiers and poured itself down their throats, then they are relieved of the responsibility. If it can be proved that the negroes were not terrified by the presence of these soldiers, in such large numbers, and did not, (as they almost invariably did) on the night of the fire, skulk away into their cabins, lying quite low, and keeping as dark as possible, we might listen to this suggestion, and perhaps admit its plausibility. But why did the soldiers prevent the firemen from extinguishing the fire as they strove to do? Why did they cut the hose as soon as it was brought into the streets? Why did they not assist in extinguishing the flames? Why, with twenty thousand men encamped in the streets, did they suffer the stragglers to succeed in a work of such extent? Why did they suffer the men to break into the stores and drink the liquor wherever it was found? And what shall we say to the universal plundering, which was a part of the object attained through the means of fire? Why, above all, did they, with their guards massed at every corner, suffer the negroes to do this work? These questions answered, it will be seen that all these suggestions are sheer nonsense. To give them plausibility, we have been told, among other mis-statements, that General Sherman himself was burned out of his own selected quarters, no less than four times. This is simply ridiculous. He was burned out in no single instance. None of his generals was burned out. The houses chosen for their abodes, were carefully selected, and the fire was kept from approaching them in any single instance.

But we have pursued our narrative very imperfectly, if our array of facts be not such as conclusively to show that the destruction of the city was a deliberately designed thing, inflexibly fixed from the beginning, and its fate sufficiently well known to be conceived and comprehended by all the army.

Long before the army left Savannah, a lady inquired of one of the Federal Generals in that city, whither she should retire—mentioning her preference of Columbia. His reply was significant. "Go anywhere but to Columbia." We have stated the conference between the Lady Superior of the Ursuline Convent, and a certain Major of the Federals, who originally belonged to the press gang of Detroit. He warned her at 11 o'clock of Friday, "that she would need all the guard he had brought, as Columbia was a doomed City."

A lady in one of our upper districts, expressing surprise at the treatment of Columbia in this nineteenth, or boasted century of civilization, was answered: "South Carolina has been long since the promised boon of Sherman's army."

Masonic brethren told others in the city that an order had been issued to the troops before they crossed the river, giving them license to sack, plunder and destroy for the space of thirty-six hours, and that Columbia was destined to destruction. A sick Federal soldier, who had been fed, nursed and kindly treated by a city lady, told her, on Friday morning, that the place would be destroyed that night. The simultaneous breaking out of the fires, in the heart of the city, and in the suburbs in twenty places besides, should conclude all doubt.

1. Enough that Sherman's army was under perfect discipline. They were, as an army, completely in the hands of the officers. Never was discipline more complete—never authority more absolute.

2. That the fire was permitted, whether set by drunken stragglers or negroes, to go on, and Sherman's soldiers prevented, by their active opposition, efforts of the firemen, while thousands looked on in perfect serenity, seeming totally indifferent to the event.

3. That soldiers, quite sober, were seen in hundreds of cases busily engaged in setting fire, well provided with all the implements and agencies.

4. That they treated with violence the citizens who strove to arrest the flames.

5. They when entreated and exhorted by citizens to arrest the incendiaries and prevent the catastrophe, at the very outset, the officers, in many cases, treated the applicants cavalierly, and gave no heed to their application.

6. That, during the raging of the flames, the act was justified by a reference to the course of South Carolina in originating the secession movement.

7. That the general officers themselves held aloof until near the close of the scene and of the night. That General Sherman knew what was going on, yet kept aloof and made no effort to arrest it, until daylight on Saturday, ought of itself, to be conclusive.

8. That, with his army under such admirable discipline, he could have arrested it at any moment; and that he did arrest it, when it pleased him to do so, even at the raising of a finger, at the tap of a drum, at the blast of a single trumpet.

But, what need of these and a thousand other suggestive reasons, to establish a charge which might be assumed from a survey of Sherman's general progress, from the moment when he entered South Carolina? The march of his army was a continued flame — the tread of his horse was devastation. On what plea was the picturesque village of Barnwell destroyed? We had no army there for its defence; no issue of strength in its neighborhood had excited the passions of the combatants. Yet it was plundered every house — and nearly all burned to the ground; and this, too, where the town was occupied by women and children only. So, too, the fate of Blackville, Graham, Bamberg, Buford's Bridge, Lexington, &c., all hamlets of most modest character, where no resistance was offered — where no fighting took place — where there was no provocation of liquor even, and where the only exercise of heroism was at the expense of women, infancy and feebleness. Such, too, was the fate of every farm-house of six in seven, at least. Surely, when such was the fate and treatment in all cases, there need be no effort now to show that an exception was to be made in favor of the State capital, where the offences charged upon South Carolina had been necessarily of the rankest character; and, when they had passed Columbia — greatly bemoaning the cruel fate which, under stragglers and whiskey-drinkers and negroes, had brought her to ruin — what were the offences of the villages of Allston, Pomaria, Winnsboro, Blackstock, Society Hill, and the towns of Camden

368 / From *Sack and Destruction of the City of Columbia, S.C.*

and Cheraw? Thus weeping over the cruelty which so unhappily destroyed Columbia, was it that she should enjoy fellowship in woe and ashes, that they gave all these towns and villages to the flames, and laid waste all the plantations and farms between? But enough. If the conscience of any man be sufficiently flexible on this subject to coerce his understanding even into a momentary doubt, all argument will be wasted on him.

Our task has ended. Our narrative is drawn by an eye-witness of much of this terrible drama, and of many of the scenes which it includes, but the chief part has been drawn from the living mouths of a cloud of witnesses, male and female, the best people in Columbia.

Copy-text: *Sack and Destruction of the City of Columbia, S.C.,* ed. A. S. Salley, 2d ed. (Atlanta, 1937), 34–43, 47–54, 65–69, 74–75, 79–82, 83–87.

Poetry

Sonnet——To My Books

Ye chaste creators of the youthful mind,
  Picture of man in each extreme of fate,
  Nations may fade——but yours no endless date——
For immortality design'd,
Then let me foster with a filial care,
  Your fairy pleasures and historic scenes,
  Where nations long forgot retain some gleams
Of former lustre, new created glare,
Which like the relics in Pompeii found——
  Point out the various beauties there that reign'd,
  And tho' all strew'd with ashes, yet the ground,
The lustre of a former day retain'd!
  Is there, my Books, a charm which ye have not,
No!——When with you, the world is all forgot.

Date: 1823.

The Broken Arrow

Ye warriors! who gather the brave to deplore,
  And repine for the Chief who shall conquer no more,
Let the hatchet of fight, still unburied remain,
  Whilst we joy in the glory of him that is slain.

Unbounded in soul, as unfearing in fight;
  Yet mild as the dove, when, untempted to smite;
His arm was resist less, his tomahawk true,
  And his eye, like the eagle's, was lightning to view.

Far down in the valley, when evening was still,
  I heard the deep voice of the Wolf on the hill:
And "hark!" said the Chief, as it echoed below,
  "'Tis the voice of Menawe! the cry of my foe!

"He comes not, the coward, to mingle in fight,
  "When the Day-God can offer one streak of his light;
"But in darkness, that emblems his bosom's own hue,
  "He seeks to perform, what he trembles to do!"

The Chief took his rifle, unerring as fate,
    His eye glow'd as proud, as his bosom was great;
I heard the flint strike on the steel, but in vain,
    For I heard not the rifle re-echo again.

Go, sigh not away, as the coward has done,
    The remnant of life, o'er the fields we have won;
But a mournful farewell, to our fruit trees we'll leave,
    They o'ershadow our fathers, and honor their grave.

Farther West! farther West! where the buffalo roves
    And the red deer is found in the valley he loves;
Our hearts shall be glad, in the hunt once again,
    'Till the white man shall seek for the lands that remain.

Farther West! farther West! where the Sun as he dies,
    Still leaves a deep lustre abroad in the skies;
Where the hunter may roam, and his woman may rove,
    And the white man not blight, what he cannot improve!

One song of regret to the wilds that we leave,
    To the Chief, o'er whose grave still his warriors must grieve;
He died as a hero—and equall'd by few—
    Himself his worst foe, to the white man too true!

Farther West! farther West, it is meet that we fly,
    Where the red deer will bound at the glance of an eye:—
And lonely and sad be the strain that is sung,
    For the arrow is broken, the bow is unstrung!

Date: 1825.

The Wilderness

He whose proud intellect forbids to rove
In nature's wild recesses, nor can taste,
From the deep waters of forgotten times,
Of feeling or of joy, with grateful thirst,
Scorning the deeply cavern'd rock, the stream
That glideth with a prattling whispering
O'er pebbly beds, or dasheth listless down,
From the far precipice, I would not seek
Much converse with. He may own a heart

Of subtler intricacy, more remote,
From nature's open book of fruits and flow'rs,
Which all may be acquainted with, but to me
There is a chilliness in lofty thoughts,
That like the mountain's brow, forever wears
A wreath of frostwork, that forbids approach.
I would mark its base, where falls the stream
And buds make merry with the gliding drops,
That steal into their open bells, at morn,
To hide, from the fierce thirstings of the sun at noon.
There is a melody in waterfalls,
A sweetness of repose in solitude,
In the far windings of untrodden wilds—
Where nature is the same, as at her birth,
I love to riot in. My heart forgets
The chains of social life, and I become
A member of the scene, I but survey!
'Tis a fond mystery to hold converse,
With the sweet warbler, who at noon tide heat,
Whispers soft carols to the blushing rose,
That opens by the wayside, yet untouch'd
By wanton or uncaring hands, alone.
Nor is it solitude as man may deem—
But a wide glance at all existing nature,
Who sits within a tangled bower, and speaks
To the reposing earth, who straight casts down
His mantle redolent with flowers and fruits
Of mingled sweetness, and of varying hue.
'Twas a deep Indian forest, where I laid
My form, reposing from the noonday sun
Listless. A lowly green grass-plat, my couch,
And a small tuft of flowers, my pillow form'd
Which, cautiously I press'd upon, as not
To crush them, so delicate and soft they grew.
A torrent tumbling from a neighboring hill,
Incessant murmur'd, as it reach'd the base,
Where straight diverging into several streams,
It found a passage thro' a rising rock,
Furrow'd by time in his irregular course.
The tangled flow'rs and vines, a zephyr fill'd,

Discoursing, as the wind-harp, touch'd at night,
By the soft language of the enamour'd sea;
Holding such pleasant music, that it came,
Like fairy spells upon me, and I slept.
Straightway, transported to a by-gone age,
I seem'd to be—tho' still the scene, the same.
But in the distance could I hear the roar
Of the wide waste of waters, and at length,
My vision more expansive grew, and soon
The far Atlantic, created o'er with foam,
And shining, like the sky with many stars,
Torn from the sun, which the disporting waves,
Leaping continual from their boundless bed,
Divided into brilliants, filled my view.
A speck was seen, tho' scarce perception-noted,
Upon the verge of the pale grey horizon,
Like a hand upon the wall at midnight.
It grew in swift proportion as it rose,
Upon the bounding billow, cleaving on
Its cresting foam, and rising at each leap,
With newer energy, and tenser nerve,
Till o'er the waters, with resistless force,
It bore wide way, as up its yellow sides,
The struggling billows leap'd. The ship drew near,
And now upon her deck, might many a face
Awe-fill'd, and wond'ring at the new found land
Be seen—They look'd around on all;
The sky that wore a different aspect,
A clearer blue, and the wide forest,
That unbounded seem'd, in the blue world
Of distance. The trees of giant height,
Mantled in foliage, and the sparkling sand,
Of Ophir seeming, and the mountains vast,
That the extended eye grew pain'd to search
Their summits capp'd with clouds.

       The Chief he came,
Pensive, but calm, as fill'd with grateful pride,
And prostrate on the earth, to him who gave
That earth, before a waste, untrod, unknown,

He bent his soul in pray'r, whilst all around
Spoke audible the same; accepted then
The voice of nature, thro' her thousand echoes,
Straightway repeated it again, again,
Whilst tears of sweet communion fill'd each eye.

Date: 1826.

Carolina Woods

These woods have all been haunted, and the power
Of spirits still abides in tree and flower;
They have their tiny elves that dance by night,
When the leaves sparkle in the moonbeam's light;
And the wild Indian often, as he flew
Along their water in his birch canoe,
Beheld, in the soft light of summer eves,
Strange eyes and faces peering through the leaves;
Nor, are they vanish'd yet.—The woodman sees,
Even now, wild forms that lurk behind the trees;
And the pine forests have a chanted song,
The Indians say, must linger in them long.

Date: 1836, 1847.

Ashley River

i

Still, still, thou gentle river,
    A long, a last farewell:
I fly from thee forever,
    In other climes to dwell;
And never more, thus roving,
    Along thy banks, shall I,
Behold a stream so worthy loving,
    Beneath the blessed sky.

ii

Thou hast bless'd me with a beauty
 Like a smile from the Most High;—
Thou hast cheer'd me with a murmur
 Of music melting by—
I have seen thee in thy glory,
 When the loved ones saw thee too,
But we see them now no longer,
 To them and thee, adieu.

iii

Sad parting with thy waters,
 Sweet waters of my youth;
When every hour was gladness,
 When every tone was truth—
Dark clouds have come about me,
 Thou, too, hast felt the change,
And thy billows only flout me,
 With a murmur stern and strange.

iv

Yet, well my heart has loved thee,
 And, alas! it loves thee still;
It cannot soon forget thee,
 Let me roam where'er I will—
Thou still art to my spirit,
 Like a smile from the Most High—
Thou art still most worthy loving
 Beneath the blessed sky.

Date: 1838.

Invocation

Come, Chevillette, my own love, come with me,
 No idle pomp, no bustling world, I seek;
Enough, if in the shadow of the tree,
 I watch thy glistening eye and glowing cheek.

Enough, if in thy gentle heart and eye,
 Mine own may find a warm, responsive flame,
Enough, if in thy murmur and thy sigh,
 Breathed out from love's own lips, I hear my name.

Thy hand in mine, thy spirit watchful still,
    Of what mine own hath spoken, and thy heart
Fill'd with that hope which love can best fulfil,
    We feel how sweet to meet, how sad to part.

Come, be a dweller in this quiet grove,
    And teach the wild vine how to gather round,
While, with thy lips, still breathing songs of love,
    To the deep woods thou lend'st a genial sound.

Things gentle shall be won to gather near,
    Solicitous of all the sweets thou bring'st,
And the young mock-bird, bending down his ear,
    Shall emulous listen whensoe'er thou sing'st.

Toward eve, the frisking rabbit 'neath thine eyes,
    Shall overlay the grass plat near our cot;
The squirrel, as from tree to tree he flies,
    Fling the dismember'd branches o'er the spot.

Thy gentle nature, winning as their own,
    Theirs all unwronging, shall a favorite be;
And they will gather round thy forest throne,
    And own thy sway, and love thy chains, like me.

Come, be a dweller in this quiet grove,
    Sweet heart! and with thy spirit true as fine,
Attune the sleeping chords of life to love,
    Till the high harmonies shall kindle thine.

Shut out the world's coarse discords, till no more
    Thy heart shall hear of violence or grief,
And heaven, in mercy to our lot, restore
    The bloom of Eden, blissful, but how brief!

Date: 1838.

Taming the Wild Horse

    Last night he trampled with a thousand steeds
The trembling desert. Now, he stands alone—
His speed hath baffled theirs. His fellows lurk,
Behind, on heavy sands, with weary limbs
That cannot reach him. From the highest hill,
He gazes o'er the wild whose plains he spurn'd,

And his eye kindles, and his breast expands,
With an upheaving consciousness of might.
He stands an instant, then he breaks away,
As revelling in his freedom. What if art,
That strikes soul into marble, could but seize
That agony of action,— could impress
Its muscular fulness, with its winged haste,
Upon the resisting rock, while wonder stares,
And admiration worships? There,—away—
As glorying in that mighty wilderness,
And conscious of the gazing skies o'erhead,
Quiver for flight, his sleek and slender limbs,
Elastic, springing into headlong force—
While his smooth neck, curved loftily to arch,
Dignifies flight, and to his speed imparts
The majesty, not else its attribute.
And, circling, now he sweeps, the flow'ry plain,
As if 'twere his, gathering up
His limbs, unwearied by their sportive play,
Until he stands, an idol of the sight.

      He stands and trembles! The warm life is gone
That gave him action. Wherefore is it thus?
His eye hath lost its lustre, though it still
Sends forth a glance of consciousness and care,
To a deep agony of acuteness wrought,
And straining at a point—a narrow point—
That rises, but a speck upon the verge
Of the horizon. Sure, the humblest life,
Hath, in God's providence, some gracious guides,
That warn it of its foe. The danger there,
His instinct teaches, and with growing dread,
No more solicitous of graceful flight,
He bounds across the plain—he speeds away,
Into the tameless wilderness afar,
To 'scape his bondage. Yet, in vain his flight—
Vain his fleet limbs, his desperate aim, his leap
Through the close thicket, through the festering swamp,
And rushing waters. His proud neck must bend
Beneath a halter, and the iron parts
And tears his delicate mouth. The brave steed,
Late bounding in his freedom's consciousness,

The leader of the wild, unreach'd of all,
Wears gaudy trappings, and becomes a slave.

He bears a master on his shrinking back,
He feels a rowel in his bleeding flanks,
And his arch'd neck, beneath the biting thong,
Burns, while he bounds away—all desperate—
Across the desert, mad with the vain hope
To shake his burden off. He writhes, he turns
On his oppressor. He would rend the foe,
Who subtle, with less strength, hath taken him thus,
At foul advantage—but he strives in vain.
A sudden pang—a newer form of pain,
Baffles, and bears him on—he feels his fate,
And with a shriek of agony, which tells,
Loudly, the terrors of his new estate,
He makes the desert—his own desert—ring
With the wild clamors of his new born grief.
One fruitless effort more—one desperate bound,
For the old freedom of his natural life,
And then he humbles to his cruel lot,
Submits, and finds his conqueror in man!

Date: 1838.

The Western Emigrants

An aged man, whose head some seventy years
Had snow'd on freely, led the caravan;—
His sons and sons' sons, and their families,
Tall youths and sunny maidens—a glad group,
That glow'd in generous blood and had no care,
And little thought of the future—follow'd him;—
Some perch'd on gallant steeds, others, more slow,
The infants and the matrons of the flock,
In coach and jersey,—but all moving on
To the new land of promise, full of dreams
Of western riches, Mississippi-mad!
Then came the *hands,* some forty-five or more,
Their moderate wealth united—some in carts
Laden with mattresses;—on ponies some;
Others, more sturdy, following close afoot,

Chattering like jays, and keeping, as they went,
Good time to Juba's creaking violin.

      I met and spoke them. The old patriarch,
The grandsire of that goodly family,
Told me his story, and a few brief words
Unfolded that of thousands. Discontent,
With a vague yearning for a better clime,
And richer fields than thine, old Carolina,
Led him to roam. Yet did he not complain
Of thee, dear mother—mother still to me,
Though now, like him, a wanderer from thy homes.
Thou hadst not chidden him, nor trampled down
His young ambition;—hadst not school'd his pride
By cold indifference; hadst not taught his heart
To doubt of its own hope, as of thy love,
Making self-exile duty. He knew thee not,
As I, by graves and sorrows. Thy bright sun
Had always yielded flowers and fruits to him,
And thy indulgence and continued smiles
Had made his pittance plenty—made his state
A proud one in the honors which thou gav'st,
Almost in's own despite. And yet he flies thee
For a wild country, where the unplough'd fields
Lie stagnant in their waste fertility,
And long for labor. His are sparkling dreams,
As fond as those of boyhood. Golden stores
They promise him in Mississippian vales,
Outshining all the past, compensating—
So thinks he idly—for the home he leaves,
The grave he should have chosen, and the walks,
And well-known fitness of his ancient woods.
Self-exiled, in has age he hath gone forth
To the abodes of strangers,—seeking wealth—
Not wealth, but money! Heavens! what wealth we give,
Daily, for money! What affections sweet—
What dear abodes—what blessing, happy joys—
What hopes, what hearts, what affluence, what ties,
In a mad barter where we lose our all,
For that which an old trunk, a few feet square,
May compass like our coffin! That old man
Can take no root again! He hath snapp'd off

The ancient tendrils, and in foreign clay
His branches will all wither. Yet he goes,
Falsely persuaded that a bloated purse
Is an affection—is a life—a lease,
Renewing life, with all its thousand ties
Of exquisite endearment—flowery twines,
That, like the purple parasites of March,
Shall wrap his aged trunk, and beautify
Even while they shelter. I could weep for him,
Thus banish'd by that madness of the mind,
But that mine own fate, not like his self-chosen,
Fills me with bitterer thoughts than of rebuke;—
He does not suffer from the lack of home,
And all the pity that I waste on him
Comes of my own privation. Let him go.

There is an exile which no laws provide for,
No crimes compel, no hate pursues;—not written
In any of the records! Not where one goes
To dwell in other regions—from his home
Removed, by taste, or policy, or lust,
Or the base cares of the mere creature need,
Or pride's impatience. Simple change of place
Is seldom exile, as it hath been call'd,
But idly. There's a truer banishment
To which such faith were gentle. 'Tis to be
An exile on the spot where you were born;—
A stranger on the hearth which saw your youth,—
Banish'd from hearts to which your heart is turn'd;—
Unbless'd by those, from whose o'erwatchful love
Your heart would drink all blessings:—'Tis to be
In your own land—the native land whose soil
First gave you birth; whose air still nourishes,—
If that may nourish which denies all care
And every sympathy,—and whose breast sustains,—
A stranger—hopeless of the faded hours,
And reckless of the future;—a lone tree
To which no tendril clings—whose desolate boughs
Are scathed by angry winters, and bereft
Of the green leaves that cherish and adorn.

Date: 1836, 1853.
Copy-text: *PDDLC* 2 : 163−65.

Harbor by Moonlight

The open sea before me, bathed in light,
>As if it knew no tempest; the near shore
Crown'd with its fortresses, all green and bright,
>As if 'twere safe from carnage ever more;
And woman on the ramparts; while below
>Girlhood, and thoughtless children bound and play
>As if their hearts, in one long holiday,
Had sweet assurance 'gainst to-morrow's wo:—
Afar, the queenly city, with her spires,
>Articulate, in the moonlight,—that above,
Seems to look downward with intenser fires,
>As wrapt in fancies near akin to love;
One star attends her which she cannot chide,
Meek as the virgin by the matron's side.

Date: 1844, 1845.

Sonnet—The Age of Gold

These times deserve no song—they but deride
>The poet's holy craft,—nor his alone;
>Methinks as little courtesy is shown
To what was chivalry in days of pride:
Honor but meets with mock:—the worldling shakes
>His money-bags, and cries—"My strength is here;
O'erthrows my enemy, his empire takes,
>And makes the ally serve, the alien fear!"
Is love the object? Cash is conqueror,—
>Wins hearts as soon as empires—puts his foot
Upon the best affections, and will spur
>His way to eloquence, when Faith stands mute;
And for Religion,—can we hope for her,
>When love and valor serve the same poor brute!

Date: 1844, 1853.

Accabee——A Ballad

It was a night of calm o'er Ashley's waters,
    Crept the sweet billows with their own sad tune,
While she, the fairest of our southern daughters,
    A maid to spell the footsteps of the moon——
        As slow we swept along,
        Pour'd forth her own sweet song——
    Ah! song of rapture, not forgotten soon!

Hush'd was our breathing, still the lifted oar,
    Our spirits spell'd, our limbs no longer free,
While the boat drifting silent to the shore,
    Brought us within the shades of Accabee:
        "Ah!" sudden cried the maid,
        Of the dim groves afraid,
    Where roves the ghost of the old Yemassee.

And sure the spot is haunted by a power,
    To fix the pulses of the youthful heart;
Never was moon more gracious in a bower,
    With the green leaves delicious in her art,
        Weaving so meekly bright,
        Her pictures of delight,
That much we sorrow'd but to say depart.

"If these old woods are haunted," sudden then,
    Said she, our dear companion, "it must be,
By one who loved and was beloved again,
    And loved all forms of loveliness to see;
        Here, in these groves they went,
        With songs and worship blent,
    Their wilder toils forgot in that idolatry."

Slow sped our skiff into the open light,
    The billows grew around us, but no more,
Rose the sweet ditty on our ears that night——
    Silent the maid looked back upon the shore,
        And thought of those dark groves,
        And the wild Indian's loves,
    As they had been a truth her heart had dream'd of yore.

Date: 1845.

Heedlessness

We see the flow'r decaying as we pass,
Pale with the coming cold, and, on the grass,
    Write ruin, with our footsteps, every hour,
    Yet pause not in our progress, though a pow'r,
As much superior to ourselves, as we
    To these dumb suff'rers of the predestined earth,
    Beholds us rapidly passing from our birth,
To a like ruin with the things we see;
And, from our side, as little heeded, goes,
    Drawn by invisible cords, the treasured thing
    That has our heart, in keeping;—yet we sing
As idly as if life were free from foes,
And love were sure 'gainst danger;—there is one,
Who, speaking near me now, of death, is heard by none!

Date: 1845.

Tzelica—A Tradition of the French Broad

The following is a Cherokee tradition. The substance of the story, stripped of its poetry, is simply this:—A young man, a white, heated with travel, after descending from the mountains, came to a river whose cool waters delighted his eye and tempted him to bathe. He did so, and lingering too long in the water, he became chilled and died in consequence. The stream indicated is the French Broad, in North-Carolina,—a poetical river, whose primitive name seems to have been Tzelica or Tzellico. There was a warrior, famous among the Cherokees at their first acquaintance with the English, whose name was Telliquoo. But Tzelica, is clearly feminine.

    'Twas the noontide hour of summer time,
        And sleep was upon the vale,
    The leaves they droop'd in the burning ray,
        And sigh'd for the evening gale.

    Weary and sad, with travel sore,
        O'er the hills the stranger came,
    His eyelid droop'd, and his bounding blood,
        Through his bosom coursed like flame.

Cool rush'd the river beneath his eye,
 With a thousand rocks at strife,
Its billows tossing their foam-wreaths high,
 As if they were mad with life.

With a cheerful shout they hurried on
 And they laugh'd with a childish glee,
As they flung their limbs o'er the antique rocks,
 With a joy that was strange to see.

In the shade of the hills, by the river side,
 With a sad and failing heart,
The youth sat down, and his secret thought
 Was a yearning to depart.

"Why should I toil in this sad unrest,
 Why strive in the endless strife,
And where is the hope that came to cheer
 In the better days of life!"

The murmur thus rose in his secret soul
 As beside the stream he lay,
And watch'd its billows, that, bounding on,
 With the rocks kept fearful play.

But soon 'midst the din a song rose,
 The fainting heart to cheer,
A song as sweet as the evening bird,
 Still sings in the flowret's ear.

He look'd, and lo! in the foaming wave,
 That plays with the rocks below,
A maiden glides without stretching arms,
 And a bosom white as snow.

A glimpse he sees, a sudden gleam,
 From an eye that shone as bright,
As the single star that at midnight streams,
 Alone from the mountain height.

Dark as the night her tresses float,
 Outflung by her buoyant arms,
And, spread o'er her bosom, now half conceal,
 Now half betray her charms.

And sung she then, with a pleading voice:
    "Thou faint'st with the noonday heat,
Thy brow is sad, thine eyelids droop,
    And sore with toil thy feet.

Then come to me,—in a sweet embrace,
    I'll soothe thy heart to rest,
While thy burning cheek, as the wave flows by,
    Is pillow'd on my breast."

The syren thus—"oh! come to me!"
    And, won by her maiden charms,
He sought the wave, but shudd'ring rushed,
    From the clutch of her death-cold arms.

To the shore he fled, but alas! too late,—
    And his dying sense could hear,
The cruel notes of that syren song
    That late had won his ear.

A plaintive strain of love no more,
    It rose with a fearful glee;
"And death," she cried "to the stranger bold,
    Who seeks embrace of me!"

Date: 1845.
Copy-text: *SWMMR* 1 (Jan. 1845): 15–17.

Indian Serenade

I.

'Mong Lucayo's isles and waters,
    Leaping to the evening light,
Dance the moonlight's silver daughters,
Tresses streaming, glances gleaming,
    Ever beautiful and bright.

II.

And their wild and mellow voices,
    Still to hear along the deep,
Every brooding star rejoices,
While the billow, on its pillow,
    Lull'd to silence, sinks to sleep.

III.

Yet they wake a song of sorrow,
        Those sweet voices of the night—
Still from grief a gift they borrow,
And hearts shiver, as they quiver,
        With a wild and sad delight.

IV.

'Tis the wail for life they waken,
        By Bonita's silver shore—
With the tempest, it is shaken;
The wide ocean, is in motion,
        And the song is heard no more.

V.

But the gallant bark comes sailing,
        At her prow the chieftain stands,
He hath heard the tender wailing;—
It delights him—it invites him
        To the joys of other lands.

VI.

Bright the moonlight round and o'er him,
        And O! see, a picture lies,
In the yielding waves before him—
Woman smiling, still beguiling,
        With her dark and wondrous eyes.

VII.

White arms toss above the waters,
        Pleading murmurs fill his ears,
And the gem of ocean's daughters,
Love assuring, still alluring,
        Wins him down with tears.

VIII.

On the good ship speeds without him,
        By Bonita's silver shore—
They have twined their arms about him,
Ocean's daughters, in the waters,
        Sadly singing as before.

Date: 1846.
Copy-text: *Areytos* (1846), 30–32.

The Grape Vine Swing

Lithe and long as the serpent train,
    Springing and clinging from tree to tree,
Now darting upward, now down again,
    With a twist and a twirl that are strange to see:
Never took serpent a deadlier hold,
    Never the cougar a wilder spring,
Strangling the oak with the boa's fold,
Spanning the beech with the condor's wing.

Yet, no foe that we fear to seek,
    The boy leaps wild to thy rude embrace;
Thy bulging arms bear as soft a cheek
    As ever on lover's breast found place:
On thy waving train is a playful hold
    Thou shalt never to lighter grasp persuade;
While a maiden sits in thy drooping fold,
    And swings and sings in the noonday shade!

Oh! giant strange of our southern woods,
    I dream of thee still in the well known spot,
Though our vessel strains o'er the ocean's floods,
    And the northern forest beholds thee not;
I think of thee still with a sweet regret,
    As the cordage yields to my playful grasp—
Dost thou spring and cling in our woodlands yet?
    Does the maiden still swing in thy giant clasp?

Date: 1848, 1853.

Shakspeare

The mighty master in each page we trace,
Natural always, never common-place;
Forever frank and cheerful, even when wo,
Commands the sigh to speak, the tear to flow;
Sweet without weakness, without storming, strong,
Jest not too strain'd, nor argument too long;
Still true to reason, though intent on sport,
Thy wit ne'er drives thy wisdom out of court;—
A brooklet now, a noble stream anon,

Careering in the daylight and the sun;
A mighty ocean next, broad, deep and wide,
Earth, sun and heaven, all imaged in its tide!—
Oh! when the master bends him to his art,
How the mind follows, how vibrates the heart,
The mighty grief o'ercomes us as we hear,
And the soul hurries, hungering, to the ear;
The willing nature worships as he sings,
And Heaven is won when Genius spreads her wings.

Date: 1843.

Scott

————Not forgotten or denied,
Scott's trumpet lay of chivalry and pride;
Homeric in its rush, and, in its strife,
With every impulse brimming o'er with life,
Teeming with action, and the call to arms;—
A robust Dame, his muse, with martial charms,
To strive, when need demands it, or to love;—
The Eagle quite as often as the Dove.

Date: 1848, 1853.
Copy-text: *PDDLC* 2 : 158.

The Poet

Thou art a Poet, and thy aim has been
To draw from every thought, and every scene
Psychal, and natural, that serene delight
Wherewith our God hath made his worlds so bright,
The sense of Beauty—the immortal thrill
Of intuitions throned above our Will—
The secret of that yearning, dim, but strong
Which yields the pulse to Hope—the wings to Song.

Date: 1858.

The Edge of the Swamp

' Tis a wild spot, and even in summer hours,
With wondrous wealth of beauty and a charm
For the sad fancy, hath the gloomiest look,
That awes with strange repulsion. There, the bird
Sings never merrily in the sombre trees,
That seem to have never known a term of youth,
Their young leaves all being blighted. A rank growth
Spreads venomously round, with power to taint;
And blistering dews await the thoughtless hand
That rudely parts the thicket. Cypresses,
Each a great ghastly giant, eld and gray,
Stride o'er the dusk, dank tract,—with buttresses
Spread round, apart, not seeming to sustain,
Yet link'd by secret twines, that, underneath,
Blend with each arching trunk. Fantastic vines,
That swing like monstrous serpents in the sun,
Bind top to top, until the encircling trees
Group all in close embrace. Vast skeletons
Of forests, that have perish'd ages gone,
Moulder, in mighty masses, on the plain;
Now buried in some dark and mystic tarn,
Or sprawl'd above it, resting on great arms,
And making, for the opossum and the fox,
Bridges, that help them as they roam by night.
Alternate stream and lake, between the banks,
Glimmer in doubtful light: smooth, silent, dark,
They tell not what they harbor; but, beware!
Lest, rising to the tree on which you stand,
You sudden see the moccasin snake heave up
His yellow shining belly and flat head
Of burnish'd copper. Stretch'd at length, behold
Where yonder Cayman, in his natural home,
The mammoth lizard, all his armor on,
Slumbers half-buried in the sedgy grass,
Beside the green ooze where he shelters him.
The place, so like the gloomiest realm of death,
Is yet the abode of thousand forms of life,—
The terrible, the beautiful, the strange,—
Wingéd and creeping creatures, such as make

The instinctive flesh with apprehension crawl,
When sudden we behold. Hark! at our voice
The whooping crane, gaunt fisher in these realms,
Erects his skeleton form and shrieks in flight,
On great white wings. A pair of summer ducks,
Most princely in their plumage, as they hear
His cry, with senses quickening all to fear,
Dash up from the lagoon with marvellous haste,
Following his guidance. See! aroused by these,
And startled by our progress o'er the stream,
The steel-jaw'd Cayman, from his grassy slope,
Slides silent to the slimy green abode,
Which is his province. You behold him now,
His bristling back uprising as he speeds
To safety, in the centre of the lake,
Whence his head peers alone,—a shapeless knot,
That shows no sign of life; the hooded eye,
Nathless, being ever vigilant and sharp,
Measuring the victim. See! a butterfly,
That, travelling all the day, has counted climes
Only by flowers, to rest himself a while,
And, as a wanderer in a foreign land,
To pause and look around him ere he goes,
Lights on the monster's brow. The surly mute
Straightway goes down; so suddenly, that he,
The dandy of the summer flowers and woods,
Dips his light wings, and soils his golden coat,
With the rank waters of the turbid lake.
Wondering and vex'd, the pluméd citizen
Flies with an eager terror to the banks,
Seeking more genial natures,—but in vain.
Here are no gardens such as he desires,
No innocent flowers of beauty, no delights
Of sweetness free from taint. The genial growth
He loves, finds here no harbor. Fetid shrubs,
That scent the gloomy atmosphere, offend
His pure patrician fancies. On the trees,
That look like felon spectres, he beholds
No blossoming beauties; and for smiling heavens,
That flutter his wings with breezes of pure balm,
He nothing sees but sadness—aspects dread,

That gather frowning, cloud and fiend in one,
As if in combat, fiercely to defend
Their empire from the intrusive wing and beam.
The example of the butterfly be ours.
He spreads his lacquer'd wings above the trees,
And speeds with free flight, warning us to seek
For a more genial home, and couch more sweet
Than these drear borders offer us to-night.

Date: 1836, 1853.
Copy-text: *PDDLC* 2 : 201–3.

Hayne——Let the Death-Bell Toll

i.

Let the death-bell toll for the parting soul——
    It has paid for the pomp at a fearful price;
Spread gloom o'er the walls of your stately halls,
    And deck your homes with each drear device:
For the city lies strangled by hostile power,
And the tyrant's foot is on temple and tower;
Yet one brave heart, in that desolate hour,
    Now makes himself ready for sacrifice!

ii.

And the toll of the bell shall answer well,
    As it lifts his soul o'er the tyrant's aim;
And well he knows, that the hate of foes
    Shall win from his people a deathless name;
He sees the black coffin his couch beside,
But the hangman cowers at his glance of pride——
While he walks his cell with a sovereign stride,
    Since he feels that the morrow shall bring him fame.

iii.

With the morrow is Fame, but a death of shame——
    A mortal agony first, and then
A glad release to the realms of peace,
    And a memory living 'mongst loving men!
He hath led to the battle a noble band,
Hath fought the good fight for his father-land;
He hath won, he hath lost; but his battle brand
    Shall flash in the eyes of his foes again:

iv.

There are hands that shall wield, in the tented field,
    The weapon so sacred in Freedom's sight;
And souls that shall rise, ere the martyr dies,
    And pledge to his manés a deathless plight:
Never, while hostile foot shall tread
The soil where the sire hath fought and bled,
To sheathe the good weapon whose flash hath shed,
    For the cause of his people, a glorious light!

v.

There are friends who come in the hour of his doom—
    Of doom and of gloom—and they have no fear:
But they cower with their grief for the noble chief,
    Who answers their pleadings with words of cheer!
To the boy at his side he says: "My son,
Be true to your country!—for though but one,
You are one of a thousand, and realms are won
    Where a single great son shall in arms appear!"

vi.

And the death-bells toll for the parting soul,
    And he walks 'mid the ranks of the marshall'd foe,
And he smiles as he sees that the balconies,
    And windows, have none who would see the show.
There is silence deep in each mansion proud,
Dread as deep, with no moaning loud,
But the citizen feels as the deathly shroud
    Were wrapping himself in a common woe!

vii.

Lo! the British are here, and the Hessians there,
    And they form the square round the scaffold high,
And the martyr comes, to the sound of drums,
    And will show, by his death, how the brave should die;
He utters his prayer, that his God will spare,
But none to the Tyrant that's sovereign there;
And with brow erect, and soul above fear,
    He dies for his country's liberty.

Date: 1858, 1860.
Copy-text: *Areytos* (1860), 26–28.

'Tis True That Last Night I Adored Thee

'Tis true that last night I adored thee,
  But 'twas moonlight, the song, and the wine;
The cool morning air has restored me,
  And no longer I deem thee divine;
I confess thou art pretty and tender,
  And when thou canst catch me again,
As last night, on a desperate *bender,*
  Once more I'll submit to thy chain.

The fact is, dear Fanny, I'm human,
  Very weak, I may say, on a *spree*;
And no matter of what sort the woman,
  I'm her slave if she *cottons* to me.
But this curséd sobriety ever
  Undoes every chain of delight,
And my memory, by daylight, has never
  Any sense of what takes place by night.

I'm a man of most regular habit
  When daylight comes round, on my word;
And though loving, by night, as a rabbit,
  With the sunrise I'm cool as a curd;
I'm quite willing in moonlight for capture,
  But she's a bright woman whose skill,
Having spell'd the short hours with rapture,
  With the daylight can fetter me still.

Date: 1859, 1860.

Raisons in Law and Liquor

There needs should be reason for thinking,
To the eyes that are evermore winking,
  But, when eyes gleam with fire,
  What fool would require
A rhyme or a reason for drinking?

Leave books to the sages that make 'em,
And laws for the scoundrels that break 'em,
  But in wine we have saws
  That are better than laws,
And we're infidels if we forsake 'em.

These teach us that thinking's a trouble,
That your glory is only a bubble,
    And that study and care
    Do but end in a snare,
Making innocent students see double.

We have doctrines more genial and better,
Writ in crimson, and not in black letter;
    Madeira for ink
    Gives us freedom, I think,
While your thought only forges a fetter.

The devil take Blackstone and Vattel;
Here's the wisdom that's born of the bottle,
    And the student who drains
    The last drop, for his pains,
Shall never have pains in his throttle.

Date: 1859, 1863

[Drummond's Dithyrambic]

' Tis the milk-sop that withers in autumn,
    And shakes, in the winter, with chill,
Not he who dives down in the bottle,
    And grows warm by the fire of the still!

Date: 1852.
Copy-text: *Woodcraft*, 272.

The Voice of Memory in Exile, from a Home in Ashes

Ever a voice is pleading at my heart,
    With mournful pleading, ever soft and low,
    Yet deep as with an ocean's overflow,
"Depart! depart! Why wilt thou not depart?
Here are no blossoms such as live; no flowers,
    Such as with sacred scent and happy glow,
Recal Elysian homes, and those dear hours,
When with the breezes sporting in our bowers,
And the soft moonlight sweet'ning the old towers,
There was no tree that sheltered not its bird,
    No shrub without its song and summer bloom,
And never a fate was nigh, with threatening word,

Articulate of the terror and the doom.
Were not the wings contented there in home
   That never lacked its sunshine and its songs?
We did not lack, beneath the grand old dome,
   The joy of solitude, though bless'd with throngs,
Coming and going; blessing as they came,
   And having solace in the bliss they found:
Depart! depart! and ye shall find the same,
   Nor wither in this cold and foreign ground!"
Alas! alas! for the poor home and heart
That still from out their ashes cry "depart!"

Date: 1865.

The Kiss behind the Door

i

Methinks the stars now shine more bright,
   Than they have ever shone before;
Their beauty born of that delight,—
     My Rosalie,—
   That first sweet kiss behind the door!

ii

While mother keeps a cheerful din,
   And sister sings, and guests *encore,*
our bliss, undream'd by all within,
     Dear Rosalie,—
   Is in the kiss behind the door!

iii

In greybeard's veins, the blood still glows,
   And back to twenty bounds three score;
What's years, if beauty still bestows,—
     My Rosalie,—
   Her sweetest kiss behind the door!

iv

Ah! damsel of a glad caprice,
   Enough, if I may hope no more,—
That I have had a taste of bliss,
     Dear Rosalie,
   In that sweet kiss behind the door!

Date: 1866, 1870.

Life, Struggle and Defeat

When thou shalt put my name upon the tomb,
    Write under it—here lies the weariest man
    That ever struggled 'gainst an evil ban,
The victim from his birth-hour to a doom,
That made all nature war against his will—
    Made profitless his toil—its fruits denied,
To patient courage and ambition still;
    His task decreed—his industry decried—
And left him weary of the sun, whose flight
Brought him the gloom, but not the peace of night!
His toilsome path was ever up the hill,
    A hill forever growing;—still his draught,
Was water in a seive that could not fill,
    And bitter was his cup, or drank, or left unquaffed.

Date: 1842; undated [1867?].
Copy-text: Scrapbook A, Charles Carroll Simms Collection, South
Caroliniana Library.

Sonnet—Exhaustion

I am so weary, wounded, scant of breath,
    So dispossessed of Hope. So comfortless,
    That sometimes, in the dread of this duress,
I half persuade myself to fly to death;
But evermore springs up the generous Faith,
    Looking a Goddess! and the life renews,
    As grasses, sweetly fed by Heavenly dews;
    And I again upspring, and to the sky,
    Look, glad to bourgeon! Shall it be in vain?
I know that most of pleasures end in pain,
    And pain and pleasure in eternity;
    And thus we struggle on—so live, so die;
Happy, if yet, upon the blasted tree
There may be fruits 'twould please a God to see.

Date: 1867.

Nelly's Sex

Let not the story I tell ye vex,
    For no one in Gotham disputes it,
Nell never remembers poor Nelly's sex,
    Except when she prostitutes it.

Date: n.d.

Politician

A shallow mind, a worthless heart,
Concealed and taught by every art—
A soul without a single aim,
Worthy an honorable name—
A spirit prone to petty toils,
And still supreme in tavern broils—
That frets and fever still to be
The vulgar herd's idolatry—
To whom a shout is highest fame,
A vote the thing of fondest aim—
A whiskey speech, where reason reels,
And grammar paces on her heels—
The best performance of the mind
That, dark itself, must others blind—
And yet he bears a human shape,
And has no tail, and is no ape.

Date: n.d.

The Ballad of the Big Belly

As I walk[e]d out one morning in May
As pretty a little girl as ever I did see,
Came trudging alone by the side of me—
Crying O Lawd! my Big belly!
What will my mammy say to me,
When I go home with a big belly.
    Olaw! my big belly!
    Olaw! my big belly!

When my b[e]lly lay so low,
The boys they came through rain & snow;
But now my belly is up to my chin
They all pass by & ne'er come in.
    Olaw! my big belly!
    Olaw! my big belly!

I wish my sweet little babe was born,
A-setting on its fathers knee
And I poor girl was dead & gone,
And the green grass growing over me.
    Olaw! my big belly!
    Olaw! my big belly!

Date: 1847, 1869.
Copy-text: *CP*, 278−79.

Select Bibliography

PRIMARY SOURCES

Writings of William Gilmore Simms appearing in book form

This list includes all first publications (regardless of brevity) issued separately in book form and all book-length publications, whether or not in book form, issued during Simms's lifetime. The bibliographical information is given as it appears on the title page.

Monody, on the Death of Gen. Charles Cotesworth Pinckney. By A South-Carolinian. Charleston: Gray & Ellis, 1825.

Lyrical and Other Poems. By William G. Simms, Jun. Charleston: Ellis & Neufville, 1827.

Early Lays. By William G. Simms, Jun. Author of "Lyrical and Other Poems,"— "Monody on Pinckney," &c. Charleston: A. E. Miller, 1827. Dedication: To Charles R. Carroll, Esq.

The Vision of Cortes, Cain, and Other Poems. By W. Gilmore Simms, Jr. Charleston: James S. Burges, 1829. Dedication to James L. Petigru, Esq.

The Tri-Color; or, The Three Days of Blood, in Paris. With Some Other Pieces. London: Wigfall & Davis, 1830. [Charleston, S.C.: James S. Burges, 1831.]

Atalantis. A Story of the Sea: In Three Parts. New York: J. & J. Harper, 1832. Dedication to Maynard D. Richardson, Esq.

Martin Faber; The Story of a Criminal. New York: J. & J. Harper, MDCCCXXXIII. Dedication to the author's daughter [Anna Augusta Simms].

The Book of My Lady. A Melange. By a Bachelor Knight. Philadelphia: Key & Biddle, 1833; Boston: Allen & Ticknor, 1833.

Guy Rivers: A Tale of Georgia. By the author of "Martin Faber." New York: Harper & Brothers, 1834. 2 vols. Dedication to Charles R. Carroll, Esq.

The Yemassee. A Romance of Carolina. By the author of "Guy Rivers," "Martin Faber," &c. New York: Harper & Brothers, 1835. 2 vols. Dedication to Samuel Henry Dickson, M.D.

The Partisan: A Tale of the Revolution. By the author of "The Yemassee," "Guy

Rivers," &c. New York: Harper & Brothers, 1835. 2 vols. Dedication to Richard Yeadon, Jr.

Mellichampe. Legend of the Santee. By the author of "The Yemassee," "Guy Rivers," &c. New York: Harper & Brothers, 1836. 2 vols. No dedication; 1854 Redfield edition has dedication to Colonel M. C. M Hammond.

Martin Faber, The Story of a Criminal; and Other Tales. By the author of "The Yemassee," "Guy Rivers," "Mellichampe," &c. New York: Harper & Brothers, 1837. 2 vols. Dedication to the author's daughter [Anna Augusta Simms].

Slavery in America, being a Brief Review of Miss Martineau on that subject. By a South Carolinian. Richmond: Thomas W. White, 1838. Dedicated to the Hon. Delegates from South Carolina, in the Congress of the United States.

Richard Hurdis; or, The Avenger of Blood. A Tale of Alabama. Philadelphia: E. L. Carey & A. Hart, 1838. 2 vols. Dedication to the Hon. John A. Grimball, of Mississippi.

Pelayo: A Story of the Goth. By the author of "Mellichampe," "The Yemassee," "Guy Rivers," "The Partisan," "Martin Faber," &c. New York: Harper & Brothers, 1838. 2 vols. Dedication to William Hayne Simmons.

Carl Werner, An Imaginative Story; With Other Tales of Imagination. By the author of "The Yemassee," "Guy Rivers," "Mellichampe," &c. New York: George Adlard, 1838. 2 vols. Dedication to Prosper M. Wetmore.

Southern Passages and Pictures. By the author of "Atalantis," "The Yemassee," "Guy Rivers, "Carl Werner," &c. New York: George Adlard, MDCCCXXXIX. Dedication to William Cullen Bryant.

The Damsel of Darien. By the author of "The Yemassee," "Guy Rivers," "Mellichampe," &c. Philadelphia: Lea and Blanchard, 1839. 2 vols. Dedication to the Hon. James K. Paulding.

The History of South Carolina, from its First European Discovery to its Erection into a Republic: with a Supplementary Chronicle of Events to the Present Time. By William Gilmore Simms, Author of "The Yemassee," "The Partisan," "Damsel of Darien," &c. Charleston: S. Babcock & Co., 1840. Dedication to the Youth of South Carolina.

Border Beagles; A Tale of Mississippi. By the author of "Richard Hurdis." Philadelphia: Carey and Hart, 1840. 2 vols. Dedication to M——— L———, of Alabama. Redfield 1855 edition has dedication to the Hon. John A. Campbell, of Alabama.

The Kinsmen: or The Black Riders of Congaree. A Tale. By the author of "The Partisan," "Mellichampe," "Guy Rivers," "The Yemassee," &c. Philadelphia: Lea & Blanchard, 1841. 2 vols. Dedication to Colonel William Drayton, of Philadelphia. Revised as *The Scout or The Black Riders of Congaree.* New York: Redfield, 1854. 2 vols. Now known as *The Scout.*

Confession; or, The Blind Heart. A Domestic Story. By the author of "The Kinsmen," "The Yemassee," "Guy Rivers," etc. Philadelphia: Lea and Blanchard, 1841. 2 vols. Dedication to James W. Simmons.

Beauchampe, or The Kentucky Tragedy. A Tale of Passion. By the author of "Richard

Hurdis," "Border Beagles," etc. Philadelphia: Lea and Blanchard, 1842. 2 vols. Dedication to the Hon. James Hall, of Cincinnati. Later revised as *Charlemont* and *Beauchampe:* see under *Charlemont* below.

The Social Principle: The True Source of National Permanence. An Oration, Delivered Before the Erosophic Society of the University of Alabama, at its Twelfth Anniversary, December 13, 1842. By William Gilmore Simms, of South Carolina. Tuscaloosa: The [Erosophic] Society, 1843.

The Geography of South Carolina: Being a Companion to the History of that State. By William Gilmore Simms. Charleston: Babcock & Co., 1843. Dedication to Southern Teachers.

Donna Florida. A Tale. By the Author of "Atalantis," "Southern Passages and Pictures," &c. Charleston: Burges & James, 1843. Dedication to James Lawson, of New York.

The Prima Donna: A Passage from City Life. By W. G. Simms, author of "Guy Rivers," "The Yemassee," "Richard Hurdis," etc. Philadelphia: Louis A. Godey, 1844. No. 1 of Godey's Library of Elegant Literature.

The Sources of American Independence. An Oration, on the Sixty-ninth Anniversary of American Independence; Delivered at Aiken, South-Carolina, before the Town Council and Citizens Thereof. By W. Gilmore Simms. Aiken: Council, MD.CCC.XLIV.

The Life of Francis Marion. By W. Gilmore Simms. New York: Henry G. Langley, 1844.

Castle Dismal: or, The Bachelor's Christmas. A Domestic Legend. By the Author of "Guy Rivers," "The Yemassee," "Richard Hurdis," &c. New York: Burgess, Stringer & Co., 1844. Dedication to Richard Henry Wilde, of Georgia.

Helen Halsey: or, The Swamp State of Conelachita. A Tale of the Borders. By W. Gilmore Simms, Author of "Richard Hurdis," "The Yemassee," "The Kinsmen," &c. New-York: Burges, Stringer & Co., 1845. Dedication to Randell Hunt, Esq., of Louisiana.

Grouped Thoughts and Scattered Fancies. A Collection of Sonnets. By the Author of "Atalantis," "Southern Passages and Pictures," &c. Richmond, Va.: Wm. Macfarlane, 1845.

The Wigwam and the Cabin. By the Author of "The Yemassee," "Guy Rivers," &c. New York: Wiley and Putnam, 1845. First and Second Series. Dedicated to N. Roach, Esq.

Count Julian; or, The Last Days of the Goth. A Historical Romance. By the Author of "Guy Rivers," "The Yemassee," "The Damsel of Darien," "Richard Hurdis," "Border Beagles," "The Kinsmen," &c. Baltimore and New York: William Taylor, 1845. Dedication to the Hon. John P. Kennedy, of Baltimore, Maryland.

Views and Reviews in American Literature, History and Fiction. By the author of "The Yemassee," "Life of Marion," "History of South Carolina," "Richard Hurdis," &c., &c. New York: Wiley and Putnam, 1845. First and Second Series. Dedication to Professor E. Geddings, of the Medical College of South Carolina.

Areytos: or, Songs of the South. By W. Gilmore Simms, Author of "The Yemassee," "Confession," etc. Charleston: John Russell, MDCCCXLVI.

The Life of Captain John Smith. The Founder of Virginia. By W. Gilmore Simms. Author of "Life of Marion," "History of South Carolina," etc. New York: Geo. F. Coo-ledge and Brother [1846].

The Life of the Chevalier Bayard; "The Good Knight," "Sans peur et sans reproche." By W. Gilmore Simms. New York: Harper & Brothers, 1847. Dedication to John Izard Middleton, Esq., of South Carolina.

Self-Development. An Oration Delivered Before the Literary Societies of Oglethorpe University, Georgia; November 10, 1847. Milledgeville, Ga.: Thalian Society, 1847.

Lays of the Palmetto: A Tribute to the South Carolina Regiment, in the War with Mexico. By W. Gilmore Simms, Esq. Charleston, S.C.: John Russell, 1848.

Charleston, and Her Satirists; A Scribblement. By a City Bachelor. Charleston: James S. Burges, 1848. Two pamphlets: No. 1 and No. 2.

The Cassique of Accabee. A Tale of Ashley River. With Other Pieces. By William Gilmore Simms, Esq. Author of "Atalantis," "The Yemassee," etc. Charleston: John Russell, 1849. Almost identical copies issued in New York with Geo. P. Putnam and Harper & Brothers imprints.

Father Abbot, or, the Home Tourist; A Medley. By W. Gilmore Simms, Esq. Charleston, S. C.: Miller & Browne, 1849.

Sabbath Lyrics; or, Songs from Scripture. A Christmas Gift of Love. By W. Gilmore Simms. Charleston: Walker and James, MDCCCXLIX. Dedication to My Wife and The Mother of my Children [Chevillette Roach Simms].

The Lily and the Totem, or, The Huguenots in Florida. A Series of Sketches, Picturesque and Historical, of the Colonies of Coligni, in North America. 1562–1570. By the author of "The Yemassee," "Life of Marion," "Life of Bayard," etc. New York: Baker and Scribner, 1850. Dedication to the Hon. James H. Hammond, of South Carolina.

Flirtation at the Moultrie House: In a Series of Letters, from Miss Georgiana Appleby, To Her Friends in Georgia, Showing the Doings At the Moultrie House, and the Events Which Took Place at the Grand Costume Ball, On the 29th August, 1850; With Other Letters. Charleston: Edward C. Councell, 1850.

The City of the Silent: A Poem. By W. Gilmore Simms. Delivered at the Consecration of Magnolia Cemetery. November 19, 1850. Charleston: Walker & James, 1850 [1851].

Katharine Walton: or, The Rebel of Dorchester. An Historical Romance of the Revolution in Carolina. By the author of "Richard Hurdis," "Border Beagles," "The Yemassee," "The Partisan," "Mellichampe," etc. Philadelphia: A. Hart, late Carey and Hart, 1851. Redfield 1854 edition dedicated to the Hon. Edward Frost.

Norman Maurice; or, The Man of the People. An American Drama. By W. Gilmore Simms, Author of "The Yemassee," &c. Richmond: Jno. R. Thompson, 1851. Walker & Richards 1852 edition dedicated to Henry Gourdin, Esq. of South Carolina.

The Golden Christmas: A Chronicle of St. John's, Berkeley. Compiled from the Notes of a

Briefless Barrister. By the author of "The Yemassee," "Guy Rivers," "Katharine Walton," etc. Charleston: Walker, Richards and Co., 1852.

The Sword and the Distaff; or, "Fair, Fat and Forty," A Story of the South, at the Close of the Revolution. By the author of "The Partisan," "Mellichampe," "Katharine Walton," etc. Charleston: Walker, Richards & Co., 1852. Dedication to Joseph Johnson, M.D. Republished as *Woodcraft or Hawks about the Dovecote. A Story of the South at the Close of the Revolution*. New York: Redfield, 1854. Now known as *Woodcraft*.

As Good as a Comedy: or, The Tennessean's Story. By an Editor. Philadelphia: A. Hart, late Carey & Hart, 1852. Dedication to Harry Placide.

Michael Bonham: or, The Fall of Bexar. A Tale of Texas. By a Southron. Richmond: Jno. R. Thompson, 1852.

South-Carolina in the Revolutionary War: Being a Reply to Certain Misrepresentations and Mistakes of Recent Writers, in Relation to the Course and Conduct of this State. By a Southron. Charleston: Walker and James, 1853. Charleston: Courtenay, 1853.

Marie de Berniere: A Tale of the Crescent City, Etc. Etc. Etc. By W. Gilmore Simms, Author of "The Yemassee," "Richard Hurdis," "Guy Rivers," etc. Philadelphia: Lippincott, Grambo, and Co., 1853. Republished as *The Maroon; A Legend of the Caribbees, and Other Tales*. Philadelphia: Lippincott, Grambo, & Co., 1855.

Egeria: or, Voices of Thought and Counsel, for the Woods and Wayside. By W. Gilmore Simms, Esq., Author of "Katharine Walton," etc. Philadelphia: E. H. Butler & Co., 1853.

Vasconselos. A Romance of the New World. By Frank Cooper. New York: Redfield, 1853. Dedication to Dr. John W. Francis, of New York.

Poems Descriptive, Dramatic, Legendary and Contemplative. By William Gilmore Simms, Esq. New York: Redfield, 1853. Charleston, S.C.: John Russell, 1853. 2 vols.

Southward Ho! A Spell of Sunshine. By W. Gilmore Simms, Esq. Author of "The Yemassee"—"The Partisan"—"Mellichampe"—"Katharine Walton"—"The Scout"—"Woodcraft," etc. New York: Redfield, 1854.

The Forayers or The Raid of the Dog-Days. By W. Gilmore Simms, Esq. Author of "The Partisan"—"Mellichampe"—"Katharine Walton"—"The Scout"—"Woodcraft"—"The Yemassee"—"Guy Rivers," etc. New York: Redfield, 1855. Dedication to Gen. D. F. Jamison, of Orangeburg, S.C.

Eutaw[:] A Sequel to The Forayers, or The Raid of the Dog-Days. A Tale of the Revolution. By W. Gilmore Simms, Esq. Author of "The Partisan"—"Mellichampe"—"Katharine Walton"—"The Forayers"—"The Scout"—"Woodcraft"—"Charlemont," etc. New York: Redfield, 1856. Dedication to the Hon. John Perkins, Jr., of Ashewood, Madison Parish, Louisiana.

Charlemont or The Pride of the Village. A Tale of Kentucky. By W. Gilmore Simms, Esq. Author of "The Partisan"—"Mellichampe"—"Katharine Walton"—"The Forayers"—"The Scout"—"Woodcraft"—"Beauchampe," etc. New York: Redfield, 1856. Dedication to the Hon. James Hall, of Cincinnati.

Beauchampe or The Kentucky Tragedy. A Sequel to Charlemont. By W. Gilmore Simms,

Esq. Author of "The Partisan"—"Mellichampe"—"Katharine Walton"—"The Forayers"—"The Scout"—"Woodcraft"—"Guy Rivers," etc. New York: Redfield, 1856.

The Cassique of Kiawah[:] A Colonial Romance. By William Gilmore Simms, Esq. Author of "The Yemassee"—"The Partisan"—"Guy Rivers"—"Scout"—Charlemont"—"Vasconselos"—etc., etc. New York: Redfield, 1859. Dedication to Hon. W. Porcher Miles, M.C.

Simms's Poems[:] Areytos or Songs and Ballads of the South With Other Poems. By W. Gilmore Simms, Esq. Author of "The Yemassee," "The Cassique of Kiawah," "The Partisan," "Eutaw," "The Forayers," etc. Charleston, S.C.: Russell & Jones, 1860. Dedication to Professor James W. Miles, of South Carolina.

Paddy McGann; or, The Demon of the Stump. By W. Gilmore Simms, author of "Richard Hurdis," "The Cassique of Kiawah," "Border Beagles," "The Yemassee," etc. *Southern Illustrated News,* Feb. 14—May 30, 1863.

Sack and Destruction of the City of Columbia, S.C. to Which Is Added a List of Property Destroyed. Columbia, S.C.: Power Press of Daily Phoenix, 1865.

Joscelyn; A Tale of the Revolution. By W. Gilmore Simms, Esq. Author of "The Yemassee," "The Partizan," "The Cassique of Kiawah," &c. *Old Guard* 5 (Jan.–Dec. 1867).

Voltmeier, or The Mountain Men. By William Gilmore Simms. *Illuminated Western World* 6 (March 6–Aug. 28, 1869).

The Cub of the Panther; A Mountain Legend. By W. Gilmore Simms, Esq. *Old Guard* 7 (Jan.–Dec. 1869).

The Sense of the Beautiful. An Address, Delivered by W. Gilmore Simms, before the Charleston County Agricultural and Horticultural Association (Now the Agricultural Society of South Carolina), May 3, 1870. Charleston: The Society, 1870.

Letters

The Letters of William Gilmore Simms. Ed. Mary C. Simms Oliphant, Alfred Taylor Odell, and T. C. Duncan Eaves. 5 vols. Columbia, S.C., 1952–56.

The Letters of William Gilmore Simms. Ed. Mary C. Simms Oliphant and T. C. Duncan Eaves. Supplement, vol. 6. Columbia, S.C., 1982.

Modern Collections

Selected Fiction of William Gilmore Simms: Arkansas Edition. Ed. John Caldwell Guilds. 7 vols. to date. Fayetteville, Ark., 1993—.
  Guy Rivers: A Tale of Georgia (1993)
  The Yemassee: A Romance of Carolina (1994)
  Richard Hurdis: A Tale of Alabama (1995)

Border Beagles: A Tale of Mississippi (1996)

The Cub of the Panther: A Hunter Legend of the "Old North State," ed. Miriam Jones
   Shillingsburg (1997)

Helen Halsey: The Swamp State of Conelachita (1998)

The Wigwam and the Cabin (2000)

Selected Poems of William Gilmore Simms. Ed. James Everett Kibler, Jr. Athens, Ga.,
   1990.

Stories and Tales. Ed. John Caldwell Guilds. Vol. 5 of *The Writings of William Gilmore
   Simms: Centennial Edition.* Columbia, S.C., 1974.

Tales of the South by William Gilmore Simms. Ed. Mary Ann Wimsatt. Columbia, S.C.,
   1996.

The Writings of William Gilmore Simms: Centennial Edition. Ed. John Caldwell Guilds
   and James B. Meriwether. 4 vols. Columbia, S.C., 1969–75.

Modern Editions of Individual Works by Simms

Poetry and the Practical. Ed. James Everett Kibler, Jr. Fayetteville, Ark., 1996.

View and Reviews in American Literature, History and Fiction. First Series. Ed. C. Hugh
   Holman. Cambridge, Mass., 1962.

SECONDARY SOURCES

Biography

Guilds, John Caldwell. *Simms: A Literary Life.* Fayetteville, Ark., 1992.

Trent, William P. *William Gilmore Simms.* American Men of Letters Series. Boston
   and New York, 1892.

General Criticism and Studies: Books or Parts of Books

Davidson, Donald. "Introduction." In *The Letters of William Gilmore Simms* 1 : xxi–
   clii. Columbia, S.C., 1952. Early highly appreciative estimate of Simms's
   fiction.

Faust, Drew Gilpin. *A Sacred Circle: The Dilemma of the Intellectual in the Old South,
   1840–1860.* Baltimore, 1977. Deals extensively and perceptively with Simms
   as Southern intellectual.

Gray, Richard. *Writing the South: Ideas of an American Region.* Cambridge, 1986. See
   "To Speak of Arcadia: William Gilmore Simms and Some Plantation Novelists,"
   pp. 45–62.

Guilds, John Caldwell, ed. *"Long Years of Neglect": The Work and Reputation of William Gilmore Simms.* Fayetteville, Ark., 1988. Evaluative essays by Guilds, James B. Meriwether, Anne M. Blythe, Linda L. McDaniel, Nicholas G. Meriwether, James E. Kibler, Jr., David Moltke-Hansen, Mary Ann Wimsatt, Rayburn S. Moore, Miriam J. Shillingsburg, John McCardell, and Louis D. Rubin, Jr.

———, and Caroline Collins, ed. *William Gilmore Simms and the American Frontier.* Athens, Ga., 1997. Essays by Moltke-Hansen, Elliott West, Guilds, Moore, Jan Bakker, Collins, Thomas L. McHaney, Nancy Grantham, David W. Newton, Wimsatt, Molly Boyd, Edwin T. Arnold, Garard Donovan, Kibler, Shillingsburg, Dianne C. Luce, and Sabine Schmidt.

Holman, C. Hugh. *The Immoderate Past: The Southern Writer and History.* Athens, Ga., 1977. Chapter 2 deals with Simms's use of history in his Revolutionary novels.

Hubbell, Jay B. *The South in American Literature, 1607–1900.* Durham, N.C., 1954. Chapter on Simms (pp. 572–602) still one of the best short essays on the author.

Kibler, James E., Jr. *The Poetry of William Gilmore Simms: An Introduction and Bibliography.* Spartanburg, S.C., 1979.

Kolodny, Annette. *The Lay of the Land: Metaphors as Experience and History in American Life and Letters.* Chapel Hill, N.C., 1975. Feminist study of Simms's depiction of landscape, pp. 115–32.

Kreyling, Michael. *Figures of the Hero in Southern Narrative.* Baton Rouge, La., 1987. See "William Gilmore Simms: Writer and Hero," pp. 30–51.

McCardell, John. "Poetry and the Practical: William Gilmore Simms." In *Intellectual Life in Antebellum Charleston,* ed. Michael O'Brien and David Moltke-Hansen, pp. 186–210. Knoxville, Tenn., 1986.

McHaney, Thomas L. "William Gilmore Simms." In *The Chief Glory of Every People: Essays on Classic American Writer,* ed. Matthew J. Bruccoli, pp. 173–90. Carbondale, Ill. , 1973. Notable for its recognition of the significance of Border novels.

Meats, Stephen E. "Artist or Historian: William Gilmore Simms and the Revolutionary South." In *Eighteenth-Century Florida and the Revolutionary South,* ed. Samuel Proctor, pp. 95–108. Gainesville, Fla., 1978.

Parrington, Vernon L. *The Romantic Revolution in America, 1800–1860.* Vol. 2 of *Main Currents in American Thought.* 3 vols. New York, 1927–30. Chapter on Simms an important early assessment of his achievement.

Ridgely, J. V. *William Gilmore Simms.* Twayne's United States Authors Series. New York, 1962.

Rubin, Louis D., Jr. *The Edge of the Swamp: A Study in the Literature and Society of the Old South.* Baton Rouge, La., 1989. See "The Dream of the Plantation: Simms, Hammond, Charleston," pp. 54–102, and "The Romance of the Frontier: Simms, Cooper, and the Wilderness," pp. 103–26.

Shillingsburg, Miriam J. "Simms's Failed Lecture Tour of 1856: The Mind of the North." In Guilds, *Long Years,* pp. 183–201.

Wakelyn, Jon L. *The Politics of a Literary Man: William Gilmore Simms.* Westport, Conn., 1973.

Watson, Charles S. *Antebellum Charleston Dramatists.* University, Ala., 1976. Chapter 5 deals with Simms as dramatist.

———. *From Nationalism to Sessionism: The Changing Fiction of William Gilmore Simms.* Westport, Conn., 1993.

Wimsatt, Mary Ann. *The Major Fiction of William Gilmore Simms: Cultural Traditions and Literary Form.* Baton Rouge, La., 1989. Highly valuable study of the technique and substance of Simms's fiction.

Bibliography and Reference Guide

Butterworth, Keen, and James E. Kibler, Jr. *William Gilmore Simms: A Reference Guide.* Boston, 1980.

Titles Index

THE PUBLICATIONS OF THE

SOUTHERN TEXTS SOCIETY

An Evening When Alone:
Four Journals of Single Women in the South, 1827–67
Edited by Michael O'Brien

Louisa S. McCord: Political and Social Essays
Edited by Richard C. Lounsbury

Civilization and Black Progress:
Selected Writings of Alexander Crummell on the South
Edited by J. R. Oldfield

Louisa S. McCord: Poems, Drama, Biography, Letters
Edited by Richard C. Lounsbury

Soldier and Scholar: Basil Lanneau Gildersleeve and the Civil War
Edited by Ward W. Briggs Jr.

Louisa S. McCord: Selected Writings
Edited by Richard C. Lounsbury

A Southern Practice: The Diary and Autobiography of Charles A. Hentz, M.D.
Edited by Steven M. Stowe

The Simms Reader: Selections from the Writings of William Gilmore Simms
Edited by John Caldwell Guilds